Image and Reality
of the Israel–Palestine Conflict

# Image and Reality
# of the Israel–Palestine Conflict

## Second Edition

◆

### NORMAN G. FINKELSTEIN

**VERSO**

London · New York

First published by Verso 1995
© Norman G. Finkelstein 1995
Second edition first published by Verso 2003
© Norman G. Finkelstein 2003
All rights reserved

3 5 7 9 10 8 6 4 2

**Verso**
UK: 6 Meard Street, London WIF OEG
USA: 180 Varick Street, New York NY 10014–4606

Verso is the imprint of New Left Books

ISBN 978-1-85984-442-7

**British Library Cataloguing in Publication Data**
A catalogue record for this book is available from the British Library

**Library of Congress Cataloging-in-Publication Data**
A catalog record for this book is available from the British Library

Typeset in Monotype Bembo by Illuminati, Grosmont

Printed in the USA by Quebecor World

To my beloved parents,

Maryla Husyt Finkelstein,
survivor of the Warsaw Ghetto,
Maidanek concentration camp
and
Zacharias Finkelstein,
survivor of the Warsaw Ghetto,
Auschwitz concentration camp.

May I never forget or forgive
what was done to them.

# Contents

# Acknowledgments

Over the past decade I benefited from the generosity of many individuals; no words can adequately express my gratitude. Roane Carey, Allan Nairn and Cyrus Veeser expertly served as my personal editors. Carol Chomsky, Noam Chomsky and Samira Haj commented on all the chapters in draft form. Albeit in different ways, each also played a crucial role in ushering the book from conception to completion. I am equally grateful to Nabeel Abraham and Nawal Ragheb for being there all these years. Unless otherwise indicated, Hebrew-language periodicals are cited from Israel Shahak's invaluable *Translations from the Hebrew Press*. I want also to thank personally several individuals who gave unsparingly of themselves: Rudolph Baldeo, Harry Chomsky, Carolyn Fialkow, Joanne Koslofsky, Ellen Mastromonaco, Donald Neff, Adele Oltman, Richard Parker, William Quandt, Frank Sheed and Mariam Touba. I owe the book's title as well as its overarching structure to Noam Chomsky. All errors of fact, reasoning and judgment are my own.

The conquest of the earth, which mostly means the taking it away from those who have a different complexion or slightly flatter noses than ourselves, is not a pretty thing when you look into it too much.

Joseph Conrad, *Heart of Darkness*

# Introduction to the
# Second Edition

The logical implication of trying to create a continent neatly divided into coherent territorial states, each inhabited by a separate ethnically and linguistically homogeneous population, was the mass expulsion or extermination of minorities. Such was and is the murderous *reductio ad absurdum* of nationalism in its territorial version, although this was not fully demonstrated until the 1940s. ... The homogeneous territorial nation could now be seen as a programme that could be realized only by barbarians, or at least by barbarian means.

> E.J. Hobsbawm, *Nations and Nationalism since 1780*

## Background

To resolve what was called the 'Jewish question' – i.e., the reciprocal challenges of Gentile repulsion, or anti-Semitism, and Gentile attraction, or assimilation – the Zionist movement sought in the late nineteenth century to create an overwhelmingly, if not homogeneously, Jewish state in Palestine.[1] Once the Zionist movement gained a foothold in Palestine through Great Britain's issuance of the Balfour Declaration,[2] the main obstacle to realizing its goal was the indigenous Arab population. For, on the eve of Zionist colonization, Palestine was overwhelmingly not Jewish but Muslim and Christian Arab.[3]

Across the mainstream Zionist spectrum, it was understood from the outset that Palestine's indigenous Arab population would not acquiesce in its dispossession. 'Contrary to the claim that is often made, Zionism was not blind to the presence of Arabs in Palestine', Zeev Sternhell observes. 'If Zionist intellectuals and leaders ignored the Arab dilemma, it was chiefly because they knew that this problem had no solution within the Zionist way of thinking ... [I]n general both sides understood each other well and knew that the implementation of Zionism could be only at the expense of the Palestinian Arabs.' Moshe Shertok (later Sharett) contemptuously dismissed the 'illusive hopes' of those who spoke about a '"mutual misunderstanding" between us and the Arabs, about "common interests" [and] about "the possibility of unity and peace between the two fraternal peoples."' 'There is no example in history', David Ben-Gurion declared, succinctly framing the core problem, 'that a nation opens the gates of its country, not because of necessity ... but because the nation which wants to come in has explained its desire to it.'[4]

'The tragedy of Zionism', Walter Laqueur wrote in his standard history, 'was that it appeared on the international scene when there were no longer empty spaces on the world map.' This is not quite right. Rather it was no longer politically tenable to *create* such spaces: extermination had ceased to be an option of conquest.[5] Basically the Zionist movement could choose between only two strategic options to achieve its goal: what Benny Morris has labeled 'the way of South Africa' – 'the establishment of an apartheid state, with a settler minority lording it over a large, exploited native majority' – or the 'the way of transfer' – 'you could create a homogenous Jewish state or at least a state with an overwhelming Jewish majority by moving or transferring all or most of the Arabs out.'[6]

## Round One – 'The Way of Transfer'

In the first round of conquest, the Zionist movement set its sights on 'the way of transfer'. For all the public rhetoric about wanting to 'live with the Arabs in conditions of unity and mutual honor and together with them to turn the common homeland into a flourishing land' (Twelfth Zionist Congress, 1921), the Zionists from early on were in fact bent on expelling them. 'The idea of transfer had accompanied the Zionist movement from its very beginnings', Tom Segev reports. '"Disappearing" the Arabs lay at the heart of the Zionist dream, and was also a necessary condition of its existence. ... With few exceptions, none of the Zionists disputed the desirability of forced transfer – or its morality.' The key was to get the timing right. Ben-Gurion, reflecting on the expulsion option in the late 1930s, wrote: 'What is inconceivable in normal times is possible in revolutionary times; and if at this time the opportunity is missed and what is possible in such great hours is not carried out – a whole world is lost.'[7]

The goal of 'disappearing' the indigenous Arab population points to a virtual truism buried beneath a mountain of apologetic Zionist literature:

what spurred Palestinians' opposition to Zionism was not anti-Semitism, in the sense of an irrational or abstract hatred of Jews, but rather the prospect – very real – of their own expulsion. 'The fear of territorial displacement and dispossession', Morris reasonably concludes, 'was to be the chief motor of Arab antagonism to Zionism.' Likewise, in his magisterial study of Palestinian nationalism, Yehoshua Porath suggests that the 'major factor nourishing' Arab anti-Semitism 'was not hatred for the Jews as such but opposition to Jewish settlement in Palestine.' He goes on to argue that, although Arabs initially differentiated between Jews and Zionists, it was 'inevitable' that opposition to Zionist settlement would turn into a loathing of all Jews: 'As immigration increased, so did the Jewish community's identification with the Zionist movement. ... The non-Zionist and anti-Zionist factors became an insignificant minority, and a large measure of sophistication was required to make the older distinction. It was unreasonable to hope that the wider Arab population, and the riotous mob which was part of it, would maintain this distinction.'[8] It ought also to be remembered that Zionist leaders consistently claimed to be acting on behalf and with the support of 'world Jewry', a claim which to many Palestinians seemed increasingly credible, as first non-Zionist Jews in Palestine were marginalized during the Mandate as noted above and, especially after 1967, as non-Zionist Jews around the world became, if not a small minority, certainly an increasingly voiceless one.

From its incipient stirrings in the late nineteenth century through the watershed revolt in the 1930s, Palestinian resistance consistently focused on the twin juggernauts of Zionist conquest: Jewish settlers and Jewish settlements.[9] Apologetic Zionist writers like Anita Shapira juxtapose benign Jewish settlement against recourse to force.[10] In fact, settlement *was* force. 'From the outset, Zionism sought to employ force in order to realize national aspirations', Yosef Gorny observes. 'This force consisted primarily of the collective ability to rebuild a national home in Palestine.' Through settlement the Zionist movement aimed – in Ben-Gurion's words – 'to establish a *great Jewish fact* in this country' that was irreversible (emphasis in original).[11] Moreover, settlement and armed force were in reality seamlessly interwoven as Zionist settlers sought 'the ideal and perfect fusion between the plow and rifle.' Moshe Dayan later memorialized that 'We are a generation of settlers, and without the combat helmet and the barrel of a gun, we will not be able to plant a tree or build a house.'[12] The Zionist movement inferred behind Palestinian resistance to Jewish settlement a generic (and genetic) anti-Semitism – Jewish settlers 'being murdered', as Ben-Gurion put it, 'simply because they were Jews' – in order to conceal from the outside world and itself the rational and legitimate grievances of the indigenous population.[13] In the ensuing bloodshed the kith and kin of Zionist martyrs would, like relatives of Palestinian martyrs today, wax proud at these national sacrifices. 'I am gratified', the father of a Jewish casualty eulogized, 'that I was a living witness to such a historical event.'[14]

It bears critical notice for what comes later that, from the interwar through early postwar years, Western public opinion was not altogether averse to population transfer as an expedient (albeit extreme) method for resolving ethnic conflicts. French socialists and Europe's Jewish press supported in the mid-1930s the transfer of Jews to Madagascar to solve Poland's 'Jewish problem'.[15] The main forced transfer between the two world wars was effected between Turkey and Greece. Sanctioned by the Treaty of Lausanne (1923) and approved and supervised by the League of Nations, this brutal displacement of more than 1.5 million people eventually came to be seen by much of official Europe as an auspicious precedent. The British cited it in the late 1930s as a model for resolving the conflict in Palestine. The right-wing Zionist leader, Vladimir Jabotinsky, taking heart from Nazi demographic experiments in conquered territories (about 1.5 million Poles and Jews were expelled and hundreds of thousands of Germans resettled in their place), exclaimed: 'The world has become accustomed to the idea of mass migrations and has almost become fond of them. Hitler – as odious as he is to us – has given this idea a good name in the world.' During the war the Soviet Union also carried out bloody deportations of recalcitrant minorities such as the Volga Germans, Chechen-Ingush and Tatars. Labor Zionists pointed to the 'positive experience' of the Greek-Turkish and Soviet expulsions in support of the transfer idea. Recalling the 'success' (Churchill) of the Greek–Turkish compulsory transfer, the Allies at the Potsdam Conference (1945) authorized the expulsion of some thirteen million Germans from Central and Eastern Europe (around two million perished in the course of this horrendous uprooting). Even the left-wing British Labour Party advocated in its 1944 platform that the 'Arabs be encouraged to move out' of Palestine, as did the humanist philosopher Bertrand Russell, to make way for Zionist settlement.[16]

In fact, many in the enlightened West came to view displacement of the indigenous population of Palestine as an inexorable concomitant of civilization's advance. The identification of Americans with Zionism came easily, since the 'social order of the Yishuv [Jewish community in Palestine] was built on the ethos of a frontier society, in which a pioneering-settlement model set the tone'. To account for the 'almost complete disregard of the Arab case' by Americans, a prominent British Labour MP, Richard Crossman, explained in the mid-1940s: 'Zionism after all is merely the attempt by the European Jew to build his national life on the soil of Palestine in much the same way as the American settler developed the West. So the American will give the Jewish settler in Palestine the benefit of the doubt, and regard the Arab as the aboriginal who must go down before the march of progress.' Contrasting the 'slovenly' Arabs with enterprising Jewish settlers who had 'set going revolutionary forces in the Middle East', Crossman himself professed in the name of 'social progress' support for Zionism. The left-liberal US presidential candidate in 1948, Henry Wallace, compared the Zionist struggle in Palestine with 'the fight the American colonies carried on in 1776. Just as the British stirred up the Iroquois to fight the colonists, so today they are stirring up the Arabs.'[17]

Come 1948, the Zionist movement exploited the 'revolutionary times' of the first Arab–Israeli war – much like the Serbs did in Kosovo during the NATO attack – to expel more than 80 per cent of the indigenous population (750,000 Palestinians), and thereby achieve its goal of an over-whelmingly Jewish state, if not yet in the whole of Palestine.[18] Berl Katznelson, known as the 'conscience' of the Labor Zionist movement, had maintained that 'there has never been a colonizing enterprise as typified by justice and honesty toward others as our work here in Eretz Israel.' In his multi-volume paean to the American settlers' dispossession of the native population, *The Winning of the West*, Theodore Roosevelt likewise concluded that 'no other conquering nation has ever treated savage owners of the soil with such generosity as has the United States'. The recipients of this benefaction would presumably have a different story to tell.[19]

## Round Two – 'The Way of South Africa'

The main Arab (and British) fear before and after the 1948 war was that the Zionist movement would use the Jewish state carved out of Palestine as a springboard for further expansion.[20] In fact, Zionists pursued from early on a 'stages' strategy of conquering Palestine by parts – a strategy it would later vilify the Palestinians for. 'The Zionist vision could not be fulfilled in one fell swoop', Ben-Gurion's official biographer reports, 'especially the transformation of Palestine into a Jewish state. The stage-by-stage approach, dictated by less than favorable circumstances, required the formulation of objectives that appeared to be "concessions".' It acqui-esced in British and United Nations proposals for the partition of Palestine but only 'as a stage along the path to greater Zionist implementation' (Ben-Gurion).[21] Chief among the Zionist leadership's regrets in the aftermath of the 1948 war was its failure to conquer the whole of Palestine. Come 1967, Israel exploited the 'revolutionary times' of the June war to

finish the job.[22] Sir Martin Gilbert, in his glowing history of Israel, maintained that Zionist leaders from the outset conceived the conquered
territories as an undesired 'burden that was to weigh heavily on Israel'. In
a highly acclaimed new study, *Six Days of War*, Michael Oren suggests
that Israel's territorial conquests 'came about largely through chance', 'the
vagaries and momentum of war': they just happened. A careful review of
the historical record, however, suggests that they were just *waiting to
happen*. In light of the Zionist movement's long-standing territorial imperatives, Sternhell concludes: 'The role of occupier, which Israel began
to play only a few months after the lightning victory of June 1967, was
not the result of some miscalculation on the part of the rulers of that
period or the outcome of a combination of circumstances, but another
step in the realization of Zionism's major ambitions.'[23]

Israel confronted the same dilemma after occupying the West Bank
and Gaza as at the dawn of the Zionist movement: it wanted the land
but not the people.[24] Expulsion, however, was no longer a viable option.
In the aftermath of the brutal Nazi experiments with and plans for
demographic engineering, international public opinion had ceased granting any legitimacy to forced population transfers. The landmark Fourth
Geneva Convention, ratified in 1949, for the first time 'unequivocally
prohibited deportation' of civilians under occupation (Articles 49, 147).[25]
Accordingly, after the June war Israel moved to impose the second of its
two options mentioned above – apartheid. This proved to be the chief
stumbling block to a diplomatic settlement of the Israel–Palestine conflict.

## The 'Peace Process'

Right after the June war the United Nations deliberated on the modalities
for achieving a just and lasting peace. The broad consensus of the General
Assembly as well as the Security Council called for Israel's withdrawal
from the Arab territories it occupied during the June war. Security Council Resolution 242 stipulated this basic principle of international law in
its preambular paragraph '*emphasizing* the inadmissibility of the acquisition
of territory by war' (emphasis in original).[26] At the same time, Resolution 242 called on Arab states to recognize Israel's right 'to live in peace
within secure and recognized boundaries free from threats and acts of
force'. To accommodate Palestinian national aspirations, the international
consensus eventually supported the creation of a Palestinian state in the
West Bank and Gaza once Israel withdrew to its pre-June borders. (Resolution 242 had only referred obliquely to the Palestinians in its call for
'achieving a just resolution of the refugee problem'.)

Although Defense Minister Moshe Dayan privately acknowledged that Resolution 242 required full withdrawal, Israel officially maintained that it allowed for 'territorial revision'.[27] Israel's refusal in February 1971 to fully withdraw from the Sinai in exchange for Egypt's offer of a peace treaty led directly to the October 1973 war.[28] The basic parameters of Israeli policy regarding Palestinian territory were set out in the late 1960s in the proposal of Yigal Allon, a senior Labor Party official and Cabinet member. The 'Allon Plan' called for Israel's annexation of up to half the West Bank, while Palestinians would be confined to the other half in two unconnected cantons to the north and south. Sasson Sofer notes generally the 'fertile dualism' of Israeli diplomacy – one might rather say 'fertile cynicism' – of 'pointing to the uniqueness of the Jewish question in order to obtain legitimacy, and then stressing the normality of Israel's sovereign existence as a state which should be accorded all the international rights and privileges of a national entity'. In the case at hand Israel demanded, like all sovereign states, full recognition yet also claimed a right, in the name of unique Jewish suffering and despite international law, to territorial conquest. As shown elsewhere, invocation of the Nazi holocaust played a crucial role in this diplomatic game.[29]

The United States initially supported the consensus interpretation of Resolution 242, making allowance for only 'minor' and 'mutual' adjustments on the irregular border between Israel and the Jordanian-controlled West Bank.[30] In heated private exchanges with Israel during the UN-sponsored mediation efforts of Gunnar Jarring in 1968,[31] American officials stood firm that 'the words "recognized and secure" meant "security arrangements" and "recognition" of new lines as international boundaries', and 'never meant that Israel could extend its territory to [the] West Bank or Suez if this was what it felt its security required'; and that 'there will never be peace if Israel tries to hold onto large chunks of territory'. Referring to it explicitly by name, the US deplored even the minimalist version of the Allon Plan as 'a non-starter' and 'unacceptable in principle'.[32]

In a crucial shift beginning under the Nixon–Kissinger administration, however, American policy was realigned with Israel's.[33] Except for Israel and the United States (and occasionally a US client state), the international community has supported, for the past quarter-century, the 'two-state' settlement: that is, the full Israeli withdrawal/full Arab recognition formula as well as the creation of a Palestinian state alongside Israel. The United States cast the lone veto of Security Council resolutions in 1976 and 1980 affirming the two-state settlement that were endorsed by the Palestine Liberation Organization (PLO) and neighboring Arab states. A 1989 General Assembly resolution along similar lines passed 151–3 (Israel,

US, and Dominica). Despite the historic geo-political changes in the past decade, the international consensus has remained remarkably stable. A 2002 General Assembly resolution ('Peaceful settlement of the question of Palestine') affirming Israel's right to 'secure and recognized borders' as well as the Palestinian people's right to an 'independent state' in the West Bank and Gaza passed 160–4 (Israel, Marshall Islands, Federated States of Micronesia, US). The 2002 UN voting record on virtually every resolution bearing on the Israeli–Palestinian (and –Syrian) conflict was similarly lop-sided. In the UN Third Committee the vote was 156–3 (Israel, Marshall Islands, US) regarding 'the right of the Palestinian people to self-determination', while in the Fourth Committee the vote was 148–1 (Israel) regarding 'Assistance to Palestinian refugees', 147–4 (Israel, Marshall Islands, Micronesia, US) regarding 'Persons displaced as a result of the June 1967 war', 147–5 (Israel, Marshall Islands, Micronesia, Nauru, US) regarding 'Operations of the United Nations Relief and Works Agency for Palestine Refugees', 147–4 (Israel, Marshall Islands, Micronesia, US) regarding 'Palestine refugees' properties and their revenues', 145–5 (Israel, Marshall Islands, Micronesia, Nauru, US) regarding 'Applicability of the Geneva Convention ... to the Occupied Palestinian Territory', 145–6 (Israel, Marshall Islands, Micronesia, Nauru, Tuvalu, US) regarding 'Israeli settlements in the Occupied Territories', 141–5 (Israel, Marshall Islands, Micronesia, Nauru, US) regarding 'Israeli practices affecting the human rights of the Palestinian people', and 144–1 (Israel) regarding 'The occupied Syrian Golan.' Responding to the Syrian charge that 'Israel stood isolated' in the international community Israel's ambassador rejoined that 'to the right' it had truth and 'to the left, justice', and he did not call that isolation. Indeed, he left out Nauru, Tuvalu, Micronesia, and the Marshall Islands. This record is often adduced as proof of the UN's bias against Israel. In fact the exact reverse is true. A careful study by Marc Weller of the University of Cambridge comparing Israel and the occupied territories with similar situations in Bosnia and Herzegovina, Kosovo, East Timor, occupied Kuwait and Iraq, and Rwanda found that Israel has enjoyed a 'virtual immunity' from enforcement measures such as an arms embargo and economic sanctions typically adopted by the UN against member states condemned for identical violations of international law. Given its conflict with the 'entire world community', Israel has unsurprisingly set as a crucial precondition for negotiations that Palestinians 'must drop their traditional demand' for 'international arbitration' or a 'Security Council mechanism'.[34]

The main obstacle to Israel's annexation of occupied Palestinian territory from the mid-1970s was the PLO. Having endorsed the two-state settlement, it could no longer be dismissed as simply a terrorist organization bent on Israel's destruction. Pressures mounted on Israel to reach an agreement with the PLO's 'compromising approach'. Consequently, in June 1982 Israel invaded Lebanon, where Palestinian leaders were head-quartered, to head off what Israeli strategic analyst Avner Yaniv dubbed the PLO's 'peace offensive'.[35] With the Palestine question diplomatically sidelined after the invasion, West Bank and Gaza Palestinians rose up in December 1987 against the occupation in a basically non-violent civil revolt, the *intifada*. Israel's brutal repression (compounded by the inept and corrupt leadership of the PLO) eventually resulted in the uprising's defeat.[36] After the implosion of the Soviet Union, the destruction of Iraq, and the suspension of funding from the Gulf states, Palestinian fortunes reached a new nadir. The US and Israel seized on this opportune moment to recruit the already venal and now desperate Palestinian leadership – 'on the verge of bankruptcy' and 'in [a] weakened condition' (Uri Savir, Israel's chief negotiator at Oslo) – as surrogates of Israeli power. This was the real meaning of the Oslo Accord signed in September 1993: to create a Palestinian Bantustan by dangling before Arafat and the PLO the per-quisites of power and privilege, much like how the British controlled Palestine during the Mandate years through the Mufti of Jerusalem, Amin al-Husayni, and the Supreme Muslim Council.[37] 'The occupation contin-ued' after Oslo, a seasoned Israeli observer, Meron Benvenisti, wrote, 'albeit by remote control, and with the consent of the Palestinian people, represented by their "sole representative," the PLO.' And again: 'It goes without saying that "cooperation" based on the current power relation-ship is no more than permanent Israeli domination in disguise, and that Palestinian self-rule is merely a euphemism for Bantustanization.' The 'test' for Arafat and the PLO, according to Savir, was whether they would 'us[e] their new power base to dismantle Hamas and other violent oppo-sition groups' contesting Israeli apartheid.[38]

Israel's settlement policy in the Occupied Territories during the past decade points up the real content of the 'peace process' set in motion at Oslo. The details are spelled out in an exhaustive study by B'Tselem (Israeli Information Center for Human Rights in the Occupied Terri-tories) entitled *Land Grab*.[39] Due primarily to massive Israeli government subsidies, the Jewish settler population increased from 250,000 to 380,000 during the Oslo years, with settler activity proceeding at a brisker pace under the tenure of Labor's Ehud Barak than Likud's Benjamin Netan-yahu. Illegal under international law and built on land illegally seized from Palestinians, these settlements now incorporate nearly half the land surface of the West Bank. For all practical purposes they have been annexed to Israel (Israeli law extends not only to Israeli but also non-Israeli Jews residing in the settlements) and are off-limits to Palestinians

without special authorization. Fragmenting the West Bank into disconnected and unviable enclaves, they have impeded meaningful Palestinian development. In parts of the West Bank and East Jerusalem the only
available land for building lies in areas under Israeli jurisdiction, while the
water consumption of the 5,000 Jewish settlers in the Jordan Valley is
equivalent to 75 per cent of the water consumption of all two million
Palestinian inhabitants of the West Bank. Not one Jewish settlement was
dismantled during the Oslo years, while the number of new housing
units in the settlements increased by more than fifty per cent (excluding
East Jerusalem); again, the biggest spurt of new housing starts occurred
not under Netanyahu's tenure but rather under Barak's, in the year 2000
– exactly when Barak claims to have 'left no stone unturned' in his quest
for peace. During the first eighteen months of Prime Minister Sharon's
term of office (beginning early 2001), forty-four new settlements –
rebuked by the UN Commission on Human Rights as 'incendiary and
provocative' – were established in the West Bank.[40]

'Israel has created in the Occupied Territories a regime of separation
based on discrimination, applying two different systems of law in the same
area and basing the rights of individuals on their nationality', the B'Tselem
study concludes. 'This regime is the only one of its kind in the world,
and is reminiscent of distasteful regimes from the past, such as the Apartheid regime in South Africa.'

As Jewish settlements expand, Israel has begun corralling West Bank
Palestinians into eight fragments of territory, each surrounded by barbed
wire with a permit required to move or trade between them (trucks must
load and unload on the borders 'back-to-back'), thereby further devastating
an economy in which roughly one-third of the population is unemployed,
half the population lives below the poverty line of $2 per day, and one-
fifth of children under five suffer from malnutrition largely caused –
according to US, UN and European relief agencies – by Israeli restrictions on transporting food. 'What is truly appalling', a *Haaretz* writer
lamented, 'is the blasé way in which the story has been received and
handled by the mass media. ... Where is the public outcry against this
attempt to divide the territories and enforce internal passports ... [and]
humiliate and inconvenience a population that can scarcely earn a living
or live a life as it is?'[41]

After seven years of on-again, off-again negotiations and a succession
of new interim agreements that managed to rob the Palestinians of the
few crumbs thrown from the master's table at Oslo,[42] the moment of
truth arrived at Camp David in July 2000. President Clinton and Prime
Minister Barak delivered Arafat the ultimatum of formally acquiescing in
a Bantustan or bearing full responsibility for the collapse of the 'peace

process'. Arafat refused, however, to budge from the international consensus for resolving the conflict. According to Robert Malley, a key American negotiator at Camp David, Arafat continued to hold out for a 'Palestinian state based on the June 4, 1967 borders, living alongside Israel', yet also 'accepted the notion of Israeli annexation of West Bank territory to accommodate settlements, though [he] insisted on a one for one swap of land of "equal size and value"' – that is, the 'minor' and 'mutual' border adjustments of the original US position on Resolution 242. Malley's rendering of the Palestinian proposal at Camp David – an offer that was widely dismissed but rarely reported – deserves full quotation: 'a state of Israel incorporating some land captured in 1967 and including a very large majority of its settlers, the largest Jewish Jerusalem in the city's history, preservation of Israel's demographic balance between Jews and Arabs; security guaranteed by a US-led international presence.' On the other hand, contrary to the myth spun by Barak–Clinton as well as a compliant media, 'Barak offered the trappings of Palestinian sovereignty', a special adviser at the British Foreign Office observed, 'while perpetuating the subjugation of the Palestinians.' Although accounts of the Barak proposal significantly differ, all knowledgeable observers concur that it 'would have meant that territory annexed by Israel would encroach deep inside the Palestinian state' (Malley), dividing the West Bank into multiple, disconnected enclaves, and offering land swaps that were of neither equal size nor equal value.[43]

Consider in this regard Israel's reaction to the March 2002 Saudi peace plan. Crown Prince Abdullah proposed, and all twenty-one other members of the Arab League approved, a plan making concessions that actually went beyond the international consensus. In exchange for a full Israeli withdrawal, it offered not only full recognition but 'normal relations with Israel', and called not for the 'right of return' of Palestinian refugees but rather only a 'just solution' to the refugee problem. A *Haaretz* commentator noted that the Saudi plan was 'surprisingly similar to what Barak claims to have proposed two years ago' at Camp David. Were Israel truly committed to a comprehensive withdrawal in exchange for normalization with the Arab world, the Saudi plan and its unanimous endorsement by the Arab League summit ought to have been met with euphoria. In fact, after an ephemeral interlude of evasion and silence, it was quickly deposited in Orwell's memory hole. When the Bush administration subsequently made passing reference to the Saudi plan in a draft 'road map' for settling the Israel–Palestine conflict, Israeli officials loudly protested.[44] Nonetheless, Barak's – and Clinton's – fraud that Palestinians at Camp David rejected a maximally generous Israeli offer provided crucial moral cover for the horrors that ensued.

## Learning from the Nazi Holocaust

In September 2000, Palestinians embarked on a second *intifada* against
Israeli rule. In the 'warped thinking' of Israelis since Oslo, *Haaretz*
journalist Amira Hass wrote soon after the renewed resistance,

> the Palestinians would accept a situation of coexistence in which they were on
> an unequal footing vis-à-vis the Israelis and in which they were ranked as
> persons who were entitled to less, much less, than the Jews. However, in the
> end the Palestinians were not willing to live with this arrangement. The new
> *intifada* ... is a final attempt to thrust a mirror in the face of Israelis and to tell
> them: 'Take a good look at yourselves and see how racist you have become.'

Meanwhile, Israel, having failed in the carrot policy it initiated at Oslo,
reached for the big stick. Two preconditions had to be met, however,
before Israel could bring to bear its overwhelming military superiority:
a 'green light' from the US and a sufficient pretext. Already in summer
2001, the authoritative *Jane's Information Group* reported that Israel had
completed planning for a massive and bloody invasion of the Occupied
Territories. But the US vetoed the plan and Europe made equally plain
its opposition. After 11 September, however, the US came on board.
Sharon's goal of crushing the Palestinians basically fit in with the US
administration's goal of exploiting the World Trade Center atrocity to
eliminate the last remnants of Arab resistance to total US domination –
or, in Robert Fisk's succinct formulation, 'to bring the Arabs back
under our firm control, to ensure their loyalty'. Through sheer exertion
of will and despite a monumentally incompetent leadership, Palestinians
have proven to be the most resilient and recalcitrant popular force in
the Arab world. Bringing them to their knees would deal a devastating
psychological blow throughout the region.[45]

With a green light from the US, all Israel now needed was the pretext. Predictably, it escalated the assassinations of Palestinian leaders following each lull in Palestinian terrorist attacks. 'After the destruction of
the houses in Rafah and Jerusalem, the Palestinians continued to act with
restraint', Shulamit Aloni of Israel's Meretz party observed. 'Sharon and
his army minister, apparently fearing that they would have to return to
the negotiating table, decided to do something and they liquidated Raed
Karmi. They knew that there would be a response, and that we would
pay the price in the blood of citizens.'[46] In fact, it was plainly the case
that Israel desperately sought this sanguinary response. Once the Palestinian terrorist attacks crossed the desired threshold, Sharon was able to
declare war and proceed to beat the basically defenseless civilian Palestinian population into submission.

Only the willfully blind could miss noticing that Israel's March–April invasion of the West Bank, 'Operation Defensive Shield', was largely a replay of the June 1982 invasion of Lebanon. To crush the Palestinians' goal of an independent state alongside Israel – the PLO's 'peace offensive' – Israel laid plans in September 1981 to invade Lebanon. In order to launch the invasion, however, it needed the green light from the Reagan administration and a pretext. Much to its chagrin and despite multiple provocations, Israel was unable to elicit a Palestinian attack on its northern border. It accordingly escalated the air assaults on southern Lebanon and after a particularly murderous attack that left two hundred civilians dead (including sixty occupants of a Palestinian children's hospital), the PLO finally retaliated, killing one Israeli. With this key pretext in hand and a green light now forthcoming from the Reagan administration, Israel invaded. Using the same slogan of 'rooting out Palestinian terror', Israel proceeded to massacre a defenseless population, killing some 20,000 Palestinians and Lebanese between June and September 1982, almost all civilians. One might note by comparison that, as of May 2002, the official Israeli figure for Jews 'who gave their lives for the creation and security of the Jewish State' – that is, the total number of Jews who perished in (mostly) wartime combat or in terrorist attacks from the dawn of the Zionist movement 120 years ago until the present day – comes to 21,182.[47]

To repress Palestinian resistance, a senior Israeli officer in early 2002 urged the army to 'analyze and internalize the lessons of ... how the German army fought in the Warsaw ghetto'. Judging by Israeli carnage in the West Bank culminating in Operation Defensive Shield – the targeting of Palestinian ambulances[48] and medical personnel, the targeting of journalists, the killing of Palestinian children 'for sport' (Chris Hedges, *New York Times* former Cairo bureau chief), the rounding up, handcuffing and blindfolding of Palestinian males between the ages of fifteen and fifty, and affixing of numbers on their wrists, the indiscriminate torture of Palestinian detainees, the denial of food, water, electricity, medical treatment and burial to the Palestinian civilian population, the indiscriminate air assaults on some Palestinian neighborhoods, the systematic use of Palestinian civilians as human shields, the bulldozing of Palestinian homes with the occupants huddled inside – it appears that the Israeli army followed the officer's advice. When the offensive, supported by fully 90 per cent of Israelis, was finally over, 500 Palestinians were dead (including more than seventy children) and 1,500 wounded, more than 8,000 Palestinians detained in mass round-ups had been subjected to ill-treatment (and sometimes torture), more than 3,000 dwellings were demolished (sometimes with the residents still inside) leaving over 13,000 Palestinians homeless, while the already devastated Palestinian economy suffered more than $350 million in direct property losses.[49]

The climax of Operation Defensive Shield was the Israeli siege in early April of Jenin refugee camp. A Palestinian militant told Amnesty International that the decision to resist was 'made by the community' against the background of an Israeli incursion the month before that had met little resistance: 'And otherwise, where would we go? The Israelis had put a cordon around the town; we had no choice. We had nowhere else to fight.' Human rights organizations consistently found that in the course of the siege 'Israeli forces committed serious violations of humanitarian law, some amounting *prima facie* to war crimes' (Human Rights Watch) and 'the IDF [Israel Defense Forces] carried out actions which violate international human rights and humanitarian law; some of these actions amount to ... war crimes' (Amnesty International). Some 4,000 Palestinians, nearly a third of the camp's population, were rendered homeless in 'destruction [that] extended well beyond any conceivable purpose of gaining access to fighters, and was vastly disproportionate to the military objectives pursued' (HRW); indeed, 'in one appalling and extensive operation, the IDF demolished, destroyed by explosives, or flattened by army bulldozers, a large residential area of Jenin refugee camp, much of it after the fighting had apparently ended' (Amnesty). Some fifty-four Palestinians were killed, mostly civilians.[50] Typical of the documented Israeli atrocities in Jenin were these: a 'thirty-seven-year-old paralyzed man was killed when the IDF bulldozed his home on top of him, refusing to allow his relatives the time to remove him from the home'; a 'fifty-seven-year-old wheelchair-bound man ... was shot and run over by a tank on a major road outside the camp ... even though he had a white flag attached to his wheelchair'; 'IDF soldiers forced a sixty-five-year-old woman to stand on a rooftop in front of an IDF position in the middle of a helicopter battle' (HRW). Israeli authorities apparently didn't initiate 'proper investigations' in any of the 'unlawful killings', giving rise to fears that the IDF has been given 'a *carte blanche* to continue' (Amnesty). 'Though the IDF offensive against Nablus in April 2002 has not received the attention of Jenin', Amnesty further found, 'there were more Palestinians casualties (80) and fewer Israeli soldiers killed (four)', and a comparable pattern of human rights violations and war crimes as well as the complete or partial razing of 'religious and historical sites ... in what frequently appeared to be wanton destruction without military necessity'. In one grisly case, IDF soldiers repeatedly beat with their rifles, pummeled and flipped, and shoved off a truck and down stairs, a 'twenty-five year-old ... paralyzed from the waist down and confined to a wheelchair' (Amnesty). The IDF would later explain that the killing of a 'large number' of civilians has 'deterrent value' (senior IDF officer), and allowed for the killing of unarmed teenage boys on the grounds that they are 'people of an age to be fighters'. It's only a flea's hop to the Nazi justification for killing Jewish children on the grounds that otherwise 'a generation of avengers filled with hatred [will] grow up'.[51]

Recalling that Israel, 'frequently supported by the United States', has 'blocked all attempts to end human rights violations and install a system of international protection in Israel and the Occupied Territories', Amnesty International called on 'the international community and, in particular, the United States government to immediately stop the sale or transfer of weaponry that are used to commit human rights violations to Israeli forces'.

It wasn't only human rights organizations that criticized Operation Defensive Shield. Ehud Barak, for example, registered dissent: according to the former Prime Minister, Sharon should have acted 'more forcefully'. In the meantime, dismissing criticism of Israeli atrocities as driven by anti-Semitism, Holocaust Industry CEO Elie Wiesel lent unconditional support to Israel – 'Israel didn't do anything except it reacted … . Whatever Israel has done is the only thing that Israel could have done. … I don't think Israel is violating the human rights charter. … War has its own rules' – and went on to stress the 'great pain and anguish' endured by Israeli soldiers as they did what 'they have to do'.[52] Boasting that he 'left them a football stadium', one of Wiesel's agonized Israeli soldiers operating a bulldozer in Jenin later recounted in an interview: 'I wanted to destroy everything. I begged the officers … to let me knock it all down, from top to bottom. To level everything. … For three days, I just destroyed and destroyed. … I found joy with every house that came down, because I knew that they didn't mind dying, but they cared for their homes. If you knocked down a house, you buried forty or fifty people for generations. If I am sorry for anything, it is for not tearing the whole camp down. … I had plenty of satisfaction. I really enjoyed it.' A B'Tselem investigation in Ramallah found that, typically, at 'the Ministry of Education, not only was the computer network taken, so were overhead projectors and video players. Other equipment, including televisions and file cabinets full of records, such as student transcripts, were simply destroyed. … Hard disks were taken from civil society organizations that had invested years of work and millions of dollars to compile this material.' 'It was simply unbelievable', one young conscript recalled, 'people simply made an effort to both destroy and rob. … The sergeant major would bring a truck and load up. It was done openly.' 'The total picture', B'Tselem concluded, 'is one of a vengeful assault on all symbols of Palestinian society and Palestinian identity. This is combined with what can only be described as hooliganism: the result of thousands of teenage boys and young men in uniform allowed to run wild in Palestinian cities with no accountability for their actions.' *Haaretz* reported that Israeli soldiers occupying Ramallah 'destroyed children's paintings' in the Palestinian Ministry of Culture, and 'urinated and defecated everywhere' in the building, even 'managing to defecate into a photocopier' – no doubt with 'great pain and anguish'. It seems that this has become an IDF rite of passage: during Israel's occupation of Beirut in 1982, soldiers similarly defecated in Palestinian cultural and medical institutions.[53]

In July 2002, Israel moved quickly to avert yet another political catastrophe. With assistance from European diplomats, militant Palestinian organizations, including Hamas, reached a preliminary accord to suspend all attacks inside Israel, perhaps paving the way for a return to the negotiating table. Just ninety minutes before it was to be announced, however, Israeli leaders – fully apprised of the imminent declaration – ordered an F-16 to drop a one-tonne bomb on a densely populated civilian neighborhood in Gaza, killing, alongside a Hamas leader, eleven children and five others, and injuring 140. Predictably, the declaration was scrapped and Palestinian terrorist attacks resumed with a vengeance. 'What is the wisdom here?' a Meretz party leader asked the Knesset. 'At the very moment that it appeared that we were on the brink of a chance for reaching something of a cease-fire, or diplomatic activity, we always go back to this experience – just when there is a period of calm, we liquidate.' Yet, having headed off another dastardly Palestinian 'peace offensive', the murderous assault made perfect sense. Small wonder Sharon hailed it as 'one of our greatest successes'. And 'once again' in October 2002 'an outburst of violence' ended 'a period of relative calm in the Israeli–Palestinian conflict', the *Christian Science Monitor* reported, as Israel killed fourteen Palestinians and wounded more than a hundred (mostly civilians) in Gaza. 'The main Palestinian political faction, Fatah, was abstaining from terrorist attacks inside Israel and ... officials of the Palestinian authority were attempting to persuade militant Palestinian groups to do the same', it continued. The Israeli attack 'appeared to extinguish this initiative's chances for success' and 'may add credibility to assertions by Palestinians and others that Israel intentionally stokes the conflict'. European Union representative Javier Solana rued that the assault would undermine the Palestinians' new undertaking to 'distance themselves from violence' – which is presumably why the Israeli army commander in Gaza concluded that 'The operation was definitely successful from our point of view.'[54] Scoring a major victory on a related front, the Israeli government blocked Israeli peace activists in August 2002 from linking up with 700 of their Palestinian counterparts in Bethlehem. Reporting from

Bethlehem, Amira Hass observed that many Palestinians were endeavoring to 'open a pubic debate aimed at reducing Palestinian support for attacks inside Israel, without waiting for a change in Israeli policy'. The joint demonstration, she continued, 'was an example of that type of effort. It was an effort that failed, foiled by the Israeli authorities'.[55]

## Expulsion Redux

The Oslo process was premised on finding a credible Palestinian leadership to cloak Israeli apartheid: a Nelson Mandela to act the part of a Chief Buthelezi.[56] Camp David signaled the defeat of this strategy: Arafat refused – or, due to popular resistance, wasn't able – to play the assigned role. Without such a legitimizing Palestinian facade, the reality of Israeli apartheid stands fully exposed and subject to the same withering criticism as its South African precursor. 'If Palestinians were black, Israel would be a pariah state subject to economic sanctions led by the United States', the London *Observer* editorialized after the outbreak of the new *intifada*. 'Its development and settlement of the West Bank would be seen as a system of apartheid, in which the indigenous population was allowed to live in a tiny fraction of its own country, in self-proclaimed "bantustans", with "whites" monopolizing the supply of water and electricity. And just as the black population was allowed into South Africa's white areas in disgracefully under-resourced townships, so Israel's treatment of Israeli Arabs – flagrantly discriminating against them in housing and education – would be recognized as scandalous too.' Mainstream figures across the political spectrum, from President Carter's National Security Advisor, Zbigniew Brzezinski, to South Africa's Anglican Archbishop and Nobel Laureate, Desmond.Tutu, have since issued similar denunciations. 'I have been very deeply distressed in my visit to the Holy Land', Tutu declared. 'It reminded me so much of what happened to us blacks in South Africa. I have seen the humiliation of the Palestinians at checkpoints and roadblocks, suffering like us when young white police officers prevented us from moving about.'[57]

But paradoxically, whereas apartheid is no longer a tenable Israeli option, expulsion once again may be. Israel adopted the apartheid strategy after new precedents in international law and public opinion barred ethnic expulsions. In recent times, however, there has been a dramatic loosening of such juridical and moral constraints. Especially since September 11, the US has even ceased honoring international law in the breach, but rather effectively declared it null and void. Unlike its 1991 devastation of Iraq, the US's assault on Afghanistan was launched without any direct

UN sanction – not because it couldn't get such a sanction but because it wanted to make the point of not needing one. Unlike its use in the past of covert operations and legitimizing facades, like the Nicaraguan Contras, to overthrow nettlesome foreign governments, the US now brazenly talks about 'regime change'. And in proclaiming the doctrine of preventive war, the Bush administration has dealt a 'mortal blow' to Article 51 of the UN charter prohibiting armed attack except in the face of an imminent threat. 'Since Bush came to office', the London *Guardian* observes, 'the United States government has torn up more international treaties and disregarded more UN conventions than the rest of the world has in 20 years.'

> It has scuppered the biological weapons convention while experimenting, illegally, with biological weapons of its own. It has refused to grant chemical weapons inspectors full access to its laboratories, and has destroyed attempts to launch chemical inspections in Iraq. It has ripped up the anti-ballistic missile treaty, and appears to be ready to violate the nuclear test ban treaty. It has permitted CIA hit squads to recommence covert operations of the kind that included, in the past, the assassination of foreign heads of state. It has sabotaged the small arms treaty, undermined the international criminal court, refused to sign the climate change protocol and, last month, sought to immobilize the UN convention against torture so that it can keep foreign observers out of its prison camp in Guantanamo Bay. Even its preparedness to go to war with Iraq without a mandate from the UN Security Council is a defiance of international law far graver than Saddam Hussein.[58]

With crucial US backing, Israel is likewise now able to totally flout international conventions – as evidenced by its contemptuous and humiliating treatment in April 2002 of the UN's fact-finding mission on Jenin, and its shredding of the Oslo accord with the reoccupation of Palestinian-administered areas in the West Bank. Influential Israeli policy-makers like infrastructure minister Effi Eitam and former leftwing stalwarts like author A.B. Yehoshua openly advocate transfer, while former commander of the Air Force Eitan Ben Eliahu urges the necessity to 'thin out the number of Arabs here'. 'Every day that goes by', Amira Hass warns, 'the preachers of transfer feel ever more confident about raising their "permanent solution" in the Israeli public.' Israeli military correspondent Ze'ev Schiff points to the settlers' 'stealing and confiscating of Palestinian food' (justified by Israel's former chief rabbi on the grounds that 'the fruit from the trees planted by Gentiles on land inherited by the people of Israel does not belong to the Gentiles') as 'laying the groundwork for Transfer', and Israeli journalist Danny Rubinstein likewise observes that 'The settlers can always claim that they shoot at olive harvesters because the peasants are actually scouts meant to help prepare terror attacks – but the clear truth is that it's really a preparation for transfer.' Nearly one-half of Israelis support expulsion of West Bank and Gaza Palestinians, and nearly one-third support expulsion of Israeli Palestinians (three-fifths support 'encouraging' Israeli Palestinians to leave), while bumper stickers around Jerusalem urge the government to 'Deport the [expletives]'.[59]

The dean of Israel's 'new historians',[60] Benny Morris, explicitly justifies expulsion of the Palestinians not only in the event of a regional war but in the name of *Lebensraum*: 'This land is so small that there isn't room for two peoples. In fifty or a hundred years, there will only be one state between the sea and the Jordan. That state must be Israel.' This insight is of a piece with many of his recent pronouncements. According to Morris, the Zionist settlers had the right to expel Arabs from their homes in 1948 because 'they started shooting'. Early American settlers similarly maintained that 'We ... may now by right of Warre, and law of Nations ... destroy them who sought to destroy us: whereby ... their cleared grounds ... shall be inhabited by us.' Or, is it legitimate to expel in time of war but illegitimate to exterminate? Morris claims that Ben-Gurion's 'terrible mistake in 1948' was that he didn't 'complete the job' and expel 'one hundred percent' of the Palestinian Arabs; that Israeli Palestinians now constitute an 'existential danger' and a 'time bomb'; and that ideally 'the Arabs will leave' – exactly how he doesn't say except that 'this will become a strategic problem for the security forces'. Morris professes that as an historian his only concern is truth. Indeed, finding evidence of yet more 'massacres' of Arabs in 1948 'makes me happy'. What would one say of a German historian who expresses glee that he uncovered evidence of yet more gas chambers?

The Palestinians, according to Morris, are 'a sick, psychotic people'. They refuse to acknowledge that 'Jews have a just claim to Palestine' and that 'Zionism was/is a just enterprise'. Yet, Morris further states that this 'just claim' couldn't be redeemed and this 'just enterprise' realized without expelling the Palestinian Arabs: 'a removing of a population was needed. Without a population expulsion, a Jewish state would not have been established.' Such an 'inevitable' expulsion wasn't, however, 'morally defective. ... I morally accept the erection of the Jewish state.' This must mean that Palestinians are a 'sick, psychotic people' because they refuse to acknowledge that their expulsion wasn't 'morally defective': that it was morally just. In one remarkably disingenuous interview Morris denied statements of his already in print and went on to wax eloquent on the immorality of expulsion: 'I regard the notion of expelling a whole population as immoral and unjust and [it] will cause a grievous amount of suffering.' But if expulsion is 'immoral and unjust'; and expulsion of the

Palestinians was 'inevitable' in creating a Jewish state; how can Zionism be moral and just?

Prime Minister Sharon 'merely responds, usually with great restraint', Morris stated, and in Operation Defensive Shield 'no army has ever been more discriminating and gone to such lengths to avoid inflicting civilian casualties' and accordingly the final tally was merely 'two or three hundred deaths, mostly of Palestinian gunmen, and the destruction of several dozen homes'. It seems otherwise only because 'Western journalists' give credence to the 'never-ending torrent of Palestinian mendacity' and in particular to Arafat and the Palestinian Authority – a 'kingdom of mendacity' unlike 'straight, or far less mendacious, Israeli officials'. Putting to one side Sharon's own record on truth-telling, it bears notice that the most damning reportage on Israeli human rights violations typically comes not from Western but *Israeli* journalists; that all the major human rights reports on Operation Defensive Shield flatly contradict Morris's account of what happened; that Amnesty International found that virtually every official Israeli claim regarding its conduct during Operation Defensive Shield proved to be a flagrant lie; and that if Sharon shows 'great restraint' it's cause for wonder that – according to Israeli polls – 'everyone loves Arik' because he 'beats' Palestinians 'to a pulp'. On the other hand, Morris's inference that 'someone like Barak, coming from the left with the credit as someone coming from the peace camp, would have had a much easier time using the IDF much more liberally' is probably true – but this says much more about the brutality of Barak (and hypocrisy of the 'peace camp') than it does about the restraint of Sharon. With smug satisfaction Morris goes on to observe that once Sharon deployed the requisite force, 'Palestinians learned some lessons' and 'major acts of terrorism' ceased: 'So, force does appear to work, at least in the short term.' Indeed, the *very* short term – the day after his interview a suicide-bomber blew up a bus.[61]

Apart from mainstream Israeli support for expulsion, there's yet another cause for alarm. Throughout its history the Zionist movement has wagered against daunting odds. Victory always seemed beyond reach. 'The State of Israel owes its existence', Yael Zerubavel writes, 'to the very ethos that raises ideological commitment beyond realistic calculations.' Indeed, at each crucial juncture a 'miracle' – this word constantly recurs in Zionist historiography – saved it: the 'miracle' of the Balfour Declaration (Ben-Gurion); the 'miracle' of the Partition Resolution (Chaim Weizmann); the 'miraculous simplification of Israel's tasks' in the 1948 war (Weizmann, referring to the Arab flight); the 'miracle' of the June 1967 war; the 'miracle' of massive immigration of Soviet Jewry to Israel. A close reading of the documentary record shows, however, that these weren't really miracles. Rather, in each instance the Zionists maximally exploited a slender historical opportunity – 'revolutionary times' – by a comprehensive marshalling of their material and human assets. September 11 may yet prove to be another such occasion. The world has granted – or, has been coerced into granting – the US a kind of grace period to openly carry on like a lawless state. This means for Israel a window of opportunity to resolve the Palestine question, once and for all: it's a 'miracle' waiting to happen. Short of a full withdrawal from the Occupied Territories, Israel's only alternatives are to continue tolerating the terrorist attacks or to expel the Palestinians. One is hard-pressed to imagine, however, that Israel will absorb these attacks indefinitely. Their relentlessness might also temper the ensuing international condemnation of an expulsion.[62]

Should Israel attempt expulsion, it can probably count on support from powerful sectors in American life. House Majority Whip Tom DeLay and House Majority Leader Dick Armey sponsored a resolution supporting Israel's claim to the whole of 'Judea and Samaria', while Armey explicitly upheld that 'the Palestinians who are now living on the West Bank should get out of there'. Senator James M. Inhofe of Oklahoma intoned that 'the most important reason' the US ought to support Israel was that 'God said so. ... Look it up in the book of Genesis. ... In Genesis 13:14–17. ... This is not a political battle at all. It is a contest over whether or not the word of God is true.' When Senator Hillary Clinton, a liberal Democrat from New York, visited Israel earlier this year, she was hosted and embraced by Benny Elon, leader of Moledet, a party officially committed to 'transferring' the Palestinians. Turning to organized American Jewry, the picture becomes yet bleaker. A respected Washington attorney and Jewish communal leader, Nathan Lewin, called for the execution of family members of Palestinian suicide bombers. Reproaching critics of Lewin, prominent Harvard University Law School Professor Alan Dershowitz and national director of the Anti-Defamation League Abraham Foxman deemed Lewin's proposal a 'legitimate attempt to forge a policy for stopping terrorism'. In what might be termed the 'Lidice gambit', Dershowitz himself recommended a 'new response to Palestinian terrorism': the 'automatic destruction' of a Palestinian village after each terrorist attack (as well as the legalization of the torture of terrorist suspects). Dershowitz's proposal, however, lacks novelty. Israel pursued this strategy of murderous reprisals against Arab civilians in the early 1950s. A massacre perpetrated in 1953 by Ariel Sharon at the village of Qibya, which left some seventy villagers dead (the majority women and children), was compared by American newspapers to Lidice. Lewin and Dershowitz have teamed up to promote a new Washington-based National Institute for Judaic Law that will illuminate the Jewish roots of 'our legal system in America'. To judge by their interpretation of Jewish law, it's a wonder they didn't recommend that Timothy McVeigh's family be executed and his hometown obliterated. Inspired by Dershowitz, a group of former Israeli military officers and settlers supported by a pro-Israel charity in New York posted on its website this ingenious proposal to facilitate 'transfer': 'Israel issues a warning that, in a response to any terrorist attack, she will immediately completely level an Arab village, randomly chosen by a computer from a published list. ... The use of a computer to select the place of the Israeli response will put the Arabs and the Jews on a level footing. The Jews do not know where the terrorists will strike, and the Arabs will not know which one of their villages or settlements will be erased in retaliation. The word "erased" very precisely reflects the force of Israel's response.'[63]

Meanwhile, Joan Peters's colossal hoax, *From Time Immemorial*, which purports that Palestine was practically empty before Zionist colonization,[64] was reissued in February 2001 and, touted by American Jewish organizations and periodicals, immediately soared to the top of the Amazon sales rankings. After having disappeared into the night following the exposure of her fraud, Peters is now 'back in high demand for speaking engagements' and is getting (according to her) 'an amazingly wonderful, overwhelmingly positive response from audiences'. Alongside her forte, 'What Palestinian Land?', Peters's range of scholarly expertise has broadened to include 'Worldwide Islamic Jihad', 'Terrorism', and 'Religious Persecution by Muslims'. Christian fundamentalists rallying behind the demand for expulsion point to the Peters thesis for support, Christian Coalition founder Pat Robertson maintaining, for example, that 'the Palestinians are really Arabs who moved there a few decades ago. Their claim to that land really does not go back very far such as it is.' A documentary film based on *From Time Immemorial* is currently in the planning stages. With priceless irony, it's entitled 'The Myth'.[65] The Zionist investment in Peters's preposterous claim constitutes, incidentally, a backhanded admission that, had Palestine been inhabited (which it plainly was), the Zionist enterprise was morally indefensible.

Maintaining that Sharon 'has always harbored a very clear plan – nothing less than to rid Israel of the Palestinians', respected Israeli military historian Martin van Creveld has posited two alternative pretexts for expulsion. (1) The diversion of a global crisis such as an 'American attack on Iraq'. In this regard it bears recalling that in 1989 Benjamin Netanyahu urged the Israeli government to exploit politically favorable circumstances like the Tiananmen massacre to carry out 'large-scale' expulsions when the 'damage to Israel would have been relatively small'. (2) A spectacular terrorist attack that 'killed hundreds'. Apart from the regrettably real prospect that Palestinians (or others claiming to act in their support) might commit such an atrocity, judging from the historical record it's plainly not beyond possibility that Sharon would provoke it. Although 'some believe that the international community will not permit such an ethnic cleansing', van Creveld plausibly concludes, 'I would not count on it. If Sharon decides to go ahead, the only country that can stop him is the United States. The US, however, regards itself as being at war with parts of the Muslim world that have supported Osama bin Laden. America will not necessarily object to that world being taught a lesson.' The main US fear is that expulsion would trigger a reaction in the 'Arab street' toppling its client regimes. But twice before, on the eve of the assaults on Iraq and Afghanistan, elite American opinion harbored a similar fear. In both cases it proved unfounded. The Bush administration might try its luck again in the expectation that the 'Arab street' is a chimera. Meron Benvenisti conjured, in the pages of *Haaretz*, this nightmare scenario: 'An American assault on Iraq against Arab and world opposition, and an Israeli involvement, even if only symbolic, leads to the collapse of the Hashemite regime in Jordan. Israel then executes the old "Jordanian option" – expelling hundreds of thousands of Palestinians across the Jordan River.' Pointing up the likelihood in Israel's current state of 'moral dissolution' of a war-time expulsion ('there has never been a better opportunity'), he concludes that 'Nobody should be allowed to say they weren't warned.' 'If the US attacks Iraq and during that attack there is a mega-terrorist incident in Israel', former Shin Beth chief Ami Ayalon similarly warns, 'then Ariel Sharon could exploit the outbreak of rage in the Israeli public to conduct a mass transfer of Palestinians.' It's also possible that Israel will execute a large-scale internal transfer from West Bank villages to townships, or deport several thousand key local functionaries, leaving the Palestinian population even more leaderless than it already is. *Jane's Information Group*, taking note of the 'growing concern' that Sharon will exploit a US attack on Iraq to 'driv[e] out large numbers of Palestinians from the West Bank into neighboring Jordan', reports that already since the outbreak of the new *intifada* 'as many as 200,000 Palestinians, fleeing from the violence or the economic misery' have entered Jordan.[66]

The question remains – what would it take to effect a full Israeli withdrawal and avert this catastrophe? 'The basic tendency of Israeli policy and people', observes the perceptive Israeli writer Boas Evron, 'is to solve problems by means of force and to see force as the be-all and end-all, rather than trying diplomatic and political solutions', and to view borders with neighboring Arab states as 'nothing but a function of power relations'.

Likewise, Ze'ev Sternhell argues that a Zionist tenet is 'never giving up a position or a territory unless one is compelled by superior force'. In this regard it also bears keeping in mind what van Creveld calls 'the unique position' occupied by the military and martial values in Israeli society: 'It is comparable, if at all, only to the status the armed forces held in Germany from 1871 until 1945.' (The 'greatest compliment that anyone could receive was that he was a "fighter"' and 'the highest praise one could bestow on anything was to say that it was "like a military operation."'[67]) The reasonable inference is that Israel will withdraw from the Occupied Territories only if Palestinians (and their supporters) can summon sufficient force to change the calculus of costs for Israel: that is, making the price of occupation too high. The historical record sustains this hypothesis. Israel has withdrawn from occupied territory on three occasions: the Egyptian Sinai in 1957 after Eisenhower's ultimatum, Sinai in 1979 after Egypt's unexpectedly impressive showing in the October 1973 war, and Lebanon in 1985 and 2000 after the losses inflicted by the Lebanese resistance. In addition, it seems that Israeli ruling elites seriously contemplated withdrawal during the initial years of the first *intifada* (1987–9) due to the international and domestic costs inflicted on Israel by the Palestinian revolt.

Neither a conventional nor a guerrilla war seems a viable Palestinian option. Terrorism – apart from being morally reprehensible (if unsurprising) – will probably not budge Israel and if at all, will move it rightwards. Israeli elites accept civilian casualties as a necessary, if regrettable, price of power. They pay heed only when the Israeli military suffers losses or its deterrent capacity is undermined. Consider in this regard Sternhell's assessment of the impact on Israel of the new *intifada*:

> The number of Israeli civilian casualties in the past year is far greater than the number of soldiers who have been killed or wounded. When all is said and done, the army is waging a deluxe war: it is bombing and shelling defenseless cities and villages, and that situation is convenient for both the army and the settlers. They are well aware that if the army were to sustain casualties on the same scale as occurred in Lebanon, we would now be on our way out of the territories. We perceive the death of civilians in shooting attacks or at the hands of crazed suicide bombers in the heart of our cities, including the extinction of whole families, as a decree of fate or as a kind of act of nature. However, the death of soldiers immediately poses the critical questions: What are the goals of the war? For what end are the soldiers being killed? Who sent them to their death? As long as the conscript troops do not pay too heavily, as long as the reservists are not called up in massive numbers to protect and defend the occupation, the question of 'why' does not dictate the national agenda.[68]

Ample historical evidence – from indiscriminate bombing by Germany and the Allies during World War II to indiscriminate US bombing of

Vietnam – likewise attests that Israel's civilian population is unlikely to succumb to terrorism. Jewish terrorism no doubt catalyzed the British decision to terminate the Mandate in 1947, but the fundamental reason was Britain's financial insolvency after the war. In the Israeli case, the evidence suggests that 'when an external threat intensifies while, at the same time, there is a sense that all parts of society are exposed to that danger, a feeling of common fate emerges and the level of internal criticism declines': rather than plummeting in the face of terrorist attacks 'national morale' surges as the society closes ranks.[69]

In many respects, the current Palestinian resort to terrorism bears uncanny resemblance to the Zionist terror campaign after World War II against the British occupation. Although officially denouncing anti-British terrorism, Ben-Gurion and the Zionist authority he headed, the Jewish Agency, didn't cooperate with the British in apprehending terrorist suspects or even in calling upon the Jewish community to respect the law. On the one hand Ben-Gurion maintained that on principle he couldn't assist enforcing an unjust occupation. 'Without in the least condoning the acts committed', he wrote to British officials, 'the Executive considers the policy at present by the Mandatory Government ... to be primarily responsible for the tragic situation which has developed in Palestine. The Executive cannot agree that it can in fairness be called upon to appear in the invidious position of assisting in the enforcement of that policy.' On the other hand Ben-Gurion pleaded that he had lost control over the Jewish community, which no longer accepted occupation. A contemporary British assessment concluded that Zionist officials had fomented Jewish terrorism but also that they could no longer put a stop to it: 'By their incitement of the Yishuv through constant anti-British and anti-Government propaganda, they have so inflamed Jewish young men and women that terrorist organizations have received a fillip both in recruits and sympathy. Now the Jewish Agency find themselves no longer able to draw back without losing their authority over the Jewish community, and are being forced to greater lengths of extremism. The extent to which they cooperate with the terrorist organization is in some doubt. ... There is, however, some evidence that they have pre-knowledge of most incidents which have taken place.' Later revelations confirmed this cooperation. For example, the Jewish Agency publicly deplored the major terrorist attack on the King David Hotel killing some ninety people, although it had approved in advance targeting the hotel. The official Zionist condemnation, one historian has written, 'contained more than a smattering of hypocrisy and opportunism'.[70]

'What was intolerable – and what was in fact being done – was to attempt to have it both ways', a sympathetic British Labour MP on the scene observed, 'to claim constitutional rights for the Jewish Agency as a loyal collaborator with the mandatory, and simultaneously to organize sabotage and resistance.' While Ben-Gurion sought 'to remain within the letter of the law as chairman of the agency' by officially condemning terrorism, he also 'tolerate[d] terror as a method of bringing pressure on the administration'. Zionist leaders acquiesced in the deadly attacks for another reason as well, according to the British MP. Jewish terrorism was 'winning popular support' as 'perfectly decent Jews in Palestine cannot help somehow admiring the terrorists and even assisting them when they seek refuge in their houses'. Ben-Gurion and the Jewish Agency had to 'condone terrorism' in order to 'prevent a swing of public opinion' to extreme Zionist parties and against themselves. The only means to fight Jewish terrorism, the British MP concluded, was 'to remove the legitimate grievances of every Jew in Palestine', and to 'state objectively ... the historical causes for the growth of this beastly phenomenon in a decent people'. Were the British to do this they could 'rely on the support of moderate elements in suppressing terrorism, and I believe that the majority of the population would turn against the extremists'. If, however, the British ignored the reasons behind Jewish support for terrorism and simply demanded 'the replacement of the Jewish Agency by another organization and the disarming' of the Jewish resistance, the MP warned, it 'would merely provoke the Jews into a fanatical support of the extremists'.[71]

When the British imposed martial law in retaliation for multiple Zionist terrorist attacks ('The bestialities practiced by the Nazis could go no further', the staid *Times* of London would later editorialize), Ben-Gurion passionately condemned the draconian measures for both inflicting collective punishment on the Jewish people and effectively hindering the struggle against terrorism. If only for its current resonance, this denunciation deserves extended quotation:

> Two hundred and fifty thousand Jews of Tel Aviv and suburbs, core of country's social and industrial life, and thirty thousands of Jews in Jerusalem, mostly working-class quarters, isolated from all normal contact with outside world, facing complete breakdown of mechanism civilized life apart from food supplies and skeleton medical service. Industry crippled, trade paralyzed, unemployment threatening to become catastrophic. Industrial raw materials cannot enter, goods manufactured with available stock cannot be marketed outside. Workers cut off from places of work, children from schools. These restrictions have not affected terrorists nor stopped their outrages but instead have increased resentment of hard-hit population, created fertile soil for terrorist propaganda, frustrating community's attempt to combat terrorism by itself. Martial Law absolutely futile and senseless unless really meant to punish whole community, ruin its economy and destroy the foundations of the Jewish National Home.[72]

It also merits recalling, however, that although Jewish terrorist attacks (nearly twenty per month) left hundreds of British dead and wounded, the British 'never deliberately fired into crowds', and 'a Jewish large-scale massacre never took place and entire Jewish settlements were not demolished with explosives'. The reason behind this relative British restraint, according to van Creveld, was 'British recognition that Jews constituted a "semi-European" race.' By contrast, Palestinians suffer at the hands of Israel the lethal fate of non-Europeans.[73]

A non-violent Palestinian civil revolt creatively building on the lessons of the first *intifada* and synchronized with international – in particular, American – pressure probably holds out the most promise in the current crisis. It could bog down and neutralize Israel's army. Among Israel's chief worries during the first *intifada* was the IDF's loss of morale and élan as it sought to violently quell a civilian population, and the army's diminishing capacity to fight a '*real* war' as it trained for and engaged in 'police-type operations' (emphasis in original).[74] A reservoir of Palestinian support for such a strategy of civil disobedience perhaps already exists.[75] Should a Palestinian leadership successfully harness this constituency, there are reasonable grounds for hoping that its message will resonate among many Israelis. The refusenik movement among Israeli conscripts has prompted a national debate and, although registering massive support for Sharon's brutal repression, Israelis have supported in roughly equal numbers withdrawal from the West Bank and Gaza.[76]

The US will impose on Israelis a full withdrawal only when its vital interests are at stake or public pressure compels it to do so. Such pressures may yet be exerted. Support for Israel among ordinary as well as 'influential' Americans has markedly declined.[77] Modeled on the anti-apartheid divestment campaign in the 1980s, a movement on American college campuses calling for divestment from Israel is gathering momentum. In an unusual intervention Harvard University President Lawrence Summers labeled this new divestment campaign anti-Semitic 'in effect'. Yet, if the divestment campaign targeting South Africa wasn't anti-white 'in effect', why is a divestment campaign targeting an occupation that 'is the only one of its kind in the world, and is reminiscent of ... the Apartheid regime in South Africa' (B'Tselem), and that 'is guilty of apartheid policies' (Ami Ayalon, former Israeli head of the Shin Bet) anti-Semitic 'in effect'? Curiously, Summers has not been similarly moved to criticize a member of his own faculty urging the 'automatic destruction' of Palestinian villages. Lending his moral stature to the new divestment campaign, Archbishop Tutu exhorted 'average citizens to again rise to the occasion, since the obstacles to a renewed movement are surpassed only by its moral urgency.'[78] In fact, Europeans are contemplating a spectrum of actions from consumer boycotts to arms embargoes, while scores of courageous international volunteers (including many Jews) have journeyed to the Occupied Territories to shield Palestinian civilians from attack and publicize Israeli atrocities. Israel's apologists like Wiesel deplore these initiatives as evidence of a resurgent anti-Semitism. Disparaging similar allegations after Israel's 1982 invasion of Lebanon, the respected Israeli academician Uriel Tal responded: 'The bitter cries about anti-Semitism which allegedly raises again its head all over the world serve to cover up the fact that what is disintegrating in the world is Israel's position, not Jewry's. The charges of anti-Semitism only aim to inflame the Israeli public, to inculcate hatred and fanaticism, to cultivate paranoid obsession as if the whole world is persecuting us and that all other peoples in the world are contaminated while only we are pure and untarnished.' To be sure, world Jewry's position *will* disintegrate if it doesn't publicly dissociate from Israel's crimes. In a passionate denunciation of current Israeli policy for 'staining the Star of David with blood', a prominent Jewish parliamentarian and former British shadow Foreign Secretary lamented that 'the Jewish people ... are now symbolized throughout the world by the blustering bully Ariel Sharon, a war criminal implicated in the murder of Palestinians in the Sabra–Shatila camp and now involved in killing Palestinians once again'.[79]

'Every morning now, I awake beside the Mediterranean in Beirut with a feeling of great foreboding', the insightful Middle East correspondent Robert Fisk reflected this past year. 'There is a firestorm coming. And we are blissfully ignoring its arrival; indeed, we are provoking it.'[80] Apart from being a moral abomination, expulsion of the Palestinians can set off a chain reaction in the Arab world that will make September 11 look like a pink tea. But it's yet within our grasp to seize these fraught times and achieve a just and lasting peace for Israel and Palestine.

This edition of *Image and Reality* includes a new chapter on the 'peace process' and an appendix critically analyzing a recent study of the June 1967 war. In addition to those acknowledged in the first edition of this study, I would like to thank Michael Alvarez, Mouin Rabbani, Jennifer Loewenstein and Shifra Stern for their assistance.

*Norman G. Finkelstein*
*December 2002*

# Introduction

The origins of this book reach back to Israel's invasion of Lebanon in June 1982. I began then for the first time to read systematically about the Israel–Palestine conflict. The topic that most engaged me was the question of Zionism. Specifically, I was intrigued by the debate joined by Michael Walzer and Noam Chomsky on whether a Jewish state can also be a democratic state.[1] The research proved sufficiently fruitful that I was able to turn it into a doctoral dissertation.[2] My thesis – that Zionism is a kind of Romantic nationalism fundamentally at odds with liberal values – is synthesized in the first chapter of this volume.

Just as the research for my dissertation was completed, I came across a newly published book, *From Time Immemorial*, which, according to the pantheon of luminaries quoted on the back cover, radically undercut prevailing assumptions about the Israel–Palestine conflict.[3] So disturbing (and bizarre) was the book's main argument – that Palestinians had, individually and *en masse*, fabricated their genealogies – that I read it with more than the usual care. It quickly became obvious that the said author, Joan Peters, had concocted – and, more revealingly, that the American intellectual establishment had lent its name to – a threadbare hoax. As it happened, documenting the fraud – Chapter 2 of this volume – proved by far the easier task as compared to publicizing my findings. A small sense of the difficulties met is sketched in the chapter's postscript.

Chapters 3 and 4 consider two of the more substantial contributions to the literature on the Israel–Palestine conflict, Benny Morris's *The Birth of the Palestinian Refugee Problem, 1947–1949*, and Anita Shapira's *Land and Power*.[4] Morris's contention is that the Palestinian refugee problem was 'born of war, not by design'. Shapira maintains that a 'fundamental supposition' of the Zionist movement was that the realization of its project 'would not require the use of force'. I conclude that the research findings, however original and useful (much more so in Morris's volume), do not support these largely apologetic arguments.

In recent years, the received wisdom on the first Arab–Israeli war of 1948 has come under withering examination by the so-called new historians.[5] Israel's rationale for its joint assault with England and France on Egypt in 1956 has carried less and less conviction with time; the few myths that managed to endure have now been punctured by Morris's latest study.[6] Israel was never able to make a credible case for its 1982 invasion of Lebanon. Even Israeli scholars fairly quickly conceded that 'calling the Lebanon War "the War for the Peace of Galilee" is more than a misnomer. It would have been more honest to call it "the War to Safeguard the Occupation of the West Bank"'.[7] Yet, Israel's version of the June 1967 and October 1973 wars has shown remarkable resilience. In both instances, Israel is widely seen as the unprovoked victim of Arab aggression. Chapters 5 and 6 explore, respectively, the backgrounds to these wars. My conclusion is that the Israeli narrative does not in either case withstand close scrutiny.

My approach throughout is to use, as the foil of my critique, an influential piece, or standard body, of scholarship. The form seemed best suited to my double purpose in writing this book: to point up the systematic bias of, as well as to make a modest contribution to, the extant literature on the Israel–Palestine conflict.

Perhaps the most memorable passages of Leon Trotsky's *The Revolution Betrayed*[8] are those devoted to the 'friends of the Soviet Union': that claque of left–liberal intellectuals that served up one apologia after another for Stalin's crimes. Michael Walzer is one of the best-known 'friends of Israel'. Walzer's intellectual odyssey offers an instructive insight into the etiology of apologetics for Israel.[9]

In his early works – notably *Just and Unjust Wars*[10] – Walzer's defense of Israel is embedded in a universal ethic. The task was easy enough since a critical literature on Israel barely existed and Walzer, in any event, was able to pass scholarly muster with the barest reference to any literature at all: Israel's case was seemingly so unimpeachable that facts were almost beside the point.

Beginning in the late 1970s (but especially after the Lebanon War), new scholarship became available which cast Israel and the Zionist legacy generally in a much harsher light than hitherto. Paralleling these literary revelations were the practical, political ones of Israel's brutal occupation of the West Bank and Gaza. Defending Israel with reference to the ordinary standards of right and wrong proved increasingly difficult. Symptomatically, Walzer jettisoned the liberal project – most famously in *Spheres of Justice*[11] – as he argued that there was no universal moral code but, rather, only ethnically specific clusters of 'shared understandings': one 'national "family"' cannot be judged by applying the 'shared understandings' of another, and – more important – there is no common language to morally adjudicate between 'national "families"' should a conflict arise. Substantive moral judgments are strictly reflexive. The moral universe inhabited by a 'national "family"' is separate and disparate, homogeneous and enclosed. The liberation of one nation, as Walzer suggests in *Exodus and Revolution*,[12] is not at all tainted if achieved at the expense of another nation's extermination. Each 'national "family"' judges for itself according to its own peculiar standards and exigencies what is just and what is not. Incommensurate, juxtaposed 'national narratives' thus displaced in Walzer the embracive notion of 'just and unjust wars'.

Culminating Walzer's rupture with liberalism is *The Company of Critics*.[13] Walzer – like the fascist ideologues that Julien Benda chastised in *The Treason of the Intellectuals* – now professes that not only is there no universally applicable standard of justice but that, even if one were contrived, the 'connected' social critic would still privilege his 'own' people. Asked to explain his silence as France waged a bloody, colonial war in Algeria, the French-Algerian writer, Albert Camus, replied: 'I believe in justice, but I will defend my mother above justice.' Walzer takes Camus's apothegm as his credo. Only a hopelessly estranged intellectual would valuate abstract moral principles above the flesh and blood of one's kith and kin. Thus, Walzer's *bêtes noires* are Sartre and de Beauvoir for attaching equal weight to an Arab life as to a French one during the Algerian war and, especially, Rosa Luxemburg, for displaying the same compassion for a tormented African as for a tormented Jew. For Israel's 'friends', the ring of Walzer's message is as welcome as it is familiar: to be 'connected' is to ask, 'Is it good for the Jews?'[14]

More from sorrow than anger, a dear friend reflected one night as we sat in his Hebron home that 'history will not forgive what was done to the innocent people of Palestine'. I am less certain about what history *will* do: after all, it depends on who does the writing – the conqueror or the conquered. But I do not for a moment doubt what history *should* do. I once heard someone I greatly admire and respect lecture on her experiences in the Warsaw Ghetto and the Nazi death camps. Asked afterwards her views on the Middle East conflict, my mother briefly replied, 'What crime did the Palestinians commit except to be born in Palestine?' That is the core reality lost in all the fabricated images of the Israel–Palestine conflict. The great offense of the Palestinians was that they refused to commit auto-dispossession; they balked at 'clearing out' for the Jews. It is perhaps true that the common ethical code joining humanity is – at present, at any rate – a fairly rudimentary one; but one does not need more than such a rudimentary standard to measure that the people of Palestine have fallen victim to a colossal injustice. And I fail to see any redeeming virtue in 'connecting' with the perpetrators of that injustice as against the victims of it. Jules Roy, also a French–Algerian writer, answered Camus: 'It is not a matter of choosing one's mother above justice. It is a matter of loving justice as much as one's mother.'[15]

As the ample scholarly apparatus to this book attests, the plea of 'not knowing' cannot in good faith be entered at history's bar. Those who want to know can know the truth; at all events, enough of it to draw the just conclusion. The *mea culpa* of Hitler's adjutant, Albert Speer, applies with equal force to the case at hand:

> Whether I knew or did not know, or how much or how little I knew, is totally unimportant when I consider what horrors I ought to have known about and what conclusions would have been the natural ones to draw from the little I did know. Those who ask me are fundamentally expecting me to offer justifications. But I have none. No apologies are possible.[16]

Indeed, the Germans could point in extenuation to the severity of penalties for speaking out against the crimes of state. What excuse do we have?[17]

*Norman G. Finkelstein*
*September 1994, New York City*

# PART I

# Theory and History

# 1

## Zionist Orientations

### *The Theory and Practice of Jewish Nationalism*

In *Zionism and the Arabs, 1882–1948: A Study of Ideology*, Yosef Gorny has provided the most authoritative study to date on the crucial period when the Zionist movement made its first contacts with, struggled against and ultimately prevailed over Palestine's indigenous Arab population.[1] As its subtitle indicates, the focus is Zionist ideology. Gorny reveals in fascinating detail both the variousness of possibilities in the Zionist idea and its intransigent kernel that precluded any *modus vivendi* with the Palestinian Arabs.

### Defining the Zionist Enterprise

Gorny begins by identifying the 'ideological consensus' within which most, if not the full gamut, of Zionist thinking unfolded. One element of this consensus, he stresses throughout the study, was at the core of Zionist belief and proved to be the principal obstacle to any reconciliation with the Arabs – namely, that Palestine should one day contain a Jewish majority.

Within the Zionist ideological consensus there coexisted three relatively distinct tendencies – political Zionism, labor Zionism and cultural Zionism. Each was wedded to the demand for a Jewish majority, but not for entirely the same reasons.[2]

The touchstone of the French Revolutionary liberal idea was that a rational and just social order could and ought to be constructed on shared political – i.e. democratic – values. Hence, the nation-state was conceived above all else as a consensual relationship and the citizen as its irreducible unit and building block. Originating in the post-French Revolution reaction to Enlightenment rationalism and liberalism, political Zionism's point of departure was the presumed bankruptcy of the democratic idea.[3] Romantic nationalists argued that more profound bonds both 'naturally' united certain individuals and 'naturally' excluded others. Ideally, they concluded, each such organically connected community ought to be endowed with an independent state. Having located the thinking of Theodor Herzl, the founder of modern Zionism, in such 'German sources', Hans Kohn, probably the most eminent authority on modern nationalism (and himself a Zionist at one time), goes on to observe:

> According to the German theory, people of common descent … should form one common state. Pan-Germanism was based on the idea that all persons who were of German race, blood or descent, wherever they lived or to whatever state they belonged, owed their primary loyalty to Germany and should become citizens of the German state, their true homeland. They, and even their fathers and forefathers, might have grown up under 'foreign' skies or in 'alien' environments, but their fundamental inner 'reality' remained German.[4]

Analogous assumptions informed the distinctive Zionist approach to the Jewish Question. Throughout the Diaspora, its adherents argued, Jews constituted an 'alien' presence amidst states 'belonging' to other, numerically preponderant, nationalities. Anti-Semitism was the natural impulse of an organic whole 'infected' by a 'foreign' body (or too obtrusive a 'foreign' body).

In effect, the Zionist analysis of the Jewish Question duplicated the reasoning of anti-Semitism, which invoked the same argument to justify Jew-hatred. Indeed, the prescription it proposed for the Jewish predicament was inscribed in the logic of anti-Semitism as well. Political Zionism sought, not to combat anti-Semitism – which was viewed as, at best, a quixotic undertaking – but to achieve a *modus vivendi* with it. It proposed that the Jewish nation resolve the Jewish Question by (re-)establishing itself in a state that 'belonged' to it. To achieve this, Jews would have to constitute themselves somewhere as the majority: for, wasn't the statelessness of the Jews pointed up precisely in the fact that, everywhere in the Diaspora, they formed a numerical minority? Majority status would consequently ratify the Jews' constitutional title to a state. The Revisionist leader Vladimir Jabotinsky, who stood well within the Zionist ideological consensus (p. 165; all page references are to Gorny's book) therefore stated that 'the creation of a Jewish majority … was the fundamental aim of Zionism', since 'the term "Jewish state" … means a Jewish majority', and Palestine 'will become a Jewish country at the moment when it has a Jewish majority' (pp. 169, 170–1, 233).[5]

For labor Zionism, the Jewish Question was not only the absence of a state but the class structure of the Jewish nation, which had become lopsided and deformed in the course of its long dispersion: Galut (exile) had created a surfeit of Jewish middlemen, marginal petty entrepreneurs and *Luftsmenschen*, and a deficit of Jewish laborers. Part of Zionism's mission was to lay the basis for a healthy state by reconstituting the Jewish working class. Since the interests of this class (here labor Zionism was evidently borrowing from and adapting for its own purposes a page in Marx) required a socialist Jewish state, this was the only true solution to the Jewish predicament. Labor Zionism thus represented less an alternative than a supplement to political Zionism. The class struggle and economic development would unfold, ideally, in a field purified of 'alien' elements. In Ben-Gurion's words,

> The right to independent national existence, to national autonomy, which no reasonable person could regard as conflicting with solidarity between peoples, means above all: independent national existence on the basis of an independent national economy. (pp. 137–8)[6]

Labor Zionism imbued the demand for a Jewish majority with a dual significance: first, it would ratify the Jews' right to claim title to the state and, second, it would signal their right to radically alter the demographic balance in Palestine, clearing the way for the territorial concentration of the Jewish nation. To quote Ben-Gurion again: '[T]he majority is but a stage along our path, albeit *an important and decisive stage in the political sense*. From there we can proceed with our activities in calm confidence and concentrate the masses of our people in this country, and its environs' (p. 216; emphasis added).[7]

In general, the Zionist movement's demand for a Jewish majority was grounded in a cluster of assumptions that gainsaid the liberal idea. Cultural Zionism, however, did not explicitly deny the desirability (or viability) of a democratic polity. Its demand for a Jewish majority represented not so much a categorical rejection of liberalism as a solution for certain alleged limits within it, especially in the domain of culture.

Cultural Zionists wished to resolve not the 'problem of the Jews' but the 'problem of Judaism' in the modern world. In their view, the survival of Judaism and the Jewish people was threatened less by anti-Semitism than by an increasingly secular civilization that rendered them anachronisms. The real danger was not the Gentiles' icy rejection but, rather, their seductive embrace. The most pressing task of Zionism, therefore, was to elaborate a *Weltanschauung* relevant to the contemporary world yet still bearing the unmistakable impress of the Jewish people's resplendent legacy. The success or failure of this enterprise would determine whether the Jewish nation survived.

This new national synthesis could not unfold, however, while Jewry remained scattered throughout the Diaspora. It required a 'spiritual center' which could concentrate and unify the energies of the Jewish nation and, ultimately, serve as a centripetal force for it. To create this center, Jews had to constitute themselves as the numerical majority in some state, since the crucial cultural institutions in any society are subordinate to the state and the state always bears the imprint of the majority nation. Even in the most democratic of states, the cultural life of the minority cannot but be – in the words of the outstanding theoretician of cultural Zionism, Ahad Ha'am – 'cribbed and crammed' (pp. 102–3).[8]

Cultural Zionism thus conceived a Jewish majority as the *conditio sine qua non*, not for a state of the Jews, but for the unbridled spiritual renaissance of the Jewish nation. Palestine, with its Jewish majority, would eventually serve as a spiritual beacon for world Jewry; it would not, however, be a state to which all Jews were, perforce, politically bound.[9] Yet, the status of the demand for a Jewish majority was, for all practical purposes, defined by the hegemonic sectors of the Zionist movement. For them, the Jewish majority and the Jewish state were inextricably linked: a Jewish majority was the means and a state constitutionally beholden to world Jewry the end.

Gorny's meticulous and exhaustive analysis of the documentary record convincingly demonstrates that, for all its tactical flexibility, the Zionist leadership never wavered in its devotion to the idea of a state of the Jewish nation. What this leadership offered Palestine's indigenous Arab population was, at best, institutional safeguards that its 'civil' rights would not be violated once the Jewish state was established; but such protections for the future Arab minority did not preclude – indeed, they presupposed – that, in principle, the prospective state would belong to the Jewish people.

Consider the 'compromise' formulae put forth by the Zionist movement in the wake of the 1929 Arab riots, when the fortunes of the Zionist enterprise had reached their lowest ebb to date. Weizmann proposed the principle of parity – that is, total equality in the administrative representation of both peoples – but his intention (in Gorny's words) was 'to guarantee the civil status of the Arabs' within a state whose 'proprietorship' would be Jewish (p. 206). Likewise, the 'compromise' Ben-Gurion favored at this time was not a bi-national state but a bi-national regime, in which (in Gorny's words) 'the Jewish people would have ownership rights over Palestine and the Arab community would have the right to reside therein' (p. 212).[10] Finally, Jabotinsky promised to Palestine's Arab inhabitants full and equal rights as a national entity, in accordance with the finest traditions of Austro-Hungarian socialist thought, yet on the principle of a Jewish majority/Jewish state he would entertain no compromise (pp. 233–4).

The Zionist leadership's devotion to the principle of a Jewish state of the Jewish nation found concrete and unambiguous expression in its insistence that, *vis-à-vis* the future state, diasporan Jews would have to be accorded a privileged status. Ben-Gurion, for example, denied that a Jewish state necessarily implied domination of the (Arab) minority (pp. 306–7). The minority could still enjoy full civil and national equality, and autonomy in education, culture and religion; indeed, a member of the minority might even be elected president or premier of the state. True, the Jewish majority would determine the cultural 'image' of the state, but that was (even) true in all democratic states. However, what would distinguish the Jewish state, in his view, was its orientation towards the entire Jewish people: 'The state will exist not only for its own inhabitants ... but in order to bring in masses of Jews from the Diaspora and to assemble and root them in their homeland.'[11]

We have thus far identified the trends in Zionism that fell within what Gorny designates the Zionist ideological consensus. Gorny also devotes considerable space to those elements in the Zionist movement that stood outside the ideological consensus but were nonetheless committed to some version of Zionism.

Generally speaking, what attracted these dissidents to Zionism was its cultural dimension; politically, they favored a bi-nationalist resolution of the Palestine conflict, in which the 'total equality of political rights of the two peoples' would be recognized (p. 119). What especially interests us here, however, is not their programs and perspectives *per se* (of which there were many and all of which underwent crucial revisions over time). For, although the dissident Zionist circles (e.g. Brit-Shalom, Ihud) could count in their ranks some of the most eminent members of the Movement, including the distinguished sociologist Arthur Ruppin, first president of the Hebrew University Judah Magnes, and the renowned philosopher Martin Buber, they were, nevertheless, numerically weak and politically marginal. Rather, it is their critique – sometimes implicit, more often explicit – of the Zionist mainstream. This critique is noteworthy because it was both internal to the Zionist movement and thus not easily dismissed and, on any accounting, exceptionally cogent and incisive. Indeed, it is as pertinent today as it was when first elaborated.

The Zionist dissidents denied that the success of the Zionist project – at any rate, as they defined it – hinged on the Jews constituting themselves as the majority in Palestine. They were not in principle opposed to Jews becoming at some point the numerically preponderant element; what they objected to was the meaning conferred on the idea of a Jewish majority by their adversaries in the Zionist movement. The dissidents argued that behind the demand for a Jewish majority lurked the intention to establish a superior claim to the prospective state, one which would confer on Jews an 'advantage in rights' and implied the domination and suppression of the Arabs of Palestine (pp. 120, 145, 284). Hugo Bergmann of Brit-Shalom deftly exposed the regressive assumptions of mainstream Zionism:

> The contradiction between the political outlook of Brit-Shalom and that of its opponents is not anchored in our stand on the Arabs alone. It is much more fundamental and deep-rooted. Our political convictions stem from the perceptions of Judaism. We want Palestine to be ours in that the moral and political beliefs of Judaism will leave their stamp on the way of life in this country, and we will carry into execution here that faith which has endured in our hearts for two thousand years. And our opponents hold different views. When they speak of Palestine, of our country, they mean 'our country,' that is to say 'not their country.' This viewpoint is borrowed from Europe at the time of its decline. It is based on the concept of a *state which is the property of one people.* ... Thus several European States today believe that the existence of a State implies that one people, among the peoples residing there, should be granted priority right. ... They justify this injustice by means of the sacred egotism of the State. (pp. 122–3; emphasis in original)

Bergmann also denounced the concept of 'the people of the country' which, in his words, 'award[ed] prior right to one people over another, as if the one were the native son and the other a stepchild' (p. 123). In effect, it controverted the democratic principle of citizenship.

## Justifying the Zionist Enterprise

Zionism sought to establish a state that the Jewish people could claim fully as their own. In a state thus conceived, non-Jews, even if enjoying full rights of citizenship, could hope to figure, at best, as an excrescence on the body politic. The realization of the Zionist project in Palestine thus, in effect, implied the transformation of the indigenous Arab population into a gratuitous presence living on the sufferance of the Jewish majority.

All its apparent – or public – optimism notwithstanding, the Zionist leadership harbored few illusions that the Palestinian Arabs would ever acquiesce to such an eventuality. Jabotinsky mocked the idea that the roots of Arab objections perhaps lay in their imperfect understanding of the Zionist enterprise: the Arabs understood it only too well, which was why they were so vehemently opposed even to its modest beginnings (pp. 165–6). During the Arab Revolt of 1936–39, Weizmann conceded to his comrades assembled at the Zionist Congress that 'If I were an Arab, I would undoubtedly think as they do, although I would certainly act somewhat differently' (p. 249).[12]

Concomitantly, the Zionist leadership did not suffer from any illusions that its project would not have to be imposed on Palestine's overwhelmingly Arab majority or that its implementation could be accomplished without the egregious violation of democratic norms. Several days before his death, Berl Katznelson, for instance, admitted to a meeting of young people that a Jewish state meant forcing the will of the Jews on the Arabs, that this was reprehensible from the point of view of pure democratic morality, but that all Zionist actions had been carried out against the wishes of the majority (p. 303). Gorny also cites Jabotinsky's highly pertinent observation that ever since Herzl first proposed the idea of a charter, the Zionist movement had acted on the premise that until the Jews formed the preponderant element in Palestine, the democratic principle of majority rule would have to be honored in the breach there.[13] Nonetheless, the mainstream Zionist movement never doubted its 'historical right' to impose a Jewish state through the 'Right of Return' on the indigenous Arab population of Palestine.

Zionism grounded its preemptive right to establish a Jewish state in Palestine – a right that, allegedly, superseded the aspirations of the indigenous population – in the Jewish people's supposedly unique claim to that land. To fully understand this argument, we must first step briefly back to the genesis of Zionist ideology.

Modern anti-Semitism combined two conceptually distinguishable – if, in practice, overlapping – discourses, each of which disputed from a different angle the liberal understanding of the relationship between nation and state:

1. A *political* discourse, which suggested that the state/political superstructure belonged, not to its citizens, but to the nation (organic community) with the numerical majority. This was the basic contention of 'Romantic' anti-Semites such as Fichte in Germany.

2. A *topographic* discourse, which suggested that the state/territorial unit belonged, not to its inhabitants *per se*, but only to the nation (organic community) that could establish a singular historical–spiritual connection with it. This was the basic contention of the Romantics, as well as the 'integral' anti-Semites such as Barrès in France.

We have already seen that Zionism replicated the reasoning of the anti-Semitic political discourse and followed its logic to conclude that the resolution of the Jewish Question required a polity 'belonging' to the Jewish nation. In effect, Zionism also replicated the reasoning of the anti-Semitic topographic discourse in reaching the conclusion that resettling Jewry in its 'historical' ('organic', 'integral', etc.) homeland was the way to resolve the Jewish Question. The obvious candidate for such a home-land was, of course, Palestine ('Land of Israel'), with its manifold resonances for the Jewish people. Ideologically, the implications of in-corporating Palestine into a discourse that depicted it as the 'historical' homeland of the Jewish people were twofold. In the first place, it rendered the Jewish people 'alien' to every other state/territorial unit, thus sanc-tioning the claims of anti-Semitism.[14] Second, and more importantly for our purposes here, it rendered Palestine of only incidental importance to its resident Arab population.

As Gorny vividly illustrates, the above argument formed the keystone in the arch of Zionist ideology as well as the Movement's first, last and only line of rhetorical defense as the opposition of Palestine's indigenous Arab opposition escalated.[15] As formulated by the Zionist leadership during the period covered by Gorny's study, world Jewry's preemptive right to Palestine derived from three interrelated 'facts': (1) the Jewish people's bond with the land of Palestine was *sui generis*; (2) the Arab inhabitants of Palestine, even if they did constitute a nation, were not a separate nation but, rather, part of a greater Arab nation, for which Palestine had no distinctive resonances; ergo (3) the Jewish people had a 'historical' right to Palestine whereas the indigenous Arab population could lay claim, at best, to mere 'residential' rights there.

The cultural Zionist Ahad Ha'am was (in Gorny's words) 'firm in his insistence that both peoples in Palestine be treated justly', but he 'saw the historical rights of the Jews outweighing the Arabs' residential rights in Palestine' (pp. 103–4). Max Nordau declared that Palestine was the 'legal and historical inheritance' of the Jewish nation, 'of which they were robbed 1900 years ago by the Roman aggressors'; the Palestinian Arabs had only 'possession rights' (p. 157). Jabotinsky asserted that since the Arab nation incorporated 'large stretches of land', it would be an 'act of justice' to requisition Palestine 'in order to make a home for a wandering people'; the Palestinian Arabs would still have a place to call their own, indeed, any of fully nine countries to the east and west of the Suez (pp. 166, 168–9). In Ben-Gurion's view, Palestine had a 'national' significance for Jews and thus 'belonged' to them; in contrast, Palestinian Arabs, as constituents of the great Arab nation, regarded not Palestine, but Iraq, Syria and the Arabian peninsula as their 'historical' homeland – Palestine was of only 'individual' importance to them, the locale where they happened to dwell presently. The Jewish people were therefore entitled to concentrate in Palestine whereas the Palestinian Arab community should enjoy merely those rights redounding on residents (pp. 210–12, 217–18).[16]

Within the ranks of the Zionist movement, only the small circle of dissidents took exception to these formulations. The Brit-Shalomist Ernst Simon, for example, held that Zionism's 'historical right' to Palestine was 'a metaphysical rather than a political category'. Relating as it did to 'the very inner depths of Judaism', this 'category ... is binding on us rather than on the Arabs'. Hence, he 'emphatically' denied that it conferred on Jews any right to Palestine without the consent of the Arabs (p. 197).[17]

Zionism's preemptive claim to Palestine bore directly on two policy issues that loomed large during the British mandate period: partition and population transfer.

For the Zionist movement, the Jewish people's 'historical' homeland incorporated the whole of Palestine, including Transjordan, the Golan Heights and southern Lebanon. Given the supra-historical – indeed, fantastical – nature of this 'historical' writ, no mundane agreements could cancel it. Partition was consequently seen as a provisional compromise, useful until conditions were ripe for full realization of the Zionist *endziel*. Ben-Gurion thus carefully qualified his acceptance of the partition scheme put forth by the British in the late 1930s:

> The Jewish State now being offered to us is not the Zionist objective. Within this area it is not possible to solve the Jewish question. But it *can* serve as a decisive stage along the path to greater Zionist implementation. It will consolidate in Palestine, within the shortest possible time, the real Jewish force which will lead us to our historic goal. (p. 259; emphasis in original)

In his private correspondence, Ben-Gurion amplified this point. The Jewish state, he wrote his son, would have 'an outstanding army – I have no doubt that our army will be among the world's outstanding – and so I am certain that we won't be constrained from settling in the rest of the country, whether out of accord and mutual understanding with the Arab neighbors or otherwise' (p. 260; Gorny cites only a part of this quote).

Zionism's claim to the whole of Palestine not only precluded a *modus vivendi* based on partition with the indigenous Arab population, it called into question *any* Arab presence in Palestine. This was especially so, given that, in practice, the Zionist discourse on Palestine merged with the Zionist discourse on a Jewish polity. Both these discourses posited that (1) to 'normalize' their condition, Jews needed to relocate to a state (polity/territorial unit) that 'belonged' to them, and (2) non-Jewish inhabitants, even citizens and long-term residents, of the Jews' state (polity/territorial unit) were not intrinsically 'of' it.[18] The political and topographic discourses in Zionism thus run parallel; they are mutually reinforcing and validating. The result is a radically exclusivist ideology which renders non-Jews at best a redundant presence and easily lends itself to schemes favoring population transfer – and expulsion.

For most Zionists, Gorny observes, a mass exodus of the indigenous Arab population was always the optimum resolution of the Palestine conflict (pp. 303–4).[19] Labor Zionists, for example, did not view 'the idea of a mass transfer ... as morally deplorable at any time, and their hesitations related only to its political effectiveness' (p. 305). In the late 1930s, the revered labor Zionist Berl Katznelson avowed publicly that he could, in all good conscience, support a British-inspired proposal to forcibly uproot the native Arab population:

> A distant neighbor is better than a close enemy. They will not suffer through the transfer, and we most certainly will not. In the last analysis, this is a political settlement reform benefiting both parties. I have thought for some time that this is the best of all solutions, and during the riots I became more convinced that it must happen some day. (p. 258)

Even the extreme left of the Zionist labor movement agreed that there was nothing morally objectionable in the notion of a compulsory population transfer. True to his Zionist convictions, Aharon Zisling thus said that 'I do not deny our moral right to propose population transfer. There is no moral flaw to a proposal aimed at concentrating the development of national life; the contrary is true – in a new world order it can and should be a noble human vision.' Zisling's only reservation was pragmatic: its implementation could result in an all-out war with the neighboring Arab states (p. 262). On the other end of the mainstream Zionist spectrum, Jabotinsky likewise did not consider population exchange an historical injustice, even if forcibly applied (pp. 270–1).[20]

## Implementing the Zionist Enterprise

We have seen that the root cause of the Palestine conflict was – to quote Gorny – the Zionist aspiration 'to restore full or partial sovereignty over Palestine to the Jewish people' (p. 13). The Zionist movement sought to establish a Jewish state in Palestine – that is, a state in which non-Jews would figure, at best, as a superfluous presence. Zionist leaders were fully cognizant that the indigenous Arab population of Palestine would view with alarm any and all efforts to create such an exclusivist state. We turn now to the strategy that they elaborated to cope with the anticipated – and, subsequently, actual – resistance. Such an inquiry is useful not only for its intrinsic historical interest but also because it reveals the deep sources of present-day Israeli strategic thinking.

Within the Zionist movement, strategic consensus on the Arab Question was remarkable.[21] Essentially, this consensus was informed by three interrelated premises:

1. *The Zionist movement should neither expect nor seek the acquiescence of the Palestinian Arabs.* In his seminal series of articles, aptly entitled 'The Iron Wall', Jabotinsky insists that 'a voluntary agreement between us and the Arabs of Palestine is inconceivable, now or in the foreseeable future ... precisely because they are not a mob, but a living nation' (pp. 165–6). We have seen that, notwithstanding their public protestations to the contrary, most Zionist leaders concurred in this view. Thus, Ben-Gurion conceded that, between the Jews and Arabs of Palestine, 'there is indeed a conflict which is hard to overcome' (p. 228). What was more, the Palestinian Arabs were not even viewed as the relevant party for reaching a settlement of the Palestine conflict. As noted above, the Zionist movement regarded the indigenous Arab population's claims on Palestine as tentative at best. Accordingly, Gorny observes, Weizmann 'did not regard the Palestinian Arabs as partners in negotiations on the future of Palestine' (p. 114).

2. *The success of the Zionist enterprise was dependent on the support of one (or more) Great Power(s).* Given the anticipated – and, later, the real – resistance of Palestine's indigenous population to the Zionist project, Movement leaders recognized that they could never gain a firm foothold in Palestine without the backing of one (or more) Great Power(s). As Jabotinsky succinctly put it, 'Settlement can [only] develop under the protection of a force which is not dependent on the local population, behind an iron wall which they will be powerless to break down' (p. 166). To win the support of a Great Power for its enterprise, the Zionist movement evidently had to offer a *quid pro quo*. This was especially so, given that Zionism intended to establish the Jewish state in Palestine – a region that, at the dawn of the New Imperialism in late nineteenth-century Europe, figured crucially in every Great Power's strategic thinking.[22] In effect, before any Great Power would agree to facilitate a colonizing enterprise in Palestine, the colonizers would have to subordinate their project to its strategic interests. This is exactly what the Zionist movement set out to do from early on.

As the conflict between the Ottoman Turks and the Arabs unfolded in the early twentieth century, Jabotinsky proposed an alliance with the Turks to undermine the unity and homogeneity of the Arab world. It was Jabotinsky's insight that the Turkish imperial policy of divide and rule was congruent with Zionist interests, and that the fiercer the political competition between Turks and Arabs, the more likely the former would be 'to regard with growing favor the increase in our numbers in Palestine. The growth of Arab power will gradually increase Turkish sympathies with us' (p. 53). Jabotinsky's proposal constitutes a kind of precedent for Zionist thinking in the wake of World War I, when Great Britain replaced Turkey as the dominant power in the Middle East. Whatever disappointments and frustrations it may have given the Zionist movement along the way, from the Balfour Declaration until the termination of the Palestine mandate, the British Empire served as the 'iron wall'. Gorny stresses that Weizmann's strategy 'was based, above all, on the assumption that the alliance with Great Britain was the sole external guarantee for the achievement of Zionist goals' (p. 108). He goes on to observe that, 'In this respect there was a consensus from the first within the Zionist movement, encompassing all sectors, from Weizmann through the labor movement, to Jabotinsky and the Revisionist movement at a later date (ibid.; see also p. 176).

In effect, Zionism represented a double advantage to the imperialist overseers: on the one hand, it could serve as an imperial bridgehead in a strategically crucial but politically volatile region and, on the other, it could serve as a lightning rod for local popular discontent, thereby deflecting attention from the imperial power. Essentially this – the Jewish state as 'strategic asset' – was the *quid pro quo* that the Zionist movement offered the British. Gorny observes that Weizmann, who handled the external affairs of the Zionist movement, devoted his 'untiring efforts' to 'persuad[ing] the British Government of the identity of interests between the national goals of the two peoples' (p. 108). He thus argued that a Jewish Palestine could serve as a regional garrison to defend the Suez Canal, as well as a loyal political base amidst the newly independent Arab states. He contrasted the total devotion of the Jewish population to the British Empire with the political fickleness of the Arabs, whose movement was anti-European in orientation (pp. 114, 207). Similarly, Jabotinsky, who formulated strategy for the quasi-autonomous Revisionist wing of the Zionist movement, asserted that, 'if there is one outpost on the Mediterranean shore in which Europe has a chance of holding fast, it is Palestine, but a Palestine with a Jewish majority' (p. 234).

3. *The Palestine conflict should be resolved within the framework of a regional alliance subordinate to the interests of the Great Power(s).* In Jabotinsky's view, the Jewish state idea was so antithetical to Arab sensibilities that the Zionist movement could count only on the British to support its endeavors (p. 166). Less extreme Zionist leaders, however, articulated a more nuanced approach to the Arab world, distinguishing between the Palestinian Arabs

and their brethren who were not directly affected by the Zionist enterprise. The neighboring Arab regimes, they believed, could be convinced – however reluctantly – of the advantages of a partnership with Zionism. The Zionist movement would facilitate the Arab renaissance in exchange for the right to exercise sovereignty in a small corner of the vast territory over which the Arab people claimed jurisdiction. The Palestine conflict would thus find its resolution in an enlarged regional framework. On the one hand, once isolated from Arab politics in general, its significance would be dramatically reduced. As Weizmann put it in a letter to Balfour, 'the issue known as the Arab problem in Palestine will be of merely local character and, in effect, anyone cognizant of the situation does not consider it a highly significant factor' (p. 110). On the other hand, the Palestinian Arabs could realize their national aspirations in their 'authentic' homeland – i.e. the region that lay between the three points of the Mecca–Damascus–Baghdad triangle – which, with Zionist assistance, would soon be experiencing a rebirth. Hence, Ben-Gurion's optimistic suggestion that there was no 'inevitable contradiction' between Jewish and Palestinian Arab national aspirations, so long as the problem was viewed in its full regional scope (p. 228).

In effect, the Zionist movement was proposing to provide the linchpin of a pan-Arab confederation subordinate to the interests of the British Empire (pp. 110–11, 260). The Jewish state would both serve as Great Britain's regional gendarme and bolster the local Arab regimes. Zionism's fundamental reliance on the British to establish and maintain its foothold in Palestine restricted its options *vis-à-vis* the Arab world. It could only enter into negotiations that were consistent with the interests of Great Britain (pp. 86–7). In practice, this meant that the regional alliances that Zionism forged would have to be with dependent and therefore feckless, unpredictable and domestically unpopular Arab elites. Yet, given the very nature of Zionism's project – i.e. the intent to implant an exclusivist Jewish state in the midst of the Arab world and at the expense of the Palestinian Arabs – only the more corrupt Arab elites could, in any case, be expected to align themselves with it.[23] Clearly, alliances built on so fragile and unstable a foundation would do little to mitigate Zionism's dependence on a Great Power. Indeed, the Zionist movement's identification with, and identification of Zionism with, the most regressive and barren social forces in the Arab world (an unavoidable consequence of the alliances),[24] would tend, ultimately, to increase its regional insecurity and exacerbate its dependence on a Great Power. These considerations help to account for Ben-Gurion's deep forebodings about the fate of a Jewish state in the Arab world even in the event of a conclusive Jewish–Arab settlement on a regional basis and his injunction that such a hypothetical settlement would still have to (in Gorny's words) 'operat[e] in accordance with the interests of the British Empire' (p. 260; see also pp. 227, 255).

Just as the Zionist dissidents took exception to the *endziel* and the ideological rationalizations of the mainstream Zionist movement, so they took exception to its strategic *modus operandi*. An August 1931 Brit-Shalom editorial charged that in its quest for a Jewish majority and Jewish state, the Zionist movement had associated itself with (in Gorny's paraphrase) 'reactionary and imperialist forces against the resurgent East' (p. 194).[25] Sounding this same theme in a subsequent number of the association's journal,[26] the distinguished Brit-Shalomist Gershom Scholem suggested that the Zionist movement would one day regret the alliance it had forged with British colonialism against the oppressed peoples in the Arab world: 'either it will be swept away with the imperialist nations or burned in the furnace of the revolution of the renascent East'. The one alternative was to recast the Zionist project in such a way that the Zionist movement could identify with the 'forces of revolution'. 'If it must fall', he admonished, 'it is better to fall with those who are on the right side of the barricades' (pp. 195–6).

The Zionist movement did not heed the reprovals of its dissidents, with consequences which are all too painfully familiar today. Indeed, the scope of the Zionist enterprise has, by now, been reduced to its *modus operandi*. Israel has not resolved the Jewish Question; if anything, the enthrallment of the self-described 'Jewish state' to Western imperialism and its local satraps has exacerbated it. Israel has not become the spiritual beacon for world Jewry; indeed, it is arguably less fecund culturally than the Jewish communities in so-called Galut.[27] Israel has not remade the Jewish people into a 'working nation'; if anything, it is transforming Israeli Jews into a parasitic class – *pieds noirs* battening off cheap Arab labor and massive foreign subventions.[28]

The means have become the ends. What is the *raison d'être* of Zionism in the contemporary world save as an outpost of 'reactionary and imperialist forces against the resurgent East'?

# 2

# A Land Without a People

## Joan Peters's 'Wilderness' Image

Turnspeak – the cynical inverting or distorting of facts, which, for example, makes the victim appear as culprit.

*From Time Immemorial*, p. 173

Few recent books on the origins of the Israel–Palestine conflict evoked as much interest as Joan Peters's study, *From Time Immemorial.*[1] Virtually every important journal of opinion printed one or more reviews within weeks of the book's release. Harper & Row reported that, scarcely eight months after publication, *From Time Immemorial* went into its seventh printing. Author Joan Peters reportedly had 250 speaking engagements scheduled for the coming year.

Reviewers have differed in their overall assessment of the book. But they have uniformly hailed the research and the demographic findings that are at the core of Peters's study. Jehuda Reinharz, the distinguished biographer of Chaim Weizmann and current president of Brandeis University, acclaimed *From Time Immemorial* in *Library Journal* (15 April 1984) as a 'valuable synthesis' and 'new analysis' that 'convincingly demonstrates that many of those who today call themselves Palestinian refugees are former immigrants or children of such immigrants'. Walter Reich, who has made a career in recent years of cautioning against deniers of the Nazi holocaust, happily joined in the chorus denying Palestinians a past. In his *Atlantic* review (July 1984), Reich praised Peters's book as 'fresh and powerful ... an original analysis as well as a synoptic view of a little-known but important human story'. 'If Peters's arguments,' he perorated, 'especially the demographic one, are confirmed, they will certainly change [our] assumptions about the Arab–Israeli conflict.' In *Commentary* (July 1984), Daniel Pipes threw all caution to the wind in his appraisal of Peters's findings – her 'historical detective work has

21

produced startling results which should materially influence the future course of the debate about the Palestinian problem'. Ronald Sanders, author of a monumental study of the Balfour Declaration, likewise opined in *The New Republic* (23 April 1984) that Peters's demographics 'could change the entire Arab–Jewish polemic over Palestine'. Martin Peretz, again in *The New Republic* (23 July 1984), suggested that there wasn't a single factual error in the book, and that, if widely read, it 'will change the mind of our generation. If understood, it could also affect the history of the future.' At the other end of the mainstream spectrum, Sidney Zion gushed in *National Review* (5 October 1984) that Peters's book was 'the intellectual equivalent of the Six-Day War' and that 'the most remarkable thing about it all, the scariest thing, is that nearly everything in this book reads like hard news. No area in the world has been so heavily covered by the news media. And yet one woman walks in and scoops them all.' Timothy Foote, in the *Washington Post* (24 June 1984), acclaimed *From Time Immemorial* as 'part historic primer, part polemic, part revelation, and a remarkable document in itself'.

The accolades continued. Nazi holocaust scholar Lucy Dawidowicz congratulated Peters for having 'brought into the light the historical truth about the Mideast'. Barbara Probst Solomon called *From Time Immemorial* 'brilliant, provocative and enlightened'. Barbara Tuchman ventured that the book was a 'historical event in itself'. Saul Bellow predicted that 'Millions of people the world over, smothered by false history and propaganda, would be grateful for this clear account of the origins of the Palestinians.' Moralist Elie Wiesel promised that Peters's 'insight and analysis' would shed new light on our understanding of the Mideast conflict. Arthur Goldberg, Paul Cowan and others added their voices – and names – to the chorus of praise.

That a scholarly work meets with critical acclaim would hardly be news, were it not for the fact that *From Time Immemorial* is among the most spectacular frauds ever published on the Arab–Israeli conflict. In a field littered with crass propaganda, forgeries and fakes, this is no mean distinction. But Peters's book has thoroughly earned it.

The fraud in Peters's book is so pervasive and systematic that it is hard to pluck out a single thread without getting entangled in the whole unravelling fabric. To begin with, the fraud falls into two basic categories. First, the evidence that Peters adduces to document massive illegal Arab immigration into Palestine is almost entirely falsified. Second, the conclusions that Peters draws from her demographic study of Palestine's indigenous Arab population are not borne out by the data she presents. To confound the reader further, Peters resorts to plagiarism.

## Daunting Hercules

Peters purports to document massive illegal Arab immigration into the Jewish-settled areas of Palestine during the British mandate years (1920–48). Her thesis is that a significant proportion of the 700,000 Arabs residing in the part of Palestine that became Israel in 1949 had only recently settled there, and that they had emigrated to Palestine only because of the economic opportunities generated by Zionist settlement. Therefore, Peters claims, the industrious Jewish immigrants had as much, if not more, right to this territory than the Palestinian 'newcomers'.

Peters begins by recalling that Palestine's Arab population expanded at a remarkable rate during the years of the British mandate. She is skeptical of the generally accepted opinion – scholarly, official British, even mainstream Zionist[2] – that 'natural' increase accounts for by far the greater part of the growth in Palestine's Arab population in this period. Peters writes that 'the so-called "unprecedented" rate of "natural increase" among the non-Jews was never satisfactorily broken down or explained' (p. 223). She takes special exception to the findings of the 'population expert' (her phrase) A.M. Carr-Saunders in his 1936 study, *World Population*. In her version of his conclusions (p. 224), Peters first alleges that Carr-Saunders 'contradicted' himself by, on the one hand, claiming that 'the fall in death rate' was the 'likely' cause of the Palestinian Arabs' population increase and then asserting that 'Medical and sanitary progress has made little headway among the Palestinian Arabs as yet, and cannot account for any considerable fall in the death-rate.'

If we consult the pages in *World Population* cited by Peters, however, we discover the following:

> Medical and sanitary progress, *so far as it affects the personal health and customs*, has made little headway among the Palestinian Arabs as yet, and cannot account for any considerable fall in the death-rate. But general administrative measures, in the region of quarantine, for example, have been designed in the light of modern knowledge and have been adequately carried out. Measures of this kind can be enforced almost overnight. ... Therefore we can find in these administrative changes, brought about by the British occupation of Palestine, what is in any case a tenable explanation of the natural increase of population among Arabs. (pp. 310–11; my emphasis)

Carr-Saunders does indeed state that 'medical and sanitary progress' couldn't explain the 'fall in death rate', but only insofar as such progress impinges on the 'personal health and customs' of the Palestinian Arabs. He then goes on to say that recently implemented medical and sanitary administrative measures such as the quarantine could explain the decline in the mortality rate. The 'contradiction' evidently results, not from a lapse in Carr-Saunders's reasoning, but from Peters's (unacknowledged) deletion of the crucial qualifying phrase in her citation from *World Population*.

Next, Peters mentions the 'administrative measures' explanation only to dismiss it as a 'rather lame possibility'. She offers not a single reason for this evaluation. Peters concludes her mini-inquisition with the following summary of Carr-Saunders's position:

> In other words, the new 'phenomenal' rise in the Arab population of Palestine, which had remained sparse and static for two hundred years despite constant replenishing, was attributed to a sudden, hyped natural increase of the 'existing' long-settled indigenes. That phenomenon, or so went the rationalization, resulted from *new* conditions. Yet, it was also acknowledged that because of its recent timing, the introduction of those new conditions *could not in fact have been responsible* for the population increase in the period of time for which it was credited! (Peters's emphases)

Note that Carr-Saunders's finding is precisely the opposite of the one Peters attributes to him: the new conditions – i.e. 'general administrative measures' – offer a 'tenable explanation of the natural increase of population among Arabs'.

Having thus mangled what she now qualifies as a 'self-contradicting expert source', Peters swings her cleaver in the direction of the 1938 *Palestine Partition Commission Report*, which she reproves for 'try[ing] to reconcile contradictory "facts"' (pp. 224–5). She cites, without comment, the following excerpt from the *Report* to illustrate this supposed shortcoming:

> We thus have the Arab population reflecting simultaneously two widely different tendencies – a birth-rate characteristic of a peasant community in which the unrestricted family is normal, and a death-rate which could only be brought about under an enlightened modern administration, with both the will and the necessary funds at its disposal to enable it to serve a population unable to help itself. It is indeed an ironic commentary on the working of the Mandate and perhaps on the science of government, that this result which so far from encouraging *has almost certainly hindered close settlement by Jews on the land*, could scarcely have been brought about except through the appropriation of tax-revenue contributed by the Jews. (Peters's emphasis)

Peters is apparently unaware that different tendencies often coexist in the real world and that the observation of the Partition Commission cited above is no more than a commonplace illustration of this fact.

In this manner, Peters sets aside the conventional wisdom on the demographics of Palestine's Arab population during the Mandate years.

She is now in a position to advance her own explanation of the Arab population's unusual growth – namely, massive 'hidden' immigration. That is, Peters avers that a significant part of the population of Palestine in 1947 was not indigenous.

Peters is reluctant to specify the exact percentage of Palestinian Arabs who were not indigenous. This is a curious omission on the part of an author who elsewhere pretends to achieve scientific precision in her calculations. The few hints that Peters does give about this crucial matter are remarkable for their inconsistency. This, too, is odd in a study that devotes so much space to alleged numerical discrepancies in refugee reports, population statistics and other documents.

On two occasions, Peters suggests that the number of illegal Arab immigrants who had settled in the Jewish areas of Palestine was 'great enough to compare with [the] admittedly immigration-based increase of the Jews' (p. 275; see also p. 337). That would put total 'illegal' or 'un-recorded' Arab immigration at about 370,000. Elsewhere (p. 381), Peters seems to set her sights considerably lower – 'at least 200,000' through 1939, she reports. In a third place (p. 298), she implies that almost the entire Arab population of Palestine was immigrant and not indigenous.[3] That would put the total number of 'hidden' Arab immigrants and their descendants at roughly 1,300,000. In still a fourth place (p. 253), Peters muses whether Arab immigration into the Jewish-settled areas of Palestine between 1893 and 1947 may have been in the 10:1 ratio to Jewish immi-gration she purports to establish for the very first years of modern Zionist settlement.[4] By this calculation, Arab immigration into Palestine's Jewish-settled areas through 1947 would have been on the order of 3,700,000, that is well over 1,000 per cent greater than the second of Peters's esti-mates quoted above. What is even more astonishing is that this figure is nearly three times the *total* Arab population in *all* of Palestine in 1947.[5]

For the sake of argument, let us assume that the figure Peters wishes to propose for illegal Arab immigration is somewhere between 200,000 and 400,000. Peters is thus alleging that non-indigenous Arabs constituted fully one-half of the Arab population residing in the region of Palestine that became Israel in 1949.

The first thing to be said about this thesis is that Peters's own data refute it. Peters's demographic study (see pp. 36f. below) shows that Palestine's Arab population expanded 'naturally' by a factor of (at least) 2.7 between 1893 and 1947.[6] Peters puts Palestine's Arab population at 466,400 in 1893 (p. 255, Table G). Multiplying 2.7 by 466,400 we get 1,259,280. Palestine's total Arab population stood at 1,303,800 in 1947 (ibid.). Natural increase therefore accounts for all but (at most) 44,520 of the Arabs in Palestine in 1947. The thesis that Peters intends to prove is thus, by her own reckoning, untenable. Was Peters unaware that the results of the demographic study demolished her thesis? Did she simply elect to ignore this unpleasant fact?

Citing 'British government records' (p. 427), Peters puts the official estimate of illegal Arab immigrants who had settled in Palestine at about 10,000 for *all* thirty years of the British mandate. She herself contends, on the contrary, that on average for *each* of the thirty years of the Mandate, 10,000 Arabs had settled illegally in the Jewish areas of Palestine.

Peters's thesis is, to say the least, audacious.[7] The burden of her case is to prove the plausibility of this extraordinary revisionist figure. To do so, she draws on what reviewers have claimed is prodigious original research. Even John C. Campbell, in the one lukewarm notice to date (*The New York Times Book Review*, 13 May 1984), acclaimed Peters's 'massive research ... [which] would have daunted Hercules'. In fact, nothing could be further from the truth. A close reading of Peters's voluminous footnotes reveals that she relies almost exclusively on the standard official documents of the period – the 1930 *Hope Simpson Report*, the 1937 *Peel Commission Report*, the 1945–46 Anglo-American *Survey of Palestine*, the annual British reports to the League of Nations and so on. None of this evidence is new.[8]

This discovery raises an intriguing question. Without exception these official, mostly British-authored reports concluded that – in the words of the *Survey of Palestine* – 'Arab immigration for the purposes of settlement [in Palestine] is insignificant'.[9] Yet, Peters manages to use these *very same* documents to 'prove' precisely the contrary. How does she manage this astonishing *volte face*?

In effect, Peters uses a three-pronged strategy to supply evidence where none exists: (1) multiple references; (2) a 'tip of the iceberg' theory; and (3) major surgery.

### Multiple references

The fragments of evidence that Peters does offer the reader (almost all of which are, in any case, falsified) are repeated over and over again. Peters's wildly chaotic presentation of the relevant material manages to conceal this fact to some extent.

### 'Tip of the iceberg' theory

Peters repeatedly implies that the scant evidence she does come up with is actually worth many times its apparent value. This is because the British purportedly turned a blind eye to all but the most flagrant cases of illegal

Arab immigration into Palestine. It follows that for every *reported* Arab deported from Palestine, many other illegal Arab immigrants must have been allowed to ·stay behind.

This argument hinges on the allegation that the British were indifferent to all but the most egregious instances of illegal Arab infiltration. Unfortunately for Peters, however, save for a relatively brief period during World War II (October 1942–October 1944), there isn't a particle of evidence to support this 'theory'.

But Peters did not let this obstacle deter her. She completely falsifies a section of the 1930 *Hope Simpson Report* to secure the crucial evidence and then repeatedly refers back to this same doctored material at each critical juncture in the text to clinch her argument. Peters construes the section in question to mean that the British only deported 'flagrant' illegal Arab immigrants, letting many others stay. This is sheer invention. The document says nothing of the sort. Rather, it makes the following recommendations for handling illegal immigration – Jewish, Arab, etc. – into Palestine:

> *Discouragement of illicit entry*. – As to the treatment of such [illegal] immigrants, when they are discovered, it should be the rule that they are at once returned to the country whence they came. The rule may possibly work harshly in individual cases, but unless it is understood that detection is invariably followed by expulsion the practice will not cease. It is probable that it will cease entirely as soon as it is discovered that the rule is actually in force.
>
> The case of the 'pseudo-traveller' who comes in with permission for a limited time and continues in Palestine after the term of his permission has expired is more difficult. Where the case is flagrant, recourse should certainly be had to expulsion. In case of no special flagrancy, and where there is no special objection to the individual, it is probably sufficient to maintain the present practice, under which he is counted against the Labor Schedule, though this method does a certain injustice to the Jewish immigrant outside the country, whose place is taken by the traveller concerned.[10]

Before turning to Peters's rendering of these two paragraphs, the following points should be stressed:

(a) the *Report* evidently urges that illegal immigrants be deported 'at once';

(b) a *single* exception is made in the case of the 'pseudo-traveller' of 'no special flagrancy' – he may be reclassified as a legal immigrant;

(c) *Jews* were by far the main beneficiaries of the latter special provision;[11]

(d) the British *included*, in the total figure for recorded Arab immigration,[12] *all* Arab 'travellers' reclassified as legal immigrants.[13] The special case of the reclassified 'pseudo-traveller' is thus, for the purposes of Peters's argument, completely irrelevant. Recall that Peters alleges that, in addition to the officially registered Arab immigrants, some 300,000 *unrecorded* Arabs had entered and settled in Palestine. The only policy statement in the *Hope Simpson Report* pertinent to her thesis reads: illegal immigrants should 'at once [be] returned to the country whence they came'.

Peters makes nineteen – sometimes implicit, more often explicit – references to the section of the *Hope Simpson Report* cited above. She purports that it 'says'/'admits'/'acknowledges'/'suggests' that:

1. illegal Arab immigrants 'were addressed only when their "detection" had become "flagrant"' (p. 229);

2. 'all but the most blatant cases of illicit Arab immigration [were] overlook[ed]' (p. 232);

3. '"the case of the 'pseudo-traveller' who comes in with permission for a limited time and *continues* in Palestine after the term has expired" [is] "present practice," a method that was "*injustice*" to the *Jews*' (p. 232; Peters's emphases);

4. 'large-scale Arab immigration was a recognized "practice"' (p. 233);

5. 'it was the "present practice" of British officials to blink at all but the most "flagrant" of the thousands of Arabs immigrating into Western Palestine' (p. 296);

6. 'the illegal Arab immigration was an "injustice" that was *displacing* the prospective Jewish immigrants' (p. 296; Peters's emphasis);

7. illegal Arab immigrants were expelled 'only [in] "flagrant" cases' (p. 297);

8. the illegal immigrants subject to immediate deportation were all Arabs (p. 297);

9. only when 'flagrant' 'illicit immigrants' 'are discovered' should they be deported (p. 297);

10. Arab immigrants and in-migrants were committing an '"injustice" [because] these emigres from other areas were fill[ing] the places ... meant to provide space for the hundreds of thousands, if not millions, of Jewish refugees' (p. 326);

11. the 'sufficient' British '"practice" was [to] add ... the Arab immigrants into the "economic absorptive capacity" as though they were "indigenous Arab population for millennia"' (p. 375);

12. 'it was "injustice" for "illicit" Arab immigrants to "take the places" that Palestinian Jews created for Jewish immigrant hopefuls "outside the country"' (p. 375);

13. it was the 'casual British "practice"' to allow ' "illicit" Arab immigrants' to take the places of would-be Jewish immigrants abroad (p. 375);

14. 'illegal Arab immigrants ... [and] Arab in-migrants ... [were] all counted as "natives" unless they were "flagrant"' (p. 376);

15. 'the police were encouraged not to deport illegal Arab immigrants, and the only Arab deportees were those whose presence had become 'flagrant" (pp. 376-7);

16. 'policy only "found" those illegal Arab immigrants who were "flagrant"' (p. 378);

17. 'the Palestine authorities ... were under orders *not* to deport Arab illegal immigrants unless they were embarrassingly noticeable' (p. 379; Peters's emphasis);

18. 'the Arab demand for "justice" is ... "injustice"' (p. 394);

19. 'Arab migrants and immigrants ... committed the "injustice" of "taking the places" of Jews in the "Jewish National Home"' (p. 402).

As comparison with the full text of the cited section of the *Hope Simpson Report* shows, each and every one of the above references to its content falsifies both the letter and the spirit of the document.

To sum up, Peters argues *ad nauseam* that, since the British responded to only the most flagrant instances of illegal Arab immigration, we should assume for every illegal Arab immigrant reported deported during the Mandate years, many times more illegal immigrants must have remained in Palestine. Without the falsification of the *Hope Simpson Report*, Peters could not have sustained this thesis, which is fundamental to the argument of her book.

*Major surgery*

Peters still needs the 'tip' to prove the 'iceberg'. She still needs a fact before she can make multiple references to it. Peters resolves this problem by embarking on a falsification spree that, in John Campbell's phrase cited earlier, 'would have daunted Hercules'.

Peters does not adduce one substantive, pertinent piece of evidence to document her thesis that is not in some way mangled. But though Peters is a gross falsifier, she is not lacking in cleverness. For example, the quotations she falsifies in the text are often accurately rendered somewhere in a footnote. I suspect that Peters will at some point argue that she could not possibly have intended to conceal anything since the full quotation is right there, buried in her 120 pages of footnotes.

This is not the place to document all of Peters's crude and shameless distortions. In the space available, I will first sample and gloss Peters's characteristic methods. These are illustrated in Tables 2.1, 2.2 and 2.3.

| *Hope Simpson Report* (1930) | *From Time Immemorial* | Comments |
|---|---|---|
| In Palestine, ' … Egyptian labor is being employed in certain individual cases … ' | '[A]ccording to that *Report*, evidence of Arab immigration abounded: "Egyptian labor is being employed; … " ' (p.297) | Peters does not even insert an ellipsis after 'employed' to indicate that something – in this case, the crucial qualifier – was deleted. She corrects for her 'oversight' in the footnote where the quote appears in full. |
| '[A]rab unemployment is liable to be used as a political pawn. Arab politicians are sufficiently astute to realize at once what may appear an easy method of blocking that [Jewish] immigration to which they are radically averse, and attempts may and probably will be made to swell the list of Arabs unemployed with names which should not be there, or perhaps to ensure the registration of an unemployed man in the books of more than one exchange. It should not prove difficult to defeat this manoeuvre.' | The *Report* 'had strongly indicated … that the condition of Arab "unemployment" was being blown out of all semblance to reality by the Arab leaders who had indeed found "the method of blocking that [Jewish] immigration to which they are radically averse."' (p. 298)  'The illicit Arab immigration from "Syria and Transjordan" … had "swollen unemployment lists" and was "used as a political pawn" toward "blocking immigration to which they are radically averse". … ' (p. 374) | The entire paragraph is addressing a hypothetical situation, one which, in the *Report*'s words, 'It should not prove difficult to defeat.' |
| 'There can be no doubt that there is at present time serious unemployment among Arab craftsmen and among Arab laborers.'  'Arab unemployment is serious and general.' | 'Further, Arab unemployment was claimed when in fact such was not the case; according to the *Report*, Arab unemployment figures were inflated.' (p. 298) | For the subordinate clause ('according to … '), see above 'comments'. This is a nice example of one of Peters's unsung achievements in *From Time Immemorial* – packing multiple falsifications into a single sentence. |

**Table 2.1**

| Peel Commission Report (1937) | From Time Immemorial | Comments |
|---|---|---|
| 'A large proportion of Arab immigrants into Palestine come from the Hauran. These people go in considerable numbers to Haifa, where they work in the port. It is, however, important to realize that the extent of the yearly exodus from the Hauran depends mainly on the state of the crops there. *In a good year the amount of illegal immigration into Palestine is negligible* and confined to the younger members of large families whose presence is not required in the fields. Most persons *in this category* probably remain permanently in Palestine, wages there being considerably higher than in Syria. According to an authoritative estimate as many as ten or eleven thousand Hauranis go to Palestine temporarily in search of work in a really bad year. The Deputy Inspector-General of the Criminal Investigation Department has recently estimated that the numbers of Hauranis illegally in the country at the present time is roughly 2,500.' (my emphases) | 'The "Arab immigrants", particularly "Hauranis" from Syria, the *Report* stated "probably remain permanently in Palestine." But although the number of Hauranis who illegally immigrated was "authoritatively estimated" at 10,000–11,000 during a "bad" year in the Hauran, only the unrealistically, perhaps disingenuously low Government estimate of 2,500 were concluded to be "in the country at the present time."' (p. 310) | Recall that Peters must prove not only that massive numbers of Arabs had entered but also that they had settled in Palestine. In the original text, the Hauranis who 'remained permanently' explicitly refers, *not* to the '10,000–11,000 during a "bad" year,' but rather to a 'negligible' sum who immigrate in a 'good' year. This particular falsification serves a triple purpose: (i) 'documenting' massive illegal Arab settlement in Palestine, (ii) illustrating the bad faith and untrustworthiness of the British reports ('unrealistically, perhaps disingenuously low Government estimate of 2,500') and (iii) pointing up the alleged 'contradictions' between the facts reported in the official documents and their conclusions. (The *Peel Commission Report*, like every other document of the period, concluded that 'Arab illegal immigration is mainly casual, temporary and seasonal.') |

**Table 2.2**

The examples in Tables 2.1, 2.2 and 2.3 are typical of Peters's falsification technique. Here are some more inspired falsifications:

1. Peters writes (p. 275; her emphasis): 'From [1920,] the preoccupation of Palestine's administration would be concentrated solely upon *limiting* the immigration of the *Jews*. As a British report attested, for "Arab immigration" a "different" set of rules applied.' But the context of the quotation, in the *Survey of Palestine*, is a discussion of how Arab housing differs from Jewish housing. And the document continues:

| Anglo-American *Survey of Palestine* (1945–6) | *From Time Immemorial* | Comments |
|---|---|---|
| 'Arab illegal immigration is mainly ... casual, temporary and seasonal.' The *Survey* observes that, for example, immigration increases in 'boom' and emigration in 'bust' periods. To illustrate this particular pattern of temporary immigration, the following example is cited: '[T]he "boom" conditions in Palestine in the years 1934–6 led to an inward movement in Palestine particularly from Syria. The depression due to the state of public disorder during 1936–9 led to the return of these people and also a substantial outward movement of Palestinian Arabs who thought it prudent to live for a time in the Lebanon and Syria.' | 'Under the heading "Arab illegal immigration," a 1945–6 report noted that "...the 'boom' conditions in Palestine in the years 1934–6 led to an inward movement into Palestine particularly from Syria."' (p. 517, footnote 49) | The quote is used in Peters's section headed 'Hints of Substantial Unrecorded Immigration'. It points up one of Peters's favorite techniques for falsifying a document – wrenching an observation from its critical context. |
| The *Survey* divides Arab immigration into Palestine during World War II into two categories: first, the 3,800 Arabs who were brought in under 'official' arrangements and, second, the 'considerable numbers', of which 'no estimates are available', who were either recruited by private contractors or else 'entered individually'. | 'What the official Anglo-American *Survey* of 1945–6 definitively disclosed ... is that ... tens of thousands of "Arab illegal immigrants" [were] *recorded* as having been "brought" into Palestine. ... In addition, other *unestimated* "considerable" numbers immigrated "unofficially" or as "individuals" during the war, according to the report.' (p. 379; all emphases in Peters's text) | The latter sentence in Peters's rendering refers unmistakably to the second category of Arab immigrant workers: note, for example, the quotation marks around 'considerable', 'unofficially' and 'individuals', and the italics in '*unestimated*'. The 'tens of thousands' must then refer to the first category – those who entered 'under official arrangements'. Yet, the *Survey* records only 3,800 such immigrant workers. |
| | 'In one group of nearly ten thousand reported "foreign workers" – most of whom eventually "deserted" or "remained in Palestine illegally" – the *Survey* states that the Arab "illegal immigrants [were] Egyptians, Syrians, Lebanese ... also small numbers from Trans-Jordan, Persia, India, Somaliland, Abyssinia and the Hejaz."' (p. 378) | There is no such reference in the *Survey*. Peters fabricates it by splicing together two categories of immigrant workers listed in the document that she already tallied. Peters's falsified presentation (pp. 378–9) of the – for her purposes – crucial section of the *Survey* from which this quote is allegedly taken is, even by her exalted standards, in a class all its own. |

**Table 2.3**

Although different considerations apply to Arab immigration, special consideration need not be given to the latter as, out of a total number of 360,022
immigrants who entered Palestine between 1920 and 1942, only 27,981 or 7.8%
were Arabs. The number of room units to house Arab immigrants has, therefore, been calculated on the same basis as Jewish immigrants.

So the phrase 'different considerations', which Peters finds so sinister and
pregnant, refers *not* to immigration policy but to housing construction.
Peters repeats this same falsification on pp. 250 and 514, footnote 31.

2. Peters asserts that, in 1893, some 60,000 Jews and 92,300 non-Jews
inhabited the region of Palestine that became Israel after the 1948 war
(pp. 250–1).[14] Since 38,000 of the non-Jews were Christians, Jews were
'perhaps' a 'marginal majority'. But, according to Peters's tables in the
back of the book (pp. 424–5), not 92,300, but 218,000 Arabs resided, in
1893, in that slice of Palestine that became Israel. Peters manages this
neat little trick by dividing the region of Palestine that became Israel
into three areas and then 'forgetting' (in her text) the two areas of what
became Israel in which there was virtually no Jewish, but significant
Arab, settlement.[15]

3. To prove that the Mandatory authorities were more hostile to illegal
Jewish than illegal Arab immigration, Peters cites (pp. 346 and 548, footnote 26) the 'self-contradicting' 1933 annual *Report to the League of Nations* which states on page 35 that '[t]here was a considerable increase of
*illicit* immigration, *mostly of Jews*, entering as transit travellers or tourists'
(Peters's emphasis), yet

> on p. 180, separated from the 'immigration' material by 145 pages, was the
> report that 'The extent of illicit and unrecorded immigration into Palestine
> from or through Syria and Transjordan has been estimated at about 2,000 and
> Jewish as to fifty percent.' From 'mostly Jews,' the estimate had dropped to fifty
> percent.

This 'revelation' is simply untrue. The breakdown on p. 180 of the *Report*
refers only to illicit immigration through contiguous territories. Peters
'forgets' that there was also infiltration directly through Palestine's ports,
with would-be immigrants posing as 'transit travellers' and 'tourists'. There
is no contradiction between the two statements in the report. I would
add parenthetically that, in general, the British reports are models of
precision, clarity and internal consistency. The 'contradictions' Peters
purports to have 'uncovered' in them are all of her own making.

4. Peters tells us in her chapter on 'Official Disregard of Arab Immigration' that, contrary to popular belief, Jews were not dispossessing the indigenous Arab population but, rather, the landless Arab peasants in Palestine were 'mostly new Arab entrants' (p. 323). Her only documentation for this thesis is an article by Moshe Braver, an Israeli professor. Peters quotes Braver as follows (p. 546, footnote 76): 'landless peasants were new immigrants'. But Braver actually wrote, 'The immigrants were mostly landless laborers.' In other words, he does not say that all landless Arabs were immigrants; he says that the immigrants were landless.

5. To document the British Mandatory Government's indifference to Arab infiltration of Palestine, Peters cites the 1935 annual *Report to the League of Nations* in which, she asserts, 'only "Jewish Immigration into Palestine" was catalogued; that was the only heading' (p. 275). In fact, the British report in question meticulously and exhaustively tabulates every conceivable aspect of Arab immigration on *nine* consecutive pages. Peters could hardly have overlooked these tabulations since the comparable statistics for Jewish immigration appear *on the very same pages in parallel columns.* *Every* annual British report on Palestine – and Peters purports to have scrutinized *thirteen* of them – contains identical exhaustive tabulations of Arab immigration under the same chapter heading, 'Immigration and Emigration'.[16] In this connection, another of Peters's falsifications merits special comment. Peters, and her reviewers, make much of the alleged remarks of an anonymous 'thirty-year archivist – a specialist in the Foreign Office and Colonial Office records on the Middle East for the Public Record Office' in London. He purportedly told her that Arab immigration into Palestine 'did not exist. There was no such thing. No one ever kept track of *that*' (p. 270; Peters's emphasis). Yet, every British annual report to the League of Nations and every major official British study of the period includes an exhaustive tabulation and detailed commentary on Arab immigration. If 'no one ever kept track of' Arab immigration, how were the tables composed? Where did the numbers come from?

Finally, let me turn to the central piece of evidence that Peters brings to bear in support of her thesis. The item is tucked away in the minutes of the League of Nations Permanent Mandates Commission hearings on Britain's Palestine mandate. The first – and last – reference to it in the Commission minutes comes during a June 1935 exchange prompted by the Jewish Agency's allegation of 'considerable immigration of labor from Egypt, Syria and Transjordan'. Assistant Chief Secretary of the Government of Palestine Moody, a British government representative at the hearings, denied the allegation, stating that, whereas Transjordanians and

Syrians had indeed entered Palestine, the right to settle there had been given over almost exclusively to the Jews. I quote now the relevant minutes of the exchange in their entirety:

> Lord Lugard [a Mandates Commission member] said that *La Syrie* had published, on August 12th, 1934, an interview with Tewfik Bey El-Huriani, Governor of the Hauran, who said that in the last few months from 30,000 to 36,000 Hauranese had entered Palestine and settled there. The accredited representative would note the Governor's statement that these Hauranese had actually 'settled.' … Mr. Moody expressed the view that the statement of the Governor of the Hauran was a gross exaggeration. Mr. Orts [also a Commission member] did not know how much value could be attached to the statement, but the statement itself was definite. The Governor even referred to the large sums remitted by these immigrants to their families, who remained in the Hauran. Mr. Moody said he had read the article in question. As he had said, he thought that the figure must be grossly exaggerated, because the Palestine Government had taken special measures on the eastern and northeastern frontier with a view to keeping out undesirable people.

Peters cites the Mandates Commission reference to the report in *La Syrie* on no fewer than seven different occasions (pp. 230, 231, 272, 275, 297, 319, 431). She classifies this reference in the Commission minutes 'hard evidence' (p. 297) and lists this reported entry of 30,000–36,000 Hauranis into Palestine flat out as a fact in her chronology of significant events in the history of the British Mandate (p. 319; see also p. 272, where the item is again presented, without qualification, as a proven fact). Yet, Peters cites not a single cross-reference for a report that, in the view of the British government representative, was 'grossly exaggerated'. The representative's vigorous rejoinder, *also* cited in the Commission minutes, does not rate a single mention in Peters's book. Instead, citing these same June 1935 minutes, Peters falsely states that the Mandates Commission 'verified' (p. 231) and 'recognized' (p. 319) the influx, in the space of just a few months, of 30,000 to 36,000 Hauranis, and that the Commission 'took special "note" … that the Hauranese, not merely passing through, had indeed settled' (p. 230).[17]

To be sure, Hauranis did enter Palestine in fairly significant numbers in the mid-1930s, but they departed, in equal numbers, soon thereafter. The *Survey of Palestine* reported that 'the "boom" conditions in Palestine in the years 1934–6 led to an inward movement into Palestine particularly from Syria. The depression due to the state of public disorder during 1936–9 led to the return of these people.'[18] Peters herself devotes considerable space to documenting the 'hasty leavetaking' (p. 272) of the Hauranis in 1936.[19] She quotes one private British government memorandum to the effect that '128 Hauranis left today. Many more are expected to leave tomorrow.' According to a second memorandum, 'countrymen from Hauran' had 'applied urgently and pleadingly to be sent back to their homes for reason that there was no work ... and they did not wish to be involved in more trouble'.

Peters seems not to be aware that the batch of memoranda she cites on the frantic exodus of Hauranis between 1936 and 1939 renders her most significant find, her 'hard evidence' of massive illegal Arab immigration and settlement – namely, the (unverified) *La Syrie* report mentioned in the Mandates Commission hearings – worthless. Recall that Peters wishes to prove that fully 50 per cent of the Arabs residing in the 'Jewish-settled' areas of Palestine in 1947 were really illegal Arab immigrants. But by 1947, the Hauranis had long since departed from Palestine.

## The Strange Case of Area IV

Peters's highly touted demographic study is the centerpiece of *From Time Immemorial*. Yet, this study is marred by serious flaws: (1) several extremely significant calculations are wrong; and (2) numbers are used selectively to support otherwise baseless conclusions.

Peters claims to plot demographic growth and shifts *within* Palestine (i.e. the region bordered on the east by the Jordan River and on the west by the Mediterranean Sea) between the years 1893 and 1948. Her central thesis is that at least 170,000 of the 600,000-odd refugees in 1948 were and *had to be* recent migrants from the West Bank and Gaza Strip.

For the purposes of her study, Peters divides Palestine into five areas, three of which (I, II, and IV) correspond to the whole of pre-1967 Israel and the remaining two (III and V) to the West Bank and Gaza. Area I was the main zone of Jewish settlement between the years 1893 and 1948. Peters provides the following geographic breakdown of Palestine's indigenous Arab population in 1893 (p. 255, Table G):

|         |         |
|---------|---------|
| Area I   | 92,300  |
| Area II  | 38,900  |
| Area III | 14,300  |
| Area IV  | 87,400  |
| Area V   | 233,500 |

She next suggests that the indigenous Palestinian Arab population expanded by a factor of 2.7 between 1893 and 1947.[20] (Peters assumes for the Palestinian Arab population in the area of Jewish concentration the same rate of natural increase that she has calculated for the Palestinian

|  | A<br>Actual indigenous<br>Palestinian Arab<br>population (1947) | B<br>Projected indigenous<br>Palestinian Arab<br>population (1947) | C<br>Net in-migration (+)/<br>out-migration (-)<br>[column A − column B] |
| --- | --- | --- | --- |
| Area I | 417,300 | 249,210 | +168,090 |
| Area II | 110,900 | 105,030 | +5,870 |
| Area III | 39,900 | 38,610 | +1,290 |
| *Area IV* | *125,100* | *235,980* | *−110,880* |
| Area V | 507,200 | 630,450 | −123,250 |

*Note*: Peters uses a uniform national rate of natural growth to project the 1947 indigenous Palestinian Arab population in each of the five areas from the 1893 census. From the data from Area I (1893 pop.: 92,300; projected 1947 pop.: 249,210), a rate of 2.7 is inferred (249,210/92,300).[21] Aside from the data for Area IV, to which I will return presently, my significant calculations differ only slightly from those of the author.

**Table 2.4**

Arab population in the non-Jewish areas between 1893 and 1947.) However, actual population figures for Palestinian-born Arabs in certain of the five areas differed markedly from the projected increase. Table 2.4, based on Peters's data (pp. 424–5, Appendix V), juxtaposes the actual number of indigenous Palestinian Arabs in each of the five areas in 1947 (column A) against what the figure would have been had the indigenous population in each area expanded by natural increase alone (column B).

Peters contends that the excessive number of indigenous Palestinian Arabs in Area I (center of Jewish settlement) and the unnaturally sparse Palestinian Arab population in Area V (center of Arab settlement) can only be explained by Arab in-migration.[22] In other words, approximately 170,000 Palestinian Arabs forsook their native soil in the West Bank/Gaza region of Palestine and moved into the areas of Jewish settlement in order to take advantage of the new opportunities opened up by the thriving Yishuv economy. Peters further argues that these 170,000 Palestinian Arab in-migrants likely found themselves among the refugees in 1948 since their roots in the Jewish-settled part of Palestine were not very deep. But – and this is her crucial point – these Arabs were not really refugees since they had *followed* the Jews into this corner of Palestine and thus were not indigenous to it; their real homes were in the West Bank and Gaza areas of Palestine. Peters thus concludes:

> From the evidence, then, among the estimated 430,000–650,000 Arab 'refugees' reported in 1948, well over 170,000 are apparently Arabs who were *returning* to 'Arab areas' in ... Palestine (the West Bank or Gaza) from the land that became Israel – the Jewish-settled areas where those Arabs had recently arrived in search of better opportunities. (p. 258; Peters's emphasis)[23]

The first point to be made about this argument is that the case Peters mounts for massive illegal Arab immigration into Palestine contradicts it. Peters arrives at the figures in column A of Table 2.4 above by deducting the *officially* tabulated number of nomads and legal and illegal immigrants for each area from the total Arab population for that area. For example, Peters puts the total Arab population in Area I at 462,900. From this sum she subtracts the 8,800 nomads, 27,300 legal immigrants and 9,500 illegal immigrants officially tallied for this region (p. 425), and thus obtains the figure of 417,300. Recall, however, that Peters puts the real number of illegal immigrants in Area I at about 300,000. (Peters assumes that the Arab immigrants illegally entering Palestine all settled in the main zone of Jewish colonization, Area I; see p. 425, Appendix V, 1947, column D.) In that case, column A in Table 2.4 should actually read 126,800 and column C (-122,410). But then nothing remains of Peters's central conclusion from her demographic study. Simply put, if Arabs immigrated in massive numbers to Area I, there could not have been any in-migration to this region. Further, even if Peters's argument is evaluated on its own terms, the demographic evidence in the study does not support the 170,000 figure cited repeatedly in the text. Her actual findings are, at best, trivial.

Let us look closely at Area IV (the western Galilee, etc.) in Table 2.4 above. This region is *also* 'short' by approximately 111,000 indigenous Palestinian Arabs. Couldn't *these* 111,000 souls have migrated to Area I? But recall that this region was *incorporated* into Israel in 1948, in which case, if they did indeed flee, these Arabs were genuine refugees. In other words, Arab 'indigenes' from the western Galilee region of what became Israel migrated to the *Yishuv* area during the Mandate period and then fled (for whatever reason) in 1948 and became refugees. (It seems not to have occurred to Peters that 170,000 Arab in-migrants could not have *all* come from the West Bank and Gaza if, by her own reckoning, these areas were not 'short' by that many Arabs!) Peters offers not a single word to explain why these 111,000 migrants from Area IV (a part of Israel) should not be subtracted from the 170,000 migrants who were allegedly returning home in 1948.[24]

Not only does Peters completely ignore the significant demographic changes in Area IV when they threaten to render her findings trivial, but she actually falsifies the relevant numbers. According to Peters's chart

(p. 425, Appendix V), there were only 71,200 fewer indigenous Arabs in Area IV than the projection based on the 1893 census. The real number is closer to 111,000 (see Table 2.4 above).[25]

What is more, all the data are arranged in what can only be described as a curiously confusing manner. For no apparent reason, the regions that eventually comprised Israel are labeled I, II and IV and the remainder of Palestine III and V (see key to map, p. 246). As a result, all but the most attentive readers can easily be misled. For example, in the chart on p. 425, Areas I, II and III are boxed off from Areas IV and V. It is very easy to forget that the first of the latter two regions (IV) – from which, as we have seen, there was very significant out-migration – became part of *Israel. Why did Peters section off Area III, and not Area IV, with Areas I and II?* Another example: in the legend to Appendix V (p. 424), Areas I, II and III are bracketed off and labeled 'contained most of Jewish population'; Areas IV and V are similarly bracketed off and labeled 'contained very little Jewish population'. But, according to Peters's map on p. 246, Area III contained no Jews. By grouping in this highly misleading and altogether erroneous fashion the five regions, the distinct impression is again left that the first three areas became Israel while the remaining two fell within the jurisdiction of the Arabs in 1948: *Area IV easily gets lost in the shuffle.*[26]

Had Peters properly grouped the five areas in her charts, it would have been obvious to any attentive reader that: (1) the demographic changes *within* what became Israel could have more or less cancelled each other out; therefore, (2) the amount of in-migration from the West Bank/Gaza region could have been relatively insignificant; and finally, (3) the number of West Bank/Gaza natives among the 1948 Arab refugees could also have been relatively insignificant.

Had Peters used Roman numerals I, II and III to designate the constituent areas of Israel and IV and V for the West Bank/Gaza, as common sense would recommend, the significance of the population changes within Israel would also have been highlighted. Why did Peters choose the far more clumsy method of labeling Israel I, II and IV, the West Bank/Gaza III and V, and then section off the areas in such a way that the significant population shift within Israel is concealed?

Why did Peters include 'intermediate' areas at all in her study? Why didn't she simply divide the map of Palestine into the region that became Israel and the region that fell outside its boundaries after the 1949 Armistice Agreements? What purpose do the 'intermediate' areas serve in Peters's study other than to conceal and obscure crucial data?

The weight of the evidence suggests that Peters's demographic 'study' is a carefully contrived, premeditated hoax. How else can one explain

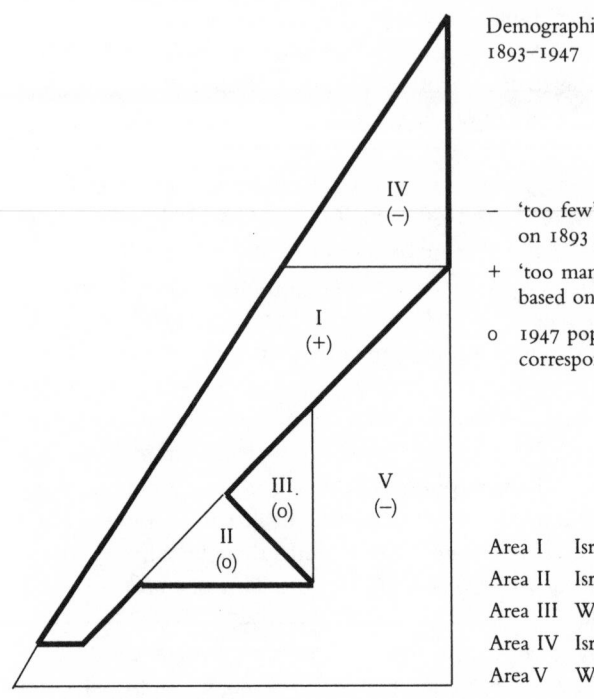

Demographic shifts in Palestine,
1893–1947

–    'too few' indigenous Arabs based
     on 1893 projection

+    'too many' indigenous Arabs
     based on 1893 projection

o    1947 population more or less
     corresponds to 1893 projection

| Area I | Israel | +168,090 |
| Area II | Israel | o |
| Area III | West Bank | o |
| Area IV | Israel | −110,880 |
| Area V | West Bank/Gaza | −123,150 |

**Peters's argument**   The 'missing' indigenous Arabs from Area V (West Bank/Gaza) must have in-migrated to Area I (Israel) during the Mandate years and then fled in 1948.

**Peters's conclusion**   Since they were indigenous to Area V (West Bank/Gaza), these refugees could not claim what became Israel as their homeland 'from time immemorial'.

**The fraud**   The 'too many' indigenous Arabs in Area I (Israel) may *just as likely* have come from Area IV (Israel). But *these* Arabs, once having become refugees in 1948, could have justly claimed that Israel was their homeland 'from time immemorial'. Hence Peters's falsification and concealment of the population change in Area IV.

**Figure 2.1**   Simplified Diagrammatic Explanation

why, in reading off the data from the very same Appendix chart (p. 425) for the table she assembles on p. 257, Peters 'remembers' to add Area IV in all the columns (e.g. in the column for 'nomads', column B in the Appendix) but 'forgets' to add Area IV in the column for 'Arab in-migrants' (E in the Appendix)?[27]

*Appendix*

| From Time Immemorial | Comments |
|---|---|
| **p. 246 (printings 1–6)**<br>Area I: 'Main areas of Jewish settlement, 98% of Jewish population'<br>Area II: 'Intermediate areas, mainly Arab, some Jews'<br>Area III: 'Intermediate areas, no Jewish settlement'<br>Area IV: 'Intermediate areas, no Jewish settlement'<br>Area V: 'Main areas of Arab settlement, no Jewish settlement' | |
| **p. 246 (printing 7)**<br>Area I: 'Main areas of Jewish settlement, 98% of Jewish population'<br>Area II: 'Intermediate areas, mainly Arab, some Jews'<br>Area III: 'Intermediate areas, some Jewish settlement'<br>Area IV: 'Intermediate areas, some Jewish settlement'<br>Area V: 'Main areas of Arab settlement, no Jewish settlement' | Areas III and IV now contain 'some Jewish settlement'. |
| **p. 254 (all printings)**<br>Peters states that she has divided Palestine 'into 1) those subdistricts that were heavily or mainly settled by Jews (68), 2) those regions that had little Jewish development (69), and 3) those areas from which Jews were being expelled [no footnote]'.<br>Footnote 68 reads: 'Areas I and II'<br>Footnote 69 reads: 'Areas III, IV and V' | Area II is now 'heavily or mainly' Jewish. Area V now has a 'little Jewish development'. Areas III, IV and V are grouped together. The last category in this tripartite classification subsumes none of the five areas – why was it included? |
| **p. 255, Table G (all printings)**<br>Area I: 'Main areas of Jewish settlement'<br>Area II: 'Some Jews, mainly Arab'<br>Area III: 'Intermediate'<br>Area IV: 'Intermediate'<br>Area V: 'Main areas of Arab settlement – no Jewish settlement' | Area II now contains only 'some Jews' and is 'mainly Arab'. Areas III and IV ('Intermediate') are now separated out from Area V ('no Jewish settlement'). Area V now has 'no Jewish settlement'. |
| **p. 424 (all printings)**<br>Area I: 'Main areas of Jewish settlement'<br>Area II: 'Intermediate areas'<br>Area III: 'Intermediate areas'<br>Area IV: 'Intermediate area'<br>Area V: 'Main area of Arab settlement'<br>*Note*: Peters brackets off Areas I-III with the label 'Contain most of Jewish population', and Areas IV-V with the label 'Contain very little Jewish population'. | Area II is now listed under the exact same rubric as Areas III and IV. The bracketing corresponds neither with the category divisions nor with the data presented on other pages in the book (see below). |
| **p. 425 (all printings)**<br>According to Peters's geographic breakdown of Jewish settlement as presented in the charts on this page:<br>1) Areas II and III contained no Jews in any years for which the breakdown is available; 2) Area IV contained 6,000 Jews in 1944 and 5,300 Jews in 1947; 3) Area V contained 3,400 Jews in 1944 and more Jews than Area II, III or IV in 1947 (Area II: 0; Area III: 0; Area IV: 5,300; Area V: 6,500). | The actual geographic and numerical breakdown of Jewish settlement in Palestine contradicts all the category divisions of Areas II–V listed above. |

**Table A1**   The Transubstantiation of Categories

## Handling the 'Mechanics of Citation'

As should now be clear, much of the 'prodigious' research praised by reviewers of Peters's book is an optical illusion. Much else is simply laughable.[28] Yet, it is difficult not to be impressed by, say, the obscure travelogues and other recondite sources that Peters apparently ploughed through to document the state of Palestine on the eve of Zionist colonization. But one's legitimate admiration for such diligence will surely vanish once it is recognized that she did not read them.

For example, both Peters (on pp. 158–9) and Ernst Frankenstein (on pp. 122–4 of his frankly partisan tract, *Justice for My People*, New York 1994) cite the reminiscences of the eighteenth-century French scholar Count Constantin François Volney, and follow their citations in the manner shown in Table 2.5 opposite.

Peters's only original contribution here – other than juggling the quotations – is to put the estimate of Syria's population in her footnote whereas Frankenstein has it in the body of the text.

When this remarkable 'coincidence' was brought to the attention of Aaron Asher at Harper & Row, he told *The Nation* magazine (13 October 1984) that this 'so-called plagiarism' was 'a teapot tempest'. Had he known about it he might, as her editor, have suggested that Peters handle the 'mechanics of citation' differently. Asher also stated that he has been assured that Peters has copies of all the relevant citations in her files. This suggests that even if she did not acknowledge her debt to Frankenstein, she had examined his original sources.

Yet, elsewhere in her book (p. 197), Peters quotes another travelogue, W.F. Lynch's *Narrative of the United States Expedition to the River Jordan and the Dead Sea*, London 1849, as follows: 'In 1844, "*the American expedition under Lynch*" recorded *fewer than* 8,000 "Turks" in Jaffa in a population of 13,000' (my emphases). Frankenstein also refers to this source (pp. 127–8): 'In 1844 the American expedition under Lynch found *fewer than* eight thousand "Turks" in Jaffa among a population of thirteen thousand' (my emphasis). Turning to Lynch's work, we read the following: 'The population of Jaffa is now about 13,000, viz.: Turks, 8,000; Greeks, 2,000.' If Peters read through Frankenstein's sources, why are her quotation marks around a phrase ('the American expedition under Lynch') that appears not in Lynch, but in Frankenstein, and how does one explain her repetition of Frankenstein's little error on the number of Turks ('*fewer than 8,000*') in Jaffa?[29]

Readers who cannot help being impressed by Peters's virtuoso performance when it comes to numbers and statistics should consider the following. On pp. 244–5, Peters claims to have calculated '[a]ccording to

| Peters | Frankenstein |
|---|---|
| Another writer, describing 'Syria' (and Palestine) some sixty years later in 1843, stated that, in Volney's day, 'the land had not fully reached its last prophetic degree of desolation and depopulation.' (1)<br><br>From place to place the reporters varied, but not the reports: J.S. Buckingham described his visit of 1816 to Jaffa, which 'has all the appearances of a poor village, and every part of it that we saw was of corresponding meanness.' (2) Buckingham described Ramle, 'where, as throughout the greater part of Palestine, the ruined portion seemed more extensive than that which was inhabited.' (3)<br><br>After a visit in 1817–8, travelers reported that there was not a 'single boat of any description on the lake [Tiberias].' (4) In a German encyclopedia published in 1827, Palestine was depicted as 'desolate and roamed through by Arab bands of robbers.' (5)<br><br>Throughout the nineteenth century the abandonment and dismal state of the terrain was lamented. In 1840 an observer, who was traveling through, wrote of his admiration for the Syrian 'fine spirited race of men' whose 'population is on the decline.' (6) While scorning the idea of Jewish colonization, the writer observed that the once populous area between Hebron and Bethlehem was 'now abandoned and desolate' with 'dilapidated towns.' (7) Jerusalem consisted of 'a large number of houses ... in a dilapidated and ruinous state,' and 'the masses really seem to be without any regular employment.' | Buckingham, who visited the country in 1816, states that Jaffa 'has all the appearances of a poor village, and every part of it that we saw was of corresponding meanness.' (1) He visited Ramleh, 'where, as throughout the greater part of Palestine, the ruined portion seemed more extensive than that which was inhabited.' (2) ...<br><br>Thereafter conditions deteriorated further. 'In his (Volney's) day,' writes Keith in 1843, (3) 'the land had not fully reached its last prophetic degree of desolation and depopulation. The population (viz., of the whole of Syria), rated by Volney at two million and a half, is now estimated at half that amount.'<br><br>This statement corresponds to the observations of other travellers, for instance Olin (1840) who is a specially valuable witness, since he admires the Palestinian ('Syrian') population ('a fine-spirited race of men') and ridicules the idea of Jewish colonization. (4) According to him 'the population is on the decline.' (5) In Hebron, 'many houses are in a dilapidated state and uninhabited'; the once populated region between Hebron and Bethlehem is 'now abandoned and desolate' and has 'dilapidated towns.' (6) In Jerusalem 'a large number of houses are in a dilapidated and ruinous state'; 'the masses really seem to be without any regular employment.' (7) ...<br><br>A German Encyclopedia published in 1827 calls Palestine 'desolate and roamed through by Arab bands of robbers.' (8) Irby, who visited the country in 1817–8, found 'not a single boat of any description on the lake (of Tiberias),' (9)…. |
| Footnotes<br><br>1. A. Keith, *The Land of Israel* (Edinburgh, 1843), p. 465. 'The population (viz., of the whole of Syria), rated by Volney at two million and a half, is now estimated at half that amount.'<br>2. J.S. Buckingham, *Travels in Palestine* (London, 1821), p. 146.<br>3. *Ibid.*, p. 162.<br>4. James Mangles and the Honorable C.L. Irby, *Travels in Egypt and Nubia* (London, 1823), p. 295.<br>5. Brockhaus, *Allg. deutsch Real-Encyklopaedie*, 7th ed. (Leipzig, 1827), vol. viii, p. 206.<br>6. S. Olin, *Travels in Egypt, Arabia Petraea and the Holy Land* (New York, 1843), vol. 2, pp. 438–9.<br>7. *Ibid.*, pp. 77–8. | Footnotes<br><br>1. J.S. Buckingham, *Travels in Palestine*, London, 1821, p. 146.<br>2. *Ibid.*, p. 162.<br>3. A. Keith, *The Land of Israel*, Edinburgh, 1843, p. 465.<br>4. S. Olin, *Travels in Egypt, Arab Petraea and the Holy Land*, New York, 1843, vol. ii, p. 438.<br>5. *Ibid.*, p. 439.<br>6. *Ibid.*, pp. 77, 88.<br>7. *Ibid.*, pp. 135, 138.<br>8. Brockhaus, *Allg. deutsch Real Encyklopedie*, 7. Aufl. Leipzig, 1827, vol. viii, p. 206.<br>9. James Mangles and Hon. C.L. Irby, *Travels in Egypt and Nubia*, London, 1823, p. 295. |

**Table 2.5**

projection of statistics of Vital Cuinet for 1895, and ... *Murray's Handbook for Travellers in Syria and Palestine*, which was reprinted in the *Encyclopedia Britannica*, 8th edition, 1860, vol. xx, p. 905' (p. 523, footnotes 40, 41), the 'settled' Muslim population in Palestine for 1882 (the eve of modern Jewish colonization) and 1895. This is no mean accomplishment since, among many other things, Palestine did not yet exist as a single national entity; numerous partial statistics thus have to be collated. Peters compares the two figures (1882: 141,000; 1895: 252,000) and concludes:

> Even if we assume a high rate of natural increase of 1.5 percent per annum for that thirteen-year period, the population would not have increased to more than 170,000 or so. ... The only plausible answer is that ... [Arab immigration] coincided exactly with the time Jewish development commenced. (pp. 244–5)

Peters's statistical *tour de force* has thus apparently produced a highly original conclusion.[30]

But Peters need not have gone to all the trouble. Ernst Frankenstein used the exact same sources (even the same edition of *Murray's Handbook!*), did the exact same calculations and derived identical figures. His conclusion reads almost word for word like Peters's:

> Even if we admit the possibility of a natural increase of 20–25 percent during these thirteen years [Frankenstein converts the 20–25 percent to the 1.5 per annum percentage used in Peters's text in his next paragraph] ... the 141,000 settled Moslems of 1882 cannot possibly, by natural increase, have exceeded the figure of 170,000 to 175,000. Here, therefore, we are confronted ... with a large immigration of Arabic-speaking people which coincides with the development of the Jewish settlements. (p. 128)[31]

One may, finally, note that the Frankenstein–Peters sources have always figured as a staple in official Israeli polemics. To cite one example at random, the Israeli representative lectured the Security Council in June 1973 that before the Jews came,

> the land of Israel stood desolate. ... Those of the conquerors who settled in the land were few, their populated localities sparse. Travellers who visited the area described it always as a dying land. The Frenchman Volney who toured Palestine in 1785 wrote that it was 'desolate.' A. Keith, writing some decades after Volney, commented: 'In his [Volney's] day the land had not reached its last degree of desolation and depopulation.'[32]

In her fulsome blurb for *From Time Immemorial*, Nazi holocaust scholar Lucy Dawidowicz congratulates Peters for having 'dug beneath a half-century's accumulation of propaganda and brought into the light the historical truth about the Middle East'. What Peters actually did was dig beneath a half-century's accumulation of pro-Zionist propaganda tracts and unearth a particularly ludicrous one, from which she proceeded to plagiarize generously.[33]


## Postscript

By the end of 1984, *From Time Immemorial* had gone through eight printings (cloth) and received some two hundred notices, ranging from ecstasy to awe, in the United States. The only 'false' notes in this crescendoing chorus of praise were the *Journal of Palestine Studies*, which ran a highly critical review by Bill Farrell; the small Chicago-based newsweekly *In These Times*, which published a condensed version of this writer's findings; and Alexander Cockburn, who devoted a splendid series of columns in *The Nation* to exposing the hoax. Otherwise, it proved impossible to open any discussion of the book. Joan Peters, via her publisher, peremptorily dismissed the findings of fraud as 'without merit' and Harper & Row senior editor Aaron Asher defended Peters's right not to reply to 'published attacks on her work, regardless of their nature or provenance'. The periodicals in which *From Time Immemorial* had already been favorably reviewed refused to run any critical correspondence (e.g. *The New Republic, Atlantic, Commentary*). Periodicals that had yet to review the book rejected a manuscript on the subject as of little or no conse-quence (e.g. *The Village Voice, Dissent, The New York Review of Books*). Not a single national newspaper or columnist contacted found newsworthy that a best-selling, effusively praised 'study' of the Middle East conflict was a threadbare hoax.

In April 1985, *From Time Immemorial* was awarded the prestigious National Jewish Book Award in the 'Israel' category. Chairing the com-mittee that honored Peters was the renowned authority on the 'Arab mind', Raphael Patai. Patai and his fellow judges discounted without explanation the copious documentation of fraud. Reaffirming that it was 'very happy' with the Peters selection, the Jewish Book Council declared the matter 'closed'.

Yet in early 1985, the disinformation effort began to unravel as Peters's book went into a British edition. The reviews in England were devastat-ing. Oxford's great orientalist, Albert Hourani, denounced *From Time Im-memorial* in *The Observer* as 'ludicrous and worthless'. (Privately, Hourani called it a 'grotesque work', noting that every quotation checked 'proved to be wrong in one way or another'.) Ian and David Gilmour, in the *London Review of Books*, concluded an exhaustive 8000-word dissection of the book by calling it 'preposterous'. The *Spectator* of London likened it to the Clifford Irving 'autobiography' of Howard Hughes. *Time Out* reported it as a 'piece of disinformation roughly the size and weight of a dried cowpat'. The Israelis also got into the act, and a Hebrew edition of the book had not yet even appeared. The Labor Party daily *Davar* compared *From Time Immemorial* to Israel's more ignoble past propaganda exercises; the liberal weekly *Koteret Rashit* published a detailed exposé of the cover-up by the US media; and the chair of the philosophy department at the Hebrew University, Avishai Margalit, derided Peters's 'web of deceit'.

Back in the United States, *l'affaire Peters* was fast becoming a singular embarrassment as word began to circulate that a major literary-political scandal was being suppressed. In February 1985, *The New York Review of Books* finally commissioned and in early March received a lengthy piece on *From Time Immemorial* by the noted Israeli scholar Yehoshua Porath. For fully nine months it was kept under wraps. Published only after a barrage of critical commentary, the Porath essay dismissed out of hand Peters's 'theses', yet scrupulously avoided any mention of her fraudulent scholarship; every effort to raise this obviously crucial issue in the *Review*'s correspondence columns proved unavailing. In October, Edward Said delivered a stinging and eloquent riposte to Peters and her acolytes in the pages of *The Nation*.

Colin Campbell of the *New York Times* had been contacted in late 1984 about the Peters hoax. Earlier, the *Times* featured a series of articles by Campbell accusing a leftist professor in Princeton's history department of misrepresenting a handful of documents in a study on Weimar Germany. The Campbell series caused such a brouhaha that the young scholar was ultimately forced to leave academia. Yet beside the Peters scandal, the questions raised by the Princeton case plainly paled by comparison. It concerned not a recondite, ivory tower historical dispute, but a colossal and multifaceted hoax directly bearing on a burning political issue. Through Campbell, the *Times* editors first predicated doing a story on a panel of scholars confirming the allegations against Peters. A jury assembled,[34] the *Times* still demurred, claiming that the fraud did not qualify as 'newsworthy': it was not the stuff of an open controversy. True enough. Indeed, *that* was the story: the concealment – crucially *by* the *Times* – of a major disinformation effort from public exposure. Faced with escalating accusations of censorship levelled mainly by the British press, the *Times* finally ran a piece in November 1985. It was placed in the Thanksgiving Day (non-)issue, on the theater page, without even a listing in the index. Indeed, all the painstakingly assembled documentation of the hoax was cut from the published version. Porath was quoted to the effect that *From Time Immemorial* 'is a sheer forgery', and that 'In Israel, at least, the book was almost universally dismissed as sheer rubbish, except maybe as a propaganda weapon', while historian Barbara Tuchman continued to insist that the Palestinian people were 'a fairy tale'. Martin Peretz, editor-in-chief of *The New Republic*, alleged that the attack on Peters was part of a calculated leftist plot and Peters herself refused, for the nth time, to be interviewed.

In January 1986, Anthony Lewis of the *New York Times* devoted a full column to the hoax, entitled, appropriately enough, 'There Were No Indians'. In the June and October numbers of *Commentary*, some thirty pages were given over to defending Peters against the mounting on-slaught on her book. In a slightly more comical vein, David Bar Illan, current executive editor of the *Jerusalem Post*, impeached Porath's findings because he once belonged to a 'lunatic fringe group' that 'declined to circumcise their sons', and this writer's because 'his area of study as an undergraduate was (surprise!) Russian and Chinese politics and Marx-ism'. But alas, by this point, there was little that could be salvaged from the *From Time Immemorial* wreckage. *Haaretz* reported in June that, at an international conference on Palestinian demography at Haifa University, virtually all the participants ridiculed Peters's demographic 'theses' and the most authoritative scholar in attendance, Professor Yehoshua Ben-Arieh of the Hebrew University, condemned the Peters enterprise for discrediting the 'Zionist cause'.

A Hebrew edition of *From Time Immemorial* was put out in 1988 by the left-wing Kibbutz Hame'uchad publishing house. The preface noted that even Yitzhak Rabin, 'so informed and experienced', had learnt some-thing new from it. (Abba Eban had given the book a similar plaudit earlier on.) Israeli critics of Peters indulged in a little historical engineering of their own as they 'reconstructed' the unfolding of the scandal. Margalit denied that criticism of Peters was suppressed in the United States, and especially not in the pages of the *New York Review of Books*. Porath, more-over, was now cast as the hero of the hour – a role that he happily accepted. *Yediot Aharonot* reported that 'the debate centering around the reliability' of Peters's data 'featured the important historian Yehoshua Porath'. Writing in *Haaretz*, Tom Segev gushed that 'Porath did something unheard of: he checked Peters's sources'. Leaving to one side that Peters's sources had been checked and the findings circulated well before Porath had ever set eyes on *From Time Immemorial*, the one thing Porath did *not* do in the *New York Review of Books* piece, as noted above, was question Peters's use of sources.

Of Peters's original endorsers, to date only Daniel Pipes and Ronald Sanders have publicly acknowledged any lapses in Peters's scholarship, if not in her central 'theses'. Sanders rejoined in the *New York Review* that, all the criticism notwithstanding, 'there is an original and significant argument at the heart of her book' and that 'it must be granted that she has achieved ample results'. Pipes likewise opined in the same issue that 'the book presents a thesis' that no 'reviewer has so far succeeded in refuting', that Peters 'supports this argument with an array of demographic statistics and contemporary accounts, the bulk of which have not been questioned by any reviewer', and that 'because it makes such good sense, I put credence in the argument'.

Brazenly asserting that none of Peters's detractors had produced 'any specific charge with citation and reference' of falsification, Barbara Tuchman ascribed the 'concerted campaign in England of vilification' to 'growing anti-Semitism', and the American 'smear campaign' to a cabal of 'committed and long-term apologists of the Palestine Liberation Organization'. (No explanation was suggested for the Israeli prong of the alleged conspiracy.) Asked informally whether he had any second thoughts about his embrace of *From Time Immemorial*, Saul Bellow replied that 'with hindsight and given another chance' he 'would do no such thing' – no doubt, since *this* time the fraud was publicly exposed. Elie Wiesel, the revered guardian of historical memory, was made privy to the hoax fairly early on, but chose silence – as in the title of his collected *pensées*, *Against Silence*. Questioned privately about his endorsement, Wiesel noted in extenuation that 'political science' was not his 'forte'. (Aside from emoting, one wonders what is.) At any rate, Wiesel cheerfully lent his name to the subsequently issued paperback edition of the book – as did all the other original endorsers, plus historian Theodore White.

Famed orientalist Bernard Lewis was the second individual thanked on Peters's acknowledgments page, specifically for his 'extended encouragement, introductions to invaluable contacts and sources, and generous sharing of his personal archival resources' – cooperation of which Peters was 'especially appreciative'. Already a few months after *From Time Immemorial* was published, Lewis had in his possession voluminous evidence that the book was a hoax. Yet, he categorically refused to comment on any aspect of the matter even with a graduate student at his own university (this writer). Oddly, Lewis later lamented that the linking of his name with the disinformation effort was 'an interesting example of how ... myths are born'.

*The New Republic* literary editor Leon Wieseltier privately communicated in October 1985 that he had his 'own doubts – severe doubts – about the Peters book for a long time'. Supplied with the evidence of fraud, Wieseltier promised that his magazine would comment on the matter 'sooner or later, probably sooner'. It never did. When challenged about the Peters hoax at a Middle East Studies Association symposium in

1987, Wieseltier happily joined in the ridicule of that 'shabby performance by an ignorant woman'. Yet as he must surely have understood, the
real issue was the herd of intellectual luminaries – including his boss,
Martin Peretz – that heralded the 'shabby performance by an ignorant
woman' as a major literary-political event.[35] Wieseltier had not a word to
say about *their* 'shabby performance'. Rather, in a textbook case of a half-
truth being more egregious than a whole lie, Wieseltier pretended that
the worst he and his colleagues could be faulted for was the sin of omission: 'Peters' book should have been refuted in my magazine, in other
magazines; it was not.' Wieseltier forgot, however, to mention that his
magazine *did* publish not one but two glowing notices (besides Peretz's
breathless comments, *The New Republic* ran the Sanders accolade) and
that, as the scandal began to unfold, enjoined further comment. One
would never have learned from the pages of *The New Republic* that Peters's flawless study, destined – according to Peretz – to 'change the history
of the future', revealed itself to be a 'sheer forgery'. Yet, it is plainly futile
to search for words of truth from someone who could shamelessly aver,
as Wieseltier did, that 'within the Jewish community and outside the
Jewish community, the Joan Peters book had no impact whatsoever'.
When extensive documentation of and a long essay on the hoax was
published in book form in 1988,[36] Wieseltier gave yet another of his
iron-clad personal commitments to review it in *The New Republic*. Six
years later, one still waits.

Even at the extreme left of the political spectrum, the question of
Palestine suffered from incredible bad faith. *Jewish Currents*, a relic of the
Stalinist left, published in May 1987 a review essay in defense of *From
Time Immemorial*. Fully apprised that it was a hoax, then president of the
Center for Constitutional Rights, Mortin Stavis, nonetheless acclaimed
Peters's book as a 'historical panorama' that was 'illuminating and useful'.
The 'vilification' Stavis pronounced 'wholly unjustified'.

As for Joan Peters herself, she has not been seen or heard from in
nearly a decade. Dispatched to Orwell's 'memory hole', her name is no
longer mentionable in polite company. Reviled or 'forgotten', Peters no
doubt finds comfort in the knowledge that, like Jonathan Pollard, she has
– in the words of Shakespeare's Othello – 'done the state some service,
and they know't'. And despite all, *From Time Immemorial* still clings to life.
Thus, Israeli Likud leader Benjamin Netanyahu recently observed in a
tome with scholarly pretensions that

> Beginning with the first wave of Zionist immigration in 1880 and continuing
> through successive waves and after World War I, [Palestine] was rapidly trans-
> formed. ... And as Jewish immigration increased their numbers, it also caused

a rapid increase in the Arab population. Many of the Arabs immigrated into the land in response to the job opportunities and the better life afforded by the growing economy the Jews had created.[37]

# 'Born of War, Not by Design'

## Benny Morris's 'Happy Median' Image

I am particularly amazed by the flight of the Arabs. This is a more extraordinary episode in the annals of this country than the establishment of a
Jewish state. ... Truly astonishing is that the Arabs have disappeared from a
whole section of the country.
Israeli Foreign Minister Moshe Sharett, 16 June 1948

So the idea [of transfer] simmered until 1948, when war, without a Jewish
master plan or indeed, without any preplanning whatsoever, brought a
Palestinian exodus of itself. With a little nudging in the right direction, the
low-key exodus could be turned into a mass flood and a fait accompli.
Benny Morris[1]

In recent years, a more or less cohesive body of work has emerged that
challenges the received wisdom on the origins of the Israeli–Arab conflict.
Variously labeled 'new history', 'revisionist history' or simply 'history' (as
against the 'pre'-history of an earlier generation), this scholarship severely
qualifies – without, however, roundly dismissing – the standard interpretation of the eve, unfolding and aftermath of the 1948 war. Its authors,
mostly Israeli, argue five major points:

1. the Zionist movement did not in principle support the partition of
   Palestine;
2. the surrounding Arab states did not unite as one to destroy the nascent
   Jewish state;
3. the war did not pit a relatively defenseless and weak Jewish David
   against a relatively strong Arab Goliath;
4. Palestine's Arabs did not take flight at the behest of Arab orders; and
5. Israel was not earnestly seeking peace at the war's end.

In this essay I want to focus on the work of Benny Morris, a former
diplomatic correspondent of the *Jerusalem Post* who received his doctorate

from Cambridge University. Morris is the most influential and prolific of the 'new' historians.[2] The central concern of his research is the most passionately disputed chapter of the 1948 war: the flight into exile of Palestine's indigenous Arab population. Morris's first study, *The Birth of the Palestinian Refugee Problem, 1947–1949*,[3] was near-universally acclaimed as a classic, a model of scholarly rigor and detachment.[4] The publication of Morris's companion volume, *1948 and After*,[5] is an especially propitious occasion for taking stock of his – and, by extension, the 'new' history's – achievement.

In *Birth*, Morris definitively shatters one of the most enduring myths about the origins of the Israeli–Arab conflict – but only to substitute another scarcely more credible one in its place.

The aim of Morris's study is to explain why roughly 700,000 Palestinians fled their homes in the wake of the November 1947 United Nations General Assembly Resolution supporting the creation of an Arab and Jewish state in Mandatory Palestine.[6] The book's central thesis is that neither of the standard accounts of the Palestinians' exodus can withstand close scholarly scrutiny: the Zionists did not expel them with premeditation, as the Arabs allege, and the invading Arab states did not urge them to leave, as the Zionists allege. The truth, as Morris sees it, rather lies 'in the vast middle ground' between these two extremes:

> The Palestinian refugee problem was born of war, not by design, Jewish or Arab. It was largely a by-product of Arab and Jewish fears and of the protracted, bitter fighting that characterised the first Israeli–Arab war; in smaller part, it was the deliberate creation of Jewish and Arab military commanders and politicians. (*1948*, p. 88; *Birth*, p. 286)

Morris further asserts that, under the given circumstances – i.e. mutual fear and hostility, war and so on – the creation of the Palestinian refugee problem was 'almost inevitable' (*Birth*, p. 286).

The results of Morris's research thus apparently belie the most damaging Arab claims[7] and exonerate Israel of any real culpability for the catastrophe that befell Palestine's indigenous population in 1948.[8] While these conclusions will not satisfy those among Israel's partisans who will accept nothing but Arab culpability, they nevertheless substitute a new version of what occurred in 1948 which as well requires judicious analysis.

In this chapter I will argue that Morris has substituted a new myth, one of the 'happy median', for the old. My contention will be that the evidence that Morris adduces does not support his temperate conclusions and that the truth lies very much closer to the Arab view.[9] The essay is divided into four sections. In the first section, I discuss Morris's handling of evidence. I suggest that his uncritical use of Israeli documents skews his conclusions. In the second section, I discuss Morris's handling of the 'Arab broadcasts' argument. I suggest that his qualified dismissal of this argument does not go far enough. In the third section, I discuss Morris's central thesis that the Arab refugee problem was 'born of war, not by design'. I suggest that Morris's own evidence points to the conclusion that Palestine's Arabs were expelled systematically and with premeditation. In the fourth section, I discuss the general framework in which Morris situates the Arab flight. I suggest that Morris's singular emphasis on the military factor – what he refers to as Israel's 'life-and-death struggle' – obscures the ideological motivations behind Israel's decision to expel Palestine's Arabs.

## Evidence

Morris bases his studies on Israeli archival materials, many of which have only recently become available, and the standard semi-official accounts of the war.[10] While these sources can provide much valuable information, the uncritical manner in which Morris handles them casts some serious doubts on his conclusions. Indeed, Morris himself has in recent years warned against a naive reliance on such materials. Documenting extensive misrepresentation in official Zionist publications on the matter of transfer (cf. note 52 below), Morris writes:

> The speeches, debates, diaries and memoranda that the Zionist bureaucrats issued wholesale passed through the sieve of political censorship on the way to publication; a large portion disappeared or were distorted. ... Historians and students using those sources would do well to employ a large measure of caution.[11]

Consider, however, the following typical examples.

Morris repeatedly warns readers to treat with extreme circumspection the diary entries and public pronouncements of Ben-Gurion, yet uncritically reports certain of his conclusions. Morris notes that Ben-Gurion's testimony cannot be trusted because he was 'driven ... by concern for his place in history and the image of himself and the image of the new state he wished to project for posterity' (*Birth*, p. 165; cf. *Birth*, pp. 136–7, 218, 292–3, 329–30, note 24, 335, note 40; *1948*, p. 113). For example, he ridicules Ben-Gurion's repeated assertion in 1948 and 1949 that 'Israel has never expelled a single Arab' as 'a lie that even the most gullible journalists and UN officials found hard to swallow' (*Tikkun*, p. 82). Indeed, Morris singles out Ben-Gurion's own 'histories' (the quotation marks are Morris's) of the Yishuv and Israel's first years as the 'purest expression' of the highly tendentious 'old' history (*1948*, p. 5).[12] Yet he cites without irony or qualification the 'major political conclusion' (Morris's phrase) Ben-Gurion drew from the Arab exodus from Haifa and elsewhere. Speaking to the People's Council in early May 1948, Israel's first prime minister made the claim that no Jewish settlement to date had been abandoned in the war – in contrast with 'some hundred Arab settlements'. The Arabs, Ben-Gurion asserted, had abandoned 'cities ... with great ease, after the first defeat, even though no danger of destruction or massacre ... confronted them. Indeed, it was revealed with overwhelming clarity which people is bound with strong bonds to this land' (*Birth*, pp. 94–5)[13] In fact, as we shall see presently, virtually every Arab settlement was abandoned precisely because of the 'danger of destruction or massacre'. What is more, at the exact moment that Ben-Gurion was sounding this 'major political conclusion', the Palmah was massacring some seventy Arab prisoners near Ein az Zeitun and several Arabs in the village itself (*Birth*, pp. 102, 321, note 133).

Morris maintains that 'Jewish atrocities', although 'far more widespread than the old histories have let on', were nonetheless 'limited in size, scope and time' (*1948*, p. 22; *Birth*, p. 231). Yet, he also reports that the official Israeli investigation of Israel Defense Forces (IDF) atrocities during the 1948 war 'remains classified and closed to historians' (*Birth*, p. 351, note 45). It is unclear, then, why Morris is so certain about the circumscribed range of 'Jewish atrocities'. Indeed, I will discuss in Chapter 4 recent evidence casting grave doubts on Morris's facile assumption.

In any event, Morris's rendering of 'Jewish atrocities' has a distinctly sanitized quality. Morris writes:

> At Sabbarin, where IZL met resistance, the villagers fled after 20 died in the firefight, and an IZL armoured car fired at the fleeing villagers. 'More than one hundred' old people, women and children, who had not fled from Sabbarin and the other villages, were held for a few days behind barbed wire at an assembly point in Sabbarin, after which they were expelled to Umm al Fahm, a village in Arab-held territory to the southeast. The Jewish troops combed the villages to ascertain that they were empty and to make sure they stayed empty. An IZL officer at Umm al Shauf later recalled searching a column of refugees and finding a pistol and rifle among their possessions. The troops detained seven young adult males and sent the rest of the column on its way to Umm al Fahm. The troops then demanded to know who the weapons belonged to. When the seven Arabs refused to own up, the IZL men threatened to kill them. When no one owned up, the IZL officer held a 'field court martial ... which sentenced the seven to death'. The seven were then executed. (*Birth*, pp. 117–18)

Morris takes for granted that the IZL 'met resistance' at Sabbarin and that the twenty villagers were killed in a 'firefight', that the seven refugees were executed because they 'refused to own up' to possessing weapons

– he takes all this for granted because the Revisionist Zionist[14] sources, which are the only ones he cites (*Birth*, p. 325, note 192), say as much. Given the grossly apologetic Revisionist Zionist accounts of, say, the Deir Yassin massacre,[15] one could reasonably expect a historian to treat such sources with a fair amount of skepticism. Morris evidently does not.[16]

Morris devotes considerable space to the large-scale IDF massacre at Lydda. Somewhere between 250 and 400 Palestinians were killed in the actual massacre and perhaps 350 more died in the subsequent forced march. Basing himself almost entirely on an official history of the Palmah and a book by Elhanan Orren, which he describes (in a footnote) as 'written under constraints of IDF censorship' and (in an altogether different context) as typical of the disingenuous 'old' history (*Birth*, p. 344, note 14; *Tikkun*, p. 20), Morris asserts that the massacre was prompted by 'sniping by armed Lydda townspeople' and the fear and confusion that ensued:

> The 300–400 Israeli troops in the town, dispersed in semi-isolated pockets in the midst of tens of thousands of hostile townspeople, some still armed, felt threatened, vulnerable and angry: they believed that the town had surrendered. 3rd Battalion OC Moshe Kelman immediately ordered his troops to suppress the sniping ... with the utmost severity. The troops were ordered to shoot at 'any clean target' or, alternatively, at anyone 'seen in the streets'. Some townspeople, shut up in their houses, under curfew, took fright at the sounds of shooting outside, perhaps believing that a massacre was in progress. They rushed into the streets – and were cut down by Israeli fire. Some of the soldiers also fired and lobbed grenades into houses from which snipers were suspected to be operating. In the confusion, dozens of unarmed detainees in the mosque and church compounds in the center of the town were shot and killed. Perhaps some of these had attempted to escape, also fearing a massacre. (*Birth*, pp. 205–6)

Yet, the figures that Morris cites suggest that perhaps *not a single* Israeli soldier was killed or wounded amid the alleged 'sniping' attacks.[17] Couldn't the official account of 'sniping', 'confusion' and so on simply have been fabricated to conceal a premeditated massacre, the intent of which was to 'facilitate' the Palestinians' flight? Indeed, circumspection is specially warranted in light of Morris's own finding that a

> strong desire to see the population ... flee already existed: the [sniping] seemed to offer the justification and opportunity for what the bombings and artillery barrages [which preceded Lydda's occupation] ... had in the main failed to achieve. (*Birth*, p. 207)

Morris, however, reports without demurral the rendering of his Zionist sources as fact.

Indeed, Morris makes no effort to reconcile the manifest untrustworthiness of his sources with his uncritical reliance on them. For instance, after describing in some detail the massacre and expulsion in the village of Eilabun, he cites the self-serving account of one Major Sulz that '[t]he village was captured after a fierce fight and its inhabitants had fled' (*Birth*, pp. 229–30). Thus, by Morris's own reckoning, Sulz's testimony is evidently not to be credited. Yet, the equally self-serving testimony of this same Major Sulz is cited by Morris to justify the expulsions from Khisas and Qeitiya (*Birth*, p. 242). Similarly, Morris documents that, contrary to the self-serving accounts of a local IDF officer and an official of a neighboring kibbutz, the villagers of Beit Naqquba did not flee at the behest of Arab orders but were ordered to leave by the IDF (*1948*, pp. 195–7). Yet, he then goes on to conclude that the 'villagers of Beit Naqquba were apparently – simultaneously – ordered by local Arab commanders to evacuate' (*1948*, p. 214).

Revealingly, Morris is much more cautious in his handling of the few Arab sources he cites. The testimony of an Arab witness to a massacre is parenthetically qualified with the phrase 'he alleged' (*Birth*, p. 228). Actually, if we are to believe Morris, Arab sources are generally not to be trusted, given the 'Arab penchant for exaggeration' (*Birth*, pp. 230–1). Illustrating this generic 'penchant', Morris cites the 'wildly inaccurate charge' of the 'Arab media ... that "Men, women and children have been murdered in Faluja"' (*Birth*, p. 354, note 27). According to a UN source cited by Morris, civilian villagers at Faluja had been 'beaten and robbed by Israeli soldiers and ... there ha[d] been some cases of rape', and Israeli troops had 'fir[ed] promiscuously' (*Birth*, p. 244). Evidently, the Arabs did exaggerate. Yet, was their exaggeration really more egregious than Ben-Gurion's when he 'emphatically' denied in April 1949 'that Israel had expelled the Arabs. ... The State of Israel expelled nobody and will never do it' (*Birth*, p. 260)? Than Menachem Begin's when he averred that his men sought 'to avoid a single unnecessary casualty' at Deir Yassin? Than the Israeli government's when it claimed for forty years that the Arabs fled Palestine on orders from the invading Arab armies? Why, then, does Morris speak only of an Arab 'penchant for exaggeration'? Ironically, Morris faults 'old' historian Shabtai Teveth for using the phrase 'that quickest of Arab telegraphs: the rumor' – which, however racist, is rather less offensive than his own.

## Arab Broadcasts

Since the birth of the refugee question, Israeli propaganda has steadfastly held that, in response to Arab radio broadcasts urging flight to clear the field for the invading Arab armies, the Palestinians departed of their own volition – indeed, despite Zionist entreaties that they remain in place. This claim was conclusively demolished by British scholar Erskine Childers and Palestinian scholar Walid Khalidi as far back as the early 1960s. They reported that the back files of the Near East monitoring stations of the British and American governments (both of which covered not only all the radio stations in the Near East but the local newspapers as well) contained no evidence of such Arab orders. This finding, however, had little, if any, impact on mainstream scholarship.[18] Benny Morris has now lent his Israeli imprimatur to the finding, making it far more difficult to ignore. As Walid Khalidi pungently observed, 'Morris ... unequivocally and commendably confirms the death of the (albeit long-deceased) Arab evacuation orders'.[19] The relevant passages of *Birth* read as follows:

> I have found no contemporary evidence to show that either the leaders of the Arab states or the Mufti ordered or directly encouraged the mass exodus during April. It may be worth noting that for decades the policy of the Palestinian Arab leaders had been to hold fast to the soil of Palestine and to resist the eviction and displacement of the Arab communities. (p. 66)

> There is no evidence that the Arab states and the AHC [Arab Higher Committee] wanted a mass exodus or issued blanket orders or appeals to the Palestinians to flee their homes (though in certain areas the inhabitants of specific villages were ordered by Arab commanders of the AHC to leave, mainly for strategic reasons). (p. 129)[20]

Yet in *Birth*'s conclusion, Morris rather revises his finding. Though he introduces no new evidence beyond what was in the body of the book, he puts a new spin on what happened, saying that:

> The Arab leadership inside and outside Palestine probably helped precipitate the exodus in the sense that it was disunited, had decided on no fixed, uniform policy vis-a-vis the civilian evacuation and gave the Palestinians no consistent, hard-and-fast guidelines and instructions about how to act and what to do, especially during the crucial month of April. The records are incomplete, but they show overwhelming confusion and disparate purpose, 'policy' changing from week to week and area to area. No guiding hand or central control is evident. ...
>
> As to April and the start of the main exodus, I have found no evidence to show that the AHC issued blanket instructions, by radio or otherwise, to Palestine's Arabs to flee. However, AHC and Husayni supporters in certain areas may have done so, on occasion, in the belief that they were doing what the AHC wanted or would have wanted them to do. Haifa affords illustration of this. While it is unlikely that Husayni or the AHC from outside instructed the Haifa Arab leadership of 22 April to opt for evacuation rather than surrender, Husayni's local supporters, led by Sheikh Murad, did so. The lack of AHC and

Husayni orders, appeals or broadcasts against the departure during the following week-long Haifa exodus indicates that Husayni and the AHC did not dissent from their supporters' decision. Silence was consent. The absence of clear, public instructions and broadcasts for or against the Haifa exodus over 23–30 April is supremely instructive concerning the ambivalence of Husayni and the AHC at this stage towards the exodus. The Arab states, apart from appealing to the British to halt the Haganah offensives and charging that the Haganah was ex-pelling Palestine's Arabs, seem to have taken weeks to digest and understand what was happening. They did not appeal to the Palestinian masses to leave, but neither, in April, did they demand that the Palestinians stay put. Perhaps, the politicians in Damascus, Cairo and Amman, like Husayni, understood that they would need a good reason to justify armed intervention in Palestine on the morrow of the British departure – and the mass exodus, presented as a planned Zionist expulsion, afforded such a reason. (pp. 289–90)

Morris thus clearly suggests that the historical record on this point is rather more ambiguous than he stated in the body of *Birth*.

Such equivocation is not warranted by the evidence, however. Through-out March and April 1948, the broadcasts of the AHC and neighboring Arab countries were consistently urging the Palestinians to remain in place.[21] Indeed, Morris himself observes that, as early as December 1947, these broadcasts were instructing Palestinians to 'stay put and fight'. Furthermore, 'by and large, the local leaderships and militia commanders, whether in obedience to the AHC or independently, discouraged flight, even to the extent of issuing formal threats and imposing penalties, but it all proved to no avail' (*Birth*, pp. 57–8). This conclusion receives con-firmation in the official IDF intelligence report covering the period December 1947–June 1948 which states that 'the AHC decided ... to adopt measures to weaken the exodus by imposing restrictions, penalties, threats, propaganda in the press [and] on the radio. ... The AHC tried to obtain the help of neighboring countries in this context' (*Birth*, p. 60). Khalidi reports that, as late as 22 April, in the midst of the massive exodus from Haifa, the AHC, far from encouraging the Arabs to leave, fervently urged them to be patient and to bear up and hold their ground. 'The duty of the defence of the Holy Land rests upon us,' one such AHC statement read, 'the people of Palestine, first and foremost' (Khalidi, 'Why Did the Palestinians Leave?'). Morris further notes that the same theme was being sounded by Palestinian and non-Palestinian leaders at the end of April and in early May (*Birth*, pp. 68–9). In fact, *all* of Morris's specu-lations about Arab ambivalence to and silent complicity with the exodus are apparently based on the absence of any explicit broadcasts urging the Palestinians to stay put during exactly *one week* of the twenty-month-long period encompassed by the Palestinian exodus.

Notice, incidentally, that Morris abandons the standard Zionist claim that the Arab leaders urged the Palestinians to flee in order to clear the field for the invading Arab armies. Indeed, he has done so with good reason. Simha Flapan highlights the absurdity of this pretense in *Birth of Israel*:

> From the point of view of military logistics, the contention that the Palestinian Arab leadership appealed to the Arab masses to leave their homes in order to open the way for the invading armies, after which they would return to share in the victory, makes no sense at all. The Arab armies, coming long distances and operating in or from the Arab areas of Palestine, needed the help of the local population for food, fuel, water, transport, manpower, and information. (p. 85)

Unfortunately, Morris has contrived an equally untenable theory – namely, that the Arab leaders 'perhaps' encouraged the Palestinian exodus to justify an invasion of the nascent Jewish state. Yet, as Mary C. Wilson observes in *King Abdullah: Britain and the Making of Jordan*, the massive flight of Palestinian Arabs came as a very unwelcome surprise to the Arab states, which had hitherto sought to 'shield their inactivity behind the ineffectual Arab Liberation Army' but were now subjected to intense popular pressure to 'move towards direct involvement'. She notes that while the 'rush of Palestinians to Amman seeking [King Abdullah's] help and protection' did serve to legitimize Jordan's secret intention to occupy Arab Palestine, it 'threatened to throw Abdullah off course' as well since the exodus prompted the direct involvement of the other Arab states (pp. 168–9).[22]

Interestingly, Morris himself undercuts his novel theory, reporting that (1) 'already in' February 1948 King Abdullah was – in the words of the British High Commissioner for Palestine – 'complain[ing] about the exodus of Palestine Arabs into Transjordan [saying] ... they were all arriving thoroughly anti-British and, hence, might give him trouble' (*1948*, pp. 225–6); (2) the Arab exodus beginning in April 'propelled the [Arab] states closer to the brink of an invasion about which they were largely unenthusiastic' (*Birth*, p. 129); and (3) 'in early May 1948 when, according to Israeli propaganda and some of the old histories such a campaign of broadcasts urging or ordering the Arabs to leave should have been at its height, in preparation for the pan-Arab invasion, Arab radio stations and leaders ... all issued calls, in repeated broadcasts, to the Palestinians to stay put or, if already in exile, to return to their homes' (*1948*, p. 18).

One may, finally, observe that Morris never explains his divination that the 'silence' of the Arab leadership in the course of the Haifa exodus signalled 'consent'. It may just as well have signalled despair, helplessness, embarrassment, confusion – as with the Zionist leadership's reaction to the Nazi holocaust. Or did the 'silence' in the latter case also equal 'consent'?

## 'Born of War, Not by Design'?

We have seen that Morris maintains that the Palestinian Arab refugee question was 'largely a by-product of Arab and Jewish fears and of the protracted, bitter fighting that characterised the first Israeli–Arab war'. Simply put, it was 'born of war, not by design'. Yet, in a note to *Birth*, Morris suggests a rather significant qualification of this view:

> The word 'expelled' was often used rather loosely by Israelis in 1948. It was quite often assumed by non-witnesses that a given community had been expelled when in fact it had left before Israeli forces arrived. The desire to see the Arabs leave often triggered the assumption that commanders – who it was presumed shared this desire – had to act overtly and directly to obtain this result, when this had not been the case. *But if denial of the right to return was a form of 'expulsion', then a great many villagers – who had waited near their villages for the battle to die down before trying to return home – can be considered 'expellees'.* (p. 343, note 7; my emphasis)

Thus, Morris agrees that, in at least one crucial sense, 'a great many' Palestinian refugees were systematically expelled from their homes.[23] This then raises the questions of whether the Zionists intended that the Arabs flee from their homes and whether they acted in a manner consonant with this intention. If the answer to these two questions is also in the affirmative, then it becomes impossible to sustain Morris's thesis that the refugee problem was 'born of war, not by design'. One could maintain that, given the armed hostilities, the Zionists had no alternative except to expel the indigenous Arab population; but one could not still maintain that the Arab flight was an unintended or unanticipated 'by-product' of the war.

Before turning to the evidence in this regard, it is not without interest to consider the Arab estimate of Zionist intentions on the eve of the war. Morris cites a British report on the conference of Arab prime ministers in December 1947, in which the Arab view of Zionist ambitions was summarized as follows:

> The ultimate aim of all the Zionists was 'the acquisition of all of Palestine, all Transjordan and possibly some tracts in Southern Lebanon and Southern Syria'. The Zionist 'politicians', after taking control of the country, would at first treat the Arabs 'nicely'. But then, once feeling 'strong enough', they would begin 'squeezing the Arab population off their lands ... [and] if necessary out of the

State'. Later, they would expand the Jewish state at the expense of the Palestinian Arab state. However, the more militant Haganah commanders wished to move more quickly. ... Exploiting the weakness and disorganization of the Arabs, they would first render them – especially in Jaffa and Haifa – 'completely powerless' and then frighten or force them into leaving, 'their places being taken by Jewish immigrants'. The Arab leaders ... thought that there existed a still more extreme Jewish plan, of the Revisionists, calling for more immediate expansion. (*Birth*, p. 24)

For all the monumental corruption and incompetence of the Arab leaders, one cannot but be impressed by the prescience of their analyses. Curiously, Morris virtually admits as much but, in a peculiar turn of phrase, describes these Arab 'prognoses' as 'in the nature of self-fulfilling prophecies' (*Birth*, p. 24). If he means that the Arabs, by electing to wage war, facilitated the expulsion, he is no doubt correct. Yet, this in no way belies the fact that it was an expulsion.

The Arab flight from Palestine divides into basically two stages, the first covering the period from the 29 November 1947 UN General Assembly resolution to the Israeli independence declaration in May 1948, and the second covering the period from June 1948 to the signing of the armistice agreements in mid-1949. I will deal with each of these stages in turn.

### November 1947–May 1948

For the period preceding Israel's birth, Morris focuses primarily on the months April–May. Morris's central conclusion reads as follows:

The main wave of the Arab exodus, encompassing 200,000–300,000 refugees, was not the result of a general, predetermined Yishuv policy. The Arab exodus of April–May caught the Yishuv leadership, including the authors of Plan D, by surprise, though it was immediately seen as a phenomenon to be exploited. (*Birth*, p. 128)

This conclusion incorporates three claims, none of which, in my opinion, can sustain close scrutiny: (1) April–May 1948 witnessed 'the main wave of the Arab exodus'; (2) the Arab exodus was 'not the result of a general, predetermined Yishuv policy'; and (3) the Arab exodus during these months 'caught the Yishuv leadership, including the authors of Plan D, by surprise'.

*April–May 1948 witnessed 'the main wave of the Arab exodus'.* Morris divides the Arab flight from Palestine into five waves: December 1947–March 1948, April–May 1948, July–October 1948, October–November 1948, and December 1948–September 1949. Of these five waves, he reports that the 'main wave' unfolded April–May 1948, as 'the bulk of the Palestinian refugees – some 250,000–300,000 – went into exile'. Morris devotes by far the largest chapter of his study ('The Second Wave: The Mass Exodus, April–June 1948') to the Arab exodus during these months.[24] The unmistakable inference is that this wave is somehow typical. Indeed, Morris describes the events in Haifa during April and May as 'illustrative of the complexity of the exodus' (*1948*, p. 18).

Yet, Morris's periodization obscures the fact that Israel's statehood declaration was actually the watershed date. In the weeks immediately preceding 14 May, the Zionist leadership was especially sensitive to international pressure because of threats (emanating particularly from the United States) to rescind or modify the Partition Resolution. This concern for world public opinion acted to some extent as a brake on Zionist policy *vis-à-vis* the Palestinian Arabs. As Avi Shlaim puts it in *Collusion Across the Jordan*:

> The flight of the Palestinian Arabs [in April 1948] served the military needs of the Yishuv but endangered its international position. A major contention of official Zionist propaganda was that peaceful relations between Arabs and Jews were possible, and Ben-Gurion himself repeatedly declared a Jewish–Arab alliance to be one of the three main objectives of his policy. Any sign of deterioration, any incident liable to plunge Palestine into a bloodbath, naturally encouraged the opponents of partition. (pp. 164–5)

In the wake of Israel's Declaration of Independence, however, this constraint was to a large extent (but not altogether) lifted. Coupled with a new military context (the invasion and subsequent rout of the Arab armies), this diplomatic breakthrough enabled the Zionists to pursue with virtual impunity a policy that, as we shall see presently, was openly and relentlessly bent on expulsion. At least as many, and probably more, Arabs fled *after* Israel's statehood declaration as before (for the various estimates, cf. *Birth*, p. 292; *1948*, pp. 30, 72, 88; Flapan, p. 89). What happened in, say, April is thus not exactly 'illustrative of the complexity of the exodus'. Morris himself concedes this point in another context, observing that the 'circumstances of the second half of the [Arab] exodus' from June onward were 'a different story' (*1948*, p. 88). In effect, the overt expulsion of Lydda's Arabs in July was no less typical of Zionist policy than the covert expulsion of Haifa's Arabs in April. One can also easily miss this crucial point inasmuch as Morris devotes one hundred pages to the first half of the exodus before May (chs 2–3) as against only about *half as many* pages to the second half after May (chs 6–8).

*The Arab exodus was 'not the result of a general, predetermined Yishuv policy'.* Morris's argument is that no single factor can explain the flight of the Palestinian Arabs during this period:

There is probably no accounting for the mass exodus ... without understanding the prevalence and depth of the general sense of collapse, of 'falling apart', that permeated Arab Palestine, especially the towns, by April 1948. In many places, it would take very little to induce the inhabitants to pack up and flee. Come the Haganah (and IZL–LHI) offensives of April–May, the cumulative effect of the fears, deprivations, abandonment and depredations of the previous months, in both towns and villages, overcame the natural, basic reluctance to abandon home and property and go into exile. As Palestinian military power was swiftly and dramatically demolished and the Haganah demonstrated almost unchallenged superiority in successive conquests, Arab morale cracked, giving way to general blind panic or a 'psychosis of flight', as one IDF intelligence report put it. (*Birth*, p. 287)

The correlative of this argument is that the Arab exodus did not result from a systematic policy of expulsion. Yet the evidence that Morris brings to bear in support of his thesis points to a different conclusion. I will first look at general Zionist policy and then focus on two key architects of Zionist policy during these months.

According to Morris, the Yishuv military leadership formulated in early March and began implementing in April Plan Dalet to cope with the anticipated Arab offensives. The 'essence' of Plan D

was the clearing of hostile and potentially hostile forces out of the interior of the prospective territory of the Jewish State. ... As the Arab irregulars were based and quartered in the villages, and as the militias of many villages were participating in the anti-Yishuv hostilities, *the Haganah regarded most of the villages as actively or potentially hostile*. (*Birth*, p. 62, my emphasis; cf. *Birth*, pp. 113, 128–9)

In short, Plan D constituted – and here I am quoting Morris – 'a strategic–ideological anchor and basis for expulsions by front, district, brigade and battalion commanders ... and it gave commanders, *post facto*, a formal, persuasive covering note to explain their actions' (*Birth*, p. 63; cf. *Birth*: pp. 113, 157).[25]

I do not see how the above admissions can be reconciled with Morris's claim that there existed no General Staff '"plan" or policy decision' to 'expel "the Arabs" from the Jewish State's areas' (*Birth*, p. 289). One can argue that Plan D was neither discussed, nor would it likely have been approved, by the official Jewish decision-making bodies – the provisional government, the National Council and the Jewish Agency Executive (cf. Flapan, p. 89). One can also argue, and I will return to this question, that Plan D was 'not a political blueprint for the expulsion of Palestine's Arabs' but, rather, 'was governed by military considerations and was geared to achieving military ends' (*Birth*, pp. 62–3). The fact still remains, however, that such an expulsion policy *was* formulated.

Furthermore, Plan D was the *operative* policy in the field. According to Morris, 'during the first half of April, Ben-Gurion and the Haganah General Staff approved a series of offensives ... embodying [Plan D's] guidelines' (*Birth*, p. 129). And again: 'The doctrinal underpinning of Plan D was taken for granted by the majority of the Haganah commanders. ... The gloves had to be, and were, taken off' (*Birth*, p. 113). And yet again:

> It was understood by all concerned that, militarily, in the struggle to survive, the less Arabs remaining behind and along the front lines, the better and, politically, the less Arabs remaining in the Jewish State, the better. At each level of command and execution, Haganah officers in those April–May days when the fate of the State hung in balance, simply 'understood' what the military and political exigencies of survival required. (*Birth*, p. 289)

That is, expulsion.[26]

In accordance with Plan D, the Haganah and dissident Zionist groups launched a series of military offensives, the fully anticipated result of which was the Arabs' flight from Palestine. The attacks themselves were

> the most important single factor in the exodus of April–June from both the cities and from the villages. ... This is demonstrated clearly by the fact that each exodus occurred during and in the immediate wake of each military assault. No town was abandoned by the bulk of its population *before* Jewish attack. (*Birth*, pp. 130–1, emphasis in original; cf. *1948*, pp. 74–7)

The widely publicized slaughter at Deir Yassin, the massacres in Khirbet Nasr ad Din near Tiberias and Ein az Zeitun near Safad, the indiscriminate and protracted mortarings in Haifa[27] and Acre, the use of loudspeakers broadcasting 'black propaganda' (i.e. terrifying) messages in Arabic, crop burnings, and so on, spurred into exile those Palestinians not sufficiently impressed by the lightning assaults of the Zionist forces (*1948*, pp. 71, 75–6, 173–90 passim). Especially outside the major urban centers, 'it was standard Haganah and IDF policy to round up and expel the remaining villagers (usually old people, widows, cripples) from sites already evacuated by most of their inhabitants' (*Birth*, p. 288). Finally, Morris reports that the Arab exodus during these months was 'certainly viewed favorably' and 'with satisfaction' by 'the bulk of the Yishuv's leadership' (*1948*, p. 87).

Given that the expressed aim of the wartime Zionist leadership was to expel the Arabs, given that its intention became operative policy in the field, given that the tactics of the Jewish commanders had the predictable result of inducing a mass flight, and given that Palestinians who fled the scene of battle were blocked from returning to their homes once hostilities were suspended, not too much significance would seem to attach to

Morris's observation — itself questionable, as we shall see below — that expulsion orders were rarely issued 'since most of the villages were completely or almost completely empty by the time they were occupied'. (*Birth*, p. 131).

Morris does acknowledge that the 'atrocity factor' (his phrase) played a major role in certain areas of the country in encouraging Arab flight (*Birth*, pp. 130, 288; *1948*, pp. 75–6). Nonetheless, there are several curious twists in his account. In the first place, he rightly points to the pivotal role of the Deir Yassin massacre, but accuses the Arab radio stations of 'luridly and repeatedly' broadcasting accounts of it 'for weeks' (*Birth*, p. 130; cf. *Birth*, p. 114 where he refers to the 'Arab media atrocity campaign'). Yet, according to an authoritative (if controversial) Israeli military historian of the 1948 war, Uri Milstein, the reports on Deir Yassin that spurred the Arabs into exile were 'mostly fabricated or exaggerated by various elements on the Jewish side' ('No Deportations, Evacuations', *Hadashot*, 1 January 1988). Furthermore, in *Birth*'s conclusion, Morris revises the meaning of the 'atrocity factor'. There it mainly refers not to Zionist brutalities but to Arab premonitions of Jewish retribution: 'Arab villagers and townspeople, prompted by the fear that the Jews, if victorious, would do to them what, in the reverse circumstances victorious Arab fighters would have done (and did, occasionally, as in the Etzion Bloc in May), to defeated Jews, took to their heels'; the 'actual atrocities committed by the Jewish forces' serve, in this reckoning, only to 'reinforce such fears considerably' (*Birth*, p. 288). In any event, Morris provides only the flimsiest of evidence — for example, a hearsay account of an American reporter's conversation with an English sergeant in which the latter surmised what the Arabs must have 'imagined to themselves' as they fled (*Birth*, pp. 363–4, note 2) — to support his tendentious redefinition of the 'atrocity factor'.[28]

Much ink has been spilled on the mass Arab exodus from Haifa in late April.[29] There is no need to rehearse all the specific arguments here. For our purposes, the important point is that events in Haifa generally conformed to the pattern of terror, assault and expulsion described above. Intercommunal strife in Haifa first peaked in December 1947 with an unprovoked attack by Irgun members on a crowd of Arab refinery workers. By April, some 15,000–20,000 of Haifa's 70,000-strong Palestinian community had already fled the city, as hostilities continued to escalate. In accordance with Plan D, the Haganah launched its major offensive against Haifa on 21 April. Attacking Jewish forces made liberal use of psychological warfare and terror tactics. We have already noted the ghastly scene near the port area. Jeeps were also brought in broadcasting recorded 'horror sounds' — including 'shrieks, wails and anguished moans of Arab women, the wail of sirens and the clang of fire-alarm bells, interrupted by a sepulchral voice calling out in Arabic: Save your souls, all ye faithful! Flee for your lives!', according to the eyewitness account of a Haganah officer – and threats to use poison gas and atomic weapons against the Arabs (Palumbo, p. 64). The Carmeli Brigade was ordered to 'kill every [adult] male encountered' and to attack with firebombs 'all objectives that can be set alight' (*Birth*, pp. 76–7). According to Morris, 'clearly th[e] offensive, and especially the mortaring which took place during the morning of 22 April, precipitated the mass exodus' (*Birth*, p. 85; *1948*, p. 21).

Amid the wrack of Haifa, negotiations convened between the local British, Zionist and Arab civilian authorities. By this time probably half and perhaps more of Haifa's Arabs had already fled in terror, many fearing a repetition of the Deir Yassin massacre. For reasons that still remain obscure, the Arabs refused to accept the surrender terms, choosing instead to evacuate the city. Haifa was the only place in April or later where civilian Zionist leaders asked the Arabs to stay put and one of only a handful of places where the local Arab leadership made an organized, considered decision to leave (*1948*, p. 20). But the pleas on one side and the demurrals on the other were largely irrelevant to the actual unfolding of events. For the atrocities continued unabated, with 'the civilian [Zionist] authorities ... saying one thing and the Haganah ... doing something else altogether' (*Birth*, p. 90). With only several thousand Arabs remaining, certain Zionist authorities did finally make a serious effort to halt the exodus, apparently for fear of diplomatic repercussions and the serious strains in the Haifa economy that the flight of Arab workers would cause.[30]

Watching the Arabs flee, Ben-Gurion, who visited the city on 1 May, reportedly exclaimed, 'What a beautiful sight!' (Palumbo, p. 76). Learning that one Zionist official in the city was trying to persuade the Arabs to stay, Ben-Gurion remarked, 'Doesn't he have anything more important to do?' (*Birth*, p. 328, note 4). The policy he announced was to treat the remaining Arabs 'with civil and human equality' but 'it is not our job to worry about the return of the Arabs [who had fled]' (*Birth*, p. 133). In July, Haifa's remaining Arab inhabitants, some 3,500, were packed into a ghetto in the downtown Wadi Nisnas neighborhood (*1948*, pp. 149–71).

Morris maintains that 'there is no evidence that the architects of, and commanders involved in, the offensive of 21–2 April hoped that it would lead to an Arab evacuation of Haifa'. He goes on to observe that 'at the level of Carmeli Brigade headquarters, no orders were ever issued to the troops dispersed in the Arab districts to act in a manner that would pre-cipitate flight' (*Birth*: pp. 85, 92; cf. *1948*, p. 84). Yet Morris himself so qualifies these claims as to render them at best trivial. First, we are told that 'clearly the Haganah was not averse to seeing the Arabs evacuate' Haifa (*Birth*, p. 86). We next learn that, notwithstanding Carmeli head-quarters orders – issued 'somewhat belatedly' – that forbade looting and urged the Arabs to remain calm and return to work, 'if not explicitly to stay in the city', there was 'certainly an undercurrent of more militant thinking akin to the IZL approach'.

> At the company and platoon levels, officers and men cannot but have been struck by the thought that the steady Arab exodus was 'good for the Jews' and must be encouraged to assure the security of 'Jewish' Haifa. A trace of such thinking in Carmeli Brigade headquarters can be discerned in the diary entries of Yosef Weitz for 22–24 April, which the JNF executive spent in Haifa. 'I think that this [flight-prone] state of mind [among the Arabs] should be exploited, and [we should] press the other inhabitants not to surrender [but to leave]. We must establish our state,' he jotted down on 22 April. On 24 April, Weitz went to see Carmel's adjutant, who informed Weitz that the nearby Arab villages ... were being evacuated by their inhabitants and that Acre had been 'shaken'. 'I was happy to hear from him that this line was being adopted by the [Haganah] command, [that is] to frighten the Arabs so long as flight-inducing fear was upon them'. ... Weitz, it appears found a responsive echo in Carmeli Brigade headquarters. It made simple military as well as political sense: Haifa without Arabs was a more easily defensible, less problematic city for the Haganah than Haifa with a large Arab minority. (*Birth*, pp. 92–3)

In short, *de facto* Zionist policy, even at the level of the Carmeli Brigade headquarters, was to press the Arab exodus from Haifa. Thus, Milstein observes that, notwithstanding the Zionists' claim that they 'wanted the Arabs to stay in Haifa, but the Arabs refused', the

> truth was different: The commander of the Carmeli Brigade, Moshe Carmel, feared that many Arabs would remain in the city. Hence, he ordered that three-inch mortars be used to shell the Arab crowds on the market square. The crowd broke into the port, pushing aside the policemen who guarded the gate, stormed the boats and fled the city. The whole day mortars continued to shell the city, even though the Arabs did not fight. ('No Deportation, Evacuation')

Indeed, the 'great efficacy' of these 'indirect methods' (among others) in Haifa is singled out by the above-cited IDF intelligence report of June 1948 in its recommendations for precipitating Arab flight (*1948*, p. 71).[31]

Recall, finally, that Morris described Haifa as 'illustrative of the com-plexity' of the Arab flight. Accordingly, *Birth* analyzes in uniquely exhaus-tive detail the unfolding drama there. No phase of the Arab exodus is better known than Haifa. Every Zionist account of the 1948 war seizes with desperate zeal on the story of the gentle Jewish mayor, Shabtei Levi, tearfully begging the Arabs to remain and the perfidious Arab leadership opting for flight. Likewise, this episode figures very prominently in

Morris's account. Yet, as noted above, Haifa was the only place that witnessed such a turn of events. Simply put, in crucial respects, Haifa was 'illustrative' of – nothing. Morris's focus, in fact, is the most equivocal case of the most equivocal period of the Arab flight.

The other Arab cities and the Arab villages besieged during the months April–May suffered roughly the same fate as Haifa – and for roughly the same reasons. The aim of Operation Yiftah, commanded by Yigal Allon, was to 'clear' the Eastern Galilee border area 'completely of all Arab forces and inhabitants'. Thus were Safad and the villages of Fir'im and Mughr at Kheit emptied of their inhabitants (*Birth*, pp. 101–2, 121–2). The aim of Operation Ben-Ami, commanded by Moshe Carmel, was 'the conquest and evacuation by the Arabs' of the Western Galilee. Carmel's operational order of 19 May to his battalion commanders read: 'To attack in order to conquer, to kill among the men, to destroy and burn the villages of Al Kabri, Umm al Faraj and An Nahr' (*Birth*, pp. 124–5). The aim of Operation Lightning, commanded by Shimon Avidan, was to cause a 'general panic' and 'the wandering [i.e. exodus]' of the Arabs in the south, bordering Egypt (*Birth*, p. 126). The villagers of Kaufakha in the Negev had, according to Morris, 'earlier repeatedly asked to surrender, accept Jewish rule and be allowed to stay, all to no avail. The Haganah *always* regarded such requests as either insincere or unreliable' (*Birth*, p. 128; my emphasis). Even villages that had 'traditionally been friendly towards the Yishuv' – for example, Huj, whose inhabitants had hidden Haganah men from a British dragnet in 1946 and whose mukhtar was shot dead by a mob in Gaza because of his 'collaboration with the Jews' – were de-populated and destroyed (*Birth*, p. 128).

The record that Morris has assembled evidently belies his central thesis that the vicissitudes of war, not an expulsion policy, accounted for the flight of Palestine's Arabs during these months. Yet it is not only Morris's evidence that works against his thesis; his own arguments work against it as well.

Morris asserts that, although right-wing Revisionist Zionists like Menachem Begin and the Irgun leadership did not 'openly espouse a policy of expulsion' during April and May, the goal was 'manifest' in the nature of the attacks they led. He elaborates on this point in a revealing footnote worth quoting at length:

> While Begin and the IZL leadership were careful not to openly espouse a policy of expulsion, it is clear that the IZL's military operations were designed with the aim of clearing out the Arab inhabitants of the areas they conquered. Following the massacre at Deir Yassin, the IZL fighters trucked out the remaining villagers to East Jerusalem. In May in the Hills of Ephraim the IZL assault ended in the flight of the majority of the villagers; and those who remained in

place were, within days, swiftly sent packing. ... In their post-operational reports, ... the IZL commanders emphasized their satisfaction with the fact that the assaults had precipitated mass civilian-Arab flight. (*1948*, p. 37)

Terror, the flight of most Arabs as an assault unfolded and the dispatch of those who remained behind, the satisfaction of the Jewish commanders with the Arab flight – this is Morris's description of the 'main wave of the Arab exodus' during April and May. But then, by Morris's own reckoning, it was not only the right-wing Revisionists who *de facto* pursued an expulsion policy.

*The Arab exodus during the months April–May 'caught the Yishuv leadership, including the authors of Plan D, by surprise'*. Morris maintains not only that the Palestinian exodus was an unintended 'by-product' of the war but that it 'surprised' – indeed, 'shocked', 'flustered' and 'astonished' (*Birth*, p. 81; *1948*, pp. 70, 90) – the Yishuv. He frequently sounds this theme, for example, in the following representative passage:

[There is] no evidence, with the exception of one or two important but isolated statements by Ben-Gurion, of any general expectation in the Yishuv of a mass exodus of the Arab population from the Jewish or any other part of Palestine. Such an exodus may have been regarded by most Yishuv leaders as desirable; but in late March and early April, it was not regarded as necessarily likely or imminent. When it occurred, it surprised even the most optimistic and hardline Yishuv executives, including the leading advocate of the transfer policy, Yosef Weitz. (*Birth*, pp. 63–4)

Inasmuch as Morris specifically names Ben-Gurion and Yosef Weitz, let us look at what the actual record reveals about them.

David Ben-Gurion was without question the major architect of the 1948 war. His thinking and actions informed, as no other Zionist leader's did, the unfolding of events. A review of his record thus provides special insight into the Zionist approach to Palestine's Arab population during that fateful year.

Morris reports that, as far back as the late 1930s, Ben-Gurion repeatedly and forthrightly expressed his support – at meetings as well as in private correspondence and diary entries – for the expulsion of the Palestinian Arabs. For instance, at a Zionist meeting in June 1938 he affirmed that 'I support compulsory transfer. I don't see in it anything immoral' (*Tikkun*, p. 83; cf. *Birth*, p. 25).

The 'idea of a transfer as a solution to the prospective Jewish state's major problem', Morris continues, 'never left the Zionist leaders' minds'; it 'simmered' until the outbreak of hostilities in 1948. Indeed, 'already in November 1947, a few days before the UN partition resolution, Ben-Gurion was thinking in terms of a "transfer" solution to the prospective

Jewish state's Arab problem'. Hence, he advised giving the Arabs of the future Jewish state citizenship in the future Arab state so as to facilitate their expulsion in the likely event of war. Then, as the Palestinians first began to flee before the Zionist assaults during the early days of the war in December 1947, Ben-Gurion grasped that the moment was at hand to implement transfer. Morris writes:

> With a little nudging, with a limited expulsion here and the razing of a village there, and with a policy of military conquest usually preceded by mortar barrages, this trickle of an exodus, he realized, could be turned into a massive outflow. (*Tikkun*, p. 82)[32]

On 7 February 1948, Ben-Gurion spoke approvingly at a Mapai council meeting of the Arab flight from West Jerusalem and anticipated its gener-alization. He was delighted that not 'since the days of the Roman destruction' was Jerusalem 'so completely Jewish as today. ... There are no strangers [i.e. Arabs]. One hundred percent Jews.' He added that

> what happened in Jerusalem and what happened in Haifa could well happen in great parts of the country – if we [the Yishuv] hold on. ... It is very possible that in the coming six or eight or ten months of the war there will take place great changes ... and not all of them to our detriment. Certainly there will be great changes in the composition of the population of the country. (*Birth*, p. 52; *Tikkun*, p. 83; *1948*, pp. 40, 90; Milstein, 'No Deportations, Evacuation')

When asked at this same Mapai meeting about the absence of Jewish-owned land in strategic areas of Palestine, Ben-Gurion replied: 'The war will give us the land. The concepts of "ours" and "not ours" are only concepts for peacetime, and during war they lose all their meaning' (*Birth*, p. 170). Indeed, throughout this month, he repeatedly expressed his intention to appropriate Arab lands in the course of the upcoming war; for example, he suggested to Weitz on 10 February that Weitz divest himself of 'conventional notions. ... In the Negev we will not buy land. We will conquer it. You are forgetting that we are at war' (*Birth*, p. 170). Morris comments on this latter exchange:

> Of course, Ben-Gurion was thinking ahead – and not only about the Negev. The White Paper of 1939 had almost completely blocked Jewish land purchases, asphyxiating the kibbutzim and blocking Jewish regional development. ... The Partition resolution had earmarked some 60% of Palestine for the Jewish State; most of it was not Jewish-owned land. But war was war and, if won, as Ben-Gurion saw things, it would at last solve the Jewish State's land problem. (*Birth*, p. 170)

Morris evidently fails to draw the obvious inference that, 'as Ben-Gurion saw things' already in early February, resolving the Jewish state's massive and seemingly intractable 'land problem' would have to entail the dispossession and displacement of the indigenous Arab peasants. Thus, on the eve of the Haganah offensive resulting in that Arab exodus which allegedly 'surprised' Ben-Gurion, the latter anticipated that the Zionists would 'enter the *empty* [Arab] villages and settle in them' (*Birth*, p. 180; my emphasis). Morris observes that Ben-Gurion then outlined 'two major characteristics of the settlement drive of the following months: settlement of the *abandoned* Arab villages and settlement in areas thinly populated by Jews' (*Birth*, pp. 180–1; my emphasis). Two days later, on 6 April, Ben-Gurion added:

> We will not be able to win the war if we do not, during the war, populate Upper and Lower, Eastern and Western Galilee, the Negev and the Jerusalem area, even if only in an artificial way, in a military way. ... I believe the war will also bring in its wake a great change in the distribution of the Arab population. (*Birth*, p. 181)

With the implementation of Plan D, Ben-Gurion presided over the intensification and generalization of precisely those policies that, already in December 1947, he knew would result in a mass flight of the Palestinian Arabs. As Morris himself tersely puts it,

> Outwardly, he continued until very late in the day to pay the requisite lip service to the grand humanist-socialist ideals. ... *On the ground, however, he made sure that what he wanted done got done*, and he carefully avoided leaving tracks; his name rarely adorns an actual expulsion directive. (*Tikkun*, p. 82; emphasis added)

In a speech to the provisional government on 16 June 1948, Israel's first prime minister observed that

> three things have happened up to now: a) the invasion of the regular armies of the Arab states, b) our ability to withstand these regular armies, and c) the flight of the Arabs. I was not surprised by any of them. (Flapan, p. 88)

The weight of the evidence overwhelmingly points to the conclusion that, at least so far as the 'flight of the Arabs' is concerned, this was not an idle boast. (Curiously, Morris does not report Ben-Gurion's claim that the Arab flight didn't come as a surprise to him.)[33]

After citing Ben-Gurion's eager anticipation in February 1948 that 'there will certainly be great changes in the composition of the country', Morris asks rhetorically: 'Are these the words of man who wishes to see the Arabs remain "citizens of a future Jewish State"? Or are these, rather, the words of leader who has long entertained ... a concept of "transfer" as the solution to the prospective Jewish state's Arab problem?' One may just as well ask rhetorically: Are these the words – is the record that Morris has assembled – of a man who was 'shocked' by the Arab flight?

Let us now turn to Yosef Weitz. Weitz was the Jewish National Fund executive responsible for land acquisition and its allocation to Jewish settlements, and the Jewish National Fund representative on the Committee of Directorates of the National Institutions and on the Settlement Committee of the National Institutions. As Morris comments, he 'was well placed to shape and influence decision-making regarding the Arab population on the national level and to oversee implementation of policy on the local level' (*1948*, p. 91).[34]

As far back as 1940, the idea of a massive Arab transfer from Palestine had 'gripped the imagination' of Weitz (*Birth*, p. 27; cf. Palumbo, p. 4). And, already in early 1948, Weitz – like Ben-Gurion – grasped that the 'state of anarchy created by the hostilities' could and should be used to solve the 'Arab problem' in Palestine (*1948*, pp. 91, 120). In an 11 January diary entry, he wrote: 'Is it not now the time to be rid of them? Why continue to keep in our midst these thorns at a time when they pose a danger to us? Our people are weighing up [solutions]' (*Birth*, p. 55). A little over a month later he returned to this theme: 'It is possible that now is the time to implement our original plan: To transfer them [to Transjordan]' (*Birth*, p. 55). Weitz personally organized numerous 'local eviction and expulsion operations' during these months preceding the major Haganah offensive, sometimes with the assistance of local Haganah units. In January–March, he oversaw the expulsion of Arabs from Ramot-Menashe, Beit Shean Valley and Western Galilee (*Birth*, p. 26; *1948*, pp. 92–7). Throughout March and April, Weitz 'desperately sought political backing and help to implement the transfer' (*Birth*, p. 135; cf. Flapan, pp. 96–7).

With the implementation of Plan D in April, the Zionist leadership in effect undertook to accomplish exactly what Weitz had, in the preceding months, repeatedly urged and already by himself attempted – i.e. to exploit the conditions of 'war and anarchy' to expel the Arabs. Given Weitz's critical place in the Zionist apparatus and his personal foreknowledge of the likely consequences of a massive and bloody assault on the Arab population, it is hard to believe that the ensuing mass exodus came as much of a 'surprise' to him.

Indeed, consider the following suggestive incident reported by Morris. On 13 April, Israel Galili, the Haganah chief, wrote Weitz: 'We regard as important to security new settlements being established in the following places ... : Beit Mahsir, Saris, Ghuweir, Abu Shusha, Kafr Misr, Khirbet Manshiya, Tantura, Bureir.' Galili asked that the establishment of the settlements at these sites be carried out 'as soon as possible' (*Birth*, p. 181). We learn in the corresponding note that: 'Most of the sites *had not yet been abandoned by their inhabitants*' (*Birth*, p. 339, note 105; my emphasis).

Morris's only pieces of evidence to support his claim that the mass flight beginning in April took Weitz by 'surprise' are two diary entries. In his diary entry for 22 April 1948, Weitz, having just arrived in Haifa, muses about the reason behind the Arab flight from there: 'Eating away at my innards are fears ... that perhaps a plot is being hatched [between the British and the Arabs] against us. ... Maybe the evacuation will facilitate the war against us.' Morris next quotes the diary entry for the following day to clinch his argument: 'Something in my unconscious is frightened by this flight' (*Birth*, p. 64).

In the first place, the fact that Weitz was not at first privy to the specific unfolding of events in Haifa scarcely proves that the overall Arab flight came as a surprise to him. Furthermore, Weitz quickly recovered his bearings. The very same day that his 'innards' were being eaten away by 'fears' and the day *before* his 'unconscious' was being 'frightened' by the Arab exodus, Weitz was already urging that the flight-prone 'state of mind' of Haifa's Arabs be 'exploited' in order to 'hound the rest of the inhabitants so that they should not surrender [and then stay put]. We must establish our state.' So reads the remainder of Weitz's diary entry for 22 April 1948, which Morris inexplicably only reports some thirty pages later in another context in *Birth* (*Birth*, pp. 92–3; cf. *1948*, p. 100). By 24 April, Weitz is gleefully recording that his 'line was being adopted by the [Haganah] command', that is, 'to frighten the Arabs [in Haifa] so long as flight-inducing fear was upon them' (*Birth*, p. 93; cf. *1948*, p. 100). Within a few more days, 'impressed by the [Arab] flight and encouraged by Ben-Gurion', Weitz 'visited the areas conquered by the Jewish forces in order to plan the creation of new Jewish settlements on the ruins of the Arab villages' (Flapan, p. 97).

Weitz, whose cynicism apparently knew no limits,[35] could still enter into his diary on 2 May, after observing first-hand the results of the Haganah's depredations in the Jezreel Valley – 'the Arab villages [are] in ruins. ... the houses and huts are completely destroyed' – that the Arabs there left 'in a psychosis of fear. ... Village after village was abandoned in a panic *that cannot be explained*' (*Birth*, p. 111; my emphasis). And Morris, whose credulity apparently also knows no limits, credits these remarks without even the slightest demurral.[36]

Thanks in no small part to Weitz's lobbying efforts, the Arab flight from Palestine was fast becoming a *fait accompli* by the summer of 1948. In mid-June, the 'decision against a return' had more or less 'crystallized' (*1948*, p. 186). Weitz now spearheaded an unofficial and then in August an official 'transfer committee' to prevent the repatriation of the Arab refugees. In this capacity, he supervised the destruction of, or resettlement of Jews in, the abandoned Arab villages. (For details, see chs 4–5 of *Birth* and ch. 4 of *1948*.) Morris observes that the 'great majority' of the Jewish settlements (including the kibbutzim) and officials supported these policies (*Birth*, pp. 167–8).

The decision to block repatriation of the Arab refugees coincided with Israel's embarkment on a headlong expulsion policy, to which I will return presently. Before doing so, however, I want to take note of a curiosity in Morris's argument.

We have seen that there is precious little evidence that the Arab flight from Palestine came as a 'shock' to the wartime Zionist leadership. Yet there is ample evidence that a crucial component of the Yishuv believed that the wartime Zionist leadership was engaged in a policy of mass expulsion. This was Mapam, the United Workers Party.

Mapam was unusually well placed to follow the unfolding of events in 1948. Much of the Haganah/IDF's officer corps was recruited from Mapam – e.g. Galili, Carmel, Rabin and Allon. Moreover, committed as it was to achieving a *modus vivendi* with the Arab world, Mapam enjoyed atypically close relations with the Palestinian Arabs. Finally, Hashomer Hatzair, which together with Ahdut Ha'avodah formed Mapam in January 1948, managed to accumulate an extensive archive on the Arab flight.

Now, according to Morris, the 'majority opinion' in Mapam throughout 1948 was that Ben-Gurion's policy was 'tending toward expulsion'. A debate did ensue in Mapam on the Arab exodus, but this debate generally assumed that the Arabs were being expelled: the only real question was whether politics or the exigencies of combat inspired Ben-Gurion's 'war of expulsion' (*1948*, pp. 184, 71).

In early May, Aharon Cohen, director of Mapam's Arab Department, wrote that 'a deliberate eviction [of the Arabs] is taking place. ... Others may rejoice – I, as a socialist, am ashamed and afraid'. A few days later he repeated that the Arabs were being expelled – a '"transfer" of the Arabs from the area of the Jewish state' was being executed – 'out of certain political goals and not only out of military necessity'. And at a Mapam meeting in June, Cohen charged that 'it had depended on us whether the Arabs stayed or fled. ... [They had fled] and this was [the implementation of] Ben-Gurion's line in which our comrades are [also] active'. At a late May Mapam Political Committee meeting, Eliezer Prai, the editor of the party's daily paper, accused elements of the Yishuv – e.g. Weitz – of carrying out a 'transfer policy' by 'blood and fire', aimed at emptying the Jewish state of its Arab inhabitants. In July, Mapam leader Ya'acov Hazan threatened that 'the robbery, killing, expulsion, and rape of the Arabs could reach such proportions that we would [no longer] be able to stand' belonging to a coalition with Ben-Gurion's Mapai. (In May 1948, Mapam had joined the newly formed government as a junior partner.) At a meeting in December 1948, Mapam leader Meir Ya'ari charged that, while the party officially repudiated a policy of expulsion, 'its' generals had helped implement it. And so on (*1948*, pp. 46–7, 52, 53, 63, 71, 113; *Birth*, pp. 159–60).

Morris dutifully reports all this without comment. He impeaches neither the motives nor the testimony of the Mapam leaders. Yet Morris never once confronts the question begging to be asked: If the Arab flight was 'born of war, not by design', where did the Mapam leaders get such strange ideas from?

## June 1948–July 1949

Until the end of April, the Zionist leadership was very sensitive to diplomatic opinion. The international consensus that favored partition in November 1947 seemed on the brink of collapsing. If the Zionists embarked on a course too openly hostile to the indigenous Arab population, it would have supplied the perfect pretext for those parties eager to preempt the founding of a Jewish state. As 14 May approached, however, these fears abated and the Zionists' anti-Arab policies became more pronounced. The state was now an irrevocable fact. Furthermore, the Arab invasion could justify an expulsion policy; and, as the IDF went from strategic offensive to rout beginning in early July, such a policy could be relentlessly pursued with total impunity. Within the next eleven months, fully half of the total Palestinian population that ultimately found itself in exile took flight.

According to Morris, although 'there was no Cabinet or IDF General Staff-level decision to expel' the Arabs, 'from July onward, there was a growing readiness in the IDF units' to do exactly that (*Birth*, p. 292; cf. *Birth*, p. 218). Ben-Gurion himself left no doubt during these months that he 'wanted as few Arabs as possible to remain in the Jewish State. He hoped to see them flee. He said as much to his colleagues and aides in meetings in August, September and October' (*Birth*, pp. 292–3). Indeed, already in July he was openly complaining to the Northern Front chief of operations that too many Arabs had remained in newly conquered Nazareth: 'Why did you not expel them?' (*Tikkun*, p. 82). On 26 September, Israel's first prime minister assured his Cabinet that, during the next offensive, the Galilee would become 'clean' and 'empty' of Arabs. On 21 October, he declared that '[t]he Arabs of the Land of Israel have only one function left to them – to run away'. Describing the Arab exodus from Galilee ten days later, Ben-Gurion commented 'and many more still will flee' – to which Morris adds 'It was an assessment – and, perhaps, hope – shared ... at the time by many key figures in the Israeli military and civil bureaucracies' (*Birth*, p. 218).

Certain exceptions were made to this now overt expulsion policy – notably, Druse and Christian Arabs were for varying reasons not forced into flight (*Birth*, pp. 198–202)[37] – but, generally, it was executed with ruthless efficiency. For example, in Operation Yoav (as in all IDF offensives during these months), 'bombers and fighter bombers, battalions of field artillery and mortars, and tanks' were 'deployed with telling effect'. The Arabs who failed to flee before the Zionist juggernaut were expelled outright (*Birth*, pp. 219–22).

Atrocities escalated, 'no doubt precipitat[ing] the flight of communities on the path of the IDF advance' (*Birth*, p. 230). Consider the massacre at Ad Dawayima in late October. A soldier eyewitness described how the IDF, capturing the village 'without a fight', first 'killed about 80–100 [male] Arabs, women and children. The children they killed by breaking their heads with sticks. There was not a house without dead'. The remaining Arabs were then closed off in houses 'without food and water', as the village was systematically razed.

> One commander ordered a sapper to put two old women in a certain house ... and to blow up the house with them. The sapper refused. ... The commander then ordered his men to put in the old women and the evil deed was done. One soldier boasted that he had raped a woman and then shot her. One woman, with a newborn baby in her arms, was employed to clear the courtyard where the soldiers ate. She worked a day or two. In the end they shot her and her baby.

The soldier eyewitness concluded that 'cultured officers ... had turned into base murderers and this not in the heat of battle ... but out of *a system of expulsion and destruction*. The less Arabs remained – the better. This principle is the political motor for the expulsions and the atrocities' (*Birth*, pp. 222–3; my emphasis).[38]

Morris reports the following (very partial) inventory of IDF atrocities committed in the October fighting, as presented to the Political Committee of Mapam:

> SAFSAF – '52 men tied with a rope and dropped into a well and shot. 10 were killed. Women pleaded for mercy. [There were] 3 cases of rape. ... A girl aged 14 was raped. Another 4 were killed.'
>
> JISH – 'a woman and her baby were killed. Another 11 [were killed?].'
>
> SA'SA – cases of 'mass murder [though] a thousand [?] lifted white flags [and] a sacrifice was offered [to welcome] the army. The whole village was expelled.'
>
> SALIHA – '94 ... were blown up with a house.'

At a Mapam meeting in November, IDF atrocities – or, as Morris sometimes calls them, 'excesses' and 'nudging' – in the Galilee were described as 'Nazi acts' (*Birth*, p. 350, note 37). Probably thinking about the Ad Dawayima massacre, Aharon Zisling of Mapam remarked at another meeting in November that 'I couldn't sleep all night. ... Jews too have committed Nazi acts' (*Birth*, p. 233). A respected Zionist official, Yosef Nahmani, similarly observed in a November diary entry regarding the atrocities: 'Where did they come by such a measure of cruelty, like Nazis? They [i.e. the Jewish troops] had learnt from them [i.e. the Nazis]. One officer told me that those who had 'excelled' had come from [the Nazi concentration/extermination] camps' (*1948, revised*, p. 192). In December, Mapam party co-leader Meir Ya'ari declared that 'many of us are losing their [human] image' (*Birth*, p. 211).[39] To be sure, Ben-Gurion, who believed that 'the Haganah and the IDF had ... to be allowed to get on with the war' and hence resisted any censure of the attacking forces, was apparently not shocked by the reported atrocities (*Birth*, p. 232).[40]

We have seen that, already during the first weeks of hostilities, Ben-Gurion and his lieutanants were intent on expelling the Arabs from Palestine. The tactics deployed in the successive offensives by the Zionist military forces were tailor-made to achieve this end. As 14 May approached, and with the majority of the Arabs who eventually became refugees still *in situ*, the full fury of the Zionist military machine was unleashed. Palestinians who fled the field of attack, even if lingering right outside their villages or towns until the terror abated, were blocked from returning. Palestinians who lagged behind or failed to 'get the message' were generally expelled outright. The villages that were home to these Palestinians were systematically razed.[41]

Thus, to distinguish between the Palestinian refugees who fled before the attacking (or approaching) Zionist forces, on the one hand, and the Palestinian refugees who were expelled outright, on the other, is, to put it most charitably, an exercise in sophistry. Occasionally, Morris comes close to conceding this point,[42] but I do not think he goes nearly far enough. Indeed he could not without abandoning his central thesis in the same breath.

Yet even if, for the sake of argument, we were to credit this dis-ingenuous distinction, Morris's account of the Arab flight is still highly misleading – or, at best, inconsistent. Consider the incongruity between his text and sources, on the one hand, and the tables he assembles at the front of *Birth*, on the other.

These tables purport to give a synoptic view of the Arab flight from Palestine. Each of the roughly 370 Palestinian villages and towns ultimately depopulated is labeled mainly according to whether the inhabitants fled because of Arab orders ('A'), Zionist military assault ('M') or Zionist expulsion ('E'). Although noting that tabulations are restricted to the 'decisive causes of abandonment' (*Birth*, p. xiv), Morris still apparently strives to achieve a high degree of precision. Thus, the infamous mass expulsions at Lydda, Ramle and Deir Yassin are each tabulated as an 'E' (expulsion) *and* 'M' (military assault), presumably because Arabs also fled as the IDF was approaching.[43] The reasonable inference is that, wherever more than one factor contributed importantly to the flight, all the factors are tabulated.

In accordance with Morris's central thesis, flight from the overwhelming number of Arab villages and towns listed is attributed solely to Zionist military assault (or fear of such an assault), with flight from only a sprinkling of towns and villages being explained by Arab orders or Zionist expulsions. Morris's tables thus conform with his preference for the 'happy median'.

The inspiration for Morris's tables was apparently the above-cited June 1948 IDF intelligence report, 'The Emigration of the Arabs of Palestine', which included a similar breakdown. Morris faults this IDF report mainly for 'minimiz[ing] the role direct expulsion orders played in bringing about the Palestinian exodus' (*1948*, p. 84). Ironically, Morris's tables are in this respect identically flawed. In effect, Morris's tables may conform with his preference for the 'happy median', but they do not conform even with his own findings or the sources he lists. Here I can only ·sample the record.[44]

Morris reports that the IDF document erred in not also assigning an 'E' classification to Khirbet Lid (al-Awadim), Fajja, Al Khalisa, As Salihiya and Beisan (Beit Shean), since expulsion did play a part in the Arab flight from these sites (*1948*, pp. 83–4). Yet in Morris's own tables, not one of them is listed with an 'E' classification.

Morris reports that in early 1948 Yosef Weitz first 'initiated or prompted the expulsion' of Arabs from Jewish-owned land, and then shifted his focus to 'large areas, such as the Beit Shean Valley, Western Galilee, and Ramot-Menashe', where he was again 'instrumental in emptying [them] of their Arab population' (*1948*, pp. 141–2). Yet of the roughly one hundred Arab villages and towns that Morris lists for these areas, only four are given an 'E' classification.

Morris reports that the Arab villagers of Beit Naqquba were given 'strong advice' by the IDF to leave. Subsequently, a 'handful' were allowed back to live in a neighboring Arab village (*1948*, pp. 192ff.). Yet in his tables Beit Naqquba is listed with an 'M'. (Even more curiously, Morris includes Beit Naqquba in a chapter of *1948* devoted to Arab villages that remained *in situ*.) Likewise, Morris reports that the Arab villagers of Jaba, Ein Ghazal, and Ijzim 'fled and/or [were] driven out'. (The official Israeli account of Arab flight was disputed by UN observers who found evidence of expulsion; *1948*, p. 212; *Birth*, pp. 213–14). Yet in Morris's charts, not one of these villages receives an 'E' classification. And again, Morris reports that the IDF 'carried out a full-scale clearing operation in the Kaufakha-Al Muharraqa area' during which 'the villages' inhabitants and [bedouin] concentrations in the area were dispersed and expelled' (*Birth*, p. 215; the second quote is from an official Israeli source). Yet in the text, Al Muharraqa-Kaufakha receives only an 'M' classification.

Morris reports that Palmah units entering Abu Zureiq 'took some 15 adult males and some 200 women and children' captive and 'sent' the women and children towards Jenin (*Birth*, p. 117). Yet in Morris's tables, Abu Zureiq receives only an 'M' classification. Likewise Morris reports that at As Sindiyana, 'the mukhtar and his family and some 300 inhabitants stayed put and raised a white flag. They were apparently expelled eastwards' (*Birth*, p. 117). Yet, in Morris's tables, As Sindiyana receives only an 'M' classification. And again, Morris reports that the IDF 'arrested some of the villagers' in Qatra, and 'within a few days, either intimidated the rest of the villagers into leaving or ordered them to leave' (*Birth*, p. 126). Yet in Morris's tables, Qatra receives only an 'M' classification. And still again, Morris reports that the 'last major wave of evictions' in the Galilee in mid-1949 caused a public scandal as the remaining inhabitants of three formerly cooperative Arab villages – Khisas, Qeitiya, Ja'auna – were brutally expelled south of Safad (*Birth*, p. 242). Yet not one of these villages receives an 'E' classification in Morris's tables.

Morris reports that a Haganah raid 'precipitated the evacuation of ... Al Manara' (*Birth*, p. 70). In the tables, the village is listed with an 'M'. The only source that Morris cites is Naffez Nazzal, *The Palestinian Exodus from Galilee, 1947–1949*.[45] Turning to Nazzal, we read that 'Zionist soldiers attacked ... El Manara (a village of 490 Arab inhabitants), chased its inhabitants out, destroyed some houses, and left leaflets behind warning the inhabitants not to return because the village had been mined' (pp. 28–9). Morris reports that a Haganah force 'captured the village of Khirbet Nasir ad Din. ... Some non-combatants were apparently killed and some houses destroyed. Most of the population fled to Lubiya or to Tiberias. ... Several dozen villagers remained in situ' (*Birth*, p. 71). In the tables, Nasir ad Din receives three classifications, none of which is an 'E'. The main source cited by Morris is Nazzal. Turning to Nazzal, we read that 'Zionists attacked the ... village of Nasr-ed-Din (with 90 Arab inhabitants) and destroyed all its houses, killing some of its inhabitants, including women and children, and expelling all the rest' (p. 29). Morris reports that '[w]hile most of Ein az Zeitun's young adult males fled ... , some of the village women, children and old men stayed put. These were apparently rounded up ... and expelled' (*Birth*, p. 102). In the tables, Ein az Zeitun is listed only with an 'M'. The only source that Morris cites is Nazzal. Turning to Nazzal, we read that, although the armed villagers fled, '[a]lmost all the old men, women and children remained in the village because the villagers had previously agreed among themselves not to leave'. They were all subsequently expelled (pp. 33–7).

Morris concludes his discussion of the IDF report with the observation that 'only a small proportion' of the Arab exodus can be accounted for by direct or even indirect expulsion (*1948*, p. 88). This reckoning perhaps has less to do with the facts than with Morris's idiosyncratic bookkeeping.

## Behind the Expulsion

To account for the unfolding strategy of the Zionist movement in 1948, Morris repeatedly invokes the contingencies of the armed conflict – i.e. the 'life-and-death struggle' with the Arabs. Even when Morris does grant that political factors informed the Zionist decision-making process, he nonetheless grounds these factors mainly in the concern with security.[46] As Morris puts it in the first pages of *Birth*:

> It cannot be stressed too strongly that, while this is not a military history, the events it describes ... occurred in wartime and were a product, direct and indirect, of that war. Throughout, when examining what happened in each area at different points in the war, the reader must recall the nature of the backdrop – the continuing clash of arms between Palestinian militiamen and, later, regular Arab armies and the Yishuv ... ; the intention of the Palestinian leadership and irregulars and, later, of most of the Arab states' leaders and armies in launching the hostilities in November–December 1947 and the May 1948 invasion to destroy the Jewish state and possibly the Yishuv ... ; and the extremely small dimensions (geographical and numerical) of the Yishuv in comparison with the Palestinian Arab community and the infinitely larger surrounding Arab hinterland. At the same time, it is well to recall that, from July 1948, it was clear to the Yishuv (and the Arab leaders) that Israel had won its war for survival, at least in the short term, and that the subsequent Israel Defense Forces' offensives were geared to securing the political–military future of the Jewish state in what continued to be a hostile geopolitical environment and to rounding out its borders. (p. 3)

Accordingly, each escalation in the Zionist movement's onslaught against the Palestinians is seen as a defensive reaction to Arab aggression. The Palestinian leadership and irregulars 'launch[ed] the hostilities in November–

December 1947'. The Haganah implemented Plan D and 'switched to the offensive' in April because of 'a sense of imminent logistical asphyxiation ... and the expected Arab invasion of Palestine by the armies of the Arab states' (Birth, p. 7; cf. Birth: pp. 30, 61–2, 288). The Israeli government barred the return of the Arab refugees in June 1948 'against the backdrop of the invasion of the new born State by the Arab armies' (Birth, p. 132; cf. Birth, pp. 153, 291). The 'destruction of the abandoned Arab villages, the cultivation and/or destruction of Arab fields and the share-out of the Arab lands to Jewish settlements, the establishment of new settlements on abandoned lands and sites and the settlement of Jewish immigrants in empty Arab housing in the countryside and in urban neighborhoods' occurred 'naturally and were integral, major elements in the overall con-solidation of the State of Israel in wartime' (Birth, p. 155). Efforts were made to establish Jewish settlements outside the UN-designated boundaries between August and December 1948 (e.g. in the Western Galilee, the Jerusalem corridor and the Lydda-Ramle district) mainly because of security and 'military–political' reasons (Birth, pp. 185–8). The IDF launched assaults well after 'it was clear to the Yishuv (and to the Arab leaders) that Israel had won its war for survival' – e.g. operations Yoav and Hiram in October–December – in order to 'conquer additional territory, giving the Jewish state greater strategic depth and pushing back hostile armies from the Jewish population centers' (Birth, p. 235). Even the multiple atrocities committed by the Haganah and the IDF must be seen within the context that 'the fate of the State had hung in the balance' (Birth, p. 232).

The obvious, if unstated, upshot of Morris's argument is that the Arabs – who, after all, were the aggressors – must bear the brunt of political (if not moral) responsibility for the birth of the Palestinian refugee problem.[47] Recall that this is the explicit conclusion of 'old' historians like Meir Pa'il and Shabtei Teveth, who are much more ready than Morris to acknowledge the systematic and premeditated character of the Arab flight.[48]

Yet, Morris's analysis is flawed in at least three crucial respects: (1) it simplifies the origins and dynamics of the first Arab–Israeli war, (2) it woefully understates the ideological–political motivations (apart from any security considerations) to expel the Arabs and enlarge the Jewish state's borders, and (3) it inverts the relationship between politics and security. All of these are common to the vast body of scholarly myth surrounding Israel's creation.

Morris suggests that primary responsibility for the original escalation of intercommunal hostilities in Palestine belongs to the Palestinian Arabs who 'intended to destroy the Jewish State and possibly also the Yishuv' (Birth, p. 3). The Haganah's national strategy until March 1948 was one that 'restrict[ed] as far as possible the scope of the conflagration and ...

[did] not strike in areas so far free of hostilities' (*Birth*, p. 33). Where it did attack, the General Staff sought 'to keep operations as "clean" as possible' (*Birth*, p. 34). Yet Morris's account of this phase in the war is belied by the actual record.

The British officials stationed in Palestine did not believe that the Palestinians initially intended any serious resistance to the Partition Resolution, if for no other reason than because, even taking into account the assistance of the 5,000 or so Arab volunteers who reached Palestine in March 1948, they were utterly unprepared militarily for such an undertaking (*Birth*, pp. 16, 20, 34–5; Palumbo, pp. 35–6). As Morris himself puts it, 'in general, the Palestinian Arabs by the end of 1947 had a healthy and demoralising respect for the Yishuv's military power' (*Birth*, p. 21). Indeed, a Jewish intelligence source cited by Morris reported in late 1947 that, in the countryside, 'the fellah is afraid of the Jewish terrorists ... who might bomb his village and destroy his property. ... The town-dweller admits that his strength is insufficient to fight the Jewish forces and hopes for salvation from the outside'. At the same time, the 'moderate majority' of Palestine's Arabs 'are confused, frightened. ... They are stockpiling provisions ... and are being coerced and pressured by extremists. ... But all they want is peace, quiet' (*Birth*, p. 21). According to Elias Sasson, the director of the Arab division of the Jewish Agency's Political Department, in early January Arab morale was low in all the main towns and in the hinterlands (*Birth*, p. 30).

What then accounted for the spiraling violence in Palestine? Flapan points to a 'clear pattern' in Arab–Jewish relations between December 1947 and March 1948, in which lethal terrorist attacks by the Irgun or LEHI resulted in Arab retaliations and then 'the Haganah – while always condemning the actions of the Irgun and LEHI – joined in with an inflaming counterretaliation' (Flapan, p. 95).[49] Already in December 1947, Ben-Gurion ordered adoption of 'the system of aggressive defense; with every Arab attack we must respond with a decisive blow: the destruction of the place or the expulsion of the residents along with the seizure of the place'. And again: 'When in action ... we ... must fight strongly and cruelly, letting nothing stop us' (Flapan, p. 90). According to the British High Commissioner, Alan Cunningham, had the Haganah not launched these (in effect) counter-reprisals – some of which he deemed an 'offence to civilisation' – the situation would not have so drastically deteriorated (*Birth*, p. 32; cf. Palumbo, p. 36).

By late March, Haganah intelligence was reporting that relations between the Arabs and Jews in Palestine had reached a nadir: 'There is almost no area of the country where we can talk with the Arabs, even on local matters, to pacify them and calm things down.' According to two senior Haganah intelligence officers, 'in large measure the situation was a product of ill-conceived Jewish military actions and over-reactions'. Morris quotes one of these two officers, Yehoshua Palmon, to the effect that, in the future, the Yishuv would generally find it difficult 'to prove that we weren't the aggressors' (*Birth*, p. 40).[50]

One reason that Morris is unable to perceive the Yishuv's large measure of responsibility for the slide into full-scale war is his predilection for casting it in a strictly defensive, reactive posture *vis-à-vis* the Arabs. In his reckoning, the Haganah, especially, was engaged during these months only in 'reprisals', in a 'strategy of forceful retaliation' (*Birth*, p. 56), in 'cautionary and punitive raids' (*Birth*, p. 156), in 'retaliatory strikes' (*Birth*, p. 156), in a 'retaliatory policy' (*1948*, p. 188), and so on – albeit 'sometimes misdirected, sometimes excessive' (*Birth*, p. 36). The result of Morris's wishful reading of the historical record is a gross distortion of it. Consider the following examples.

1. Morris reports on page 41 of *Birth* that the intercommunal strife in Haifa in December 1947 'culminated in an IZL bombing at the gates of the Haifa oil refinery, the vengeful Arab massacre of Jewish refinery workers and the Haganah reprisal of 31 December at Balad ash Sheikh, a large satellite village southeast of Haifa'. The IZL bombing does not count as a 'vengeful massacre' and the Arab attack does not count as a 'reprisal'; rather, the Arabs are guilty of the 'vengeful massacre' and the Haganah is merely held accountable for a 'reprisal'. On page 44 of *Birth*, we learn that 'the exodus from Arab Haifa was fairly closely linked to Haganah retaliatory strikes, Arab attacks and Arab fears of subsequent Jewish retaliations'. Again, on page 93 of *Birth*, Morris reports that 'Balad ash Sheikh ... had been partially evacuated on 7 January 1948, following the Haganah's retaliatory strike on the night of 31 December 1947, which was triggered by the massacre by Arabs of the 70 Jewish oil refinery workers on 30 December 1947'. Finally, we are told on page 156 of *Birth* that 'several dozen' Arab homes were 'destroyed at Balad ash Sheikh on 31 December in the revenge attack following the Arab massacre of Jewish workers at the Haifa oil refinery'. The initial IZL atrocity has completely dropped from sight.[51]

2. According to Morris, the Haganah attack on Khisas in December 1947 – in which a dozen civilians, including four children, were killed – was severely criticized by the Arab Division of the Jewish Agency's Political Department for 'unnecessarily spread[ing] the fighting to a hitherto quiet area' (*Birth*, p. 33). In a note at the back of *Birth*, Morris presents this description of the events at Khisas:

An Arab had killed a Jew in a months-old vendetta. The local Palmah commander believed that the crime had been 'political' and decided to retaliate. Local Haganah intelligence service officers and civil leaders appealed against the intended operation, which was also to have included attacks on nearby Al Khalisa and two other villages, and obtained a postponement from the Haganah General Staff. But the local commanders, who (according to Danin) wanted to 'keep up [their troops'] morale', asked for and obtained permission from Palmah OC Allon, and attacked Khisas on 18 December. The General Staff in Tel Aviv subsequently denied advance knowledge of the operation. The attacking troops mistakenly blew up a house with civilians in it. (p. 306, note 12)

In Morris's bookkeeping, the Haganah attack on Khisas counts, not as a 'vengeful massacre' but rather, first, as 'a tale of Haganah inefficiency and trigger-happiness' (ibid.), then, as a 'mistaken attack' (*Birth*, p. 34) and, finally, as a 'Haganah retaliatory strike' (*Birth*, p. 156). Notice Morris's certainty, based entirely on official Zionist sources, that the demolition of the house with civilians in it was 'mistaken'.

3. Morris reports that

The Arabs living in the prosperous western Jerusalem district of Qatamon began evacuating their homes after the Haganah bombing of the Semiramis Hotel on the night of 4–5 January 1948. The Haganah suspected, mistakenly, that the hotel served as the headquarters of the local irregulars. Several Arab families ... died in the explosion, and a sharp dispute broke out inside the Haganah and with the British authorities. The action was carried out without Haganah General Staff instruction or consent. (*Birth*, p. 50)

Morris is certain that the 'Haganah suspected, mistakenly,' because it says so in ... Ben-Gurion's diary. He begins the paragraph following the description of this atrocity with the words: 'Other [Haganah] *retaliatory* strikes hit Arab ...' (my emphasis)

Morris includes in his first chapter a lucid, if brief, discussion of 'the notion of transfer in Yishuv thinking'. He points out that 'the idea of a "voluntary" or "compulsory" transfer of all or the bulk of the Arabs inhabiting the Jewish State areas had been in the air since the mid-1930s' (*Birth*, p. 25).[52] Yet Morris's treatment of this crucial topic is deficient in at least two respects. In the first place, it barely figures in the explanatory framework he uses to account for the origins of the refugee problem. Second, on the rare occasion that this factor is introduced, it is grounded in the concern with security – e.g. the Arabs were barred from returning to their homes because they were seen as a potentially subversive element. The reality is rather more complicated.

The aim of the Zionist enterprise was to create a Jewish state in

Palestine, a state that 'belonged' to the Jewish people.[53] The *sine qua non* of such a Jewish state was seen to be a permanent Jewish majority; the ideal was a homogeneously Jewish constituency. These beliefs were anchored in a theoretical discourse that went well beyond – indeed, was entirely distinct from – security concerns. The 'compulsory transfer' of the nascent Jewish state's Arab population was thus prefigured in the ideology of Zionism. This was especially the case inasmuch as the Jewish state anticipated in the UN Partition plan yielded not a Jewish majority – let alone a stable Jewish majority – but, rather, an Arab majority (507,780 Arabs as against 499,020 Jews). The escalating hostilities and, eventually, the Arab invasion surely contributed to the Zionists' preference for expulsion; but they also served as a convenient pretext for executing it.

Furthermore, Arab opposition and resistance to the Zionist movement was rooted preeminently in the latter's intent to create a state that would, at best, marginalize – and, more than likely, expel – them. The 'security' threat posed by the Arabs thus resulted from Zionism's ideological–political agenda. Yet, in Morris's reckoning, this relationship is inverted: the Zionist leadership's ideological–political disposition for expulsion resulted from the 'security' threat the Arabs posed to the Jewish state.

Morris's failure to give real weight to the animating impulses of the Zionist enterprise also disfigures his account of the Arab invasion and its aftermath. Morris concedes that, from July onward, 'it was clear that Israel had won its war for survival' (*Birth*, p. 3) and that, henceforth, the IDF was on the 'strategic offensive' (*Birth*, p. 197). Indeed, there was never too much doubt that the Zionists would prevail in the field of battle. Save for a brief three-week period (15 May–11 June), the Haganah/ IDF generally had the edge in the 'traditional indices of [military] strength'. As Morris himself succinctly puts it, 'the truth ... is that the stronger side won' (*1948*, pp. 13–16, 33–4).

Nonetheless, Morris takes at face value the claims in official Zionist documents that the assaults from July onward were strictly defensive in nature.[54] Consider his account of Operation Dani which resulted in the sacking of Lydda and Ramle.

> While the Arab Legion had in fact only one, defensively-oriented company (about 120–150 soldiers) in Lydda and Ramle together, and a second-line company at Beit Nabala to the north, the IDF intelligence and Operation Dani OC General Yigal Allon believed at the start of the offensive that they faced a far stronger Legion force and one whose deployment was potentially aggressive, posing a standing threat to Tel Aviv itself. (*Birth*, p. 203)

Morris knows that Allon attacked Lydda and Ramle because he 'believed' – incorrectly, as it turned out – that the Arab Legion posed a 'standing threat to Tel Aviv', for so it is written in Ben-Gurion's diary and in a book 'written under constraints of IDF censorship' (*Birth*, p. 344, note 14; cf. *Tikkun*, p. 20). Surely, an equally plausible explanation is that the Zionist movement was pursuing for its own sake the expansion of the Jewish state's borders, in accordance with its enduring objective – never renounced – to create a Jewish state in all of Palestine. As Morris himself puts it early on, whereas Ben-Gurion 'was generally willing to accept Partition and the establishment of a Jewish state in part of the country, … he remained committed to a vision of Jewish sovereignty over all of Palestine as the ultimate goal of Zionism' (*Birth*, p. 3). Yet, in Morris's account, this ideological concern figures not at all as a causal factor for the Zionists' land-grab in 1948, which resulted in Jewish sovereignty over 37 per cent more of Palestine than was allotted to the Jewish state by the United Nations.

Yet, even leaving the ideological mainsprings of the Zionist project aside, the massive immigration of Jews anticipated by the Zionist movement, too, presupposed the expulsion of the indigenous Arab population. As early as 20 December 1940, Weitz wrote in his diary:

> it must be clear that there is no room in the country for both peoples. … If the Arabs leave it, the country will become wide and spacious for us. … The only solution is a Land of Israel … without Arabs. There is no room here for compromises. … There is no way but to transfer the Arabs from here to the neighboring countries, and to transfer all of them, save perhaps for [the Arabs of] Bethlehem, Nazareth and old Jerusalem. Not one village must be left, not one [bedouin] tribe. The transfer must be directed at Iraq, Syria and even Transjordan. For this goal funds will be found. … And only after this transfer will the country be able to absorb millions of our brothers and the Jewish problem will cease to exist. There is no other solution. (*Birth*, p. 27)

The same point was made by Dr Yakov Thon, a founding member of the pacifist Brit-Shalom, in 1937:

> Without transferring the Arab peasants to neighboring lands, we will not be able to bring into our future state a large new population. In short, without transfer there can be no Jewish immigration. (Palumbo, p. 4)

The dimensions of this problem are suggested by the fact that, of the 20,418,023 dunums held by the Israeli state at the war's end, only 1,475,766 were owned by Jews.

## Conclusion

Let me conclude by putting Morris's achievement in perspective. Morris has indisputably produced landmark studies. He has permanently redefined the parameters of legitimate scholarly debate on the origins of the Palestinian refugee problem, dispatching to oblivion the standard Israeli claims about 'Arab broadcasts'.[55] Indeed, Morris's devastating reply to Shabtai Teveth's recent defense of these claims can only be described as a virtuoso performance (cf. the *Commentary* and *Tikkun* articles cited above). Morris has tapped a wealth of archival material which no serious student of the Israeli–Palestinian conflict can afford to ignore. In effect, Morris's research will serve as the benchmark for all future scholarship on the topic.

Yet Morris's achievement falls well short of the estimable standard he has set himself. In *Tikkun*, Morris distances himself from 'propagandists' such as Professor Edward Said. He rather locates his calling as a scholar above the realm of crass political partisanship in the pristine heights of truth and objectivity. Said's sin was to have cited Morris for the claim that 'a sequence of Zionist terror and Israeli expulsion ... were behind the birth of the Palestinian refugee problem'. Surely, as I think I have shown, this is a legitimate interpretation of Morris's evidence – if not of his thesis. According to Morris, however, his research shows that 'war, without a Jewish masterplan or indeed, without any preplanning whatsoever, brought a Palestinian exodus of itself', and that 'with a little nudging in the right direction, the low-key exodus ... turned into a mass flood and a fait accompli'. What is this if not official Zionism's 'astonishing' flight of Palestine's Arabs now graced with Morris's imprimatur?

In the same *Tikkun* article, Morris cautions that 'the moment the historian looks over his shoulder, begins to calculate how others might utilize his work, and allows this to influence his findings and conclusions, he is well on his way down that slippery slope leading to official history and propaganda'. Morris would have done well to heed this caveat as he prepared the results of his research for publication.

# 4

## Settlement, Not Conquest

### *Anita Shapira's 'Benign Intentions' Image*

> And then they teach men that to accept an error which is of service to them
> – the 'myth' – is an undertaking which does them honor, while it is shameful
> to admit a truth which harms them.
>
> Julien Benda, *The Treason of the Intellectuals*

The focus of this chapter is the myths used by Zionism to rationalize the
conquest of Palestine. I also try to range fairly broadly across time and
space in my discussion of Zionism to illustrate the point that the same
justifications typically crop up in many, if not all, conquest enterprises.
The mythology of conquest is remarkably uniform – or, less charitably,
banal.

This is especially so of the 'virgin land or wilderness' myth that I
explore in the first section. From the British in North America to the
Dutch in South Africa, from the Nazis in Eastern Europe to the Zionists
in Palestine, every conquering regime has invoked the same claim that
the territory appointed for conquest was deserted. In the second section,
I discuss the myth of 'self-defense'. Standing reality on its head, this myth
typically inverts the role of besieger and besieged. In the clichéd American
image, the wagons circle the pioneers as the Indians attack *them*. The
Zionist version of this myth is neatly captured in the title of Conor
Cruise O'Brien's best-selling potboiler, *The Siege: The Saga of Israel and
Zionism*.[1] In the third section, I explore one of Zionism's most cherished
myths, 'purity of arms'. I conclude that its practical significance was nil
and as a doctrine its closest analogue was, ironically, Nazism. In the second
and third sections, I use as my main foil historian Anita Shapira, the
bellwether of Zionist orthodoxy. I focus on her most recent volume,
*Land and Power: The Zionist Resort to Force, 1881–1948*,[2] which effectively
summarizes the current state of mainstream Zionist scholarship.

To compare phenomena is not to equate them. In the case at hand, it is even less to equate the scale of actual crimes committed by the respective conquest regimes. Historian Marc Bloch has in fact suggested that a primary purpose of historical comparison is the identification of differences.[3] Yet, there is no point in making historical analogies if they do not bear on crucial common features; otherwise one's findings risk being dismissed, justly, as trivial.

My own view is that the similarities I point to between Zionism and other conquest mythologies are significant; indeed, disquietingly so.

## The 'Virgin Land or Wilderness' Myth

Historian Francis Jennings has proposed that there exists a 'standard conquest myth'. Its core component is the belief that the territory slated for conquest is a 'virgin land or wilderness'.[4] This conviction performs a crucial rationalizing function – often retrospective – for the colonizer, inasmuch as the right of inhabitants to the place where they and their families have lived and made a life is basic.[5] A refinement of this belief suggests that the territory, if not literally empty, is thinly peopled by unsettled tribes whose aboriginal rights of tenure are at best tenuous since they have not worked the land.

History has shown that this generic conquest myth possesses remarkable resiliency. Indeed, what is most striking about it is its banal repetition across time and space: the apologists of conquest cannot be credited with originality; yet, given the willful credulity of their intended audiences, they do not have to be. Consider the apparently disparate instances of the English conquest of North America, the Dutch conquest of South Africa, the Nazi conquest of eastern Europe, and the Zionist conquest of Palestine.

One of the first formal justifications for seizing Indian lands in North America was published in London in 1622. The author contended that 'a sufficient reason to prove our going thither to live lawful' was that, whereas England was 'full', North America was 'empty, spacious, and void'. Further, its 'few' inhabitants 'do but run over the grass, as do also the foxes and wild beasts' and lack the 'art, science, skill or faculty to use either the land or the commodities of it'. Recalling the example of the 'ancient patriarchs' who 'removed from straiter places into more roomy [ones], where the land lay idle and wasted and none used it, though there dwelt inhabitants by them', he concluded that 'it is lawful now to take a land which none useth and make use of'.[6]

One already notices in the brief compass of these remarks almost all the components of the basic conquest myth: the quasi-virgin land, the nomads that merely 'run over' it, their near savagery (like 'foxes and wild beasts'), the moral (England is 'full') and biblical or providential (the 'ancient patriarchs') sanction of the conquest enterprise, and the regenerative or civilizing mission it incorporates (they possess no 'art, science, skill' to use the land).

The Reverend Samuel Purchas, a friend of John Smith (leader of the Virginia colony), penned at roughly the same time another seminal rationalization for colonization by conquest. He urged that Christian Englishmen might rightfully seize Indian lands because God had intended his patrimony to be cultivated and not to be left in the condition of 'that unmanned wild Country, which they [the savages] range rather than inhabite'. Jennings observes that 'although Purchas's "range rather than inhabite" phrase was contrary to known fact, it held the magic of a strong incantation and the utility of a magician's smokescreen'.[7]

John Winthrop, the first Governor of Massachusetts Bay Colony, argued in 1629 that the 'Natives in New England' could claim no legal title to the land since they had neither 'any setled habytation' nor 'any tame Cattell to improve the Land by'. John Locke, whose more technical distinctions in the *Second Treatise of Government* (for example, between a 'naturall' and 'Civill' right to property) were anticipated by Winthrop, repeatedly adverts to the virginal state of the New World: the 'in-land, vacant places of America', the 'wild woods and uncultivated waste of America, left to nature, without any improvement, tillage or husbandry', the 'several nations of the Americans [that] are rich in land, and poor in all the comforts of life; whom nature having furnished as liberally as any other people, with the materials of plenty, i.e., a fruitful soil, apt to produce in abundance, what might serve for food, raiment, and delight; yet, *for want of improving it by labor*, have not one hundredth part of the conveniences we enjoy', etc. Inasmuch as, for Locke, 'labor, in the beginning, gave a right to property', the unstated conclusion was that the 'several nations of the Americans' had no legal claim to the land.[8]

This justification of the conquest of North America was, early on, inscribed in judicial enactments. The Swiss jurist Emmerich de Vattel, an eminent eighteenth-century exponent of natural law who greatly influenced American thought, rendered the classic opinion in this regard. The crucial passage, worth quoting at length, reads as follows:

> There is another celebrated question to which the discovery of the New World has principally given rise. It is asked, if a nation may lawfully take possession of a part of a vast country, in which there are found none but erratic nations, incapable, by the smallness of their numbers, to people the whole. We have already observed in establishing the obligation to cultivate the earth, that these nations cannot exclusively appropriate to themselves more land than they have

occasion of, and which they are unable to settle and cultivate. Their removing their habitations through these immense nations cannot be taken for a true and legal possession; and the people of Europe, too closely pent up, finding land of which these nations are in no particular want, and of which they make no actual and constant use, may lawfully possess it and establish colonies there. We have already said that the earth belongs to the human race in general, and was destined to furnish it with subsistence. ... People have not, then, deviated from the views of nature, in confining the Indians within narrow limits.

Leaving aside that the Indians did make 'actual and constant use' of the soil, historian Albert Weinberg notes that 'the American people, as no one denied, had at the time an extent of territory which was beyond their own capacity to cultivate'; and, even if one were to plea, as did John Quincy Adams, that Americans were entitled to territory to accommodate future generations, so too were the Indians.[9]

Upholding, in a landmark case of 1810, the rights of states as against the national government to the so-called western territories, Chief Justice John Marshall ignored any and all claims of the indigenous population to what he deemed '*the vacant lands within the United States*'. (Thomas Paine had earlier campaigned for the claims of the Federal government to 'the vacant western territory of America', similarly oblivious to the property rights of the indigenes.) In 1823, Marshall rendered another landmark decision stating that the laws that ordinarily regulate relations between conqueror and conquered did not apply in the case of North America, since the Indians were 'fierce savages whose occupation was war and whose subsistence was drawn chiefly from the forest'. This sort of legal reasoning reached the outermost bounds of absurdity in the case of the Cherokee Indians. The Cherokees were dispossessed of their land even though they had fully adopted as their own the sedentary, agricultural way of life of the white settlers. The reason given — to quote a former US Attorney General who represented them — was 'the strange ground ... that they had no right to alter their condition and become husband-men'.[10]

As the European conquerors swept westward displacing the indigenous population, the conquest myth continued to serve as the chief weapon of ideological self-defense. Andrew Jackson asked rhetorically, 'What good man would prefer a country covered with forests and ranged by a few thousand savages to our extensive Republic, studded with cities, towns, and prosperous farms?' William Henry Harrison likewise queried, 'Is one of the fairest portions of the globe to remain in a state of nature, the haunt of a few wretched savages, when it seems destined by the Creator to give support to a large population and to be the seat of civilization, of science, and of true religion?'[11]

The 'virgin land or wilderness' image has, until very recently, dominated the historiographic literature on North America before European 'settlement'. The first, crucial move was to reduce by perhaps as much as 90 per cent the actual population of North America in the pre-Columbian era, putting it at one million when the true figure is probably closer to ten million. Francis Parkman, perhaps the greatest of American historians, described the Indian as 'a true child of the forest and the desert. The wastes and solitudes of nature are his congenial home'. Frederick Jackson Turner, in his highly influential *The Frontier in American History*, conceived the West as 'free land'. Stannard, surveying a raft of recent histories, notes that the United States before European conquest is typically described as a 'vast emptiness', a 'void', as inhabited by 'handfuls of indigenous people' who were 'scattered' or 'roamed' across a 'virgin land'.[12]

Hitler's biographers report that the Nazi leader's *Lebensraum* policy was inspired by the conquest of North America. According to John Toland, Hitler 'often praised to his inner circle the efficiency of America's extermination – by starvation and uneven combat – of the red savages who could not be tamed by captivity'. Joachim Fest observes that Hitler's 'continental war of conquest' was modeled 'with explicit reference to the United States.' Thus, gearing up for the war in the East, Hitler declared that 'there's only one duty: to Germanise this country by immigration of Germans, and to look upon the natives as Redskins'. Faced with unexpected resistance, he compared 'the struggle we are waging there against the Partisans' to 'the struggle in North America against the Red Indians'.

Typically, Hitler depicted Eastern Europe as a virgin land or wilderness: 'thinly settled', 'desert', 'desolate', 'wide spaces', 'immense spaces', 'huge open spaces', 'empty spaces', etc. Behind the Nazis' very coinage for this area – 'Eastern Space' (*Ostraum*) – was an intent 'to show the average German that he would move into a historical–cultural vacuum which he would have to model for the first time in modern history' (Weinreich). Bracing, however, for the practical exigencies of conquest, Hitler dropped the 'virgin land' pretense. 'The history of all ages', Hitler lectured his generals at a closed-door meeting in 1937, 'proved that expansion could only be carried out by breaking down resistance. ... There had never in former times been spaces without a master, and there were none today; the attacker always comes up against a possessor.' Indeed, Hitler knew full well that, far from being wilderness, the East was 'notoriously overpopulated' (Weinberg). To resolve this 'demographic problem', Hitler's grand design called for the Slavs to be in part exterminated, in part expelled ('transfers of population'), the remnant confined to undeveloped enclaves ('we will isolate them in their own pig-sties'), serving the German master race as a

helot population. Meanwhile, millions of ethnic Germans would be relo-
cated to the East until 'our settlers are numerically superior to the natives'.[13]

In *Mein Kampf*, Hitler offered a rationale for his 'continental war of
conquest' that was eerily reminiscent of the apologetics for the North
American conquest. Noting that it 'can certainly not be the intention of
Heaven to give one people fifty times as much land and soil in this world
as another', Hitler exhorted Germans not to 'let political boundaries
obscure the boundaries of eternal justice. If this earth really has room for
all to live in, let us be given the soil we need for our livelihood.' Recall
that the Swiss jurist Vattel had similarly maintained that, inasmuch as the
'people of Europe [are] closely pent up' and the Indians have 'more land
than they have occasion of', Europeans 'have not ... deviated from the
views of nature, in confining the Indians within narrow limits'. After all,
'the earth belongs to the human race in general, and was destined to
furnish it with subsistence'.[14]

The comparison between Hitler and his European and American
precursors can be made still more exact. In his so-called *Secret Book,*
Hitler lucidly spelled out the ultimate logic of his Social Darwinist views.
The 'earth', he wrote,

> is awarded by providence to people who in their hearts have the courage to
> conquer it, the strength to preserve it, and the industry to put it to the plough.
> Hence every healthy, vigorous people sees nothing sinful in territorial acquisition,
> but something in keeping with nature. ... The primary right of this world is the
> right to life, so far as one possesses the strength for this. Hence, on the basis of
> this right, a vigorous nation will always find ways of adapting its territory to its
> population size.

Yet, Hitler's defense of conquest was but an anemic facsimile of the one
given by the man who coveted not the East but the West. Theodore
Roosevelt mused that the extermination of the American Indians and the
expropriation of their lands 'was as ultimately beneficial as it was inevitable'.
'Such conquests', he continued in an evocation of Nietzsche's 'blond beast',
are 'sure to come when a masterful people, still in its raw barbarian prime,
finds itself face to face with the weaker and wholly alien race which holds
a coveted prize in its feeble grasp.' Hitler could not have put it better.[15]

Indeed, Hitler explicitly located his *Lebensraum* project within the long
trajectory of European racial conquest. The 'white race ... established for
itself a privileged position ... [and] economically privileged supremacy',
Hitler accurately observed in a speech deserving of extended quotation:

> in the closest of connections to a political concept of supremacy which has
> been peculiar to the white race ... for many centuries and which it has upheld
> as such to the outer world. ... England did not acquire India in a lawful and
> legitimate manner, but rather without regard to the natives' wishes, views, or

declarations of rights; and she maintained this rule, if necessary, with the most brutal ruthlessness. Just as Cortés or Pizarro demanded for themselves Central America and the northern states of South America not on the basis of any legal claim, but from the absolute, inborn feeling of superiority. The settlement of the North American continent was similarly a consequence not of any higher claim in a democratic or international sense, but rather of a consciousness of what is right which had its sole roots in the conviction of the superiority and thus the right of the white race. If I imagine things without this frame of mind which, in the course of the last three or four centuries of the white race, has conquered the world, then the fate of this race would in fact be no other than that, for instance, of the Chinese: an immensely congested mass of people in an extraordinarily restricted territory – overpopulation with all its inevitable consequences. If Fate allowed the white race to take a different path, it was because this white race was of the conviction that it had a right to organize the rest of the world.

'Regardless of what external disguise this right assumed in a given case', Hitler concluded, 'it was the exercise of an extraordinarily brutal right to dominate. From this political view there evolved the basis for the economic takeover of the world.' Hitler's simple plea was that Germans – belonging as they after all did to the same racial family of 'inborn superior value' – be granted as well 'the exercise of an extraordinarily brutal right to dominate'.[16]

The earliest Dutch officials and Cape colonists did not doubt that the indigenous African population had lived in southern Africa from time immemorial. Yet Afrikaner political mythology eventually came to maintain that Africans did not arrive in South Africa much – if at all – before the first Dutch settlers. One standard nineteenth-century claim had it that they originated among 'nomadic', 'Bedouin' tribes of the Arab world and only 'in relatively recent times have reached the South Coast of Africa over land'. Consequently, they had no valid claim to the land. In the words of one important scholarly treatise, *A Historical Geography of the British Colonies* (1897), 'The ownership which the Bantu tribes could claim had no deep roots in the past. It was won by force, and as it was won and as it was upheld, so it could with no glaring injustice be swept away.'

This mythology has endured to the present day. As the Afrikaner National Party began to apply its policy of apartheid in 1948, the official South African *Yearbook* series included elaborate chapters on 'The Peoples of South Africa' which argued, *inter alia*, that the Africans had no greater historical claim to the land than whites because 'the Blacks started settling in the northern part of the country more or less at the same time as the first White people began settling at the southern tip of the country during the 17th century'. The tenure claims of these alleged recent arrivals were yet more flimsy inasmuch as they never actually worked the land. Typical was the assertion of the *South African Digest* (1980) that the

> Black settlements in South Africa were not purposive or permanent in the Western sense. All tribes relied heavily on hunting and their cattle. ... They selected the best-watered regions for their cattle, and as soon as one parcel of cultivated land was exhausted they moved on in search of virgin soil.

Standard South African textbooks continue to present the *voortrekkers* (European immigrants) as heroic figures whose 'task was to tame the wilderness' as they migrated into an 'empty land'. There were – as one official formulation puts it – 'no native blacks in South Africa, only some nomadic tribes, including the Hottentots, who were of Arabic origin'.[17]

Until World War I, Israel Zangwill's slogan 'A land without a people for a people without a land' typified Zionist propaganda on Palestine. The influential Zionist publicist Moshe Smilansky recalled in 1914 that, 'From the first moment of the Zionist idea, Zionist propaganda described the land to which we were headed as desolate and forsaken, impatiently waiting for its redeemers'; a 'feeling of certainty' was created 'that Palestine was a virgin country'. (For Smilansky, this myth accounted for the 'attitude of contempt' which the Zionist settlers harbored for the indigenous population.)

Such propaganda, however, was meant mostly for foreign Zionist consumption. (It was also not taken seriously abroad outside Zionist circles.) Zionists who had already settled or sojourned in Palestine were keenly aware that it was not a 'land without a people' and the internal debates of the Zionist movement even at this early date reflected such an awareness. In 'Truth from Palestine' (1891), Ahad Ha'am observed that, contrary to Zionist myth, Palestine was not desolate and all the land available for cultivation was already being worked by the indigenous Arab population. In 'A Hidden Question' (1905), Yitzak Epstein sarcastically chided the Zionist leadership for 'overlooking a rather "marginal" fact – that in our beloved land there lives an entire people that has been dwelling there for many centuries and has never considered leaving it'. In 'The Crisis' (1905), Hillel Zeitlin charged that what the Zionists bent on settlement in Palestine 'forget, mistakenly or maliciously, is that Palestine belongs to others, *and it is totally settled*'. Indeed, according to Anita Shapira, already in the early 1900s, the 'worst problems' of the Zionist movement bore on the purchase of land owned and worked by the Arab indigenes (pp. 42, 45, 46, 50–1, 58, 62; emphasis in original).

Between the issuance of the Balfour Declaration and the Israeli declaration of independence, Palestine's indigenous population loomed large in all Zionist fora: it could hardly have been otherwise, given the intensity of the conflict that unfolded during those years between the Arab indigenes and the Zionist colonizers who sought to displace them.

After Israel's establishment, Zionist literature systematically and with considerable effect rewrote the history of Palestine – in particular, by writing the Arabs and the Arab presence out. The mythology served a double, interrelated, purpose: it delegitimized any Arab claim to Palestine, and it validated the central Zionist dogma of a *sui generis* connection between Jews and Palestine in that only the Jewish people could establish an authentic, organic bond with the 'Land of Israel' and cause it to blossom forth. This genre had its roots in the Yishuv in the 1930s when, according to Shapira, 'it became popular to maintain that the Arabs in Palestine had forfeited any right to the land because they had neglected it, allowing it to become a desolate wasteland' (p. 215).[18] The view of Palestine as a virgin land or wilderness during the 1,800 years of Jewish 'exile' was also a staple of the ideological preparation of the socialist–Zionist youth then. Palestine, they were told, had turned into a wasteland and lost its fertility: 'summer droughts, desolation of generations, eternal swamps'. The new Jewish settlements were said to have 'redeemed' the land; the areas 'densely populated by Arab villages' were regarded – in Shapira's words – 'as though they were empty of inhabitants' (pp. 271–4).

With the effective expulsion of the indigenous population from what became Israel and the systematic physical destruction of its former presence, the post-1948 Zionist literature reiterated these themes with renewed force and confidence. In David Ben-Gurion's monumental *A Personal History*, Palestine on the eve of Zionist colonization is described as 'in a virtual state of anarchy ... primitive, neglected, and derelict'. Jewish settlements 'revitalize' the 'Land of Israel' as they are built on 'desolate tracts, on swamps and sands, on deserted and barren hillsides'. The indigenous population barely figures in Ben-Gurion's 'personal history' even of the Mandate period, except as 'rioters' and an ominous, if ungrounded, 'Arab problem'.[19]

In *The Jews in their Land*, Izhak Ben-Zvi, Israel's second president, provides a copiously detailed accounting of the Jewish communities – minuscule and overwhelmingly anti-Zionist, although one would never know it from this record – in Palestine during the pre-Mandate period. The Arabs, generally cast as bedouins, are variously depicted as 'ransacking', 'looting', 'pillaging', 'robbing', 'cheating', 'vandalizing', 'plundering' or 'terrorizing' the Jews. The one thing that they apparently did not do is *live and labor* in Palestine, which must await the Jewish colonists to be 'rebuilt'.[20]

Abba Eban recalls in *My Country* that the 'physical link' between Jews and Palestine was 'never broken' as 'a thin but crucial line of continuity had been maintained by small Jewish settlements'. On the other hand, Palestine 'never became the cradle of another independent nation' and 'the association of the land with Jewish history was never obscured or superseded'. Indeed, Palestine on the eve of Zionist colonization is described by Eban as 'a backward and desolate place ... stagnant ... constantly ravished by malaria and pestilence ... squalid ... unpromising, almost repellent' – aside, presumably, from that 'thin but crucial line' of Jewish 'continuity'.[21]

Even in Zionist literature more sensitive to the presence of an indigenous non-Jewish population, the emphasis remains on the unique Jewish connection to Palestine and the tenuousness of the Arab one. In his authoritative *A History of Zionism,* Walter Laqueur states that the departure point of any discussion of Zionism is the 'central place' of Palestine 'in the thoughts, the prayers, and the dreams of the Jews in their dispersion'; and that 'physical contact between the Jews and their former homeland was never completely broken'. Yet, although much space is given over to the 'Unseen [Arab] Question', Laqueur still describes pre-Mandatory Palestine as 'in a state of utter decay', a 'desolate province'. One is reminded of Jennings's paradox that the very same historians who launch their narratives with the encounter between the European colonist and the indigenous Indian population go on to 'repeat identical mythical phrases purporting that the land-starved people of Europe had found magnificent opportunity to pioneer in a savage wilderness'.[22]

Nonetheless, it took the unique moral climate of the American Jewish intellectual community to produce that *ne plus ultra* of the conquest genre, Joan Peters's *From Time Immemorial.* Marshalling nearly 2,000 footnotes and a wealth of exacting demographic data, Peters purported to prove with all the rigors of scholarship what Zionist propaganda had hitherto only bandied as a rallying cry or suggestively hinted at: that Palestine was, literally, 'uninhabited' on the eve of Zionist colonization; and that if the Arab population did not materialize, literally, *ex nihilo* in Palestine, it did surreptitiously enter to exploit the economic opportunities that the Jews created when they made the 'desert bloom'.[23] The upshot of Peters's thesis, then, was that the 4.5 million souls calling themselves Palestinian had, each and all, falsified their genealogies. The only lacuna in her massive tome was the modalities of the conspiracy's parturition. Did a cabal of 'elders of Araby' converge on a graveyard in the dead of night as per another 'conspiracy'?

*From Time Immemorial* was quickly shown to be a threadbare hoax – what else could it have been? – but that did not prevent Israel's more prominent American 'supporters' from catapulting it into best-sellerdom. The reception they accorded Peters's book recalls an observation by

Norman Cohn in his classic (and remarkably pertinent) study of the *Protocols of the Elders of Zion*. 'The Protocols', he wrote, 'are such a transparent and ludicrous forgery that one may well wonder why it was ever necessary to prove the point', yet 'multitudes of people who were by no means insane took them perfectly seriously'.[24] *New Republic* editor-in-chief Martin Peretz, for example, exulted that Peters's book contained not a single factual error – which was true, but only in the trivial sense that it contained no facts period; and that, if widely read, it could alter the 'history of the future' – which, alas, *From Time Immemorial* did not do, although it did alter the 'history of the past', indeed, impressively so.[25]

By pushing the 'virgin land or wilderness' myth to its logical conclusion, Peters and her cronies performed the useful, if unwitting, service of exposing its sheer absurdity. Paradoxically, no single work more conclusively established the existence of an indigenous population in Palestine displaced by Zionist conquest. As Zionism embarked on a new round of colonization in the West Bank and Gaza, it was almost inevitable that the 'virgin land or wilderness' myth would be resurrected. One index of the current effort's farcicality, however, is that Peters's volume is being touted as the authoritative text.[26]

### The Myth of 'Self-Defense'

In *Land and Power*, Israeli historian Anita Shapira remains faithful to the conventional view of Palestine on the eve of Zionist colonization. Thus, it is depicted as 'a wild landscape devoid of trees and shade ... where the inhabitants were strange and alien, wild like the land itself', as 'desolate under Arab rule', etc. (pp. 53, 214). Nonetheless, the focus of Shapira's book is the encounter between the Zionist settlers and the indigenous Arab population. As a result, the myth of the 'virgin land or wilderness' does not figure prominently in her history.

Rather, Shapira's main aim is to validate another of Zionism's conquest myths. The mainstream, labor Zionist movement long publicly maintained that it did not anticipate or intend resorting to force against the indigenous population to achieve its aims, but only did so as the result of an accumulation of intractable circumstances. Shapira does not put the myth of Zionism's 'peaceful intentions' – or, as she dubs it, 'defensive ethos' – in quite such crude terms. Indeed, she cannot; even within the dwindling circle of Zionist faithful, it carries less and less conviction with time. Thus, she repeatedly qualifies and contradicts her main thesis. The result is a book at war with itself: on the one hand, sustaining the myth of Zionism's 'defensive ethos', but on the other, conceding that the 'defensive ethos' was simply a mask for what was, from the inception, a mission of conquest.

This internal conflict is, I think, the main significance of Shapira's book. It contains no original research, makes little use of recent scholarship, and extensively resorts to such dubious sources as the official *History of the Hagana*.[27] Even as a work of interpretation or synthesis, *Land and Power* offers few original insights. The main outline of Shapira's story – Zionism's initial strategy of gradual settlement and its eventual resort to outright armed conquest – has been described many times before. Shapira writes in the wooden, bombastic style of most official histories. Hers is the over-wrought prose of the Zionist initiate – endlessly repetitious and barely coherent, often impenetrable and replete with arcane references.[28] In a word, *Land and Power* is in all respects a party-spirited work. Yet, that is precisely what makes it so interesting. It vividly captures the crisis of Zionist ideology – or, at any rate, the withering of another of Zionism's central myths.[29]

Shapira places the Jewish settlement of Palestine within the framework of the Zionist idea. Zionism, Shapira observes, originated in the 'Romantic–exclusivistic' (also: 'German', 'volkisch') brand of nationalism that purported that 'blood ties, common ethnic origin', etc., not citizenship or 'agreement', were the proper foundations of community. Accordingly, its aim from the outset was to create a Jewish state in 'all of Palestine', that is, to 'alter the demographic, economic, and cultural balance of power' so that Jews would be its 'rulers and masters', 'lords and masters' (also: 'to change the character of the land from an Arab country to a Jewish one'). The minimum requirement for such a state was a Jewish majority that would 'rule over' the Arabs. The ideal was a state that was homogeneously Jewish, since Zionism's ultimate purpose was 'to liberate Jews from the burden of living in the midst of another people' (also: 'liberation from a multinational situation ... from the obligation to take the existence of others in their country into consideration') (pp. 6–7, 84, 112, 125, 138, 170, 280, 283, 321).[30]

Throughout *Land and Power*, Shapira puts on an equal ethical plane – or, at any rate, makes no ethical distinction between – the Zionist aim to transform Palestine into a Jewish state and the resistance of the indigenous Arab population to such a conquest mission. Hence she refers to 'rivals laying claim to the land'; to Jews as the 'other contenders for Palestine'; to the Arabs as a 'second full claimant of the land'; to the 'struggle between two national movements for one and the same piece of territory'; to a 'fundamental clash between two national movements fighting to gain sovereignty and control over the same country'; and so on (pp. 107, 115, 117, 125, 356). For Shapira, the conflict was essentially a clash between 'two rights', more or less equal. This puts her ahead of mainstream Zionist historiography, which typically attaches a far greater value to the Zionist claim – but behind what I think any objective valuation shows.

The Zionist claim to Palestine rests on one or a combination of the following arguments: (1) divine right, (2) historical right, (3) compelling need. None of these can withstand close scrutiny, however.

Shapira makes little if any mention of the Jewish people's providential claim to Palestine – rightly so, I think, especially since colonizing projects have typically invoked the same rhetoric of a 'divinely-ordained mission', 'chosen people', etc., and the same authority of the Old Testament to justify themselves. In the case of the United States, Thomas Jefferson suggested that the new national seal should show the children of Israel led by a pillar of light from the heavens, since he was 'confident that Americans were the new chosen people of God'. In later years, the same pretense was captured in the doctrine of 'Manifest Destiny', which – in the words of the journalist who coined the phrase – signalled that the North American continent was 'allotted by Providence for the free development of our yearly multiplying millions'. Arnold Toynbee once observed that it was the same 'biblically recorded conviction of the Israelites that God had instigated them to exterminate the Canaanites' that sanctioned the British conquest of North America, Ireland and Australia, the Dutch conquest of South Africa, the Prussian conquest of Poland, and the Zionist conquest of Palestine.[31]

The full gamut of the Zionist movement made much of what was dubbed the 'historical right' (Shapira also refers to it as the 'proprietary right') of the Jews to Palestine. It was a 'right that required no proof … a fundamental component of all Zionist programs'. Steeped in German Romanticism, the claim was that because the forefathers of the Jewish people had originated and been buried in Palestine, Jews could only – and only Jews could – establish an authentic, organic connection with the soil there. Noting its 'German source', Shapira points to the 'recurrent motif' in Zionism of the 'mysticism that links blood and soil', the 'cult of heroes, death and graves', the belief that 'graves are the source of the vital link with the land, and they generate the loyalty of man to that soil', and that 'blood fructifies the soil (in an almost literal sense)', and so on. Even so sober a thinker as Ahad Ha'am could aver that Palestine was 'a land to which our historical right is beyond doubt and has no need for far-fetched proofs'. The veteran Zionist leader, Menahem Ussishkin, pushed the logic of the argument to its ultimate, if fantastic, conclusion, stating that 'the Arabs recognize unconditionally the historical title of Jews to the land' (pp. 40–1, 45, 47, 73–4).[32]

This sort of 'historical right' was also seized by the Romantic precursors of Nazism and, with a vengeance, by the Nazis themselves, to justify the conquest of the East.[33] Germany was said to have legitimate claims on Slavic territory (especially but not limited to Poland) since it was 'already inhabited by the Germans in primeval times', 'fertilized by the most noble ancient German blood', 'germanic for many centuries and long before a Slav set foot there', 'teutonic-German *Volksboden* for 3,000 years as far as the Vistula. ... In the 6th and 7th century after Christ the Slavs pushed outwards from their eastern homelands and into the ancient German land ... – admittedly only for a few hundred years', etc. The Slavic 'interlopers', by contrast, were seen as 'history's squatters' who merely 'existed' in surroundings that they 'could not master'. Only the remnant or newly settled German communities were supposedly able to 'shape' the environment and by so doing make it 'their own' in the course, ephemeral as it was, of Slavic rule. Poland under the Slavs, for example, was depicted as an artificial entity, more a melange of inchoate nationalities than a cohesive nation, that had fallen into a state of abject decay – 'untilled fields surrendered to the thorny clutches of wild nature, desolate farm buildings, soil erosion' – with the notable exception of the German enclaves that managed to endure and even thrive despite all. Substitute the proper nouns and one could be reading any standard Zionist history of Palestine. Indeed, so profound is the affinity of these two literatures that it is registered even in specific phraseology. Thus in 1939, the eminent pro-Nazi historian, Albert Brackmann, portrayed Germany as Europe's 'defender' and 'bulwark' against the 'East', and the 'bearers of civilisation' against 'barbarism'. A half century earlier, Theodor Herzl portrayed the prospective Jewish state as Europe's 'wall of defense against Asia', and 'an outpost of civilization against barbarism'.[34]

In any event, Zionism's 'historical right' to Palestine was neither historical nor a right. It was not historical inasmuch as it voided the two millennia of non-Jewish settlement in Palestine and the two millennia of Jewish settlement outside it. It was not a right, except in the Romantic 'mysticism' of 'blood and soil' and the Romantic 'cult' of 'death, heroes, and graves' (the quoted phrases are Shapira's).

The Zionist claim as against the indigenous Arab population also rested on compelling need. This argument took two, overlapping forms. The first was the ideological, Romantic one that the Jewish 'nation' suffered persecution on account of its 'homelessness'; and only the 'restoration' of the Jewish 'nation' to a state of its 'own' in its 'ancestral homeland' would end the persecution. Yet, the claim of Jewish 'homelessness' is founded on a cluster of assumptions that both negates the liberal idea of citizenship and duplicates the anti-Semitic one that the state belongs to the majority ethnic nation. In a word, the Zionist case for a Jewish state is as valid or invalid as the anti-Semitic case for an ethnic state that marginalizes Jews.[35]

The non-ideological, humanitarian kernel of the above argument was that Jews suffering persecution needed and were entitled to a place of refuge. Why shouldn't Palestine, which was surely able to accommodate an influx of Jews, have served as such a haven? Why shouldn't the indigenous Arab population have shared Palestine with the Jews suffering persecution?

Shapira makes the most of this argument. The Arabs are repeatedly cast as making an 'exclusive claim to Palestine' and the Jews as merely demanding 'their right to settle side by side with the Arabs in Palestine'. Yet, as we have seen, she also acknowledges – indeed, often on the very same pages! – that the Zionist aim was to create a Jewish state in 'all of Palestine' that would at minimum politically 'rule over' the Arabs and ideally physically displace them altogether so as to 'liberate Jews from the burden of living in the midst of another people'. Even Berl Katznelson – the revered 'living conscience' of Labor Zionism – 'denied', according to Israeli historian Ze'ev Sternhell, 'the Arabs a collective right to the land on which they lived' and 'considered the view that ... two national movements had equal claim' to Palestine an 'existential threat to Zionism' (pp. 115–16, 134, 138–9, 356).[36]

One can imagine an argument for the right of a persecuted minority to find refuge in another country able to accommodate it;[37] one is hard-pressed, however, to imagine an argument for the right of a persecuted minority to politically and perhaps physically displace the indigenous population of another country. Yet, as Shapira forthrightly acknowledges, the latter was the actual intention of the Zionist movement.

In this connection, consider Shapira's murky discussion of the partition and 'transfer' issues. Regarding the 1937 partition proposal of the Peel Commission, Shapira juxtaposes the 'Arab side' which 'rejected [it] out of hand' because 'they still viewed themselves as the exclusive owners of Palestine', against the 'Jewish side' where 'a stormy debate developed' between proponents and opponents of partition. She does admit that 'at least a segment' of the Zionist proponents of partition viewed the creation of a Jewish state as a 'bridgehead for continuing the expansion of Jewish settlement in Palestine' (p. 271). In fact, as shown above, the mainstream Zionist movement was as united in its exclusivist claim to all of Palestine as the Arab side. For example, Ben-Gurion – the central advocate of partition – viewed it as merely a 'stage' along the 'path to greater Zionist implementation', a 'means toward' the 'final aim of Zionism'.

Shapira further maintains that the 'topic of force was marginal' to the Zionist debate surrounding the partition proposal, with all sides desiring above all 'to avoid the need for the use of force' (p. 271). Yet as noted in Chapter 1, Ben-Gurion observed on the eve of the twentieth Zionist congress in 1937 that the Jewish state being offered them by the British 'will consolidate in Palestine, within the shortest possible time, the real Jewish force which will lead us to our historic goal'. The Jewish Agency Executive was similarly apprised by Ben-Gurion in 1938 that, 'after we become a strong force, as a result of the creation of a state, we shall abolish partition and expand to the whole of Palestine'. Recall also that in his private correspondence, Ben-Gurion anticipated that the Jewish state 'would have an outstanding army ... and so I am certain that we won't be constrained from settling in the rest of the country, whether out of accord and mutual understanding with the Arab neighbors or otherwise'.[38]

For a study that is centrally concerned with the 'Zionist resort to force' (the book's subtitle) and is nothing if not verbose, Shapira's work gives the crucial topic of 'population transfer' in Zionist thinking remarkably short shrift. Shapira dispatches it in a little over one page (pp. 285–6). By comparison, fully twenty pages are devoted to the early Zionist frontier settlement of Tel Hai. This is all the more noteworthy inasmuch as the culmination of the 'Zionist resort to force' was, after all, a massive 'transfer' of the indigenous Arab population in 1948.

Shapira's discussion of the Zionist 'transfer' conception is, for all its brevity, remarkably disingenuous. She contextualizes it as 'based on what was assumed as [the] positive experience' between Turkey and Greece, and of the Volga Germans and Tartars by the Russian government. There is not even a hint at the terrifying brutality that accompanied the 'positive experience'. Another enlightened antecedent she points to was 'the lesson of the 1930s' that 'states should aspire to ethnic uniformity' – indeed, Hitler's lesson. One is hard-pressed to reconcile these precedents with Shapira's asseveration that Zionist leaders like Berl Katznelson were committed only to a 'peaceful transfer of population based on mutual agreement'. In fact, Katznelson repeatedly placed himself on record as 'with an absolutely clear conscience' favoring the compulsory 'transfer' of the Palestinian Arabs. Ben-Gurion is said by Shapira to have 'firmly opposed the idea of an imposed transfer plan' in the 1940s. Yet, as seen in Chapters 1 and 3 above, already in the late 1930s Ben-Gurion openly declared himself a strong partisan of an 'imposed transfer'. When the opportunity for such an expulsion arose in 1948, he showed no scruples about implementing it; rather the contrary.[39]

Shapira concludes that the 'traditional', 'mainstream' Zionist view was that there was 'enough room' in Palestine for Jews and Arabs. 'Transfer' was thus viewed as merely a 'good thing' that one could just as well 'do without'. Yet the benign spin that Shapira puts on Zionist thinking is not supported by recent scholarship. Historian Benny Morris observes, for example, that, from the mid-1930s, 'transferring the Arabs out' was seen as the 'chief means' of 'assuring the stability and "Jewishness" of the proposed Jewish State'.[40]

We have seen that none of the Zionist movement's standard rationales – divine right, historical right, compelling need – could justify its aim to transform Palestine into a Jewish state. A violent conflict with the indigenous Arab population was thus inevitable. As the dissident Zionist intellectual Judah Magnes succinctly put it, 'The slogan Jewish state ... is equivalent, in effect, to a declaration of war by the Jews on the Arabs.'[41]

Yet, it is Shapira's central contention that, until the late 1930s, the mainstream Zionist movement was animated by a 'defensive ethos' which had as its 'fundamental supposition' that 'the realization of the Zionist project would not require the use of force' (p. 175). She enumerates the main components of the 'defensive ethos' as follows:

> The Jews have no aspirations to rule in Palestine – they are coming to colonize the wilderness and to develop regions that to date have gone unploughed. They bring tidings of progress and development to the land, for the benefit of all its inhabitants. The clash of interests between Jews and Arabs is not the product of a genuine contradiction of interests between two peoples. Rather, it is the result of agitation and incitement by the reactionary elements among the Arab people, who are motivated by the fear of the progress and change now being ushered in by the Zionist colonization. In addition, the ruling power, guided by imperialist motives, has acted to undermine relations between the two peoples in Palestine: In order to maintain power, it is pursuing a policy of 'divide and rule'. (p. 117)[42]

Shapira's discussion of the 'defensive ethos' reveals her deep ambivalences about the justice of the Zionist enterprise. Especially in the book's conclusion, she admits that the ethos was a sham from start to finish. She states that it disguised the 'reality' that 'European[s]' were 'usurping the rights of the native population' and 'blurred the fact that there was a basic clash of interests in Palestine between the Jewish immigrants and the people already settled there'. Zionism is similarly described as not only a national movement but also 'a movement of European colonization in a Middle Eastern country' that 'had to be prepared to enter into confrontation with another people and to demand [its] national rights, even at the point of a gun'. 'Aggressiveness,' she concludes, 'was an integral component of the process' (pp. 356, 355).[43]

Accordingly, Shapira suggests that the 'defensive ethos' served simply as a cynical public relations device to assuage world and especially British opinion as well as the concerns of potential Jewish immigrants, and a psychological defense mechanism to salve the conscience of labor Zionism, which was in theory opposed to colonialism. She quotes the Zionist leader Tabenkin to the effect that 'Political necessities are forcing the leaders of Zionism to foster the illusion that we can settle the land peacefully and in agreement with the Arabs.' The pretense that Zionism would bring 'progress' to Palestine is described as 'self-persuasion' to deny the inevitability of conflict with the native population. The claim that anti-Semitism, effendi agitation and British machination, not basic interest, lurked behind the mass Arab opposition to Zionism is said to have been motivated by a need to 'strengthen the conviction about the righteousness of the movement against all its contenders, to preserve the sense of inner truth' (pp. 49, 51, 115, 122–3, 126, 185, 227, 229).

Half-hearted as it is (see below), Shapira's concession that the rhetoric of socialist–Zionism during the Mandate years was an exercise in cynicism and more or less conscious self-deception is still remarkable for a historian plainly beholden to the mainstream, labor Zionist tradition. She is not the only one to make such an admission, however. Shabtai Teveth, Ben-Gurion's current biographer, devoted a companion study to Ben-Gurion's evolving views on the Arab question during the Mandate years. For nearly two hundred pages, Ben-Gurion is cast as heroically and guilelessly wrestling with formulae to reconcile Arab and Jewish interests in Palestine. In the epilogue of his much-acclaimed book, however, Teveth abruptly discounts Ben-Gurion's posturings as sheer opportunism:

> A careful comparison of Ben-Gurion's public and private positions leads inexorably to the conclusion that this twenty-year denial of the conflict was a calculated tactic, born of pragmatism rather than profundity of conviction. The idea that Jews and Arabs could reconcile their differences … was a delaying tactic. Once the Yishuv had gained strength, Ben-Gurion abandoned it. This belief in a compromise solution … was also a tactic, designed to win continued British support for Zionism.

Yet, Teveth seems blissfully unaware that this acknowledgment cancels the value of his book, save as a study in the cynicism of Zionist diplomacy: Ben-Gurion's public positions which Teveth so minutely scrutinizes were, by Teveth's own admission, never meant seriously.[44]

Shapira likewise wants to have it both ways. She denies in one breath what she concedes in the next. Thus, the bulk of *Land and Power* is given over to proving the authenticity of the 'defensive ethos'. She argues that mainstream Zionism was, from its inception until World War II, not a 'conquest' movement but one committed to gaining Palestine 'by virtue of labor'. The embodiment of this approach was supposedly the example of Tel Hai, an early Zionist settlement attacked by Arabs. Its martyred

Jewish defenders quickly emerged as the main subject of Zionist iconography. According to Shapira, Tel Hai 'had a clearly defensive message' summed up by her as 'We have no aspirations for the domain of others or to conquests by the sword. The Hebrew worker came to Tel Hai with the *plough*, was driven out from there by the sword, and returned to Tel Hai with the *plough*.' And again: Tel Hai 'symbolized ... that Palestine would not be conquered ... by the sword. The land would be "conquered" by settling it, by making a stubborn stand in each and every place'. (Note the inverted commas around the word 'conquered'.) In this reckoning of Shapira's, the Zionist – or, for that matter, British – recourse to armed force becomes not 'aggression' but rather the 'necessity', 'obligation', 'moral duty', etc. of 'self-defense' against the 'waves of Arab assault' (pp. 98, 106, 108, 180, 223; emphases in original).

It may be true that labor Zionism was wont to view matters in this way. That scarcely alters the factual reality, however, that Tel Hai was part and parcel of a conquest enterprise made possible in the first place by the 'foreign bayonets' (Ben-Gurion's phrase) of Great Britain in which 'Europeans' were 'usurping the rights of the native population' (Shapira). Settlements were not in lieu of but an integral means to that conquest. Shapira suggests that Tel Hai's 'clearly defensive message' is shown by its central image of the pioneer who also fights as against 'the fighter, whose only craft is warfare' (p. 254). Yet in *The Winning of the West*, Theodore Roosevelt invokes the identical image of the 'early settlers' whose 'only two implements' were the 'axe and rifle, for they were almost equally proud of their skill as warriors, hunters, and wood-choppers', of these 'hunters, woodchoppers, and farmers' who were also 'their own soldiers', etc. Yet Roosevelt – unlike Shapira – frankly admits that 'this great westward movement of armed settlers was *essentially one of conquest*, no less than of colonization'. Indeed, as he formulated plans for 'pushing out the population that's there [in the East] now', Hitler instructed that 'the German colonist will be the soldier-peasant'.[45]

Consider even Shapira's description of Tel Hai's symbolic meaning. It captured the Jewish settler's willingness to relocate in regions of 'considerable Arab presence' that were 'remote from the main centers of Jewish settlement' in order to establish the 'principle of settlement in general' and stake out the 'frontiers' of a future Jewish state. One may excuse, I think, the indigenous Arab population for being blind to the 'clearly defensive message' of Tel Hai (pp. 106, 108, 254).

Every mission of conquest conceives its use of force as a justifiable act of 'self-defense' against 'aggression'. Thomas Jefferson defensively declared that, if 'constrained' by the Indians resisting American expansion to 'lift the hatchet ... , we will never lay it down till the tribe is exterminated, or is driven beyond the Mississippi'. Adlai Stevenson told the United Nations Security Council that the US invasion of South Vietnam was actually a case of resisting 'internal aggression'. Albert Camus defended the French war against Algeria on the grounds that the revolt of its North African colony was really an integral part of a 'new Arab imperialism' led by Egypt and an 'anti-Western' offensive orchestrated by Russia to 'encircle Europe' and 'isolate the United States'. No single phrase appeared more frequently in Nazi publications after September 1939 than 'the war that was forced upon us'. Hitler claimed that his attack on the Soviet Union was a preemptive strike against the threat posed by 'Bolshevik barbarism'. Indeed, the Nazis justified the genocide against the Jews as an act of self-defense. Thus, amidst the Nazi holocaust in 1942, Hitler recalled in apparent extenuation his earlier 'prophecy' that 'if Jewry should plot another world war in order to exterminate the Aryan peoples of Europe, it would not be the Aryan peoples which would be exterminated, but Jewry'. Himmler, in his infamous Posen speech on the Nazi extermination campaign, declared that 'we had the moral right, we had the duty to our people, to destroy this people which wanted to destroy us'. Even the murder of Jewish children was rationalized by Himmler in another speech on defensive grounds: 'We as Germans, however deeply we may feel in our hearts, are not entitled to allow a generation of avengers filled with hatred to grow up with whom our children and grandchildren will have to deal because we, too weak and cowardly, left it to them.'[46] One may also recall in this regard Joseph Schumpeter's crucial insight in *The Sociology of Imperialism* that a characteristic, indeed unique, feature of the modern world is precisely that 'every war is carefully justified as a defensive war by the government involved, and by all the political parties, in their official utterances'.[47]

There is, moreover, no *a priori* reason not to credit the 'sincerity' of these defensive protestations. Raul Hilberg observes that 'in Hitler's eyes, the Jews were Germany's principal adversary. The battle he fought against them was a "defense".'[48] And the Zionist leader Moshe Sharett perhaps truly believed that 'preventing Arab rule in Palestine is defense' (p. 287). Noam Chomsky has noted that it is not unusual for policy makers to get 'caught up in the fantasies they spin to disguise imperial interventions' and even for the 'delusional system' to 'present a faint reflection of reality. It must, after all, carry some conviction'. Yet the point of the serious historian, Chomsky pertinently observes, is 'to disentangle motive from myth'. Shapira is, for the most part, unwilling or unable to do so, however. For her, Zionism, whose aim was to transform 'all of Palestine' into a Jewish state that would at minimum 'rule over' the Arabs, was nonetheless not a movement of 'conquest' but one committed to gaining Palestine

'by virtue of labor' as typified in the 'clearly defensive message' of Tel
Hai, where force was used only when 'necessary' in 'self-defense'.
Ironically, Ben-Gurion himself had no difficulty disentangling the rhetoric
of self-defense from the reality of conquest. Thus in 1938, he stated:

> When we say that the Arabs are the aggressors and we defend ourselves – that
> is only half the truth. As regards our security and life we defend ourselves. ...
> But the fighting is only one aspect of the conflict which is in its essence a
> political one. And politically we are the aggressors and they defend themselves.[49]

Aside from the 'clearly defensive message' of Tel Hai, the only piece
of evidence Shapira adduces for the genuineness of the 'defensive ethos'
is Ben-Gurion's allegedly tireless efforts to 'forge an alliance between
Arab and Jewish workers'. Shapira would have it that Ben-Gurion served
as the 'tribune' for the 'revolutionary idea' of a 'joint union' that would
'vault national lines, underscoring the superiority of class identity over
national identity' (pp. 135–8, 182–3, 283). Yet, as Shapira also half admits,
his support for a joint union with the Arabs was purely pragmatic. Ben-
Gurion was a veteran of the Second Aliya, which was fully committed
to the principle of Jewish labor – i.e. to the 'building of a Jewish society
by Jews alone, from foundation stone to rafter' (p. 64; cf. p. 220). The
main obstacle posed to the 'conquest of labor' by Jewish workers was
the competition of cheap Arab labor. In the sectors of the Palestinian
economy financed by Jewish capital, the principle of Jewish labor was
eventually established – more often than not, coercively – by the Histadrut. Especially in public works and government service under the
auspices of the British Mandate administration, however, such a discrimi-
natory principle could not be imposed by the Yishuv. *In this exceptional
instance*, Ben-Gurion proposed to free up spaces for Jewish workers with
higher wage demands by organizing the Arab workers as well, thereby
making Jewish labor more competitive. The 'revolutionary idea' of a 'joint
union' was plainly not a principled commitment to 'vault' national lines.
It did not contradict the labor Zionist aim of an exclusively Jewish
economy in an exclusively Jewish state. The 'joint union' was merely a
lesser evil where the principle of Jewish labor could not – yet – be
enforced. And, in any event, almost nothing ever came of it. Indeed, so
little was labor Zionism committed to 'vaulting' national lines in the
interests of 'class solidarity' that it was given to 'stressing the *national*
component of the Jewish–Arab conflict' in order to dissuade Jewish land-
owners from using Arab labor (p. 67, emphasis in original).[50]

The 'defensive ethos' was never the operative ideology of mainstream
Zionism. From beginning to end, Zionism was a conquest movement.
The subtitle of Shapira's study is 'The Zionist Resort to Force'. Yet,

Zionism did not 'resort' to force. Force was – to use Shapira's apt phrase in her conclusion – 'inherent in the situation' (p. 357). Gripped by messianism after the issuance of the Balfour Declaration, the Zionist movement sought to conquer Palestine with a Jewish Legion under the slogan 'In blood and fire shall Judea rise again' (pp. 83–98). When these apocalyptic hopes were dispelled and displaced by the mundane reality of the British Mandate, mainstream Zionism made a virtue of necessity and exalted labor as it proceeded to conquer Palestine 'dunum by dunum, goat by goat'. Force had not been abandoned, however. Shapira falsely counterposes settlement ('by virtue of labor') to force ('by dint of conquest'). Yet, settlement was force by other means. Its purpose, in Shapira's words, was to build a 'Jewish infrastructure in Palestine' so that 'the balance of power between Jews and Arabs had shifted in favor of the former' (pp. 121, 133; cf. p. 211). To the call of a Zionist leader on the morrow of Tel Hai that 'we must be a force in the land', Shapira adds the caveat: 'He was not referring to military might but, rather, to power in the sense of demography and colonization' (p. 113). Yet, Shapira willfully misses the basic point that 'demography and colonization' were equally force. Moreover, without the 'foreign bayonets' of the British Mandate, the Zionist movement could not have established even a toehold, let alone struck deep roots, in Palestine.[51] Toward the end of the 1930s and especially after World War II, a concatenation of events – Britain's waning commitment to the Balfour Declaration, the escalation of Arab resistance, the strengthening of the Yishuv, etc. – caused a consensus to crystallize within the Zionist movement that the time was ripe to return to the original strategy of conquering Palestine 'by blood and fire'.[52]

Mainstream Zionism adapted its tactics to accommodate new contingencies.[53] But force was a constant throughout. Zionism did not come to use force despite itself. The recourse to force was not circumstantial. It was 'inherent' in the aim of transforming Palestine, with its overwhelmingly Arab population, into a Jewish state.

The scant evidence that Shapira marshals to demonstrate a rupture in mainstream Zionist ideology – its mutation from a 'defensive' to an 'offensive' ethos – proves just the opposite. She purports that a new, more militant 'myth of Hanita' displaced the 'myth of Tel Hai' in the late 1930s. To illustrate the 'change that had taken place', she points to 'Hanita's distance from any other point of Jewish settlement and its location in an area of danger' in 'the heart of an Arab area' (p. 253). Yet, she earlier described Tel Hai as 'remote from the main centers of Jewish settlement' in a region 'characterized by dubious government control and considerable Arab presence' (p. 108).

According to Shapira, 'up until the world war, the only organization that regarded physical force as a decisive factor in the "conquest" of Palestine' was the Revisionists (p. 283). It is true that Jabotinsky viewed as inevitable a violent clash with the indigenous Arab population in Palestine. In 1923, he observed that

> [t]here can be no kind of discussion of a voluntary reconciliation between us and the Arabs, not now and not in the foreseeable future. ... Everyone, with the exception of those who were blind from birth, already understood long ago the complete impossibility of arriving at a voluntary agreement with the Arabs of Palestine for the transformation of Palestine from an Arab country to a country with a Jewish majority.[54]

Yet, how different is the sentiment expressed in these words written five years earlier, in 1918?

> Everybody sees a difficulty in the question of relations between Arabs and Jews. But not everybody sees that there is no solution to the question. No solution! There is a gulf and nothing can fill this gulf. It is possible to resolve the conflict between Jewish and Arab interests [only] by sophistry. I do not know what Arab will agree that Palestine should belong to the Jews. ... We, as a nation, want this country to be *ours*; the Arabs, as a nation, want this country to be *theirs*.

The author was David Ben-Gurion.[55]

## The Myth of 'Purity of Arms'

A second major theme of *Land and Power* is the metamorphosis in the Jewish attitude to physical violence from a 'self-image' that 'abhors violence in any form' to one that is 'identified with military might' and 'does not hesitate to resort to force when deemed necessary' (p. viii).

It is true that, in this regard, the Zionist movement traversed a considerable distance in a brief time span. One may recall Sartre's classic depiction of the modern European Jew as 'often as not a weak creature who is ill-prepared to cope with violence and cannot even defend himself'.[56] Yet by 1948, the Jew was able not only to 'defend himself' but to commit massive atrocities as well. Indeed, according to the former director of the Israel army archives, 'in almost every Arab village occupied by us during the War of Independence, acts were committed which are defined as war crimes, such as murders, massacres, and rapes'. The number of large-scale massacres (more than 50 murdered) is put by the archivist at a minimum of 20 and small-scale massacres (an individual or a handful murdered) at about 100. Uri Milstein, the authoritative Israeli military historian of the 1948 war, goes one step further, maintaining that 'every skirmish ended in a massacre of Arabs'.[57]

*Land and Power* points to several sources for the – in modern Jewish history – unprecedented facility with violence demonstrated by the Jews who conquered Palestine. I will address two here: racism and the variety of socialism espoused by labor Zionism.

Shapira maintains that, in Palestine, unlike colonial encounters elsewhere, 'hatred of the "natives" among immigrants ... did not surface except among certain fringe groups' (p. 130; cf. pp. 305, 310). Yet, the evidence of her study suggests that the Zionists succumbed to the typical paternalistic contempt of the 'natives' that easily glided into hatred when the 'natives' resisted encroachment. The humanist ideals of socialist Zionism no more mitigated these racist attitudes than, say, France's humanist ideals mitigated them in Algeria. Indeed, what was Ben-Gurion's peroration in the 1920s that the task of the 'Hebrew worker [is to] stand at the vanguard of the movement of liberation and reawakening of Near Eastern peoples' – Shapira heralds it as 'the great socialist mission ... the challenge of advancing the lot of the Arab worker' – except the '*mission civilisatrice*' in socialist guise (p. 135)?[58]

Shapira reports that already the first Zionist settlers in 1882 acted as if 'they were the rightful lords and masters of this land'. Their 'first impression' of the Arab was 'that this stranger respected strength and that the language of physical force was the only idiom he understood'. Accordingly, the 'tendency of colonists' was 'to reach quickly for the whip and beat the offender for every transgression, large and small'. A correspondent from Palestine in 1886 wrote that his Zionist comrades did not 'regard the fellahin as human beings; and for every small thing, they beat and punish them with whips'. Ahad Ha'am similarly observed in 1891 that '[t]hey behave hostilely and cruelly toward the Arabs, encroaching upon them unjustly, beating them disgracefully for no good reason, and then they do not hesitate to boast about their deeds'; and in 1903 that 'the attitude of the colonists toward their land tenants and families is really very much like their attitude towards their animals'. Negative stereotypes of Arabs as 'sly', 'underhanded', 'cruel', 'cunning', 'immoral', 'lazy', etc. were pervasive. Arabs were typically described as 'a people like a donkey', echoing the Talmudic description of the Canaanite slaves. On disembarking at Haifa harbor, the eminent Hebrew writer Y.H. Brenner reflected 'So ... once again ... there's *another* sort of alien in the world that one must suffer from. ... Even from that filthy, contaminated lot, you have to suffer.' Shapira adds that, 'for Brenner, the dirt and filth symbolized the characteristic feature of that society' (pp. 43, 53–9, 69, 77, 377, note 14; emphasis in original).[59]

In the 1920s, Uri Zvi Greenberg was at one and the same time the preeminent 'author of a Hebrew hate literature against Arabs' and 'one of the most outstanding poets and publicists of the Labor movement'. He stereotyped the Arab as 'a murderer, knife honed and dipped in poison' and the Arab fields abutting Jewish settlements as 'boils'. According to Shapira, socialist Zionist leaders like Tabenkin and Ben-Gurion were

> not repelled by the inherent violence of Greenberg's style or even by his maliciously malevolent descriptions of Arabs. ... Even if, as committed socialists, they professed the brotherhood of all peoples and advocated universalist ideas, still in the Jewish sphere, Greenberg's manichaean description of the world answered to their 'gut perceptions' of reality.

Tabenkin apparently divided his time between lectures on the importance of the struggle for peace, on the one hand, and the barbarism of the Arabs who 'understood only one thing, namely, force', on the other (pp. 100, 143–6, 150–2, 259).

As the conflict between the Jewish settlers and indigenous Arab population reached new peaks of violence in 1929 and 1936, the labor Zionist press 'endlessly' denounced the Arabs as 'murderers', 'bands of robbers', 'bloodthirsty rioters', 'desert savages', 'jackals', 'highway robbers', 'treacherous murderers', 'barbarians', 'savages', 'shedders of blood', etc. Even Eliezer Yaffe, an avowed anarchist who first conceptualized the idea of the moshav and an acknowledged moral authority of the Yishuv, viciously condemned the Arabs in Palestine:

> You trampled my peace for many generations, as savages of the desert, who live by the sword, by robbery. ... And you retreated to your deserts, like jackals in the morning light. ... [When Rome attacked Judea,] once more you came out from your holes and attacked us, you wagged your tails before pagan Rome. ... Extend your hand and be a good neighbor in my land.

Shapira reckons these last words as a 'vision ... of peace' since, *inter alia*, Yaffe 'would not have seen' the 'negative characteristics he attributed to the Arabs ... as a biased view but, rather, as the plain and simple truth. ... They expressed the internal truth of a socialist – a man known to be sensitive to moral issues, with pacifist leanings' (pp. 181, 214–15, 237). One comprehends more fully the spirit of Shapira's above-cited claim that labor Zionism was unique among colonial movements inasmuch as 'hatred of the "natives" ... did not surface'. It was not hatred, it was the 'internal truth ... '.

It is generally assumed that labor Zionism was fettered by the ethical imperatives of its socialist ideology. Yet, as Shapira notes, the brand of socialism embraced by the Yishuv leaders was inspired by Stalinist Russia. Effectively this meant that, for them, 'a historical mission liberates its bearers from the restrictions of simple morality in the name of higher justice', the 'use of force' was legitimate 'for the sake of generating the desired revolutionary change', 'every revolutionary ideology harbors within it the legitimation for the use of violence, since the end justified the means', etc. Terror was thus explicitly condoned as a legitimate 'means of struggle'. The highly respected kibbutz leader Yitzak Tabenkin was fond of quoting that favorite Stalinist stand-by, 'when trees are felled, the chips will fly' (pp. 70, 203, 299, 301, 349, 351, 364, 367).[60]

Shapira concludes that labor Zionism and the dissident right-wing Zionist organizations were in basic accord so far as the deployment of physical force against the Arabs was concerned. One need hardly stress that, coming as it does from a mainstream Zionist historian, such an acknowledgment is remarkable. Shapira reports that, during the Arab Revolt of 1936–39, the Irgun Zvai Leumi engaged in 'uninhibited use of terror'; 'mass indiscriminate killings of the aged, women and children'; the execution of Jews 'suspected of informing, even though some of these persons were totally innocent'; 'the extortion of funds and acts of robbery ... in the Jewish community in order to finance their actions'; 'attacks against British without any consideration of possible injuries to innocent bystanders, and the murder of British in cold blood', etc. (pp. 247, 249, 350). Yet Shapira observes that, although labor Zionism's approach to violence 'was more "civilized" than' the Irgun's, 'they did not differ in essential respects' (p. 252). Comparing the elite labor Zionist shock troops of the Palmah and the Irgun, she again maintains 'It is doubtful whether [the] external differences in framework and patterns of behavior were sufficient to create a different attitude toward fighting or to develop "civilian" barriers to military callousness and insensitivity' (p. 365).[61]

The reality of labor Zionism's fabled 'purity of arms' is pointed up in Shapira's discussion of Yishuv policy during the Arab Revolt. As is well known, Ben-Gurion initially urged a policy of 'self-restraint' (*havlaga*) that barred attacks on innocent Arab civilians. In accordance with recent historiography, Shapira concludes that 'pragmatic', not moral considerations were 'the decisive element' in shaping this policy – namely, to force the British to fulfill the terms of the Mandate or, at any rate, not to provide them with a pretext for abandoning it. As Ben-Gurion succinctly put the issue, 'Arab terror is directed toward achieving the Arab objective' of terminating the British Mandate, whereas 'Jewish terror contradicts the Jewish objective' of preserving it (pp. 234–6, 247).[62]

Yet, Shapira significantly adds that 'the policy of self-restraint underwent various modifications and changes over the course of the three years of the Arab revolt'. In fact, with British sanction, it was effectively abandoned. The British officer Charles Orde Wingate, who 'rumor had it used to line up in a row villagers suspected of murder and then select every tenth one to be executed', recruited field squads from the labor Zionist settlements for 'merciless raids' on Arab villages.[63]

The 'approach prevalent among the ranks of the fields squads' was that 'if a village had served as a hiding place for an Arab gang, it was permissible to place collective responsibility on the village.' The 'boundaries of the permissible and impermissible in the treatment of these villagers' was 'vague and intentionally blurred'. As we have seen, Shapira concludes that, in practical effect, these boundaries did not differ from the avowedly terrorist Irgun's (pp. 249, 251–2).

Ideologically, labor Zionism's approach to violence was distinguished by the kindred values of impersonality and rationality. Shapira suggests that these sensibilities rendered labor Zionism, if not practically different, still morally superior to the Revisionist movement. Thus she favorably contrasts labor Zionism with Revisionism for not 'consciously cultivating hostile feelings toward Arabs', 'rejecting education to inculcate hatred of the enemy', 'a pedagogical conception that was not intended to teach young people to hate', etc. Indeed, she credits labor Zionism with 'misgivings' as it executed its unsavory, if appointed, tasks (pp. 76, 251, 300, 305, 310). Similarly, Shapira suggests that labor Zionism is deserving of praise because, unlike Revisionism, it curbed 'excesses,' 'abuses,' 'indiscriminate' violence, etc., as a premium was put on the 'efficiency of power.' In the words of one Palmah veteran of the 1948 war quoted by Shapira, 'We were not thirsty for blood and did not turn death into a value. We were efficient based on a sense of conviction' (pp. 157, 242, 252, 348–9, 357, 365).

A canonical text of labor Zionism's distinctive ethos is *The Seventh Day*, an oral history of the June 1967 war based on the 'soldiers' talk' of 'a group of young kibbutz members'.[64] An overarching theme of the volume is that the Israeli soldier did not harbor any personal animus toward – indeed, was tormented by the violence he inflicted on – the Arabs. The appointed task was a dirty one but, alas, had to be done. The book's moral anxiety is due not to the effects of the violence on the victim, however, but the victor: the corruption of the Jewish soul.

Barely a page of *The Seventh Day* passes without one kibbutznik or another avowing that he 'didn't hate' the Arabs, in fact, 'above all, felt pity for the poor wretches'. They take pride that 'we fight decently and morally, suppressing the sadism and the instinct to kill which is in all of us', indeed, in a manner 'so humane and kind-hearted', even '"abnormal" in the sensitivity ... expressed', that 'it cost us quite a bit'. Accordingly, the soldiers ponder 'if we were really educated properly' for war. But they also recognize that circumstances force them to be 'strong, strong to the brink of tears ... efficient ... quick, strong, and silent, like fiends'.

These are fate's reluctant, tragic warriors. One notes that the visions of Jewish martyrdom 'compel us to fight and yet make us. ashamed of our fighting. The saying, "Pardon us for winning" is no irony – it is the truth.' Another observes that

> we fought the enemy because it was vital to do so – but we don't hate them....
> I felt an awful repugnance about pulling the trigger. There were times when it
> was almost absurd; times when it was absolutely essential and when I still hesi-
> tated. I'm convinced that it had nothing to do with fear; it was simply an
> unwillingness to kill. You felt that both you and the enemy were taking part in
> some clash of forces on a much more generalized scale. When he fired at you
> or you fired back, it wasn't meant personally.

A third soldier suggests that 'one of the things that characterizes us is the tragedy of being victors. We're simply not used to it. It's got something to do with our education'. A fourth opines that 'the whole business of war is terrible', especially for Jews who are 'not a people that glories in war', yet reluctantly concludes that 'anyone who wants right to be something more than simply an abstract idea – anyone who wants to live by that right – has to be strong'.

Asked how it felt to be 'conquerors in Gaza', a soldier replies:

> It's an absolutely lousy feeling ... a really stinking feeling. ... I remember, as
> soon as they told us our objective was to capture Gaza, spontaneously, right that
> minute, most of the men said: 'Give us anything else to do, any other positions
> to take. We're prepared to do anything rather than be policemen!' ... Later, the
> second-in-command of the brigade came over and asked what I thought of it
> all. 'I'm only asking for one thing,' I told him, 'Get us out of here. It's a
> horrible job, really, horrible. I'm a kibbutznik. It's not for us, we haven't been
> brought up to it. We haven't been trained for it.'

A soldier ordered to 'evacuate' an Arab village finds evidence of a 'Jewish consciousness' in the 'very uncomfortable feeling' he experienced. 'It's very hard, simply on the human level. ... I agreed that it had to be done. I just couldn't stand being on the spot. I took my jeep and drove off, there and back.' His interlocutor concurs that, although the Arabs were expelled, 'the fact that this moral conflict exists is very important'.

The ethical qualms of *The Seventh Day* arise not from what Israel may have done to the Arabs, however, but from what it may have done to itself. Indeed, the soldier is seen as the war's salient victim, the one truly deserving of pity. The book's editor points to the constantly recurring theme of the 'fear of the brutalizing effects of war, and the danger of "losing the semblance of man"'. The hesitant conqueror of Gaza laments that, 'Above all, it destroys human dignity. It destroys the semblance of man.' The soldier anguished by his expulsion of Arab villagers fears that 'Our people, our soldiers, have a special spirit that's liable to be distorted under the conditions of a conquering nation.' The ultimate expression of this sentiment is given by writer Amos Oz (one of the interviewers), who chastises the Arabs for corrupting Israel's soul by forcing it to hate them:

> The question is how long we, as ordinary flesh and blood, can bear it. Can we go on holding the sword in one hand only? ... Can you imagine living this way and still being the same person, the same nation in a few years' time? Can it be done without our getting to the stage in which we'll quite simply hate them? Just hate them. I don't mean that we'll take a delight in killing or turn into sadists. Simply deep bitter hatred for them for having forced such a life on us.

We have seen that, for Shapira, the ethos exemplified in *The Seventh Day* morally redeemed labor Zionism. Yet (1) its practical moral significance was nil, and (2) the same ethos informed Nazism.

As noted above, labor Zionism was not averse to breaking any moral threshold in fulfillment of its 'historical mission'. Its ethos meant only that the violence used must be suited to the desired end and impersonally administered. The decisive point is nicely, if perhaps unwittingly, made by the scholar Robert Alter in a review of Shapira's book in *The New Republic*. Alter credits Ben-Gurion with condemning the 'gratuitous torture' of Arabs during the 1948 war. He observes that 'the abuse of force, as Ben-Gurion understood, was nothing less than a betrayal of Zionism'. The key word is 'gratuitous': torture was permissible, but not 'gratuitous' torture, which was an 'abuse of power'.[65] Only the 'gratuitous' use of torture was, for Ben-Gurion (and presumably Alter), a 'betrayal of Zionism'.[66]

Consider now Nazi ideology. Historian Heinz Höhne observes that, contrary to widespread belief, abusive force was not truly integral to the Final Solution. 'The fact that brutes and sadists made use of the extermination machine does not mean that they were typical of it. Sadism was only one facet of mass extermination and one disapproved of by SS headquarters.' 'Himmler's maxim', he continues, 'was that mass extermination must be carried out cooly and cleanly; even while obeying the official order to commit murder the SS man must remain "decent".' Historian Joachim Fest similarly comments that 'the new type of man of violence recruited by Himmler was concerned with the dispassionate extermination of real or possible opponents, not with the primitive release of sadistic impulses'. Sadism was seen as an example of 'human weakness' that contradicted the ideal type. Himmler's 'perpetually reiterated moral admonishments', notes Fest, were 'in no way a merely feigned moral austerity not "meant seriously": they are founded on the principle of rational terrorism'. Ideological concerns also meshed with pragmatic ones as Himmler worried that sadistic 'excesses', if left unchecked, would undermine military discipline and competence. 'Efficiency', writes Hilberg, 'was the real aim of all that "humaneness".'

'We shall never be rough or heartless where it is not necessary; that is clear', Himmler told an assembly of Nazi murderers at Posen. His lieutenants were exhorted to be 'hard' but 'not become hardened', and to 'intervene at once' should 'some Commander exceed his duty or show signs that his sense of restraint is becoming blurred'. The SS leader even issued definite instructions forbidding his subordinates to indulge in gratuitous torture. An order of August 1935 laid down that 'any independent, individual action against the Jews by any member of the SS is most strictly forbidden'. Concentration-camp guards had to sign a declaration every three months that they did not mistreat prisoners. In autumn 1942, Himmler declared that, in the case of 'unauthorised shootings of Jews', 'if the motive is purely political there should be no punishment unless such is necessary for the maintenance of discipline. If the motive is selfish, sadistic or sexual, judicial punishments should be imposed for murder or manslaughter as the case may be'. And he did on occasion actually have SS sadists punished. In effect, there were two distinct categories of murder: the Final Solution, which, however ghastly, was sanctioned by Germany's 'historical mission', on the one hand, and the gratuitous torture of prisoners or 'excesses', on the other. 'Against the latter category', according to Höhne, the 'SS judicial machine [was] set in motion'.[67]

In his postwar memoir, *Commandant of Auschwitz*, the exemplary 'ultra-Nazi' Rudolf Hoess underlines that he 'never personally hated the Jews', indeed, that 'the emotion of hatred' was 'foreign' to his 'nature'. He reports never having sanctioned the 'horrors of the concentration camps' – by which he evidently intends, not the systematic mass extermination supervised by him, but the sadistic outbursts he claims to have 'used every means at my disposal to stop'. Hence, he continues, 'I myself never maltreated a prisoner, far less killed one. Nor have I ever tolerated maltreatment by my subordinates.' 'I was never cruel, and I have never maltreated anyone, even in a fit of temper.'

Repeatedly, Hoess professes profound disgust at those SS guards who gratuitously tortured camp inmates. 'They did not regard prisoners as human beings at all. ... They regarded the sight of corporal punishment being inflicted as an excellent spectacle, a kind of peasant merrymaking. I was certainly not one of these.' He notes that his 'blood runs cold' as he recalls the 'fearful tortures that were enacted in Auschwitz'. Unfortunately, he confides, 'Nothing can prevail against the malignancy, wickedness and brutality of the individual guard, except keeping him constantly under one's personal supervision.' Special contempt is reserved for the prisoner collaborators given to orgies of violence: 'They were soulless and had no feelings whatsoever. I find it incredible that human beings could ever turn into such beasts. ... It was simply gruesome.'

Hoess delineates the SS ideal negatively as to act from neither 'criminal intent' nor from 'pity'. Both these last motives were seen as 'equally reprehensible'. In his own case, the internal battle is to achieve 'self-mastery and unbending severity' despite an instinctive sympathy for the wretched victims. In the SS, Hoess observes, '"hard necessity" must stifle all softer emotions'. Yet, he returns again and again to the war within himself between the ideal and his own inner fragility. 'I should have ... explained that I was not suited to concentration camp service, because I felt too much sympathy for the prisoners ... [But] I did not wish to reveal my weakness ... that I was too soft.' 'I never grew indifferent to human suffering. I have always seen it and felt for it. Yet because I might not show weakness, I wished to appear hard, lest I be regarded as weak, and had to disregard such feelings.' 'In the face of Eichmann's grim determination I was forced to bury all my human considerations as deeply as possible. ... I had to continue this mass murder and coldly to watch it, without regard for the doubts that were seething deep inside me.'[68]

For the Nazis, Germany had been singled out for a fate at once cruel and glorious. It was the appointed instrument of a task as grisly as it was imperative. Himmler, for instance, viewed his role in the Nazi Judeocide as a 'personal sacrifice' for Germany's 'great historical mission'. At public meetings, the SS leader typically declared that the 'Final Solution' had become 'the most painful question of my life'; that he 'hated this bloody business' that had aroused him to the 'depth of his soul', but everyone must do his duty, 'however hard it might be'; that 'we have completed this painful task out of love for our people'; that it was 'the curse of the great to have to walk over corpses'; that 'we have been called upon to fulfill a repulsive duty' and he 'would not like it if Germans did such a thing gladly'; etc. To assuage his unhappy executioners as they performed their 'heavy task' in the East, Himmler pointed to the moral conflicts that wracked them as evidence of an elevated 'German consciousness':

> I can tell you that it is hideous and frightful for a German to have to see such things. It is so, and if we had not felt it to be hideous and frightful, we should not be Germans. However hideous it may be, it has been necessary for us to do it and it will be necessary in many other cases.[69]

Accordingly, the Nazi mass murderers imagined that they, not the Jews, were the war's authentic victims. 'While mowing down their Jewish victims', Höhne writes, 'the Einsatzgruppen believed that they were entitled to the sympathy of all good Aryans.' As he proceeded with mass murder in Serbia, Gruppenführer Turner lamented that 'the job is not a pretty one'. Paul Blöbel, leader of Einsatzkommando 4A, maintained after the war that the real unfortunates were the liquidators themselves: 'The strain was far heavier in the case of our men who carried out the executions than in that of their victims. From a psychological point of view they had a terrible time.' Himmler praised the Einsatzgruppen for preserving their humanity – the 'semblance of man', as it were – despite the terrible ordeal they had been put through:

> Most of you will know what it means to see a hundred corpses – five hundred – a thousand – lying there. To have gone through this and yet – apart from a few exceptions, examples of human weakness [i.e. sadism] – to have remained decent, this has made us hard. This is a glorious page in our history that has never been written and never shall be written.[70]

Hoess records that he was 'deeply marked' and 'tormented' by the 'mass extermination, with all the attendant circumstances' of 'this monstrous "work"'. Regarding the 'Extermination Order' for the Gypsies – 'my best-loved prisoners, if I may put it that way' – the Auschwitz commandant muses, 'Nothing surely is harder than to grit one's teeth and go through with such a thing, coldly, pitilessly and without mercy.' Forced to bear personal witness to the Final Solution yet suppress the paroxysms of guilt and disgust convulsing him, Hoess's suffering scales exquisite peaks of tortured sublimity. Like a latter-day St Augustine, he confesses:

> I had to exercise intense self-control in order to prevent my innermost doubts and feelings of oppression from becoming apparent. I had to appear cold and indifferent to events that must have wrung the heart of anyone possessed of human feelings. I might not even look away when afraid lest my natural emotions got the upper hand. I had to watch coldly, while the mothers, with laughing or crying children went into the gas-chambers. ... My pity was so great that I longed to vanish from the scene: yet I might not show the slightest trace. I had to watch hour after hour, by day and by night, the extraction of the teeth, the cutting of the hair, the whole grisly, interminable business. I had to stand for hours on end in the ghastly stench, while the mass graves were being opened and the bodies dragged out and burned.[71]

One need not entirely gainsay the moral anxiety of the Nazis[72] to recoil at their repulsive, perverted sanctimoniousness. For, beyond the grotesque pretense they made of being victims, let alone the preeminent victims,[73] what were the Nazis' cloying public displays of angst if not duplicitous exercises in self-extenuation and self-exculpation? Höhne excoriates the 'spurious self-pity' and 'ineradicable ... philistine self-righteousness' of the Nazi executioners that 'prevented them [from] regarding themselves as murderers', indeed, 'enabled them seriously to believe that in fact they were tragic figures'. 'From their grotesquely exaggerated sense of righteousness in the fulfillment of their civic duty', he continues, 'sprang the notion that basically in the midst of all this murder they were men of compassion who had every sympathy with those who must die.'

Recalling Hoess's avowal in his memoir that he 'never grew indifferent to human suffering ... I have always seen it and felt for it', Fest scathingly comments that 'what he believed to be sympathy for his victims was nothing but sentimental pity for himself, who was ordered to carry out such inhuman acts'. 'Thus', Fest further notes, 'he was able to claim merit for a completely self-centered sentimentality, which placed him under no obligation to take any action, and to credit himself with the mendacious self-pity of the "sorrowful murderer" as evidence of his humanitarianism.'[74]

In an essay on Israeli 'kitsch', Hebrew University philosopher Avishai Margalit points to the egregious example of *The Seventh Day*. 'The clear but unstated message of the book', he observes, 'was one of rueful moral self-congratulation: we are beautiful, but we must shoot to kill – but not before we go through an agonizing search of our tormented soul.' We may now add that the 'soldiers' talk' of the 'group of young kibbutzniks' was as unoriginal as it was revolting. Indeed, as Dostoyevsky long ago recognized, 'the most refined shedders of blood have been almost always the most highly civilized gentlemen', to whom all the official terrorists 'could not have held a candle'.[75]

# PART II

# War and Peace

# 5

# To Live or Perish

## *Abba Eban 'Reconstructs' the June 1967 War*

So on the fateful morning of 5 June, when Egyptian forces moved by air and land against Israel's western coast and southern territory, our country's choice was plain. The choice was to live or perish, to defend the national existence or to forfeit it for all time.

Abba Eban, United Nations General Assembly

Propaganda is the art of persuading others of what you do not necessarily believe yourself.

Abba Eban, in Contemporary Aphorisms

The June 1967 war marked a decisive crossroads in the history of the modern Middle East. It redefined the contours of the Arab–Israeli conflict as well as the terms of its settlement. Yet, for all the importance rightly attached to the June war, it has come to be viewed as a remarkably uncomplicated affair – indeed, as the *locus classicus* of a virtuous David prevailing, against all odds, over an odious Goliath.

In this essay, I want to consider the main premises that underpin the standard depiction of the June war. To do so, I will use as my foil the copious body of commentary produced by Abba Eban. Eban is Israel's most authoritative and eloquent voice on foreign affairs. In his varied capacities – ambassador to the United States, UN permanent representative, minister of foreign affairs, memoirist, lecturer, professor, elder statesman, documentarian – Eban more than any other single individual has shaped American perceptions of the Middle East conflict.

Eban's soaring rhetoric in the spring of 1967 was arguably his finest – or, at any rate, most influential – hour. I will juxtapose Eban's rendering of the war's origins and aftermath against what the documentary record and scholarship reveal. My purpose is not *per se* to expose Eban as a liar and fraud – an interesting but not very significant revelation, especially inasmuch as one almost expects a diplomat to prevaricate in the heat of battle and to preserve his and his country's reputation as best he can in retrospect. Rather, it is precisely because the imagery that Eban conjured up in 1967 is not dismissed as partisan but typically informs – indeed, constitutes the *summa summarum* of – conventional wisdom that it merits close scrutiny. One may add that the exposure of the fragile foundations of Eban's interpretive edifice offers insight not only into the mythology surrounding the June war but also into the dominant culture that sustains that mythology.

In the first section, I will examine the main junctures on the road to the June war. I will argue that Eban's account effaces Israel's provocation of Nasser and its responsibility for the failed diplomacy. In the second section, I will examine Eban's justifications for Israel's preemptive attack. I will argue that none of Eban's rationales can withstand critical scrutiny. In the third section, I will examine the international consensus that crystallized in the war's wake as embodied in United Nations Resolution 242. I will argue that Eban's interpretation of 242 stands well outside that consensus.

## Diplomacy

A massive Israeli 'retaliatory' strike has more than once ignited the fuse that ended in an explosion in the Middle East.

E.L.M. Burns, chief of staff of United Nations forces in the Middle East during the mid-1950s, testifies that before Israel's raid on Gaza in February 1955, 'the facts did not indicate … a critical situation'. Kennett Love likewise reports that 'violence was infrequent on the Egyptian–Israeli frontier before Gaza'. Indeed, according to Donald Neff, 'Nasser since coming to power two-and-a-half years earlier, had shown scant interest in the usual Arab expressions of hatred for Israel'. The Arab nationalist leader's energies were focused inward as he sought to shepherd Egypt into the modern world. But the unprecedentedly bloody Israeli assault, which left thirty-eight Egyptian soldiers and civilians dead and nearly as many wounded, changed everything. It was – in Burns's words – the 'decisive event [that] set a trend which continued until Israel invaded the Sinai in October 1956'.[1]

In mid-November 1966, Israel embarked on its largest military action since the Suez war. An armored brigade of nearly 4,000 men attacked the West Bank town of Samu in the Hebron hills, methodically destroying 125 homes, a clinic, a school, and a workshop, and killing eighteen Jordanian soldiers as well. (One Israeli soldier was killed.) Condemning the raid at the United Nations, US Ambassador Arthur Goldberg noted that the toll it took 'in human lives and in destruction far surpasses the cumulative total of the various acts of terrorism conducted against the frontiers of Israel'. 'I wish to make it absolutely clear,' he pronounced, 'that this large-scale military action cannot be justified, explained away or excused by the incidents which preceded it and in which the Government of Jordan has not been implicated.'[2]

The ostensible purpose of the Israeli attack was to punish King Hussein for, and force him to curb, Palestinian infiltration. Guerrillas operating from Jordanian territory had killed three Israelis in October and early November. Yet, leaving to one side that Israel's 'reprisal' policy was not only contrary to international law but counterproductive as well,[3] the fact is that, as Odd Bull, chief of staff of UN forces in the Middle East at the time, recalled, 'the Jordanian authorities did all they possibly could to stop infiltration'. A UN military observer on the Israel–Jordan border noted even more emphatically that 'Jordan's efforts to curb infiltrators reached the total capabilities of the country'. Indeed, until the June 1967 war, more Palestinians were killed by Jordanian soldiers attempting to enter Israel than by the Israelis themselves. And, only a few months before the Samu attack, King Hussein had taken the extraordinary step of arresting most of the Palestine Liberation Organization staff in Amman and closing its offices.[4]

Samu's main legacy was the poisoning of relations and exacerbating of already bitter rivalries in the Arab world. As one historian observed, 'by its raid on Samu, Israel, as it no doubt calculated, sharpened Arab divisions, radicalized opinion, and set its lamentably weak and hopelessly quarrelsome neighbors lurching amid mutual plots and accusations, to the very edge of the precipice'. In particular, a new round of mutual recriminations was fueled with Radio Jordan, for example, taunting Nasser for his 'empty rhetoric' in not rising to the Kingdom's defense and for using the United Nations Emergency Force (UNEF) stationed in Sinai and Gaza as a pretext for not confronting Israel.[5]

In early April, a border incident between Israel and Syria climaxed in a major aerial engagement. Six Syrian planes were shot down, one over Damascus. Tensions between the two countries continued to mount in the ensuing month. In the second week of May, Israeli officials threatened to launch a full-scale attack on Syria. General Yitzak Rabin, the chief of staff, was alleged to have announced on Israeli radio that 'the moment is coming when we will march on Damascus to overthrow the Syrian government'. The Israeli chief of military intelligence menacingly warned of a 'military action of great size and strength' against Syria. Prime Minister Eshkol declared that Israel 'may have to teach Syria a sharper lesson' than that of early April. In a front-page dispatch headlined 'Israelis Ponder Blow at Syrians – Some Leaders Decide That Force Is the Only Way to Curtail Terrorism', the *New York Times* reported that 'some Israeli leaders have decided that the use of force against Syria may be the only way to curtail increasing terrorism. ... This has become apparent in talks with highly qualified and informed Israelis.' Citing 'authoritative sources', the *Jerusalem Post* reported that 'a major military clash with Syria seemed inevitable', in the form of a military expedition that would 'take the wind out of the Syrians' sails once and for all'.[6]

The Israeli threats were not viewed as idle in Arab capitals, or elsewhere. In a report to the Security Council on the escalating Middle East crisis, Secretary-General U Thant observed that, 'in recent weeks, ... reports emanating from Israel have attributed to some high officials in that State statements so threatening as to be particularly inflammatory in the sense that they could only heighten emotions and thereby increase tensions on the other side of the lines'. U Thant later recalled that

> rumors of an impending blow against Syria were current throughout Israel. ... [T]hey reached Cairo and other Arab capitals, where they generated the belief that Israel was about to mount a massive attack on Syria. ... Bellicose statements by Israeli leaders ... created ... panic in the Arab world.

The US State Department 'cautioned' Israel against the 'unsettling effects' of its 'threatening statements', and the US *chargé d'affaires* in Cairo advised Egypt's Foreign Minister that the Israeli threats should be taken 'most seriously'. *Le Monde* editorialized that 'it was only a matter of time' before Israel launched an attack on Syria.[7]

Eban ridicules the rumors of an impending Israeli assault on Syria as 'one of the most effective false alarms in history', as if it were not the 'bellicose statements by Israeli leaders' (U Thant) that fomented these rumors. Indeed, Eban himself conceded that, 'if there had been a little more Israeli silence, the sum of human wisdom would probably have remained intact'. What is more, the alarms were almost certainly *not* false. According to Eban, Israel 'never ... intended, or even conceived' attacking Syria. He heaps scorn on the Soviet intelligence report passed to Egypt and Syria of an imminent Israeli attack and deems 'the "information" supplied by the Soviet Union' the 'proximate cause of the 1967 war'. Yet, although apparently erring in details, the Soviet intelligence report was not wide of the mark in its general thrust. Richard Parker reports that, by mid-May, 'the question was not whether Israel was going to strike' at Syria, but 'when and how', and that 'everyone knew [it] was about to happen'. Michael Brecher states flatly in his authoritative study that Israel's Cabinet had decided in early May that, if 'noncoercive methods of persuasion' against Syria failed, it 'would launch a limited retaliation raid'. The Soviets, according to Parker, had 'gotten wind' of the Israeli Cabinet decision.[8]

Coming fast on the heels of the Samu raid and the aerial battle over Syria, the Israeli threats against the Damascus regime compelled Nasser to act. Egypt had entered into a military pact with Syria the previous November. Syria was now calling on its ally to respond with more than fiery rhetoric. Radio Jordan was again mocking Nasser's pretensions, daring the Egyptian leader to close the Gulf of Aqaba and 'hit Israel where it hurts'.[9]

On 14 May, Nasser moved Egyptian troops into the Sinai and subsequently requested the complete withdrawal of UNEF from Sinai, the Gaza and Sharm-el-Shaykh overlooking the Straits of Tiran. Within days, the UNEF had completed its withdrawal from Sharm-el-Shaykh, Egyptian troops moved in to occupy it and Nasser announced that the Straits of Tiran would be closed to Israeli shipping.

The Egyptian leader apparently did not intend so dramatic a concatenation of gestures. He wanted only that UNEF readjust its deployment in the Sinai but did not desire a UNEF withdrawal, especially from Sharm-el-Shaykh. Confronted with an all-or-nothing ultimatum from UN Secretary-General U Thant that left him with no 'face-saving device' (Rikhye), Nasser opted for complete withdrawal.[10]

To Eban, 'the wanton irresponsibility' of Nasser's action 'defies indulgence'. Indeed, he rates it 'one of the most unprovoked actions in international history'. Yet in a memo to President Johnson, National Security Advisor Walt Rostow recognized that Nasser 'probably feels his prestige would suffer irreparably if he failed a third time to come to the aid of an Arab nation attacked by Israel'. Odd Bull, chief of staff of the UN forces, similarly recalled in his memoir that Nasser 'was obliged to act if his reputation in the Arab world was not to suffer, because he had been subjected to a lot of criticism on the ground that he was sheltering behind UNEF'. Even Moshe Dayan conceded that 'the nature and scale of our reprisal actions against Syria and Jordan had left Nasser with no choice but to defend his image and prestige in his own country and throughout the Arab world, thereby setting off a train of escalation in the entire Arab region'.[11]

Acknowledging its legality, U Thant nonetheless expressed 'deep misgivings' about Nasser's decision to terminate the UNEF mission, especially in light of 'the prevailing tensions and dangers throughout the area'. The Secretary-General did not, however, reserve criticism for Egypt alone. First, he recalled that the Egyptian–Israeli Mixed Armistice Commission (EIMAC), established as part of the agreements that ended the 1948 war, 'could, as it did prior to the establishment of UNEF, provide a limited form of United Nations presence in the area'. Yet, EIMAC had become a dead letter because Israel 'unilaterally' withdrew from it at the time of the Suez war in an action that, unlike Nasser's, was a 'clear defiance of U.N. resolutions'. Throughout the 1967 crisis, Egypt expressed a strong willingness to reactivate and even expand the role of EIMAC. The Israeli Cabinet in late May officially rebuffed any and all such proposals.[12]

U Thant also proposed that Israel allow the UNEF to be repositioned on its side of the border. Indeed, the Secretary-General pointedly recalled that the original February 1957 General Assembly resolution mandating deployment of the UNEF 'envisaged' that it would be stationed on 'both sides' of the Egyptian–Israeli armistice demarcation line. (Egypt had acceded to the General Assembly request; Israel had not. U Thant also noted that, in the course of the decade that had since elapsed, Israeli troops 'regularly patrolled alongside the line and now and again created provocations by violating it'.) But Israel dismissed as 'entirely unacceptable' U Thant's recommendation. Repeated entreaties by the United States, Britain and especially Canada all fell on deaf ears. Even an alternative proposal at the end of May to reactivate UNEF on both sides of the Egyptian–Israeli frontier and along the Gaza Strip was peremptorily dismissed by Israel.[13]

In his memoir, U Thant conjectured that 'if only Israel had agreed to permit UNEF to be stationed on its side of the border, even for a short duration, the course of history could have been different. Diplomatic efforts to avert the pending catastrophe might have prevailed; war might have been averted'. His speculation received an authoritative endorsement from Odd Bull, who stated that 'it is quite possible that the 1967 war could have been avoided' had Israel acceded to the Secretary-General's request.[14]

For Eban, however, 'there is no validity' to such a surmise. He argues that UNEF 'had relevance to Sharm el-sheikh and Gaza and to nowhere else'. Yet, Eban himself maintained that 'the effect' of UNEF's withdrawal was 'to make Sinai safe for belligerency', and that 'Egyptian preparations in the Sinai' posed the 'chief danger' to Israel. It is unclear, then, why a UNEF presence on the Israeli border with Sinai would have lacked 'relevance'. Indeed, at a news conference in late May, Eban had pointed to the 'buildup of forces in Sinai' as a 'main symptom' of the crisis and assailed U Thant's withdrawal decision precisely because 'in 1957, the object of the U.N. presence was to insure that ... there would be a less explosive situation regarding the balance of forces in Sinai'. Eban also does not explain why the UNEF could not have been redeployed on the Israeli side of the Gaza border.[15]

In late May, the UN Secretary-General journeyed to Cairo personally to mediate the crisis. His minimum aim was to get both parties to agree to a 'breathing spell' which would 'allow tension to subside from its present explosive level' and give the Security Council time 'to deal with the underlying causes' and 'seek solutions'. In this spirit, U Thant presented Nasser with a proposal reportedly backed by the United States. Essentially, it called for a two-week moratorium in the Straits of Tiran similar to the one that U Thant had arranged during the Cuban missile crisis – Israel would refrain from sending and Egypt from inspecting ships – and a renewed effort at diplomacy. A special UN representative would be appointed for the area. Egypt assented, a gesture that the Secretary-General reckoned as 'very significant'. There was, however, one insuperable hitch. As U Thant recalled: 'Israel did not agree to either of these conditions.' The rationale adduced by Israel's ambassador was that Egypt 'was bent on war'. Indeed, he got the motive right – but the country wrong. Brian Urquhart, a senior UN official, concluded in his memoir that 'Israel, no doubt having decided on military action, turned down U Thant's ideas'.[16]

The United States also tried its hand at mediation. Robert Anderson, a former Treasury Secretary, and Charles Yost, a retired ambassador, met with Egyptian officials in late May and early June. A 'breakthrough in the crisis' – in Neff's words – was apparently reached. Nasser indicated that he was open to World Court arbitration of the dispute over the Straits of Tiran, and perhaps also – accounts are very contradictory – to an easing of the blockade that would allow for the passage of oil pending the Court's decision. Crucially, the Egyptian leader agreed to send his vice-president to Washington by week's end to explore a diplomatic settlement.[17]

The Washington meeting never happened. Israel struck before it could take place. In so doing, it not only preempted negotiations but broke a pledge given to Johnson at the end of May not to take unilateral action before two weeks. Dean Rusk, then Secretary of State, later recalled that, between the Egyptian vice-president's anticipated trip and Israeli assurances of restraint, the mood in Washington in early June was that 'we had a good chance to de-escalate the crisis'. But the Israeli attack put a stop to that. 'We were shocked ... and angry as hell', Rusk continued in a passage worth quoting in full,

> when the Israelis launched the surprise offensive. They attacked on a Monday, knowing that on Wednesday the Egyptian vice-president would arrive in Washington to talk about re-opening the Strait of Tiran. We might not have succeeded in getting Egypt to reopen the strait, but it was a *real possibility*. (my emphasis)[18]

Rusk's speculation that Egypt may have been amenable to compromise is sustained by a most improbable source. *Middle East Record* is a quasi-official Israeli publication assembled by the Shiloah Center for Middle Eastern and African Studies in Tel Aviv. In volume 3, a comprehensive synthesis of the June war, the editors observe that 'a number of facts seem to indicate Abdel Nasser's belief in the possibility of terminating ... the conflict through diplomacy'. Specifically, they point to 'the display of his willingness to revive' EIMAC; 'his suggestion that the issue of navigation through the Straits of Tiran be taken to the international Court of Justice'; and 'his vagueness' at the end of May 'on the exact definition of the materials that were not to be permitted through the Straits to Israel'.[19]

Eban asserts that 'Israel has never worked harder to prevent a war than it did' in June 1967. Indeed, with the Israeli victory in mind, he told the Knesset that 'wars are most often won by those who have made the greatest efforts to prevent them'. Yet, the one – and only – diplomatic undertaking that Israel embraced in 1967 was with gunboats. It lent support to a US-backed plan, ultimately abortive, to break Nasser's blockade with a multinational armada. In view of the record surveyed above – repudiation of UN mediation efforts on the one hand, and preemption of US mediation efforts on the other – Eban's testimonial that 'Israel has never worked harder' casts an unwonted light on the actual history of Israeli diplomacy.[20]

## Deception

The central rationale Israel adduced for preemptively attacking Egypt was that it faced imminent destruction. Eban recalled June 1967 as 'the month of decision' in which 'the "final solution" was at hand'. 'Israel's defensive action', he emphasized on another occasion, 'was taken when the choice was to live or to perish, to protect the national existence or to forfeit it for all time'. Indeed, the chapter of his most recent memoir devoted to the war is entitled 'To Live or Perish: 1967'. The prologue of the Cabinet decision to launch a preemptive strike read that 'the Government ascertained that the armies of Egypt, Syria and Jordan are deployed for immediate multi-front aggression, threatening the very existence of the state'. Prime Minister Levi Eshkol later told the Knesset that 'the existence of the state' had 'hung in the balance'.[21]

Eban enumerates three threats to Israel's 'national existence' on the eve of the June war: (1) 'Syrian-based terrorism', (2) 'Egyptian troop concentrations in Sinai after the departure of the United Nations forces', and (3) 'the blockade of the Straits of Tiran'. I will examine each of these claims in turn.[22]

## 'Syrian-based terrorism'

According to Eban, the threat posed by 'Syrian-based terrorism' assumed two forms: 'bombardments of our northern settlements' and 'terrorist raids'. The combined effect of these attacks was purportedly to render the 'security predicament' of Israel 'acute'. Although the issues raised by the bombardments and raids are not unrelated, I will, for clarity's sake, address each separately.[23]

Syrian shelling from the Golan Heights of Israel's northern settlements had its provenance in the Israeli–Syrian armistice agreement that ended the 1948 war. The accord established demilitarized zones (DMZs) between the two countries. 'The situation deteriorated', according to Odd Bull, 'as the Israelis gradually took control over that part of the demilitarized zones which lay inside the former national boundaries of Palestine' in blatant violation of the UN-brokered accord. Arab villagers residing in the DMZs were evicted and their dwellings demolished, 'as the status quo was all the time being altered by Israel in her favor.' The Security Council called on Israel to let the villagers return, but Israel held fast. 'In the course of time,' Bull observed, 'all the Arab villages disappeared' in wide swaths of the DMZs.[24]

Major-General Carl Von Horn, who served as chief of staff of the UN forces before Bull, similarly recalled that, inside the Syrian–Israeli DMZs, 'property changed hands, invariably in one direction', so that before long Israel was 'claiming the right to exploit all the land'. 'Gradually', he continued, 'beneath the glowering eyes of the Syrians, who held the high ground overlooking the zone, the area had become a network of Israeli canals and irrigation channels edging up against and always encroaching on Arab-owned property.' 'This deliberate poaching was bitterly resented by the Syrians.' Israel's 'premeditated' policy, Horn concluded, was 'to get all the Arabs out of the way by fair means or foul'.[25]

US consular cables from Jerusalem told much the same story. One from July 1964 stated that 'Arabs concerned selves basically with preservation situation envisioned in [the UN armistice agreements] while Israel consistently sought gain full control.' Israel, it continued, was 'emerging victorious largely because UN never able oppose aggressive and armed Israeli occupation and assertion actual control over such areas, and Arab neighbors not really prepared for required fighting'. The cable concluded that UN observers generally credited Syria for 'restraint over long period in face Israel seizure control in [DMZs] by force or constant threat using it'.[26]

Syrian shelling from the Golan Heights aimed to deter the Israeli encroachments. 'There was a certain pattern', a recent study reports, 'of action and reaction. Israeli tractors would move into disputed areas, often with the support of armed Israeli police. The Syrians would fire from their high ground positions, and would often shell Israeli settlements in the Huleh valley. By trying to oppose the Israeli challenge, Syria drew on its head punitive Israeli raids, including air strikes.' Undoubtedly, the shelling was also occasionally vindictive. On the latter point, Bull's reflections are worth quoting in full:

> I imagine that a number of those Arabs evicted settled somewhere in the Golan Heights and that their children have watched the land that had been in their families for hundreds of years being cultivated by Israeli farmers. From time to time they opened fire on these farmers. That, of course, was a violation of the armistice agreement, though I could not help thinking that in similar circumstances Norwegian peasants would almost certainly have acted in the same way.[27]

One hastens to add that Syrian shelling from the Heights was desultory, indeed, largely symbolic. This was in no small part due to the punishing Israeli 'retaliatory' strikes. Using the flimsiest of pretexts, these attacks occasionally even reached beyond the DMZs into Syria proper. In one notorious case in December 1955 that was soundly condemned by the Security Council as a 'flagrant violation' of the armistice agreements, fifty-six Syrians were killed. In this regard, it should be noted that the strategic advantage that Syria enjoyed from the Golan Heights 'disappeared completely', according to U Thant, 'when the military exchange escalated to the level of air battles, in which Israel had a decided advantage'. At any rate, there was not one civilian casualty on Israel's northern border due to Syrian shelling for the six-month period leading up to the June 1967 war.[28]

The most exhaustive review to date for the 1949–67 period concludes that the standard depiction of Israel as the innocent victim of 'Syrian firing from the Golan Heights' is basically 'historical revisionism':

> Indeed, some Syrian shells did fall on settlements as well as military positions inside Israel, along with many more inside the demilitarized zone. There is, however, no Security Council resolution condemning Syria for aggressive actions against Israel during this period, nor is there a veto of such a resolution. There are four Security Council resolutions condemning Israel. UN observers in the field and UN votes in New York are unanimous in holding that principal responsibility for the Syrian–Israeli border hostilities belongs to Israel.[29]

Syrian-backed Palestinian commando raids against Israel began in earnest after a radical coup in Damascus in February 1966. Incendiary rhetoric emanating from Syria – fueled by inter-Arab rivalries – urged that a 'people's war' be mounted to liberate Palestine. Yet, the basic motive behind Syrian support of the Palestinian guerrillas seems to have been rather more prosaic – the Israeli incursions in the DMZs. UNEF head Rikhye reports that the intensification of Palestinian attacks on Israel 'resulted from the controversy over cultivation rights in the Demilitarized Zone between Israel and Syria'. Indeed, General Aharon Yaariv, head of Israeli military intelligence, frankly acknowledged a few weeks before the June war that Syria 'uses this weapon of guerrilla activity' because 'we are bent upon establishing ... certain facts along the border'.[30]

To be sure, Palestinians harbored real grievances of their own against Israel. In particular, Israel continued to ignore a December 1948 General Assembly resolution – affirmed at every subsequent session of the Assembly – which mandated that 'refugees wishing to return to their homes' should 'be permitted to do so', or, if they so elected, receive compensation for lost property. Thus, U Thant causally connected the Palestinians' decision to 'form their own independent guerrilla organizations to harass Israel' with Israel's 'consistent refusal to comply with the recommendations of the General Assembly regarding the Palestinian refugees'.[31]

U Thant scored the Syrian-backed Palestinian raids – deplored by him as 'insidious' and 'contrary to the letter and spirit of the Armistice Agreements' – as a 'major factor' aggravating the Middle East crisis. Indeed, Palestinian and Israel leaders both ascribed a lethal potency to the guerrilla attacks. Yet, the true picture seems to have been rather more humble. In a notably sober analysis soon after the June war, former chief of Israeli military intelligence Yehoshaphat Harkabi concluded that the 'operational achievements' of the Palestinian guerrillas 'in the thirty months from its debut to the Six-Day war' were 'not impressive by any standard' and certainly posed no danger to 'Israel's national life'. He reports that there were all of 14 Israeli casualties (4 civilians, 4 policemen and 6 soldiers) for the entire two-and-a-half-year period. Indeed, in that same time span there were more than 800 Israeli fatalities in auto accidents. Conceding – with inimitable hyperbole – that the guerrilla attacks did not 'affect thousands' of lives or bring about 'a collapse' of national life, Eban goes on to acknowledge that it would be 'absurd to imagine' that they could have endangered 'anything as solid as the State of Israel'.[32]

The illusoriness of the threat posed by Syria – in the Golan Heights as well as through its support of Palestinian commandos – was pointed up in the actual unfolding of the June war. The 'opening of the northern front', reflect two historians, 'came as an afterthought.' Several days of fighting elapsed before a decision was even taken to attack Syria. Moreover, it was an independent initiative of Moshe Dayan's, reportedly reached with great reluctance. Rabin wrote in his memoir that he has 'never grasped the reasons' for Dayan's decision to launch the assault. Ezer

Weizman, who likewise could give 'no explanation' for Dayan's action, rhetorically asked years later, 'if indeed the Syrian enemy threatened to destroy us, why did we wait three days before we attacked it?'[33]

### 'Egyptian troop concentrations in the Sinai'

Eban points to the Egyptian troop concentrations in the Sinai as Israel's 'chief danger' on the eve of its preemptive attack. If so, one is forced to conclude that the known danger facing Israel could not have been very great at all. For the only two issues in the otherwise highly contentious literature on the June 1967 war on which a consensus seems to exist are: (a) there was no evidence at the time that Nasser intended to attack; and (b) even if he did, it was taken for granted that Israel would easily thrash him.[34]

In the midst of its June offensive Israel informed the Security Council that it had 'documentary proof' that Egypt 'had prepared the assault on Israel in all its military details'. Yet, all the available evidence at the time pointed to the conclusion that Egypt did not intend to attack. In late May, Rabin, who was chief of staff, told the Israeli Cabinet that the Egyptian forces in the Sinai were still in a defensive posture. An exhaustive US intelligence review at the end of the month could find no evidence that Egypt was planning to attack. US President Johnson told Eban that even after instructing his 'experts to assume all the facts that the Israelis had given them to be true', it was still 'their unanimous view that there is no Egyptian intention to make an imminent attack' – a conclusion, according to Eban, also reached by Israeli intelligence. Rikhye, who toured the Egyptian front, confirms that Egyptian troops were not poised for an offensive. Reporting from Cairo for the *New York Times* on the eve of Israel's assault, James Reston observed that Egypt 'does not want war and it is certainly not ready for war'. Reston's assessment was so widely held that it was echoed by Mossad chief Meir Amit in almost identical terms: 'Egypt was not ready for a war; and Nasser did not want a war.'[35]

Rabin remarked after Israel's victory that he 'did not believe that Nasser wanted war'. 'The two divisions he sent into Sinai on May 14', the chief of staff surmised, 'would not have been enough to unleash an offensive. He knew it and we knew it.' The Israeli-compiled *Middle East Record* states that 'most observers agree' that Nasser did not intend to launch an attack 'and that his pledges to U Thant and to the Great Powers not to start shooting should, therefore, be accepted at their face value'. Menachem Begin, who was a member of the National Unity government in June 1967, conceded many years later that 'we had a choice'. 'The Egyptian army concentrations in the Sinai approaches', he cautioned, 'do not prove that Nasser was really about to attack us. We must be honest with ourselves. We decided to attack him.'[36]

Yet, the most impressive testimony that Israel did not believe Nasser intended to give battle comes from Eban himself. Told by U Thant of Nasser's promise not to attack Israel, Eban recalls that he 'found this assurance convincing', quipping, 'Nasser did not want war; he wanted victory without war'.[37]

The mortal threat that Nasser allegedly posed to Israel in 1967 is as chimerical as his intention to attack it. The CIA estimated in late May that Israel would win a war against one or all of the Arab countries, whichever struck the first blow, in roughly a week. Richard Helms, then chief of the CIA, took special pride that 'we predicted almost within the day how long the war would last if it began'. Johnson told Eban that 'all our intelligence people are unanimous that if Egypt attacks, you will whip the hell out of them'. Former Defense Secretary Robert McNamara reports in his recent memoir that, as of 2 June, the estimates of British and US intelligence concurred that Israel would win 'beyond a shadow of a doubt'; the only question was whether it would take Israel closer to seven or ten days. Nicholas de B. Katzenbach, then Undersecretary of State, reminisced that, on the basis of the information furnished them, Cabinet and sub-Cabinet officers were so certain of an Israeli victory that they made absolutely no contingency plans for either a protracted contest or the even more unlikely prospect of an Israeli defeat.

Menachem Begin recalled that, in the penultimate Ministerial Committee on Defense meeting before the surprise attack, the IDF commanders 'had no doubts of victory' and 'expressed their belief not only in the strength of the army but also in its ability to rout the enemy'. Eban confirms that 'our military advisers were ... fervent in the promise of victory'. In his standard military history of the Arab–Israeli conflict, Dupuy reports that, as war loomed on the horizon in June 1967, 'there were no doubts in the minds of Israeli military leaders that their own troops were technologically more sophisticated, or that they would be victorious in the event of another conflict'. Indeed, 'they expected to be as successful as in the 1956 War'.[38]

Eban alleges that the pact that Jordan signed with Egypt in the last days of May marked a 'most serious aggravation of our condition'. It was a 'sensational development', the effects of which 'would be no less profound, and even more lasting, than anything we might face on the Egyptian front'. 'Our fortunes', Eban solemnly intones, 'were declining and our flame was burning low.' Yet as noted above, it was foreseen that Israel would easily prevail even against a joint Arab attack. Indeed, as a military historian of the June war recently observed, not only had Israel 'not grown weaker' after the pact's signing, Egypt 'had not grown one iota stronger'. The addition of Jordanian (and other Arab) forces 'actually created more military problems than it had solved political ones'. One may further note that the Jordanian 'front' possessed as much reality as Eban's expiring flame. The Royal Jordanian Army was basically a 'showpiece' whose 'primary function was to serve as a palace guard'. The Jordanian infantry was 'armed mainly with British rifles of World War II vintage', and the bulk of the artillery consisted of 'old British guns'. As for the Royal Jordanian air force, 'its entire striking power was represented in the form of 24 obsolete British fighter-bombers'.[39]

General (res.) Mattityahu Peled, one of the architects of the June war, observed in 1972 that the claim that Israel was under the menace of destruction was a 'bluff', adding that, for all the pretense that Israel is 'in the midst of an anguished struggle for its existence and can be exterminated at any moment', the truth is that, already 'since 1949' no country has been able to mortally threaten it. Ezer Weizman, who did much of the operational planning for the June war, concurred that 'there was no threat of destruction' against Israel in 1967 and that 'the threat of destruction was already removed from Israel during the War of Independence'. He further noted that, 'had the Egyptians attacked first, they would have also then suffered a complete defeat', with 'maybe 13 hours being needed instead of only three' to 'command control of the air'.[40]

In his maiden speech to the Security Council after Israel's preemptive strike, Eban purported that, 'as time went on, there was no doubt that our margin of general security was becoming smaller and smaller'. Yet, the chair of the US Joint Chiefs of Staff told Johnson at the end of May that Israel could remain at its current level of mobilization for two months without jeopardizing its security. The United States had also committed itself to fully footing the bill for Israel's mobilization.[41]

Indeed, the most convincing witness against Eban is – again – Eban himself. In his memoirs, Eban reveals that, not only did Israel not face mortal danger from an Arab attack, but its prospects steadily improved with each day's passing. He reports that in the final days before the preemptive strike Israel's 'military position' became 'predictably better, and that of Egypt unexpectedly worse'; that the 'Arab states' were 'vastly enlarging their own vulnerability'; and that 'stories of chaotic dislocation among Egyptian forces in the Sinai were becoming more frequent and authoritative' while 'equipment we previously ordered from Europe was reaching us every day'.

Eban also cites an 'impressive' US military intelligence review at the end of May which found that 'the days and hours that were passing did not ... increase the inability of Israel to defend herself successfully', but, 'on the contrary, it was Egyptian forces who were increasing their vulnerability'. 'Israel's lines of supply and communication were short and efficient' whereas 'Egypt's were a nightmare of distance and complexity'. 'Israel's immediate security was in good shape', it concluded, while 'Egyptian difficulties would grow every hour.' Dupuy's chapter subheading for the Sinai mobilization on the eve of the war reads 'CONFUSION CONFOUNDED'.[42]

### 'Blockade of the Straits of Tiran'

One of Eban's central claims was that Egypt's blockade of the Straits of Tiran preventing access to the port of Eilat was an 'attempt at strangulation'. In effect, it constituted an 'act of war'. Israel's preemptive attack accordingly was 'a reaction, not an initiative'.[43]

Until the Suez war, the Straits of Tiran were closed to ships headed for Israel's port city of Eilat. Nasser's avowed reason for imposing the blockade was Israel's refusal to honor the UN resolutions calling on it to allow the Palestinian refugees expelled during the 1948 war to return home.[44]

Israel tried to pry open the Straits in the course of the 1956 invasion when it occupied Sinai and Sharm-el-Shaykh. However, it was compelled to terminate the occupation without international sanction of its right of passage. To be sure, Israel did reach understandings with the United States that forcefully upheld its claims, but these were strictly bilateral. The United Nations, declared Secretary-General Dag Hammarskjold, could not 'condone a change of the *status juris* resulting from military action contrary to the provisions of the Charter'. Accordingly, he stipulated that 'the *status juris* existing prior to' Israel's attack must be 're-established by a withdrawal of troops, and the relinquishment or nullification of rights asserted in territories covered by the military action and depending on it'. The Israeli withdrawal, Hammarskjold subsequently reported, 'was un-conditional in accordance with the decision of the General Assembly'. This view was echoed in the United Nations by the US representative, Henry Cabot Lodge. Indeed, President Eisenhower had delivered perhaps the most impassioned defense of the principle that Israel's withdrawal must be without conditions, asking rhetorically if 'a nation which attacks and occupies a foreign territory in the face of United Nations disapproval should be allowed to impose conditions on its withdrawal?'[45]

As Israeli troops withdrew from Sharm-el-Shaykh, UNEF moved in to replace them. But the deployment of UNEF, cautioned Hammarskjold, 'should not be used so as to prejudge the solution of the controversial questions involved' in the Straits of Tiran. The Secretary-General's own view was that the unusual issues posed by the Straits had not yet been adjudicated. Thus, 'a legal controversy exists as to the extent of the right of innocent passage through these waters'.[46]

Although reckoning Nasser's decision 'at this moment' to reimpose the blockade of the Straits a 'blunder', U Thant also acknowledged that the 'legal aspects' of the case had been far from settled. Indeed, he cited as a 'powerful statement' the defense of Egypt's position put forth by Harvard Law Professor Roger Fisher. Fisher's opinion is worth quoting at length as both a lucid and authoritative exposition of the legal questions at issue. Noting that 'the United States press reports about the Gulf of Aqaba situation were grossly one-sided', Fisher continued:

> The United Arab Republic had a good legal case for restricting traffic through the Strait of Tiran. First, it is debatable whether international law confers any right of innocent passage through such a waterway. Despite an Israeli request, the International Law Commission in 1956 found no rule which would govern the Strait of Tiran. Although the 1958 Convention on the Territorial Sea does provide for innocent passage through such straits, the United States Representative, Arthur Dean, called this 'a new rule' and the U.A.R. has not signed the treaty. There are, of course, good arguments on the Israeli side too, and an impartial international court might well conclude that a right of innocent passage through the Strait of Tiran does exist.
>
> But a right of innocent passage is not a right of free passage for any cargo at any time. In the words of the Convention on the Territorial Sea: 'Passage is innocent so long as it is not prejudicial to the peace, good order or security of the coastal state.'
>
> In April Israel conducted a major retaliatory raid on Syria and threatened raids of still greater size. In this situation was Egypt required by international law to continue to allow Israel to bring in oil and other strategic supplies through Egyptian territory – supplies which Israel could use to conduct further military raids? That was the critical question of law.

Although 'the U.A.R. would have had a better case if it had announced that the closing was temporary and subject to review by the International Court', Fisher significantly concluded,

> taking the facts as they were, I, as an international lawyer, would rather defend before the International Court of Justice the legality of the U.A.R's action in closing the Strait of Tiran than to argue the other side of the case, and I would certainly rather do so than to defend the legality of the preventive war which Israel launched.[47]

As suggested above, the official US position held that, barring a 'contrary decision' by the World Court, Israel had a right of 'free and innocent passage' through the Straits. Nonetheless, Secretary of State Dulles acknowledged that it was a 'highly complicated question of international law' and that there was a 'certain amount of plausibility' to the Egyptian view. This was also the opinion of US legal scholars, who advised World Court adjudication. Charles Yost, the US envoy sent to negotiate with Nasser, conceded that Egypt's case was 'at least' arguable and, ultimately, urged referring the issue to the International Court of Justice. J. William Fulbright, chair of the Senate's Foreign Relations Committee, similarly recommended at the end of May that the conflict be moved to the World Court. And indeed, as we saw above, Nasser had acquiesced in World Court arbitration. As to the other party to the conflict, Quandt conjectures with considerable understatement that Israel would have found intervention by the World Court 'impossible to accept'. Finally, in the opinion of the State Department's legal adviser, international law almost certainly did not confer on Israel the right to initiate the use of armed force against the UAR in the absence of an armed attack by the UAR on Israel. A blockade, he observed in a memorandum to Rusk, did not of itself constitute, an armed attack, and self-defense did not cover general hostilities against the UAR.[48]

The legal issue aside, Israel claimed that it had come to be mortally dependent on trade through Eilat. In a Knesset speech on the morrow of Nasser's announcement, Prime Minister Eshkol pointed to Eilat as the port of 'hundreds of sailings of ships under dozens of flags' and the hub of a 'far-flung network of commerce and transport'. Israel's UN ambassador, Gideon Rafael, described Eilat as a 'thriving port and industrial center' with 'considerable trade passing through this essential maritime route'. Without free passage through the Straits, Eban asserted, Israel would be 'stunted and humiliated'. In a yet more vivid image, Eban charged that Israel was being 'strangled' by Nasser's blockade as it was condemned to 'breathe with a single lung'. 'The choice for Israel', Eban perorated, 'was drastic – slow strangulation or rapid, solitary death.'[49]

In the real world, the picture was rather less forbidding. The official terms of the blockade barred all Israeli-flagged vessels, and non-Israeli-flagged vessels carrying strategic cargo, from passing through the Straits. Yet, according to the UN Secretariat, not a single Israeli-flagged vessel had used the port of Eilat in the previous two and a half years. Indeed, a mere 5 per cent of Israel's trade passed through Eilat. The only significant commodity formally affected by the blockade was oil from Iran, which could have been re-routed (albeit at greater cost) through Haifa. What is more, it is not even clear that Nasser was rigorously enforcing the blockade. Rikhye asserts – and the available evidence seems to support him – that the Egyptian 'navy had searched a couple of ships after the establishment of the blockade and thereafter relaxed its implementation'. Recall, finally, that there was a 'real possibility' (Dean Rusk) that the blockade would have been formally lifted or modified after the Egyptian vice-president's visit to Washington in early June.[50]

Eban states that, in the wake of Israel's preemptive strike and rapid victory, 'no one questioned the responsibility of Nasser for the war'. Yet, not one government in the world took Eban's view that Israel was an innocent victim of aggression. In the international deliberations that ensued, opinion was divided between the belief that Israel was the aggressor, on the one hand, and that all parties shared some responsibility or that adjudicating responsibility served no useful purpose, on the other.

At a special emergency session of the General Assembly convened on account of the Middle East crisis, France reiterated its view that 'the first state to take up arms ... would not have its approval, still less its support'. (The day before, De Gaulle officially 'condemned' Israel 'for the opening of hostilities'.) India juxtaposed the 'incontrovertible fact that Israel struck the first blow' against the 'letter and spirit of the United Nations Charter' which barred 'pre-emptive strikes'. Tanzania stated bluntly that 'Israel has committed aggression against the Arab states', a view shared by Greece, which concluded that 'the invaded countries were the victims of an act of aggression committed by the State of Israel'. Even Israel's closest allies did not subscribe to the notion of Israel's virginal innocence – or, as Eban typically put it, that 'never in the history of nations has armed force been used in a more righteous or compelling cause'. (The latter view, incidentally, is pervasive in US scholarship, with moral theorist Michael Walzer, for example, listing Israel's preemptive strike as one of a handful of unambiguous cases of self-defense in the twentieth century – 'one about which we can, I think, have no doubts'.) Thus, at the extreme end of the spectrum, the US representative, Arthur Goldberg, refused to sign on to a Soviet-sponsored condemnation of Israel but only because the resolution censured 'Israel alone' for aggression. Canada, probably Israel's staunchest ally after the United States in the United Nations, declared that 'no one Government ... can be held responsible for what has happened'.[51]

Indeed, Eban himself seems uncertain about the solidity of Israel's case in 1967. For how else can one explain his almost manic insistence throughout 1967 and down to the present day that Egypt struck first on 5 June? In his maiden speech to the Security Council following Israel's preemptive strike, for example, Eban held that

> on the morning of 5 June, when Egyptian forces engaged us by air and land, bombarding the villages of Kissutim, Nahal-Oz and Ein Hashelosha, we knew that our limit of safety had been reached, and perhaps passed. In accordance

with its inherent right of self-defense as formulated in Article 51 of the United Nations Charter, Israel responded defensively in full strength.

A week later he informed the Security Council that 'they opened the hostilities. Egypt, Jordan, Syria, Iraq, one after the other, moved against Israel. They were repelled, and were driven back into their territory'. Even in his autobiography, written fully a decade after Israel freely admitted to its preemptive strike, Eban still maintained that Israel engaged in a 'counterattack' against the Egyptian air force which was 'sighted on the radar screens advancing toward us'.[52]

That Israel launched a preemptive strike on that fateful morning is not in dispute. As a 'friendly commentator of the Six-Day War' (Eban's phrase) reported:

By far the greater part of the Egyptian Air Force was caught on the ground. The only Egyptian craft airborne at the time the Israeli strike went in was a training flight of four unarmed aircraft flown by an instructor and three trainees.[53]

The blips Eban spotted on the screen were perhaps registering not oncoming Egyptian planes but the palpitations of a nagging conscience.

Israel faced no significant threat, let alone mortal danger, in June 1967. Furthermore, diplomacy seemed – despite Israel – to be working. Why then did Israel attack when it did? Indeed, why did Israel attack at all?

The first question is not difficult to answer. Two convergent developments acted as a fillip for Israel's decision to preemptively strike on 5 June. First, Israel received a green – or, in a more cautious formulation, yellow – light from the United States in early June. Israel's biggest fear in the weeks leading up to the war was a repetition of the 1956–57 Sinai 'trauma' when – in Eban's words – 'we had been victorious in battle but had then faced immense American pressure, which had made it difficult to reap the fruits of victory'. The intimations from the White House that it would not look unfavorably on – indeed, might positively welcome – an Israeli assault annulled that fear. On the other hand, there was acute anxiety in Tel Aviv that the Egyptian vice-president's imminent visit to Washington might produce a diplomatic breakthrough, squandering from another direction Israel's chance to reap the 'fruits of victory'. Eban, for instance, seems to have voted along with his colleagues for war at the crucial Cabinet meeting partly for fear that a face-saving compromise with Egypt was in the works. Dean Rusk later rued telling Israeli ambassador Harman of the Egyptian vice-president's travel plans since 'perhaps this was the spark that touched off the Israeli attack'. In sum, Israel struck on 5 June before it could be denied, and confident that it would reap, the 'fruits of victory'.[54]

But what gains did Israel want to reap? Historian Avi Shlaim reports that Ben-Gurion's 'greatest fear' in the immediate aftermath of Israel's victory in 1948 was that the Arab world might bring forth a leader like Ataturk who would achieve real independence for his country and embark on a program for transforming it into a modern, Westernized, secular state. 'By a curious touch of historic irony', Shlaim adds, 'at the very moment when Ben-Gurion was articulating this fear, surrounded by Israeli troops in the enclave of Faluja, there was a young brigade major who would later emerge as an Arab Mustafa Kemal – Gamal Abdul Nasser.'[55]

Indeed, soon after the Sinai invasion, Ben-Gurion acknowledged the same anxiety in almost identical terms. The crucial redeeming feature of the war, he asserted, was that 'it diminished the stature of the Egyptian dictator, and I do not want you or the entire people to underestimate the importance of this fact'. 'I always feared', he confided,

> that a personality might arise such as arose among the Arab rulers in the seventh century or like [Kemal Ataturk] who arose in Turkey after its defeat in the First World War. He raised their spirits, changed their character, and turned them into a fighting nation. There was and still is a danger that Nasser is this man.

The aim of Israel's joint invasion with Britain and France in 1956, according to US officials, was to 'destroy Nasser's prestige', nipping in the bud the twin bogies of Arab independence and modernization. But that job was left only half done in the 'Sinai campaign'. A decade later, a unique opportunity arose to complete it. Indeed, one cannot but be struck by the exact symmetry between the unfolding of the 1956 and 1967 wars. Benny Morris notes that 'from some point in 1954', Israel's 'retaliatory strikes' were designed to goad Nasser into attacking – what the British ambassador in Tel Aviv called a strategy of 'deliberately contrived preventive war'. Accordingly, Israel launched, as noted above, a massive assault against Gaza in February 1955, prefiguring the Samu raid. 'And', Morris continues, 'on 11 December, with Ben-Gurion's approval, the IDF launched a massive, more-or-less unprovoked strike against Syria ... in which IDF units destroyed a string of Syrian positions along the northeastern shore of the Sea of Galilee. A few weeks before, on 10 October, Syria and Egypt had signed a mutual defence pact, providing for a joint military command under Egyptian leadership. The aim [of the IDF attack] was to activate and provoke the Egyptians into retaliating against Israel – thus precipitating an Israeli-Egyptian war' – a precise anticipation of the lead-up to the June 1967 war.[56]

On the eve of the June 1967 war, the CIA appraised Israel's objectives as, first and foremost, 'destruction of the center of power of the radical Arab Socialist movement, i.e. the Nasser regime', second, 'destruction of the arms of the radical Arabs', and, last, 'destruction of both Syria and Jordan as modern States'. In a word, Israel's overarching aim was to extirpate any and all manifestations of Arab 'radicalism' – i.e. independence and modernization. To do so, the Egyptian upstart had to be put in his proper place, cut down to size. Most seriously, Nasser had openly defied Israel's monopoly on the use of force. By closing the Straits of Tiran, Egypt – in the trenchant aphorism of Mohammed Heikal, an influential Egyptian editor and Nasser confidant – 'succeeded for the first time, *vis à vis* Israel, in changing by force a *fait accompli* imposed on it by force'. 'To Israel', Heikal continued, 'this is the most dangerous aspect of the current situation: who can impose the accomplished fact and who possesses the power to safeguard it?' That an Arab leader should even raise the question 'Who is in charge?', was, for Israel, tantamount to a *casus belli*. Nasser – the Arab world – had to be taught the lesson that 'what we say goes', to quote President Bush's highly pertinent formulation on the eve of the Gulf slaughter.[57]

Eban is unusually candid in this regard, forthrightly observing: 'For us, the importance of denying Nasser political and psychological victory had become no less important than the concrete interest involved in the issue of navigation.' Indeed, Eban dates Israel's resolution to go to war from 'Nasser's blockade announcement on May 22' – with its potent 'political and psychological' resonances.[58]

War with the Arab world also offered Israel an opportunity to fulfill its territorial destiny. The Zionist leadership did not regard the borders that Israel achieved in the 1948 war, let alone those designated by the UN partition resolution, as permanent. 'In Ben-Gurion's eyes', Shlaim writes, 'they were not the end but only the beginning.' The 'future generation' was charged with the Zionist mandate of creating a Jewish state over the whole Land of Israel. Yet already in 1956, Ben-Gurion sought to telescope the future with the present. His plans for the post-'Sinai campaign' settlement envisaged the seizure of wide swaths of neighboring Arab territory, for example, the West Bank and Sharm-el-Shaykh. Alas, he overstepped – or, more exactly, stepped on US toes – and got nothing. But in 1967 the mistake was not repeated and the 'future generation' redeemed the Zionist project. Indeed, in an article composed on the eve of the June attack, influential Cabinet minister Yigal Allon stressed that, 'in case of a new war', Israel must set as one of its central aims 'the territorial fulfillment of the Land of Israel'.[59]

Finally, the June war enabled Israel to recover its spent élan. By 1966, immigration to Israel was at an ebb, unemployment had reached 10 per cent, and the intellectual and scientific elite was emigrating to greener pastures in the United States. In a remarkably prescient passage, E.L.M. Burns, former chief of UN forces in the Middle East, observed in 1961 that 'Israel's economic position is likely to deteriorate within the next few years'. In this 'very frustrating state of affairs', he darkly anticipated, Israel's leaders, who 'have a habit of putting down her economic difficulties' to the 'Arab states', may succumb to the 'great temptation to find an excuse to go to war ... to force a peace on Israeli terms'. It was perhaps these contingencies that Ezer Weizman had in mind in 1972 when Israel's preemptive strike was justified by him on the extraordinary grounds that Israel would otherwise 'have ceased to exist according to the scale, spirit, and quality she now embodies'. A Zionist scholar similarly reflected that 'the Six Day War turned out to be more in the nature of a salvation than a crisis'.[60]

## Deadlock

In the wake of the June war, attention shifted from the battlefield back to the diplomatic arena. The main venue of deliberations was the United Nations and the main outcome was UN Resolution 242. Controversy has swirled around 242 since its adoption principally due to the varying interpretations given the clause that calls for 'withdrawal of Israel armed forces from territories occupied in the recent conflict', in .accordance with the principle 'emphasize[d]' in the preambular paragraph of the 'inadmissibility of the acquisition of territory by war'. In this section, I will review the documentary record on the 'withdrawal clause', juxtaposing Israel's interpretation against the interpretation upheld by the rest of the world.

As the Security Council moved to adopt 242 and in subsequent years, Abba Eban invested considerable effort in elucidating the resolution's meaning. Chief among his claims have been the following:

1. *Withdrawal was not a 'central and primary' concern.* The resolution's 'central and primary affirmation', according to Eban, was 'the need for "establishment of a just and lasting peace" based on secure and recognized boundaries'. 'There is a clear understanding', he stated, 'that it is only within the establishment of permanent peace with secure and recognized boundaries that the other principles can be given effect.'[61]

2. *The preambular principle of the 'inadmissibility of the acquisition of territory by war' was 'not relevant' to the Middle East.* 'It is not relevant', Eban informed the Security Council in a disquisition that would surely have

resonated with Saddam Hussein, 'to transfer the territorial doctrines and experiences of another hemisphere to an area in which the only territorial agreements which have ever existed have been based on military considerations alone.' 'Regional doctrines', he cautioned, 'cannot be transplanted from one continent to another without regard to the different juridical circumstances which prevail. We must work within the law and the necessities which apply to our region.' In a later elucidation Eban claimed that the 'inadmissibility' principle was inserted 'in deference to Latin American pressure', yet had no pertinence except in Latin America, which was – Eban further alleged – uniquely prone to 'chaotic controversy' when boundaries were 'not safeguarded against volatile and transient military successes'. Israel's UN representative in June 1967, Gideon Rafael, maintained that the 'inadmissibility' principle referred only to 'territorial conquests resulting from wars of aggression' and was incorporated in 242 'only for the sake of parliamentary convenience'.[62]

3. *The operative paragraph calling for 'withdrawal of Israel armed forces from territories occupied' allowed for 'territorial revision'.* Eban contended that 242 left the 'scope and dimension' of Israel's withdrawal 'vague'. Accordingly, the resolution 'gave us a chance of territorial revision'. The principle of withdrawal was 'not applicable to all the territories involved'.[63]

Not one of Eban's propositions is sustained by the documentary record.

The Fifth Emergency Special Session of the General Assembly convened in mid-June 1967. It marked the first international effort in the wake of the war to reach consensus on resolving the Arab–Israeli conflict. Summarizing the main point of agreement that emerged from the otherwise contentious debate, the General Assembly president reported that 'there is virtual unanimity in upholding the principle that conquest of territory by war is inadmissible in our time under the Charter'. 'The affirmation of this principle', he continued,

> was made in virtually all statements and – I should add with some emphasis – by none more emphatically than all the big Powers – which bear the primary responsibility in the United Nations for the peace and security of the world. In this sense, virtually all speakers laid down the corollary that withdrawal of forces to their original position is expected.[64]

U Thant distilled the same essence from the General Assembly proceedings. 'There is near unanimity', the Secretary-General observed, on 'the withdrawal of the armed forces from the territory of neighboring Arab states occupied during the recent war' because 'everyone agrees that there should be no territorial gains by military conquest'. 'It would', he added in a rare personal aside, 'lead to disastrous consequences if the United Nations were to abandon or compromise this principle.'[65]

Remarkably, Eban reports that the consensus reached at the General Assembly special session 'specifically turned down' on repeated occasions 'the concept of withdrawal to the June 4 lines'.[66]

Towards the end of 1967, responsibility for finding the right formula to resolve the Arab–Israeli conflict was invested in the Security Council. Lord Caradon of Great Britain devised the language that was ultimately embodied in 242. Regarding the withdrawal clause, at the critical Security Council session, Caradon cited verbatim the words of Foreign Secretary George Brown as 'the policy which has repeatedly been stated by my Government': 'Britain does not accept war as a means of settling disputes, nor that a State should be allowed to extend its frontiers as a result of war. This means that Israel must withdraw.'

Caradon explicitly denied that there was any ambiguity in the withdrawal clause by juxtaposing the resolution's operative and preambular paragraphs:

> In our resolution we stated the principle of the 'withdrawal of Israel armed forces from territories occupied in the recent conflict' and in the preamble emphasized 'the inadmissibility of the acquisition of territory by war.' In our view, the wording of the provisions is clear.[67]

Caradon's caveat was echoed by virtually all the members of the Security Council as they cast their votes in favor of the resolution. The French delegate underlined that,

> on the point which the French delegation has always stressed as being essential – the question of withdrawal of the occupation forces – the resolution which has been adopted, if we refer to the French text which is equally authentic with the English, leaves no room for any ambiguity, since it speaks of withdrawal 'des territoires occupés,' which indisputably corresponds to the expression 'occupied territories.'

The representative from India reported that 'the principle of the inadmissibility of territorial acquisition by force is absolutely fundamental to our approach' and

> it is our understanding that the draft resolution, if approved by the Council, will commit it to the application of the principle of total withdrawal of Israel forces from all the territories – I repeat, all the territories – occupied by Israel as a result of the conflict which began on 5 June 1967.[68]

In a symposium many years later, Lord Caradon recalled that, without the preambular reference to the inadmissibility of acquiring territory by war, 'there could have been no unanimous vote'. The definite article was omitted from the operative paragraph ('occupied territories' as against 'the occupied territories'), he explained, due to the irregularities of the pre-5 June borders which 'were based on the accident of where exactly the Israeli and Arab armies happened to be' at the time of the original 1948 armistice agreement. This omission did not at all, however, mitigate the force of the preambular reference:

> Knowing as I did the unsatisfactory nature of the 1967 line, I wasn't prepared to use wording in the Resolution that would have made that line permanent. Nonetheless, it is necessary to say again that the overriding principle was the 'inadmissibility of the acquisition of territory by war' and that meant that there could be no justification for annexation of territory on the Arab side of the 1967 line merely because it had been conquered in the 1967 war. The sensible way to decide permanent 'secure and recognized' boundaries would be to set up a Boundary Commission and hear both sides and then to make impartial recommendations for a new frontier line, bearing in mind, of course, the 'inadmissibility' principle.

Maintaining at the same symposium that the withdrawal clause 'was not made applicable to all the territories involved,' Eban inferred that 'Lord Caradon's recollection has been dimmed by the passage of time'. To which Caradon politely, if pointedly, rejoined, 'Not at all. I remember it well.'[69]

At the Fifth Emergency Special Session, the United States voted for a Latin American draft resolution which urgently requested 'Israel to withdraw all its forces from all the territories occupied by it as a result of the recent conflict'. This resolution, like several others presented, failed for lack of a two-thirds majority.[70] (The General Assembly split on whether or not to make Israel's total withdrawal conditional on Arab recognition of its right to peace and security.)

In late July the United States and the Soviet Union undertook a joint last-ditch effort to fashion a resolution that would win wide enough approval to salvage the General Assembly special session. In the version supported by the United States, the 'parties to the conflict' were called on, *inter alia*, to withdraw 'without delay' from 'territories occupied by them in keeping with the inadmissibility of the conquest of territory by war'. 'Once again', a State Department study reports, 'Israel rejected the formula.' Israel's UN representative argued that the 'inadmissibility' principle had an 'ominous connotation' and that – the UN Charter notwithstanding – 'there was nothing wrong with territorial conquest if it came in a just war fought against aggression'.[71]

As the Security Council moved to debate various draft resolutions in November 1967, the United States further delineated its position on the territorial question. Israel's withdrawal had to be total, aside from 'minor' and 'mutual' border adjustments. Arthur Goldberg affirmed to Egypt that any territorial settlement would require Israel to return the Sinai and that, although Gaza raised separate issues, the United States did not consider that it belonged to Israel. Jordan was informed by Goldberg that 'some territorial adjustments would be required' but that 'there must be a mutuality in adjustments'. In a separate, joint meeting with the Egyptian and Jordanian foreign ministers, Goldberg maintained that the United States did not support Israeli claims to Sinai and the West Bank and that, although 'territorial adjustments would undoubtedly be necessary', the boundaries resulting from the agreement 'need not be of prejudice to the Arabs'. In yet a third meeting with officials from Iraq, Lebanon and Morocco, Goldberg averred that 'the United States did not conceive of any substantial redrawing of the map'. Dean Rusk also promised King Hussein that the United States supported the return of a 'substantial part' of the West Bank to Jordan and would 'use its influence to obtain compensation to Jordan for any territory it was required to give up'. Finally, the commitments Hussein received from Goldberg and Rusk were confirmed in a personal meeting with President Johnson.

According to the above-cited State Department study, American officials 'made known the content' of 'these assurances' to the British and Israeli governments. To be sure, in deference to Israeli pressures, the United States 'strongly and successfully resisted attempts to introduce more specific language into the withdrawal clause' of 242 and also 'chose not to emphasize its own position on the limited nature of boundary adjustment'. Yet, as late as two days before Goldberg cast his vote in favor of 242, the State Department explicitly committed itself to 'relatively small' and 'mutual' territorial adjustments.

In his memoir, Dean Rusk recalls that the United States favored omitting the definite article in the 'withdrawal clause' only because 'we thought the Israeli border along the West Bank could be "rationalized," certain anomalies could easily be straightened out with some exchanges of territory, making a more sensible border for all parties'. 'But', he stresses, 'we never contemplated any significant grant of territory to Israel as a result of the June 1967 war. On that point, we and the Israelis to this day remain sharply divided.' Yet, according to Eban, the United States was 'advocating' in November 1967 the Israeli position of 'territorial revision'.[72]

Abba Eban once observed that the United Nations is basically a 'theater' which 'can "act" only in the histrionic sense'. As a portrait of the United Nations, it is an open question. Yet as a self-portrait, it is remarkably fitting. In the United Nations as elsewhere, Eban's role has been basically dramaturgical. He has served with distinction as both playwright and thespian. No one can gainsay that Eban's prose and poise have made for very stirring histrionics. Unfortunately, they have made for very bad history. Perhaps his performance is what one should expect from a diplomat. But what does it say about an intellectual culture when Eban's 'reconstruction' of the June 1967 war becomes the received wisdom?[73]

# 6

# Language of Force

## The Real Meaning of the October War and its Aftermath

The Arabs will make peace only with a strong Israel.

Moshe Dayan, November 1970

The historian will find that Israel has never been the element to block peace moves.

Chaim Herzog, *The War of Atonement*[1]

The standard depiction of the 'peace process' in the wake of the June 1967 war goes something like this: 'There was a more intensive Israeli quest for peace after 1967 than in any other period' of its history. Yet, 'no peace offer' from the Arab states 'was in the offing,' as 'real diplomacy was evaded'. Fundamentally, the Israeli quest proved abortive because the Arabs only understood 'the language of force'. Believing 'it would be possible to destroy the state of Israel' or, at a minimum, impose a solution 'after a military success', the Arabs launched an 'unprovoked' attack in October 1973. Faced with the 'incredible military victory gained' by Israel 'on the battlefield', however, Anwar Sadat reached the 'revolutionary decision' that there was 'no hope of solving the Arab conflict with Israel' through force of arms and that his 'objectives should be sought by political, not military, means.' The Egyptian leader accordingly 'turned in a totally different direction: peace with Israel instead of war'. 'For the first time the Arab world was presented by one of its leaders with a vision of the Middle East that did include the sovereign state of Israel.' And once he 'crossed the psychological barrier' with the 'dramatic appearance before the Knesset in November 1977', Sadat's 'reward was immediate and dramatic'. Israel, which had always 'intended' to return 'all of Sinai' in exchange for Egyptian recognition of 'the fact of its existence', promptly agreed to withdraw. At long last Israel had arrived at 'destination peace'.[2]

Simply put, my thesis is that the above image exactly reverses the reality: Egypt (and Jordan) desperately sought a negotiated settlement after the 1967 war. Israel, however, refused to budge from the conquered territories in exchange for peace. With all diplomatic options exhausted, Egypt went to war, displaying impressive – and unexpected – military prowess. Israel accordingly agreed after the war to the same diplomatic settlement Sadat had offered it before the war. In a word, it was Israel, not Egypt, that ultimately bowed to the language of force.

I will first sketch the diplomatic record of Israel and the Arab states (in particular Egypt, generally regarded as the main protagonist on the Arab side) until the eve of the October 1973 war. I will argue that Egypt, unlike Israel, fully embraced the international consensus for resolving the conflict. I will then explore why Israel accepted only in 1977 the peace settlement with Egypt already offered it in 1971. As suggested above, I will argue that the crucial factor was Egypt's decisive show of force in the October war.


## Diplomatic Overtures

In the wake of the June 1967 war, an international consensus gradually crystallized for resolving the Israeli–Arab conflict. On the Israeli side, it called for a full withdrawal from the Arab territories occupied in the course of the war. On the Arab side, it called not only for a negative peace in the form of a pledge of nonbelligerency but a positive peace in the form of an official treaty with Israel. In accordance with Resolution 242, which was adopted by the Security Council on 22 November 1967, the Swedish diplomat Gunnar Jarring was appointed by the United Nations to mediate a resolution of the conflict. A review of the diplomatic record suggests that as Israel moved further from the international consensus, the major Arab states moved closer to it.[3]

Israel's first policy decision regarding the conquered territories was taken on 19 June 1967, when a divided Cabinet (11:10) proposed a settlement on the pre-June 1967 borders with Syria and Egypt (Israel keeping Gaza), but made no mention of Jordan and the West Bank. Several days earlier, Defense Minister Moshe Dayan declared in his 'private capacity' that Gaza would not be returned to Egypt or the West Bank to Jordan. Meeting with UN Secretary-General U Thant on 22 June, US representative Arthur Goldberg speculated that Israel had 'no interest' in Sinai (wrongly adding, however, Gaza), but would want to 'retain' Old Jerusalem and 'the area of the West Bank of Jordan'. Note that Israel's security concerns were presumably fresh in the mind of the Cabinet when it drafted, right after the June war, the proposal to withdraw from the Sinai and the Golan Heights. Yet as seen below, the Labor government adamantly maintained in subsequent years that Israel's continued presence in the Sinai and the Golan was vital to its national security.[4]

Rabin reports that Israel hardened its 19 June position already in August in response to the 'Arab intransigence' displayed at Khartoum, with its famous 'Three Noes' to 'peace', 'recognition' and 'negotiations' with Israel. Yet the Khartoum summit resolutions were not issued until September. Indeed, the highly respected head of UN forces in the Middle East, Odd Bull, suggests that it was Israel's openly avowed determination to annex the conquered territories that accounted for the rhetorical excesses at Khartoum. The official Israeli chronology effectively reverses – not for the last time, as we shall see – cause and effect. In the immediate aftermath of the June war, according to Bull, there was a 'genuine wish' by the Arabs to 'find a solution to the Arab–Israeli conflict'. But, 'by showing itself unyielding, Israel encouraged the Arabs to adopt a similar attitude' at Khartoum.[5]

In February 1968, Israel announced a carefully qualified acceptance of 242. Notably silent on the crucial issue of withdrawal, it deemed the resolution not more than a 'framework' for 'the promotion of agreement on the establishment of peace with secure and recognized boundaries'. Another formulation designated 242 as merely 'a list of principles which can help the parties and guide them in their search for a solution because it lists the claims, the main claims, which both parties make against each other, but it has no life of its own'. Publicly and in 'confidential' negotiations with Jarring, Eban insisted that 242 did not require Israel's withdrawal to the pre-June 1967 borders. Summarizing Israel's peace overtures in 1968, the quasi-official Israeli publication *Middle East Record* underlined that they precluded 'withdrawal to the 4 June lines, which were not considered ... secure borders'. As Eban typically put it in June, 'We need a better security map, a more spacious frontier, a lesser vulnerability.' In concrete (but not officially acknowledged) terms, this meant annexation of 'all, or a substantial part, of the Golan Heights', and between one-quarter and one-third of the West Bank in accordance with the modalities of the Allon Plan. Regarding the crucial Egyptian sector, the Israeli Cabinet approved in October a secret resolution stating that Israel would not withdraw from Gaza or from Sharm-el-Shaykh, and that it would keep roughly one-third of Sinai connecting Sharm-el-Shaykh to Israel proper. A few months earlier Dayan had declared that 'I regard Sharm-el-Shaykh as an eternal base of the State of Israel. We must be there forever in a suitable place where we can prevent the entry of Egyptian forces from beyond Suez.' Just as the Cabinet was covertly sanctioning an annexationist agenda, Eban announced a 'nine-point' peace proposal at the United Nations that was once again deliberately elusive on the matter of withdrawal: 'It is possible to work out a boundary settlement compatible with the security of Israel and with the honour of the Arab States.' Although acclaimed with considerable self-congratulation by Eban as the 'most moderate possible formulation of Israel's position', commentators have been less impressed. U Thant observed that it 'lacked the essential information about Israeli intentions without which the Arab Governments would not even consider any form of negotiations' and that it was 'not surprising' that Egypt rejected it. Korn similarly dismisses it as 'short on details' and not 'commit[ting] Israel to anything of significance that it had not already accepted'.[6]

To elicit where each of the main parties stood on the key provisions of 242, Jarring distributed in March 1969 a detailed questionnaire. Asked if Israel would 'agree to withdraw its armed forces from territories occupied by it in the recent conflict?', Foreign Minister Eban evasively responded: 'When permanent, secure and recognized boundaries are agreed upon and established between Israel and each of the neighboring Arab states, the disposition of forces will be carried out in full accordance with the boundaries determined in the peace treaties.' A few months later Eban pronounced that 'there is no international authority for the proposal to restore the position and lines of 4 June 1967. ... Israel will never agree to put herself again in that position of peril and vulnerability'. In a verbal elaboration of its August 1969 electoral platform – the so-called 'Oral Torah' – the Labor Party reiterated Israeli claims on large swaths of the conquered territories. Significantly, along the entire mainstream Israeli political spectrum – from Gahal (Menachem Begin, Ezer Weizman, Ariel Sharon) on the right through Labor to Mapam on the left – there was consensus that Sharm-el-Shaykh must be held. Gahal, which in its Likud incarnation would return Sharm-el-Shaykh along with the rest of Sinai to Egypt after the October war, for example, called in 1969 for Israel's retention of 'most of the occupied territories in Sinai'. Israeli journalist Amnon Kapeliouk pointed to the title of a book published by Dayan in 1969, *New Map, New Relations*, as capturing the – contradictory – essence of Israel's position: it wanted both conquered land and peace.[7]

Israel's refusal to even consider a nonannexationist settlement was highlighted in early December 1969 when US Secretary of State William Rogers unveiled a plan – roughly approximating the international consensus – that called for an Israeli withdrawal from the conquered territory on the Egyptian front in exchange for Egypt's signature on a binding peace agreement. The plan's announcement, according to Brecher, 'caused a sense of panic within the Israeli Government'. Summoned to an emergency session, the Cabinet issued an 'unqualified rejection' of it. Several days later, the United States put forth a similar initiative to settle the conflict between Israel and Jordan. In an 'intensified atmosphere of crisis', the Cabinet was called yet again into emergency session and stingingly condemned the new plan as 'prejudic[ing] the chances of establishing peace' and a 'very grave danger' to 'Israel's security and peace'. Prime Minister Golda Meir claimed that 'any Israeli government that would adopt and implement' the American proposals 'would be betraying its country'. Ambassador Yitzak Rabin likewise savaged them as 'an attempt on the very existence of Israel'. In his standard study of the period, Whetten lucidly points up the real source of Israel's hostility to the US initiatives. Earlier that year Nasser had launched the so-called 'war of attrition' to compel Israel's withdrawal from Sinai: 'Israel was winning the war and thus had no incentive to alter its policy.' In a word, the 'language of force' dictated policy.[8]

Responding in August 1970 to a new Rogers proposal to suspend hostilities with Egypt and resume peace negotiations under Jarring's aegis, Israel for the first time in an official document acknowledged the 'withdrawal' principle, giving *qualified* approval to it. The gesture signalled no substantive departure in policy, however, Labor never having intended to retain *all* of the conquered territories. On the Egyptian front, Israel remained firm as Jarring prepared to launch a new initiative. Earlier that year Eban had underscored that 'without a continued Israeli presence' at Sharm-el-Shaykh, 'a blockade, and consequently a war, would be inevitable'.[9]

On the eve of the meeting of Arab states at Khartoum in fall 1967, Egyptian President Nasser called for an early peace settlement with Israel and threatened to 'go it alone' if rebuffed at the summit. As noted above, the Arab leaders passed a resolution opposing 'peace' and 'negotiations' with and 'recognition' of Israel, and upheld 'the rights of the Palestinian people in their own country'. Significantly, it also called for joint 'political efforts at the international and diplomatic level' to 'ensure' Israel's withdrawal from the territories conquered in the June war. *Middle East Record* reports that, 'within the framework' of the 'three noes', a 'number of concessions were mooted' by the Arab states. Indeed, Marshall Tito of Yugoslavia formulated a peace plan at that time that called basically for a full Israeli withdrawal from the conquered territories in exchange for full demilitarization and other security guarantees in the evacuated areas, as well as an 'end to the call for an Arab state of Palestine'. Egypt and Jordan agreed, but Israel did not, deeming it 'one-sided'. Asked in October about recognition of Israel, Jordan's King Hussein replied that 'we are not against the existence of any nation. Israel is a nation, whether we like it or not'. An Egyptian government official similarly declared that 'the right of Israel to exist is self-evident'. With Nasser's concurrence, Hussein stated in November that, although 'diplomatic recognition' would not be granted, the Arab states were prepared, as part of a settlement, to 'recognize Israel's right to live in peace and security'. Jordan embraced UN Resolution 242 immediately after its promulgation, interpreting it to mean a full Israeli withdrawal in exchange for an end to the state of belligerency. More cautious at first, Egypt too soon announced its acceptance.[10]

'Except when referring to the Khartoum resolutions', *Middle East Report* summarizes for 1968, 'Egyptian spokesmen spoke frequently of the desirability of a "peaceful solution", but expressly rejected the possibility of concluding a peace treaty with Israel.' Analyzing the diplomatic 'deadlock' in April 1968, Jarring observed that, in Egypt's interpretation of 242, Israel's complete withdrawal must precede implementation, and 242 did not call for 'a peace-treaty, or for other contractual arrangements'. By August, Jarring was able to report that Egypt had conceded the former point, accepting a 'package deal': 'withdrawal of Israeli troops no longer a precondition; no priority for the different provisions of the resolution'. On the latter point, however, Nasser proved not as flexible: 'will not accept "peace-treaty" ... is ready to issue a declaration of termination of state of belligerency, simultaneously with Israel, but not a joint declaration. ... these declarations to be endorsed and guaranteed by the Security Council or by the four Great Powers'. Egypt also continued to insist on a comprehensive settlement with Israel, rejecting any separate deal: 'peace ... could only be achieved by Israeli withdrawal from all Arab territories' (Egyptian Foreign Minister, Mahmoud Riad).[11]

Responding to Jarring's March 1969 questionnaire, Egypt (as well as Jordan) pledged nearly full acceptance of all the main provisions of 242 subject to a 'withdrawal of Israel's forces from all Arab territories occupied as a result of Israel's aggression of 5 June 1967': 'termination of all claims or state of belligerency', 'the right of every State in the area to live in peace', 'respect for and acknowledgment of the sovereignty, territorial integrity and political independence of every State in the area', 'freedom of navigation in international waterways', etc. Asked its 'conception of secure and recognized boundaries held by Israel', Egypt's technical response ambiguously read: 'When the question of Palestine was brought before the United Nations in 1947, the General Assembly adopted its resolution 181 of 29 November 1947, for the partition of Palestine and defined Israel's borders.' Note, however, that Egypt had called for an Israeli withdrawal only from the territories conquered in the June war. And in lieu of a peace treaty, Egypt proposed a binding 'instrument' signed by Egypt and Israel that would be deposited with and endorsed by the Security Council.[12]

Throughout 1969, the Arab states took a series of initiatives basically conforming to the March reply. All were peremptorily dismissed by Israel. The most important of these was King Hussein's 'six-point' settlement presented in a speech to the National Press Club in April. Publicly affirming all commitments made in the Jarring questionnaire, Hussein – with the 'personal authority' of Nasser – stated that 'in return ..., our sole demand upon Israel is the withdrawal of its armed forces from all territories occupied in the June 1967 war, and the implementation of all other provisions of the Security Council Resolution'. The 'challenge' of the plan, perorated Hussein, was that Israel can have either 'peace or territory – but she can never have both'. But 'on the next day', reports U Thant, 'the hopes inspired by this dramatic offer were dashed'. Deriding it as 'nothing new', Israel underlined that 'it was unable to treat earnestly a demand of complete withdrawal'.[13]

Egypt's first official reaction to the 1969 Rogers Plan calling for full withdrawal/full peace was 'noncommittal' (Quandt). Mainly concerned that the United States was proposing a bilateral deal ('piecemeal settlement'), it withheld endorsement until the United States took a similar initiative on the other Arab fronts. By the time the United States presented an equivalent plan to Jordan in mid-December, however, Israel had already denounced the Rogers initiative in the strongest possible terms (see pp. 153–4 above). Egypt then effectively (if not explicitly) rejected the American proposal as well because, as the Egyptian foreign minister explained, 'I saw no point in our accepting it, for it would mean further concessions within the framework of a settlement which we were doubtful the U.S. could get Israel to accept.' (Hussein expressed satisfaction with the American initiative.) Egypt continued to suggest, however, that the US proposals 'could serve as the basis for a solution in the Middle East, and are worth exploring further', the Soviet Union reporting in mid-January 1970 that it had obtained Nasser's agreement to them.[14]

In the final year of his life, Nasser – who, according to Eban, 'refused' to the bitter end 'to give any thought to the prospect of restoring his territory by a diplomatic settlement with Israel' – was still desperately pressing to break the diplomatic stalemate. In a February 1970 *Le Monde* interview, he speculated that 'a durable peace is possible, not excluding economic and diplomatic relations', if 242 were fully implemented: 'Diplomatic relations are not possible immediately but no outstanding differences will remain so it will eventually come. Full normalization can only be attained in stages.' Two months later, he suggested to the US assistant secretary of state for the Near East and South Asia, Joseph Sisco, that Egypt and Israel could jointly sign at the United Nations a document ending the state of war in accordance with the terms of 242. All that remained for Nasser's successor (Anwar Sadat replaced Nasser after he died suddenly of a heart attack in September) was to make the final leap: a full – and, if need be, bilateral – treaty with Israel.[15]

## The Jarring Initiative

In January 1971, Jarring prepared a comparison of the latest Israeli and Egyptian positions on 242. On the question of withdrawal, Israel held that military forces must be withdrawn 'from territories lying beyond positions agreed to in the peace treaty', and that the boundaries must be 'secure, recognized, and *agreed* [to]' (emphasis in original). On the question of a peace document, Egypt 'did not comment', Jarring filling in that 'previously it expressed the view that all instruments of peace should be signed by the parties and addressed to the Security Council; the endorsement by the Security Council of those documents would constitute the final multilateral document'. To be sure, just as Jarring was compiling the memorandum, Foreign Minister Riad signalled Egypt's willingness to 'sign a peace treaty with Israel, provided that it included Israeli withdrawal from all the occupied territories'.[16]

At any rate, Jarring – coaxed by the United States to take a more aggressive approach – undertook on 8 February to break the diplomatic deadlock by making 'clear my views on what I believe to be the necessary steps to be taken in order to achieve a peaceful and accepted settlement in accordance with' 242. He accordingly sought 'from each side the parallel and simultaneous commitments which seem to be inevitable prerequisites of an eventual peace settlement between them'. From Egypt he requested a 'commitment to enter into a peace agreement with Israel'. From Israel he requested a 'commitment to withdraw its forces from occupied United Arab Republic [i.e. Egyptian] territory to the former international boundary between Egypt and the British Mandate of Palestine'.[17]

On 15 February, Egypt gave what was uniformly interpreted as an affirmative reply to Jarring's aide-mémoire, explicitly stating its readiness to 'enter into a peace agreement with Israel'. Noting that 'at the beginning of February 1971, President Sadat ... responded favorably to a plan for a peace settlement by Ambassador Jarring', Israel's distinguished UN representative, Gideon Rafael, characterized the Egyptian reply in his memoir as a 'far-reaching development': 'For the first time, the government of an Arab state had publicly announced its readiness to sign a peace agreement with Israel in an official document.'[18]

Israel was taken off guard by Jarring's initiative and even more so by Egypt's affirmative reply. Told by *Newsweek*'s Arnaud de Borchgrave in early February that Sadat was prepared to make peace, Meir replied, 'That will be the day.' Furious at Jarring and U Thant – allegedly for over-stepping 242's mandate, but in reality for specifying a full withdrawal as the *quid pro quo* for a peace treaty – Israel nonetheless submitted at February's end its reply. The fateful clause read: 'Israel will not withdraw to the pre-June 1967 lines.' Pointing to the 'boundary issue' as the 'root cause' of the conflict, an authoritative government statement issued in March was yet more emphatic on the matter of withdrawal: 'As its condition for peace, Egypt would have Israel restore its past territorial vulnerability. This Israel will never do.' And again: 'Israel will never accept and will be even prepared to fight over if necessary ... the issue of total withdrawal.' And yet again: 'Israel will not flinch in its insistence on the establishment of new and secure boundaries.'[19]

Israel's refusal to join Egypt in acceptance of the international consensus killed any prospects for a diplomatic settlement. It also made war all but inevitable. In March 1971, U Thant issued an 'appeal ... to the Government of Israel to ... respond favorably to Ambassador Jarring's initiative'. In the introduction to his annual report for 1971, U Thant more extensively observed:

> The United Arab Republic accepted the specific commitments requested of it, but so far Israel has not responded to the Special Representative's request. Ambassador Jarring feels, and I agree with him, that, until there has been a change in Israel's position on the question of withdrawal, it would serve little purpose to reactivate the talks. It is still my hope that Israel will find it possible before too long to make a response that will enable the search for a peaceful settlement under Ambassador Jarring's auspices to continue.

U Thant further warned that 'there can be little doubt that, if the present impasse in the search for a peaceful settlement persists, new fighting will break out sooner or later.'[20]

With Israel's flat rejection of the crucial commitment on withdrawal, Jarring decided against any new initiatives on the other Arab fronts. Jordan nonetheless avowed its readiness as well to formally end the state of war with Israel. In a mid-February memorandum to Jarring, Jordan proposed signing an 'international instrument' once Israel effected a 'complete evacuation of occupied Arab territories'. In late February, Hussein volunteered in an interview with the London *Observer* that Jordan was ready to sign a peace treaty with Israel if there were a comprehensive Israeli withdrawal (the formula of 'minor rectifications on a reciprocal basis' applicable on the Jordanian frontier), and was also prepared to recognize Israel. Jordan's view on signing a treaty with Israel, Hussein underlined, was 'identical with that of the UAR'.[21]

Before turning to the aftermath of the Jarring initiative, it is instructive to examine how this episode – which, beyond its intrinsic interest, provides the pivotal context for the October war – has entered the official history of the 'peace process' via memoirs and academic scholarship. The first point to make is that it has just barely done so. Quandt's now stand-ard study of the peace process running to some 600 pages devotes all of *two paragraphs* to the Jarring initiative.[22] Quandt at any rate has the merit of getting the basic facts generally correct. Meir observes in her memoir that, except for 'talk about reopening the Suez Canal', the 'Arabs refused to meet us or deal with us in any way ... in 1971 or 1972'. In a March 1971 interview with the London *Times* Meir had whistled a different tune as she acknowledged that 'Anwar Sadat was the first Egyptian leader to say that he was prepared to make peace'. Possessing more derring-do than Meir, Dayan brazenly states in his memoir that Egypt's reply to Jarring's initiative was 'that she was prepared to end the state of war but not to sign a treaty with Israel'. Back in February 1971, Dayan – declaring that he would prefer 'Sharm-el-Shaykh without peace to peace without Sharm-el-Shaykh' – had acknowledged that 'if we return all the territories the Egyptians would be ready for peace'. And in March, he had cautioned that 'there must be careful assessment of the situation because this is the first time that Arab leaders have openly talked about peace and lasting borders with Israel'. Turning to mainstream scholarship, Touval's study (the 'standard work on mediation in the Middle East', according to Eban) discerns that the 'obvious answer' to the question of why the Jarring initiative failed is that 'the parties' – note the plural – 'refused to make the necessary concessions'. Whetten illumines that 'the response of both parties' – note again the plural – 'to Jarring's initiative indicated the futility of using the good offices of the United Nations'. Similarly blaming the messenger for the message, Herzog waxes philosophical that 'it is a sobering reflection on the relation of personalities to the creation of history to realize that a more able and decisive negotiator than Dr Jarring could well have achieved a breakthrough in 1971'. Israeli strategic analyst Shimon Shamir muses profoundly that the 'precise significance' of Sadat's reply to Jarring is 'debatable' but was 'probably more than a propaganda ploy'. Tillman's important study devotes not a word to the Jarring initia-tive, instead reporting that, 'in the wake of the psychological victory of the October War it become possible, *as it had not been before*, for respon-sible Arab leaders to contemplate peace with Israel'. In his monumental history of the Israeli–Palestinian conflict, Tessler tucks away a vague allusion to the initiative in an endnote.[23]

The main brief in defense of Israel's posture at the time of the Jarring initiative has been filed by Eban. At the General Assembly debate in December 1971, he spoke of the 'widely diffused international legend which asserts that in February 1971 Egypt made a positive response to the aide-mémoire of Ambassador Jarring while Israel made a negative response or none at all'. Neither this assertion nor the one that Israel's response accounted for the diplomatic 'deadlock' were, according to Eban, 'well founded'. In his more recent memoir, Eban similarly decries the 'mythology' that 'there were chances of peace that were lost in 1971 as a result of Israeli obduracy'.[24]

Eban's central claim is that it was Egypt's, not Israel's, response that derailed the Jarring initiative. Thus he purports that the initiative 'misfire[d]' because Egypt was 'not prepared to be satisfied with a peace engagement concerning Sinai alone ... [and] insisted on an Israeli undertaking to withdraw from the Gaza strip and from all other "Arab territories" to the boundaries that existed on June 4, 1967'. Yet the decision that Sadat took in February 1971 effectively committed Egypt – whether for the better or for the worse is another matter – to a *separate* peace with Israel, as at Camp David. Committed as Egypt was in 1969 to a comprehensive settlement, it withheld approval of the Rogers Plan until a similar initiative was taken on the other Arab fronts. This time round, however, Egypt – looking out only for its own interests – immediately signed on. True, it penciled in at the very bottom of its reply to Jarring after consenting to a peace treaty that the 'United Arab Republic considers that the just and lasting peace cannot be realized without ... the withdrawal of the Israeli armed forces from all the territories occupied since the 5th of June 1967'. But Sadat manifestly did not condition his acceptance of the Jarring initiative on such a comprehensive withdrawal. Thus in a minute comparison between the commitments requested and Egypt's reply, Jarring noted only that 'in relation to the withdrawal commitment sought from Israel, the United Arab Republic feels that it should apply to the Gaza Strip, as well as Sinai'. Indeed, no one doubted at the time that Sadat was prepared to treat, if need be, bilaterally with Israel, the London *Observer*, for example, reporting that Egypt's 'current objective was a signed peace treaty, not with "all states in the area", but specifically with Israel' and that 'by making this treaty conditional on Israeli withdrawal from Sinai – and Sinai alone – Egypt had apparently agreed to seek its own peace with Israel, separately from other Arab states, if necessary'. Riad, who had for many years advocated the principle of a comprehensive settlement as foreign minister, effectively conceded in his memoir that it had been discarded with the Jarring initiative, the Egyptian position then being that 'a durable peace necessitated that agreements should be concluded with all concerned Arab countries, *although this did not mean they should all be signed on the same day*' (my emphasis). Similar airy phraseology calling for the eventual conclusion of agreements with all concerned Arab countries, incidentally, was written into the bilateral accords signed at Camp David in 1978, and the Egyptian–Israeli treaty of 1979.[25]

Eban alleges several further limitations of Egypt's February 1971 reply. I will consider the significant ones[26]:

• 'Egypt insisted on a commitment from Israel for the achievement of a settlement of the refugee problem as a condition of the peace agreement.' Indeed, Dayan conjured the specter in his memoir of a mass repatriation of refugees 'undermining the very foundations of [Israel's] existence'. Resolution 242 called for a 'just settlement of the refugee problem'. Jarring accordingly held that the replies of Egypt and Israel to his aide-mémoire were 'subject' to the 'eventual satisfactory' resolution of the refugee question. In its response, Egypt called for a 'just settlement of the refugee problem in accordance with United Nations resolutions'. The relevant UN resolution passed in December 1948 provided for the options of repatriation or compensation. As seen above, however, there was already a consensus that compensation was the only realistic option for the mass of Palestinian refugees. Indeed, Sadat explicitly stated at the time of the Jarring initiative that he considered 'compensation and a referendum on the future of the Palestinians, *without reference to repatriation to their former homes in Israel*' as a 'reasonable way to solve the problem' (my emphasis). One may further note that Jarring 'relegated the Palestinian refugee problem to a subsidiary position on the peace agenda' (Rafael), and Sadat mentioned the refugee question only 'indirectly' (Shamir) in his reply. Finally, the Camp David accords also enter a reservation in favor of 'establish[ing] agreed procedures for a prompt, just and permanent implementation of the resolution of the refugee problem' ('Framework').[27]

• Egypt's position on 'freedom of navigation in the Suez Canal' was that it 'would be ensured "in accordance with the 1888 Constantinople Convention." Now that Convention has been invoked by Egypt for 23 years, not as a justification for allowing Israeli ships and cargoes through the Canal, but as a pretext for obstructing their passage.' Yet, Egypt had already consented to amend the Convention to accommodate all of Israel's concerns. Even more to the point, the Egyptian–Israeli Treaty of 1979 also explicitly situates Israel's 'right of free passage through the Suez Canal ... on the basis of the Constantinople Convention of 1888' (Article V).[28]

- Egypt insisted on '"the establishment of demilitarized zones astride the borders in equal distances". ... This reduces the proposal for demilitarized zones to sheer mockery. If massive demilitarization in the Sinai Peninsula is to be achieved – and without it how can a final peace between Egypt and Israel be envisaged? – Israel would have to undertake the total demilitarization of itself.' Yet Egypt had already privately conceded that 'more of the demilitarized zones along the reestablished 1967 borders would consist of Arab territory'. Indeed, Jarring speculated at the time that 'it might be possible to demilitarize the whole of Sinai'. Eban alleges that the 'most important' reason the Jarring initiative 'misfired' was that Egypt 'insisted on a military presence east of the Canal. Such a presence, however small, would have compromised the principle of demilitarization without which no Israeli government has ever agreed to evacuate areas of importance to security'. Amazingly, Eban seems unaware that Egypt consented to a full demilitarization of only about one quarter of the Sinai in the 1979 treaty with Israel (Article IV and Annex I).[29]

Eban's counterclaims are evidently devoid of substance. The one and only obstacle to a negotiated settlement in 1971 was Israel's refusal to fully withdraw from the Sinai. Indeed, Eban himself privately admitted as much. In a mid-March meeting with U Thant devoted to the Egyptian reply, Eban stated:

> There [are] some areas of obscurity, for example, concerning the freedom of navigation in the Canal and the UAR reference to Article X of the 1888 [Constantinople] Convention, or the rights of the Palestinians. But these [can] be cleared up quickly in direct negotiations. Of course, *the crux of the matter [is] the question of withdrawal and boundaries.* (emphasis added)

Leaving no room for doubt, Eban underscored: 'Israel [will] not accept a solution based on Israeli withdrawal from Sharm-el-Shaykh.'[30]

### After Jarring

Official US policy through 1971 fully backed the Jarring initiative and put full responsibility for its derailment on Israel. Rabin recalled as 'the most painful talk I ever had with Rogers' a meeting at which the Secretary of State berated him because 'Egypt's attitude is positive, but Israel's is negative'. At a March news conference, Rogers reiterated American policy as 'the 1967 boundary should be the boundary between Israel and Egypt'. (In a report on the news conference, the *New York Times* pointed to

Israel's insistence on keeping Sharm-el-Shaykh and a corridor to it as 'the central point of the present impasse'.) In April, Rogers informed Jarring that the United States was urging Israel 'to come forward with a response to your February 8 aide-mémoire expressed in positive, negotiable terms. We have instructed Ambassador Barbour this week to make clear to Mrs Meir that we consider the next move is up to Israel.' Expressing 'support of the Jarring initiative' in June, the Big Four powers – the United States, United Kingdom, France, and the Soviet Union – 'welcomed the positive reply to this démarche of the UAR', and 'express[ed] the hope that Israel would give a similarly positive reply to this démarche'. U Thant laconically observes: 'It was one of the rare occasions in my experience, however, that a formula that was agreed to by the four permanent members of the Security Council did not go through.' UN representative George Bush reaffirmed in July that the United States 'consider[ed] the reply of the UAR to Ambassador Jarring's proposal to be positive' and that it 'hope[d] that Israel will make a similarly positive reply'.[31]

The United Nations issued similar appeals to Israel to respond positively to the Jarring initiative. All fell on deaf ears. When the UN Security Council moved from entreaty to condemnation in 1973, however, the US representative – now acting at Kissinger's behest – exercised the veto, blocking action. Reaffirming 'that the acquisition of territories by force is inadmissible and that, consequently, territories thus occupied must be restored', the General Assembly in late 1971 passed a resolution that 'notes with appreciation the positive reply given by Egypt' to the Jarring aide-mémoire and 'calls upon Israel' to 'respond favorably' as well. U Thant observes that 'one very important feature of the vote was that every European country – East and West – voted for the resolution'. A yet more forceful General Assembly resolution the next year that 'deplores' Israel's failure to 'respond favorably' to Jarring's 'peace initiative', and 'invites Israel to declare publicly its adherence to the principle of non-annexation of territories through the use of force' garnered even more affirmative votes. Meeting in special session in July 1973, the Security Council debated a new resolution on the Middle East conflict. The crucial paragraphs read as follows:

> Strongly deplores Israel's continuing occupation of the territories occupied as a result of the 1967 conflict, contrary to the principles of the Charter;
> Expresses serious concern at Israel's lack of co-operation with the Special Representative of the Secretary-General...

The British ambassador deemed the draft – note, incidentally, that it included the definite article before 'territories' – a 'reasonable distillation of the view of the bulk of the members'. Thirteen votes were cast in favor, zero abstentions. The resolution did not pass, however. Beginning in 1971, Kissinger managed to sabotage Secretary of State Rogers's initiatives and redefine US policy toward the Middle East. As seen below, Kissinger aligned himself completely with the Israeli position. The US delegate accordingly vetoed the Security Council resolution. The last hope of averting a war was dashed.[32]

Flouting the international consensus, Israel moved to consolidate its hold on the conquered territories. In a 13 March 1971 interview with the London *Times*, Prime Minister Meir for the first time officially delineated the new boundaries that her government sought: Israel 'must have' Sharm-el-Shaykh and an overland connection to it, the border round Eilat 'must be' negotiated, Egypt 'could not return' to Gaza, the Golan Heights and a united Jerusalem must remain under Israeli control, and border adjustments on the West Bank would be necessary. Responding to Rogers's March press conference, Meir stated that Israel would 'definitely and categorically' not withdraw from Sharm-el-Shaykh, Gaza and important parts of the West Bank. Addressing the World Zionist Congress in January 1972, Eban stressed that he 'could not envisage any peace settlement without the permanent presence of Israeli forces in the Golan Heights and at Sharm-el-Shaykh'. (That month Eban also revealed that a 'further obstacle has been added on the road to peace': not Israel's intransigence, but the 'tyrant' Quaddafi, with whom Egypt was confederating.) In February 1972, Dayan publicly stated that the new border with Egypt should run from Sharm-el-Shaykh 'somewhere through Sinai to the Mediterranean', while Meir told *Time* magazine that 'Sharm-el-Shaykh is of absolutely no use to the Egyptians. ... For us it is a lifeline'. In March Eban reportedly conditioned resumption of UN-sponsored talks on the cancellation of the Jarring initiative. Speaking on Israeli radio in April, Meir avowed that 'Israel will never leave Jerusalem, the Golan Heights, Sharm-el-Shaykh or Gaza'. Interviewed by a Swedish journal in June, Eban stated that 'Jarring adopted a position that Israel cannot accept. ... Without control [of Sharm-el-Shaykh] a new war would start immediately'. Dayan declared in August that 'on the Egyptian border ... the key to security is the desert – the Sinai desert'. In March of the new year, Meir informed the National Press Club that the Golan Heights and Sharm-el-Shaykh were 'non-negotiable'. Next month Meir opined that Egypt should recognize the importance of Sharm-el-Shaykh to Israel 'just as we should recognize the vital importance of the Suez Canal to Egypt'. Come August, Israel's Cabinet gave the stamp of approval to the Galili Plan. An 'openly annexationist' (Kapeliouk) blueprint, it envisaged the intensification of settlement building in the West Bank, a new city of 230,000 christened Yamit in northeast Sinai, a deep sea port in southern Gaza, a civilian–industrial settlement in the Golan Heights ... [33]

Eban's widely acclaimed memoir encapsulates the record just sampled as follows: 'Between 1967 and 1973 the Arabs could have recovered all of Sinai, and the Golan, and most of the West Bank and Gaza without war by negotiating boundaries and security arrangements with Israel.'[34]

With all avenues for a diplomatic settlement blocked, Sadat confronted essentially two options: unconditional surrender – or war. He chose the second.[35] Beginning in summer 1972, Egypt, along with Syria, began preparations for a conventional attack with the limited aim of recovering the Israeli-occupied territories. Indeed, Sadat (unbeknownst to Assad of Syria) intended no more than the seizure of a small beachhead on the East Bank of the Suez Canal in order to demonstrate that Egypt was still a power to reckon with.[36] Ironically, probably no war in history has been launched with as much advance publicity as the 'surprise' attack of October 1973. Sadat repeatedly warned that, if Israel remained obdurate, Egypt would have no recourse but to launch an attack. To cite one of literally scores of examples, in a 9 April 1973 *Newsweek* interview, Sadat declared: 'The time has come for a shock. ... Everything is now being mobilized in earnest for the resumption of the battle – which is now inevitable.' The threats went unheeded, however, partly because one 'deadline' after another had passed without Sadat acting, but more so because Israel simply did not believe that Egypt had a war option. In this last calculation, Israel proved wrong – indeed in the war's first days, it appeared fatally so.[37]

In his account of the roots of the October war, Eban makes – albeit obliquely – a remarkable admission:

> If Dayan had wanted to put through a program based on exchanging Sinai for peace, he could have done so from his position of strength in the Labor Party, which had already espoused that principle through the Eshkol government in June 1967. This would have prevented the Yom Kippur War.

Leaving aside the unjustifiably *ad hominem* nature of the attack (who among Israel's leaders did not suffer from purblind triumphalism after the June victory?), Eban effectively concedes that Israel *could* have 'exchang[ed] Sinai for peace' before the October war. The *singular* obstacle to a diplomatic settlement – and cause of the October war – was Israel's refusal to evacuate the Sinai. Yet, Eban's admission begs another crucial question: Why did Israel 'put through a program based on exchanging Sinai for peace' after the October war at Camp David but not before it through Jarring's offices? I want now to address this issue.[38]

## The Language of Force

As suggested above, the Camp David Accord did not substantively differ from the Jarring initiative. In effect, what differences did exist proved inconsequential and cancelled each other out. On the one hand, Rabin points to Egypt's big concession of granting not only a peace treaty but 'full, normalized relations'. Yet, as Shimon Shamir euphemistically puts it, 'normalization, however, did not go very far'. On the other hand, Eban points to Israel's big concession of having 'virtually signed the West Bank and Gaza away'. That too proved a dead letter. What remains of the Camp David Accord – its core – is what Sadat offered in February 1971: the 'full exercise of Egyptian sovereignty up to the internationally recognized border between Egypt and mandated Palestine' and the concomitant 'withdrawal of Israeli armed forces from the Sinai' in exchange for a 'peace treaty' ('Framework for the Conclusion of a Peace Treaty Between Egypt and Israel'). In sum, 'Sinai for peace'. Indeed, as Eban himself suggests, the Camp David accord issued not from a new peace initiative but Israel's acquiescence in the old one: 'Once Begin and Sadat agreed on the principle of trading Sinai for peace, the treaty was only a matter of short time.'[39]

Articulating the Israeli consensus, Rabin recalls in his memoir that 'I certainly supported the government's opposition to withdrawal from the whole of the Sinai and found no difficulty in arguing that a "peace" of this nature was a sure recipe for another war'. How, then, did 'a sure recipe for another war' metamorphose into a 'sure recipe for a real peace'? On the rare occasions that this intriguing question is even suggested – it is never directly addressed since the Jarring initiative has been deposited in Orwell's memory hole – the standard reply is the magic worked by Sadat's journey to Jerusalem. As Rabin puts it in typically florid prose:

> The idea of delivering the offer to the Israeli people in person, in Jerusalem, was a stroke of genius, and I don't believe that without it there would have been much readiness on the part of the Israeli public to make so many concessions. ... The psychological impact of Sadat's visit was enormous. ... [H]is appearance before the Knesset forced Israel's government, as well as its citizens, to reassess what they had formerly considered to be their minimal demands for peace. Then Mr. Begin came out with his famous peace plan, in which the Israeli government agreed openly, for the first time, to the restoration of Egyptian sovereignty over every inch of Sinai.[40]

Yet, there is one tiny flaw with the dramatic tale of Sadat's 'stroke of genius'. According to Avraham Tamir, who coordinated all of Israel's strategic planning after the October war, Israel agreed to return Sinai *before* Sadat's genial trip to Jerusalem. Referring to the secret talks between Dayan and an Egyptian representative in September 1977, Tamir reports: 'Through this roundabout channel, the message was conveyed from Begin to Sadat that Egypt could expect to regain all of Sinai in exchange for peace. On 19 November, Sadat journeyed to Jerusalem on the historic visit that made world news.' Indeed, even the 'official' version of these events strains credulity. Immediately after Sadat's Knesset speech, Begin explicitly agreed at the one meeting between them to the 'formal restoration of sovereignty over the Sinai peninsula to Egypt'. Yet, Begin surely did not find much comfort in Sadat's speech. Over and over again the Egyptian president demanded not only the 'end [of] the Israeli occupation of the Arab territories occupied in 1967', but also the 'achievement of the fundamental rights of the Palestinian people and their right to self-determination, including their right to establish their own state'. *These* are the magical words that bridged the 'psychological barrier' and caused Israel to make a concession that it had withheld for fully a decade?[41]

There is, incidentally, an instructive lesson in Israel's handling of the Sinai issue. Although formally agreeing to restore Egypt's sovereignty, Israel haggled until the very end to retain parts of Sinai. Specifically, it sought to maintain control of the settlements, airfields and oil refineries that it had built. Yet Sharm-el-Shaykh – that 'vital' 'lifeline' that Israel 'definitely and categorically' would not evacuate – figured not at all in these intense, often bitter, negotiations. Indeed, Israel bargained to keep the settlements mainly for fear that dismantling them would set a bad precedent for the West Bank. It bargained to keep the airfields mainly to force the United States to foot the bill for building new ones within Israel proper. And it bargained to maintain the oil refineries mainly to force the United States to guarantee its future petroleum supplies. Israel's one and only supposed 'security' interest in the Sinai – Sharm-el-Shaykh – was quietly abandoned without even a whimper. One may, I think, learn something from this episode about the substance – or lack thereof – of Israel's avowed security concerns. Indeed, Israel's control of Sharm-el-Shaykh proved 'of no use' (Schiff) during the October war. Predictably, Egypt simply blockaded the Bab el-Mandab Straits below Sharm-el-Shaykh to prevent Israeli ships from entering Eilat.[42]

In any event, what made a diplomatic settlement possible in 1977 but not 1971 was the breakthrough, not of Sadat's journey, but of Egyptian troops. In an important study, *Israël: la fin des mythes*, Amnon Kapeliouk points to a cluster of pervasive assumptions that underpinned Israeli security doctrine after 1967. Central among these was the belief that 'war is not an Arab game'. In a word, Arabs could not fight. Typically, General Ezer Weizman sneered 'War, that's not for the Arabs'. General and Professor

Yehoshafat Harkabi 'diagnosed' that Arabs were congenitally incapable of battle solidarity: 'At the crucial moment of combat, an Arab soldier finds himself not supported by a tightly-knit unit but abandoned to his own devices. The combat unit disintegrates as each soldier looks out only for himself.' Two months before the October war, Dayan lectured the Israeli army's general staff that 'the weakness of the Arabs arises from factors so deeply rooted that they cannot, in my view, be easily overcome: the moral, technical and educational backwardness of their soldiers', and that 'the balance of forces is so much in our favor that it neutralizes the Arab considerations and motives for the immediate renewal of hostilities'. General Uzi Narkiss proclaimed that 'Israel's principal enemy in the 1970s is the Soviet Union. The Arabs are merely secondary enemies who harass Israel in the area of relatively minor defence problems'. Eban derisively recalls the 'official doctrine ... that an Egyptian assault would be drowned in a sea of blood, that the Arabs had no military option'. He quotes from an article by Rabin in July 1973 that 'reads like an anthology of all the misconceptions that were destined to explode a few weeks later':

> Our present defense lines give us a decisive advantage in the Arab–Israel balance of strength. There is no need to mobilize our forces whenever we hear Arab threats. ... The Arabs have little capacity for coordinating their military and political action. ... Israel's military strength is sufficient to prevent the other side from gaining any military objective.

'An atmosphere of "manifest destiny", regarding the neighboring people as "lesser breeds without the law"', Eban adds, 'began to spread in the national discourse.' Schiff casually mentions that the Israeli soldier's 'nickname' for his opposite number in the Egyptian army was 'monkey'. Indeed, it was precisely these arrogant, racist assumptions that enabled Egypt and Syria to achieve such a degree of surprise in October. 'The Israelis' overconfidence', observes a military historian, 'made them so certain that the Arabs would not dare attack, that they simply could not believe the abundant evidence that was inconsistent with their perceptions.'[43]

Crucially, Kissinger – who effectively dictated US policy, and thereby held a veto over Israeli policy, in the Middle East – shared the belief that 'war was not an Arab game'. In a conversation with Meir shortly after the war, Kissinger reportedly recalled:

> Do you remember what we all thought before the war? – that we never had it better, and therefore there was no hurry? We and you were both convinced that the Arabs had no military option which required serious diplomatic action. Instead of doing something we joked about the shoes the Egyptians left behind in 1967.

Told by an Egyptian diplomat that 'if there weren't some agreement then there would be war', Kissinger further rued, 'in my heart I laughed and laughed. A war? Egypt? I regarded it as empty talk, a boast empty of content'.[44]

Israeli society was dealt a devastating blow by the Arab attack. Tamir recalls it as the 'most shattering experience in the history of Israel. ... Within a few days the tide had turned, but the initial shock remained'. Schiff similarly observes that 'the Day of Judgment War shook Israel from its foundations to the very summit. A deep lack of confidence suddenly replaced the exaggerated arrogance, and was most noticeable among leaders and senior officers'. Eban painfully recalls that in the first days of the war 'it was plain that we were in military disarray'. Rating the early days 'without a doubt ... the worst defeat in the history of the Israeli army', Dupuy reports that the 'Israeli government was close to panic'. Indeed, Dayan uttered such 'horrifying comments' as 'This is a war for the "Third Temple", not for Sinai'. It was, according to Schiff, 'the IDF's first war in which doctors ha[d] to treat numerous shock cases'. Then there was the 'moral crisis' that 'after years of fostering the tradition of not leaving wounded on the battlefield, the IDF now found itself having to abandon both wounded and fit in enemy territory'.[45]

The balance-sheet at war's end was a sobering one. Shlaim observes that the October war 'radically changed the whole political and psychological balance of power to Israel's disadvantage'. Indeed, according to Schiff, Israel's most knowledgeable and influential military correspondent, Israel suffered from a 'post-war trauma' that it 'had returned overnight to square one – where it all started. Despite all her past victories, Israel suddenly found herself again pondering dangers and realizing that defeat in large-scale local battles can endanger her existence'.[46]

Worse still, the war had significantly enhanced the prospect of yet another round – with Israel's victory at best uncertain. 'The October 1973 war had fortified the Arabs' self-confidence,' Weizman underlined.

> Above all, it had reduced the deterrent capacity of our armed forces. Previously, we could expect the Arabs to think twice before allowing their fingers to curl around the trigger; but in the Yom Kippur war the Arabs learned that, under certain conditions, they were capable of achieving some battlefield gains.

Weizman's somber assessment was echoed by Schiff:

> Clearly, the results of the ... war will contribute to a 'morale revolution' in the Arab armies. ... This is the first time in the history of the Arab–Israeli conflict that Arab armies have recorded any kind of military achievement. They will obviously be spurred on to additional investment and effort ... to narrow the

quality gap. ... Despite her victories and growing military power, Israel cannot deter her enemies from attacking. ... The Arabs broke the fear barrier. They weren't victorious but, for the first time, they didn't fail.

Schiff's forecast about the outcome of the next war was equally ominous: 'Exact prediction of the nature of a future war is impossible, but the general trends may be deduced. It will obviously be more difficult than its predecessor, more vicious and bloodier. The civilian rear will be hit, and Israel must assume that she will have immediately to fight on three fronts.' And again, under the dire heading 'Doubtful Supremacy': 'Israel's military supremacy has been placed in doubt by the Day of Judgment war, and she cannot foresee the future to the degree that was possible in and after the Six Day War.'

Schiff centrally concluded that 'in the new conditions, the importance of a political settlement obviously increases. Time isn't on Israel's side, and she must make greater efforts to achieve a true peace'. This is exactly what Israel moved to do – if only with the one country that had proven itself capable of speaking the 'language of force'.[47]

The United States predictably reached much the same conclusions as Israel. Quandt reports that the October war 'challenged the prevailing attitude of policymakers toward the Arab world'. Israel's 'military power had not ensured stability' and the Arabs 'had apparently fought quite well'. The United States accordingly 'for the first time ... committed its top diplomatic resources to a sustained search for a settlement of the Arab–Israeli conflict'. 'Politics', Kissinger lectured the Egyptian journalist Mohamed Heikal in the war's aftermath, 'in our age is not a question of emotions, it is the facts of power.' Put simply: to count, you must speak the 'language of force'.[48]

Addressing an international colloquium, Chief of Staff Mordechai Gur speculated with remarkable caution, 'I really think – and I do not want to be too outspoken – I really think we have a good basis to assume that we can win a war; the question is how best to do it.' Indeed, a consensus quickly crystallized 'on how best to do it': neutralize Egypt. The Arab battlefield successes in the October war were largely credited to the Egyptian account. Sadat's 'prestige was ... enhanced', Dupuy reports, 'by the brilliant military success of the war, and by the fact that, despite later setbacks, the Egyptian armed forces ended the war intact with clearly one of the most powerful military machines in the world'. For the deputy Israeli commander on the Egyptian front, the war had made 'one thing clear: the Egyptian army can be considered a good army, and there is no room for contempt'. Schiff reckons that the Egyptians had achieved 'a kind of territorial draw' with Israel. Yet, 'on the Syrian front', Schiff continues, 'Israel undoubtedly won a major victory. ... The Syrian Army wasn't destroyed, but damaged and decimated'. Addressing the same colloquium as Gur, Rabin brusquely dismissed the threat posed by Syria: 'Militarily, Syria alone is no problem whatsoever for Israel.' Ditto the Palestinians: 'Terrorism is not a threat to Israel's existence. ... I wish that the so-called PLO would be the only problem Israel would have to face – then Israel would have no problem.' 'Egypt', Rabin stressed, 'is the key country.'[49]

The inexorable conclusion was that, for Israel to sustain its regional hegemony, Egypt – but Egypt alone – must be removed from the Arab front. At the colloquium, Rabin pointed to 'relations between Egypt and Israel' as the 'key to the Arab–Israeli conflict'. Dayan quipped to Carter before Sadat's journey that 'the future is with Egypt. If you take one wheel off a car, it won't drive. If Egypt is out of the conflict, there will be no more war'. The US analysis once again mirrored Israel's. Carter observes in his memoir that 'it was fairly obvious that the key to any future military threats against Israel was the Egyptians, who could provide the most formidable invading force and who had always been in the forefront of previous battles'. The logical inference, Quandt reports Carter reasoning, was that Israel must reach an accord with them: 'Peace between Egypt and Israel would not make war impossible in the Middle East, but it would dramatically change its nature.'[50]

Egypt's basic formula for a settlement had not changed one whit since February 1971: 'Sinai for peace.' Ratification of the formula followed in short order at Camp David, Kissinger's razzmatazz 'shuttle diplomacy' largely an irrelevant sideshow. The other Arab states were left out in the cold. For Quandt, 'the disregard of Syria's position seems hard to understand'. Eban similarly muses that 'the refusal of other Arab leaders to follow Sadat's journey and to reap similar fruits is one of the mysteries of the years that followed the Egyptian–Israeli peace treaty'. The mystery is easily solved once one recalls that to pass Jerusalem's gates Sadat had first to learn the keeper's 'language'. Jordan and Syria did not – at any rate, not sufficiently well to impress. So entry was barred.[51]

With Egypt neutralized at Camp David, Israel sought to consolidate its control of the West Bank and Gaza. The big club could now be wielded with relative impunity. Indeed, removing Egypt from the Arab front was the crucial precondition for the war plans now set in motion. In 1982, Israel moved to destroy the political nexus of the Palestinian national movement based in Lebanon. Some twenty thousand Lebanese and Palestinian souls perished between June and September – ample testimony that, so far as Israel was concerned, nothing had changed in the Middle East. The operative language was still force.[52]

# 7

## Oslo:
## The Apartheid Option

This chapter will assess the significance of the 'peace process' inaugurated by the September 1993 Oslo I agreement. I will first examine the September 1995 Oslo II agreement, the definitive document for the interim period until a final settlement is reached, and then consider the likely outcome of the 'peace process'. To clarify the issues at stake, I will refer to two illuminating critiques of Oslo I, Edward Said's *Peace and its Discontents* and Meron Benvenisti's *Intimate Enemies*.[1]

The essence of the September 1993 Oslo agreement, according to Edward Said, was that it gave 'official Palestinian consent to continued occupation.' Indeed, the PLO agreed to serve as 'Israel's enforcer'.[2] 'The occupation continued' after Oslo I, Meron Benvenisti similarly observes, 'albeit by remote control, and with the consent of the Palestinian people, represented by their "sole representative", the PLO'.[3] A close reading of the September 1995 Oslo II agreement only reinforces these judgments.[4]

Until Oslo, the international consensus supported a complete Israeli withdrawal from the West Bank and Gaza, and the right of Palestinians to form an independent state within the evacuated areas. The PLO accepted these terms. Israel and the US rejected them. Oslo II states that 'Neither Party shall be deemed, by virtue of having entered into this Agreement, to have renounced or waived any of its existing rights, claims, or positions'.[5] Seemingly balanced, this provision actually signals a most crucial concession by the Palestinians. In effect, the PLO grants a legitimacy to Israel's pretence of possessing 'existing rights' in the West Bank and Gaza, and to Israel's rejectionist 'claims, or positions', including those denying Palestinians the right to sovereignty in the West Bank and Gaza, which need not be 'renounced or waived'. The broadly affirmed title of the Palestinians to the occupied territories is now put on a par with the broadly denied title of Israel to them. 'The West Bank and Gaza', writes Said, 'have now become "disputed territories." Thus with Palestinian assistance Israel has been awarded at least an equal claim to them.'[6] Once beyond dispute, Israel's withdrawal will now be subject to the give-and-take of 'permanent status negotiations'. With Palestinians on one side, and Israel and the US on the other, little imagination is needed to predict who will give and who will take.

## The Oslo Agreement

On all crucial issues – Jerusalem, water, reparations, sovereignty, security, land – Palestinians, according to Said, 'have in effect gained nothing.'[7] The actual picture is, if anything, even bleaker than Said suggests.

*Jerusalem*: Amid an analysis of Jerusalem as the nexus of Israel's conquest strategy ('an ever-expanding Jerusalem [is] the core of a web extending into the West Bank and Gaza'), Said presciently observes that 'in the history of colonial invasion … maps are instruments of conquest'.[8] Turning to Oslo II, we find that, although the text defers Jerusalem's fate to the permanent status negotiations,[9] to judge by the map appended to the accord, Jerusalem is already a closed issue. The official map for Oslo II implicitly places Jerusalem *within* Israel. Said also laments that the PLO agreed to 'cooperate with a military occupation before that occupation had ended, and before even the government of Israel had admitted that it was in effect a government of military occupation'.[10] In fact, the so-called Green Line demarcating pre-June 1967 Israel from the occupied West Bank has been effaced on the official Oslo II map. The area between the Mediterranean and Jordan now constitutes a unitary entity. Seamlessly incorporating the West Bank, Israel has ceased to be, in the new cartographic reality, an occupying power. On the other hand, the textual claim that Oslo II preserves the 'integrity' of the West Bank and Gaza as a 'single territorial unit'[11] is mockingly belied by the map's yellow and brown blotches denoting relative degrees of Palestinian control awash in a sea of white denoting total Israeli sovereignty. In sum, the official map for Oslo II ratifies an extreme version of the Labour Party's Allon Plan and gives the lie to the tentative language of the agreement itself. [12]

*Water*: Although Palestinians will be granted an increment to meet 'immediate needs … for domestic use', the overarching principle on water allocation for the interim period is 'maintenance of existing quantities of utilization', that is, 'average annual quantities … shall constitute the basis and guidelines'.[13] Turning to Schedule 10 ('Data Concerning Aquifers'), we learn that these 'average annual quantities' give Israelis approximately 80 per cent and Palestinians 20 per cent of West Bank water.[14] Prospects after the interim period seem even dimmer. Although Israel does 'recognize Palestinian water rights in the West Bank', these rights do *not* include the 'ownership of water', which will be subject to the permanent status negotiations.[15] Indeed, Israel already claims legal title to most of the West Bank water on the basis of 'historic usage'.[16] That is, having stolen Palestinian water for nearly three decades, Israelis now proclaim it is theirs. The anarchist Proudhon, at any rate, would not have been surprised: 'Property', he famously quipped, 'is theft.'

*Reparations*: Juxtaposing the cases of Germany and Iraq, Said repeatedly deplores the absence of any provision for Israel to pay reparations: 'The PLO leadership signed an agreement with Israel in effect saying that Israelis were absolutely without responsibility for all the crimes they committed'.[17] Indeed, Oslo II explicitly imposes on the newly-elected Palestinian Council 'all liabilities and obligations arising with regard to acts or omissions' which occurred in the course of Israel's rule. 'Israel will cease to bear any financial responsibility regarding such acts or omissions and the Council will bear all financial responsibility.' In what might be called the *chutzpah* clause, the Palestinian administration must 'immediately reimburse Israel the full amount' of any award that 'is made against Israel by any court or tribunal' for its past crimes. To be sure, Israel will provide 'legal assistance' to the Council should a Palestinian sue the latter for losses incurred during the Israeli occupation.[18] Washing its hands of all responsibility for nearly three decades of rapacious rule, Israel – Said rues – 'crowed' while 'an ill-equipped, understaffed, woefully incompetent Palestine National Authority struggled unsuccessfully to keep hospitals open and supplied, pay teachers' salaries, pick up garbage, and so on', and 'dumped' Gaza 'in Arafat's lap ... even though it had made the place impossible to sustain'.[19] As we shall see, South Africa's apartheid regime displayed rather more magnanimity after its comparable withdrawal from and institution of 'self-rule' in areas of black settlement. Even after conceding the Bantustans independence, South Africa continued to cover much more than half their budgets through grants.

*Sovereignty*: Oslo II refers only to an Israeli 'redeployment', not a withdrawal, from the West Bank.[20] Excluded from the Palestinian Council's purview are 'Jerusalem, settlements, specified military locations, Palestinian refugees, borders, foreign relations and Israelis'.[21] Israel retains full 'criminal jurisdiction ... over offences committed' anywhere in the West Bank 'by Israelis' or 'against Israel or an Israeli'.[22] Regarding internal

Palestinian affairs, the Council effectively cannot 'amend or abrogate existing laws or military orders' without Israel's acquiescence.[23] There is even an explicit proscription on the wording of postage stamps which 'shall include only the terms "the Palestinian Council" or "the Palestinian Authority"'.[24] On a related matter, the Palestinian National Council must 'formally approve the necessary changes in regard to the Palestinian Covenant'.[25] No comparable demand is put on Israel to renounce its long-standing claim to the West Bank – and much beyond.

*Security*: Israel retains 'responsibility for external security, as well as responsibility for overall security of Israelis'.[26] In the name of 'security', Israel is thus free to pursue any Palestinian anywhere.[27] Although duty bound to protect Israeli settlers and settlements that are illegal under international law,[28] the Palestinian police cannot – 'shall under no circumstances' – 'apprehend or place in custody or prison' any Israeli.[29] Israel preserves the right 'to close the crossing points to Israel'.[30] Palestinians who, due to Israel's systematic destruction of their economy, are dependent on work in Israel are thus still left to the latter's mercies. Israel retains 'responsibility for security' at the border crossings to the West Bank and Gaza. Accordingly, it can detain or deny passage to any person entering through the 'Palestinian Wing', and enjoys 'exclusive responsibility' for all persons entering through the 'Israeli Wing'. Said dismisses these arrangements as a 'one-sided farce'.[31] Yet, Palestinians do get to post a policeman and hoist a flag at their entrance and provision is made for the expeditious processing of Palestinian VIPs.[32] The 'Palestinian side' also gets to issue new ID numbers for residents of the West Bank and Gaza – which, however, 'will be transferred to the Israeli side'.[33]

*Land*: The first phase of Israel's redeployment leaves Palestinians with territorial jurisdiction over only 30 per cent of the West Bank. Further redeployments are promised in the future but their extent is not specified.[34] And within the areas coming under Palestinian territorial jurisdiction, Israel continues to claim undefined 'legal rights'.[35] Moreover, the Palestinian areas are non-contiguous. A caricature of South Africa's Bantustans, the Palestinian territorial jurisdiction comprises scores of tiny, isolated fragments.

## Palestinian Incompetence or Israeli Obduracy?

Said is plainly right that Israel 'achieved all of its tactical and strategic objectives at the expense of the Palestinians'.[36] More problematic, however, is his explanation of how this defeat came to pass. Perhaps because

*Peace and its Discontents* was written with an 'Arab audience in mind',[37] Said puts the onus on PLO bungling. With unfortunate echoes of Abba Eban's famous quip, 'the Palestinians have never missed an opportunity to miss an opportunity for peace', Said ruefully recalls Arafat's 'catastrophic misjudgments and failures', running from the 'folly of Palestinian involvement in Lebanese affairs [that] was to lead to the disasters of 1982', through peace overtures of the Carter Administration that 'Arafat categorically turned down', to 'the misguided policies of the PLO leadership during the Gulf crisis'.[38] Not only are these judgments open to question[39] but cumulatively they tend to obscure US–Israeli culpability for the undermining of Palestinian national aspirations. For all its corruption, criminality and incompetence, the PLO did endorse, from the mid-1970s, a full peace with Israel in exchange for a full Israeli withdrawal from the West Bank and Gaza. Notwithstanding the international consensus favoring such a two-state settlement, the US and Israel blocked implementation. Oslo signaled the complete triumph of US–Israeli force. Consider as an illuminating comparison the Camp David accord of 1977, an earlier milestone in the 'peace process'.

In February 1971, Egypt offered Israel a full peace treaty in exchange for a full Israeli withdrawal from the occupied Sinai. Claiming security imperatives, Israel obdurately refused. Note the exact symmetry of Arab offer and Israeli response on the Egyptian and Palestinian fronts. What then accounts for Israel's acquiescence in full withdrawal at Camp David in 1977 but not at Oslo in 1993? Said opines that 'for the Arabs, war has had disastrous effects'.[40] This is not altogether true. What brought Israel around at Camp David was not an Egyptian diplomatic offensive but the offensive of Egyptian troops in the October 1973 war.[41] Israel, like all conquering powers, only understands the language of force. Said no doubt knows all this. Indeed, he himself insists that the 'struggle over Palestine is principally' a 'real or material one', not a 'psychological misunderstanding'. To prevail, Palestinians must match Israel tit-for-tat in the hardball politics of power.[42] A quantitative juxtaposition of the Camp David and the Oslo II accords also points up the reality of Israeli intentions in the West Bank. Specifying in simple, lapidary phrases a full Israeli withdrawal and reciprocal Egyptian pledge of peace, the historic Camp David accord runs to barely seven pages. The 1979 Egyptian–Israeli peace treaty comes to less than ten pages. Yet, the Oslo II accord fills more than three hundred folio-size pages. With its multiple, chapter-length annexes and appendices and multitude of pettifogging, obscure, ambiguous and mutually contradictory details, Oslo II presages, not the emancipation, but the emasculation of Palestine.

## Consequences of the Agreement

One may want to argue that, the letter of Oslo notwithstanding, implementation of the accord's provisions for a Palestinian council, police force and so forth, will still put Palestinians in a better position to achieve true self-determination. The tacit, Pollyannaish assumption is that *any* new reality must improve on the present state of affairs. Yet, the new reality will more than likely allow for the tightening of Israel's grip on the Palestinians. This is the 'Bantustanization' scenario projected not only by Said but seasoned Israeli analysts as well. 'It goes without saying', Benvenisti writes, 'that "cooperation" based on the current power relationship is no more than permanent Israeli domination in disguise, and that Palestinian self-rule is merely a euphemism for Bantustanization'.[43]

Before considering this prospect, it is important to first take note of another significant Palestinian loss at Oslo. Said recalls the opinion of Walter Sisulu that 'one reason for the African National Congress's victory was its *international* campaign against apartheid'.[44] Every effort South Africa made to normalize its global standing through cosmetic concessions such as Bantustan 'self-rule' and subsequent independence proved unavailing. Its isolation only deepened. Yet, Oslo has allowed for the full rehabilitation of Israel. No longer condemned as an occupying power, Israel rather stands beyond reproach as a full-fledged peacemaker. Indeed, all the United Nations resolutions which, as Said observes, 'although ... paper resolutions ... represented the only international guarantee that [Palestinian] claims would not be ignored',[45] have been effectively nullified by Oslo. This contrast suggests that, in the short term at least, Bantustanization will prove more stable in the West Bank and Gaza than it did in the South African setting. I will return to this point presently.

After World War II, South Africa embarked on the path of separate development or apartheid to ease the conflict between an ethnically exclusivist state and an ethnically heterogeneous population. Hendrik Verwoerd, post-war Prime Minister and architect of apartheid, conceived the new initiative primarily as a political expedient to abate foreign criticism.[46] Using the vocabulary of decolonization, the South African government contrived a political separation in which whites took the lion's share of material resources and blacks were effectively consigned to a state of total thraldom. Technically free of South African domination through the creation of Bantustans, blacks – Verwoerd imagined – would have only themselves to blame for their abject state. Slow to see the merits of this scheme, skeptical whites (including Cabinet ministers) feared that the homelands or Bantustans would enhance black political power and undermine security, giving free rein to 'Mau Mau'-type terrorism. On the other side, sincere opponents of South African rule at first looked favorably on the Bantustans as a step toward justice.

Comprising multiple fragments of barren land encircled by white settlements, each Bantustan was originally cast not as an independent state – a prospect the Republic officially ruled out – but rather as an area of ethnic 'self-rule'. The South African government forcibly removed from the designated homelands white residents, who angrily charged that they had been 'sold down the river'.[47] The first homeland granted 'self-rule' was Transkei in 1963. Maintaining that 'more was to be achieved by supporting separate development than by opposing it', the leader of the new entity, Chief Matanzima, could point to the trappings of self-determination such as a Transkeian flag and national anthem.[48] Its power narrowly circumscribed by the South African-imposed constitution, the Transkei government was vested only with such civil responsibilities as tax collection, education, local public works, agriculture, courts and welfare. South Africa reserved for itself jurisdiction over external and internal security (Transkeian units performing basic police functions), foreign affairs, communications, transportation, financial institutions, and population movement. It also retained a veto on all Transkei legislation and jurisdiction over whites within Transkei's borders. Note that Oslo II is a veritable carbon copy of the Transkei constitution. As even an observer sympathetic to the Bantustan experiment conceded, 'The central Government holds the whip hand.'[49]

Although Matanzima, with a nod from South Africa, kept an iron grip on power in Transkei, political dissent was marginally tolerated. Indeed, 'deeply concerned that self-government should not be seen as a puppet show', South Africa even encouraged 'a certain amount of opposition. ... It shows that the figures are alive.'[50] Creating 'growth points' with tax concessions and especially cheap labour as incentives, South Africa sought to lure foreign investment on the periphery of and later inside Transkei. In fact, only a 'tiny percentage of the population' benefited from these policies, while the Transkei economy, tightly monitored by South Africa, became ever more closely linked and subordinate to it.[51] The identical strategy with identical results is, as Said shows, now unfolding in the West Bank and Gaza, with 'growth points' rechristened 'industrial parks'.[52] Such an economic strategy serves the dual purpose of allowing for the exploitation of cheap indigenous labour while maintaining an exclusivist ethnic state, and enhancing the credibility of the Bantustan alternative by making it financially solvent.

## Sovereignty Without Justice

As international pressures mounted, South Africa moved to grant Transkei independence in 1976. Arguing that it would legitimate a division of wealth grossly unfavorable to the interests of blacks, opposition leaders rejected the South African initiative. Through adept political maneuvering, Matanzima was able, however, to muster a popular electoral mandate for independence, although only a small minority truly supported it.[53] An emergent entrepreneurial class, together with the traditional, conservative elites and a privileged – and corrupt – official class administering the bloated bureaucracy, undergirded the new order. Matanzima maintained that the Transkeian 'nation' had successfully rid itself of colonial domination. Indeed, it did enjoy the same legal status as any other state. Yet no foreign power recognized Transkei's independence, the United Nations General Assembly declaring it 'invalid' by a vote of 134 to zero, with only the US abstaining.

After independence, the Transkei government did, to its credit, abolish the most egregious apartheid regulations,[54] but it also muzzled all political opposition. One observes a similar dynamic in the West Bank and Gaza, with the arbitrary humiliations, curfews and so forth typical of Israeli rule curtailed, yet with Arafat putting in place – in Said's words – a 'system of dictatorial rule ... in which citizens' rights, especially in the realm of civil freedoms, will be absent.'[55] South Africa's refusal to cede additional land to Transkei evoked angry denunciations and threats to sever ties from Matanzima. Shackled by its total economic thralldom to the white republic, the Transkei regime was in no position, however, to make good on its threats.[56] Willingly or not, it remained what it had always been: a servant of South African power.

The case of the KwaZulu Bantustan is equally revealing. Through the mid-1970s, Chief Buthelezi of KwaZulu won guarded praise from the African National Congress and even the militant South African Students' Organization, and the enmity of South African whites alienated by his defiant posturing. Situating participation in the Bantustan scheme within a wider strategy of creating a 'liberated area from which I can engage in the liberation struggle on South African soil', and offering 'some hope for the Zulu', Buthelezi claimed that cooperation with South Africa did not signify support of apartheid but rather acquiescence in the only available option: 'What will be more gratifying to us ... than to think that we did our best in the circumstances and to the very limit of what was possible?'[57] Like Transkei, KwaZulu abolished the most obnoxious features of apartheid. Indeed, demanding a more equitable distribution of South African resources, Buthelezi – unlike Matanzima – balked at independence on the Republic's terms. Eventually, however, KwaZulu reeked of massive political and financial corruption, with Buthelezi in the thrall of a messianic complex and an obsessive concern with status.[58]

As mass resistance to apartheid mounted, Bantustan leaders made common cause with the South African government. Homeland defense forces, trained and equipped by, and pledged to the security of South Africa, repeatedly clashed with African National Congress guerrillas. South Africa's repressive rule was partially concealed behind the veil of 'black-on-black' violence. Bantustans did not serve as a transit point to true emancipation; rather, they proved a major obstacle to it. Calling for the dismantling of apartheid and political reunification with South Africa, even the leaders of the Bantustans ultimately denounced them as a sham.

## The Question of Statehood

Edward Said writes that 'there is a gigantic and inherent difference between "limited self-rule" and "independence"' and that the Oslo accords 'do not include any reference, not one sentence, about the Palestinians' right to self-determination'.[59] The clear implication is that the crucial issue is Palestinian statehood. This emphasis, I think, is misplaced. If the South African precedent is any guide, Israel will eventually grant Palestinians full independence within the patchwork areas of 'self rule' adumbrated in Oslo II. This is especially so since pressures will undoubtedly build to 'normalize' the status of Palestinians and a relatively stable Palestinian elite beholden to Israel will undoubtedly crystallize. If cast in terms of statehood, the Palestinian question will then be technically resolved. At any rate, there will be no further basis for complaint.

Yet, even the conservative critique of apartheid was anchored in the more substantive, albeit more abstract, principle of equity: the white regime had engineered an unfair division of South Africa's resources. Consider the argument of a basically sympathetic critic of the Bantustan experiment. 'The principal deficiency', Kenneth Stultz wrote:

is that ... no African could see that the whites of South Africa had given up anything of substance in order that Transkei independence should occur. On the contrary, it appeared that the whites had *gained* greater respectability for their exclusion of blacks from equal treatment in the cities. Nor could it be believed that the Transkei representatives enjoyed effective leverage in the negotiations themselves. Certainly Pretoria wished Transkei to seek independence in order to validate its policy of separate development, but there is no evidence that the Vorster government was made to pay a high price to ensure its happening. In short, Transkei independence lacks the legitimizing element of real and material sacrifices on the part of the white population. ... Although political power has exchanged hands in consequence of Transkei independence, if only the power Transkeians now have ... to police themselves and administer their own poverty, there has been no shifting in the ownership of great amounts of wealth.[60]

Note the issue was not that Transkei was a 'neo-colony'. Even if true, it was irrelevant: many an African state, alas, exercised little real independence. Indeed, Stultz was at pains to show that the Transkei state fared no worse economically than neighbouring countries. If Transkei was, by virtue of its material dependence, illegitimate, so were they. Rather, the critical principle for Stultz was equity. True, Transkei's blacks achieved independence. So weak was their bargaining position, however, that South Africa kept for itself everything worth keeping. All Transkeians won was the right to 'police themselves and administer their own poverty'. Bantustanization was, for white South Africans, basically cost-free and therefore unjust.

Compare now Meron Benvenisti's authoritative assessment of Oslo:

> while Israel is free to act independently in its own sovereign area, it insists on 'coordinating' the usage of natural resources by the Palestinians, so that Israeli interests will not be harmed. This asymmetry perpetuates the existing inequality in the distribution of common natural resources and re-emphasizes the impression of a victor's peace. For the Israelis, it is peace without pain or sacrifice, a bargain proposition ... [61]

Thus, by the standard of even a conservative critique of apartheid, the Oslo accord, even if it culminates in independence for the marginal areas currently reserved for Palestinian 'self-rule', lacks legitimacy. Significantly, in the matter of apartheid, the international community acknowledged that the fundamental issue was not statehood but equity. As noted above, no country recognized Transkei's independence. Accordingly, international pressures on the apartheid regime did not relax. Yet, the enthusiastic reception accorded Oslo suggests that equity is no longer a concern of the world community. Recall that the two-state settlement hitherto supported by the global consensus was predicated on a *full* Israeli withdrawal. Such a division was arguably equitable. Israel is now called on to withdraw only from *parts* of the West Bank and Gaza, in effect, the parts it doesn't want.[62] The PLO's capitulation crucially legitimized this reversal. If Israel eventually grants independence to the hodgepodge areas that now exercise 'self-rule', the Palestine question will probably be dropped altogether from the international agenda. Palestinians will no longer be able to benefit from the kind of international solidarity that contributed so mightily to the collapse of the apartheid regime.

## The Chimera of Separation?

The critique of apartheid ultimately rested, however, not on a moral but rather a political, indeed, pragmatic foundation: separation was a pipe dream. 'The theory of apartheid in its pure form', wrote Christopher Hill:

> was that there should be *total* separation of White and Black, the Africans being returned to their Reserves, which though small would become highly industrialized states. Their economies would complement that of White South Africa, which would entirely dispense with African labour and rely for manpower upon greatly increased White immigration.

Yet, the basic premise that the 'existing economic integration between the races can be unscrambled' proved to be – in Hill's word – a 'fiction'.[63] South Africa could not free itself of dependence on black labour and the Bantustans could not free themselves of dependence on South African employment and subventions. Every appreciable enterprise in South Africa continued to employ, and relied on the Bantustans as a reservoir for, cheap African labour. On the other side, migrants labouring in South Africa accounted for fully 70 per cent of the gross national income in the Bantustans. Over half of the economically active Transkei male labour force, for instance, was annually recruited for work in the Republic. Without the remittances dispatched home by the migrant workers, the Bantustan economies – such as they were – would have collapsed. Indeed, the Bantustans depended, even after independence, on South African grants for fully 60–80 per cent of even current expenditures.[64]

Israel has been less reliant than South Africa on indigenous labour. Due to Israel's systematic ruination of the West Bank/Gaza economy, Palestinians in these areas are still reliant on work in Israel, a fact highlighted by the devastation wrought on their economy by the closures. Meron Benvenisti forcefully argues that the Oslo-contrived 'unscrambling' of Israel and Palestine is equally illusory. The accord, he observes:

> provided for the establishment of a permanent committee to supervise co-operation in a long list of areas, such as water, electricity and energy, finance and international investment and banking, the port of Gaza, communication and transport, industry, labor relations, human resources, and protection of the environment. The long list of areas in which cooperation and coordination is essential points to one basic fact that the advocates of 'separation' have yet to grasp: the country, from the Jordan to the sea, can perhaps be divided politically, but not physically.[65]

In fact, it is uncertain whether the two-state settlement itself is feasible. Benvenisti thinks it isn't. Although Said clings, throughout most of the book, to the two-state settlement,[66] there is a notable change of emphasis in the concluding chapter:

> Palestine/Israel ... is the place where two peoples, whether they like it or not, live inextricably linked lives, tied together by history, war, daily contact, and suffering. To speak in grandiose geopolitical terms, or to speak mindlessly about 'separating' them is nothing less than to provide prescriptions for more violence and degradation. There is simply no substitute for seeing these two communities as equal to each other in rights and expectations, and then proceeding from there to do justice to their living actualities.[67]

As Said's parting words suggest, the inevitable if very distant future is one in which Palestinian Arabs and Israeli Jews, enjoying reciprocal communal and individual rights, coexist within a unitary entity. Whether a two-state settlement might in the interim ease the suffering of Palestinians and provide a point of transition to a more desirable and feasible resolution of the conflict remains an open question. But there can be little doubt that, consigned to a footnote, Oslo will one day be dismissed as a sordid detour on the path to a just and lasting peace.

# Abba Eban with Footnotes

A Critical Review of Michael Oren's *Six Days of War:*
*June 1967 and the Making of the Modern Middle East* [1]

I

Michael Oren's new study of the June 1967 war has enjoyed unusual success in the United States. Although weighed down with nearly a hundred pages of endnotes and bibliography, this 'most comprehensive history ever published' (book blurb) of the June war immediately leapt to the top of best-seller lists. *The New York Times* lavished unstinting praise on the book ('gripping', 'fascinating', 'staggering', 'masterly', 'engrossing', 'fabulous', 'thrilling', 'powerful') in several reviews, while *Newsweek* reported that even President Bush had been greatly influenced by it.[2]

In his introduction Oren, an American-born Israeli historian, professes that his account of the June war is uncommonly detached (*SDW*: pp. xiv–xv). Were this the case it would surely be an achievement, especially in light of the author's own pronounced right-wing political biases.[3] In fact, Oren basically reiterates the official Israeli version of the June war. Notwithstanding his claim that the book's conclusions are based on massive new research findings culled from multiple, recently opened state and United Nations archives, it happens that all the Arab and most of the crucial Israeli (and Soviet) archives remain closed, while the UN archives have been accessible for many years.[4] The only substantially new documentation Oren brings to bear comes from US archives, yet none of his cited findings significantly alter the known picture of American policy during these fateful months while, on the most controversial questions – e.g., Did the US give Israel a 'green light' on the eve of its pre-emptive strike? – no new light is shed.[5]

It would seem that Oren's main achievement is lending a scholarly veneer to, as it were, the Abba Eban version of the June war. To reconcile the historical record with this apologetic narrative he resorts to several distinct, if overlapping, procedures:

- attaching equal weight to a public statement (or memoir) and the hard evidence of an internal document contradicting it;
- burying in an avalanche of dubious evidence a crucial counter-finding;
- minimizing, misrepresenting, or suppressing a crucial piece of evidence.[6]

In the ensuing pages, I will illustrate how Oren skews the historical record of the June war by deploying these techniques.

## 2

Reaching back to the Zionist movement's struggle for statehood, Oren begins with the broader historical context of the June war. This partisan account sets the book's tone. He reports that the Zionist movement re-acted with 'restraint' to Palestinian guerrilla attacks in the months follow-ing UN approval of the 1947 Partition Resolution (*SDW*: p. 4), whereas senior Haganah intelligence officers on the ground pinned responsibility for the escalation of hostilities on the 'ill-conceived Jewish military actions and over-reactions' (pp. 82–3 in this volume). In one place he rightly suggests that Israel stopped short of conquering the West Bank and Gaza due to fears of incorporating densely populated Arab areas and triggering a war with Great Britain. Yet, just two pages later he contrives the fanci-ful explanation that Israeli leaders refrained from further conquest because they 'had been duped' (he never says by whom) into believing that in exchange 'they could retain the territories they had conquered beyond the Partition borders, and keep the refugees out' (*SDW*: pp. 5, 7). He recalls Ariel Sharon's murderous assault on Qibya in October 1953 (the wrong year is given), which left sixty-nine Arab civilians dead, but then enters the apologetic caveat 'inadvertently, he claimed', and sanitizes the covert Israeli firebombing of public institutions in Egypt to thwart Nasser's rapprochement with the West as 'vandalizing' (*SDW*: p. 9).[7] Crediting Israeli public statements and representations during arms talks with West-ern powers, Oren maintains that successive Israeli leaders 'panicked' at Israel's imminent destruction by Arab states – even when the Western and Israel intelligence estimates he himself cites belied these alleged threats (*SDW*: pp. 16–17, 25–6).

## 3

A massive Israeli 'reprisal' against the Jordanian village of Samu in November 1966 marked the onset of the crisis culminating in the June war. Although Jordan was taking maximum steps to curb infiltration from its border (Oren seems to doubt this on p. 31, but cf. p. 125 in this volume), the IDF methodically razed Samu and killed eighteen Jordanian soldiers and civilians (one Israeli soldier died). Harshly condemned in the United Nations, including by the US delegate, the assault poisoned inter-Arab relations as Jordan denounced Egypt for sheltering behind the United Nations Emergency Force (UNEF) rather than coming to its assistance. In early April 1967, long-simmering tensions between Israel and Syria reached a head in a major aerial engagement in which six Syrian planes were shot down. In Oren's account, a prime 'catalyst' of the June war was Syrian belligerence culminating in this dogfight: 'The calculus of Syrian attacks, whether direct or through Palestinian guerrilla groups, had become overwhelming for the Israelis' (*SDW*: p. 49). His extensive discussion of these direct and indirect 'Syrian attacks' merits close analysis.

The armistice agreement between Israel and Syria at the close of the 1948 war called for the creation of demilitarized zones (DZs) along their common border, and an Israeli-Syrian Mixed Armistice Commission (ISMAC). Oren initially states that the DZs constituted 'areas of Israel evacuated by the Syrian army' but then quickly backpedals, designating them as areas 'over which Israel claimed total sovereignty' (*SDW*: p. 23) – a claim lacking any international sanction. In his account of the unfolding conflict punctuated by armed clashes over the DZs, Oren occasionally implies that Israel acted the belligerent (*SDW*: pp. 9, 14) or that both sides were equally blameworthy (*SDW*: pp. 23, 48–9), but overwhelmingly he portrays Israel as the innocent victim of Syrian aggression: Israel 'thwarted Syria's ... attempts to dominate the DZs'; 'Obstructing [ISMAC's] work was Syria's demand for control over the DZs [and] Israel's rejection of that demand'; 'Israel was indeed preparing the groundwork for a reprisal against Syria ... At the next Syrian provocation, Israel would send armored tractors deep into the DZs, wait for them to be fired on, and then strike back. The provocation was not long in coming'; and so forth (*SDW*: pp. 27, 44, 45–6; cf. pp. 29, 42, 64). In fact, all independent observers on the scene recalled that – in the words of Odd Bull, chief of staff of UN forces in the Middle East – 'the status quo was all the time being altered by Israel in her favor' as Arab villagers were evicted, their dwellings demolished, and 'all Arab villages disappeared' in wide swaths of the DZs. Oren frequently quotes from Bull's essential memoir but omits mention of these observations, and similar ones by numerous other eye-witnesses (pp. 131–2 in this volume).[8] Indeed, he suppresses what is surely the most revealing source on the root cause of these border clashes. In an interview that created a stir in Israel after its belated publication, Defense Minister Moshe Dayan declared:

I know how at least 80 percent of all of the incidents there started. In my opinion, more than 80 percent, but let's speak about 80 percent. It would go like this: we would send a tractor to plow ... in the demilitarized area, and we would know ahead of time that the Syrians would start shooting. If they did not start shooting, we would inform the tractor to progress farther, until the Syrians, in the end, would get nervous and would shoot. And then we would use guns, and later, even the air force, and that is how it went. ... We thought ... that we could change the lines of the cease-fire accords by military actions that were less than a war. That is, to seize some territory and hold it until the enemy despairs and gives it to us.[9]

It was just such a staged provocation – an Israeli tractor plowing through a disputed field despite Syrian pleas for compromise – that sparked the April 1967 aerial battle.[10] In Oren's reckoning, however, the battle ensued after a pattern of 'Syrian provocation' (*SDW*: p. 46).

Denied the right to return home or compensation, Palestinian refugees organized commando raids against Israel and, after a February 1966 coup in Syria, the new 'radical' regime escalated support for them. According to Oren, the 'reasons for this upsurge [of Syrian support] were obscure, as inscrutable as the Syrian regime itself' (*SDW*: p. 42). Yet in a statement not quoted by Oren, head of Israeli military intelligence General Aharon Yariv bluntly acknowledged shortly before the June war that Syria backed these raids 'because we are bent upon establishing ... certain facts along the border' – i.e., in retaliation for Israel's land-grab in the DZs (p. 133 in this volume; Oren alludes to this explanation on pp. 24, 27). Oren's narrative is replete with references to these Syrian-backed Palestinian attacks supposedly causing Israel's 'security situation' to deteriorate 'from worse to insufferable': 'Over the course of 1965 ... the armed wing of al-Fatah received Syria's support in carrying out thirty-five attacks according to Israel's reckoning, 110 by Palestinian accounts'; 'Over the course of 1966, Israel recorded ninety-three border incidents – mines, shootings, sabotage – while the Syrians boasted seventy-five guerrilla attacks in the single month of February–March';[11] in late 1966 'eleven guerrilla attacks, most of them from Jordan, ensued in rapid succession – seven Israelis died and twelve were wounded. ... Then ... a paramilitary police vehicle struck a mine. Three police were killed, one wounded'; 'the first months of 1967 saw some 270 incidents – an increase, Israel acknowledged, of 100 per cent ... Al-Fatah issued a series of thirty-four communiques describing its actions in great detail and praising the courage of its martyrs'; during April–May 1967 'al-Fatah undertook no less than fourteen operations. Mines and explosives were planted not only on the Israeli side of the Syrian and Jordanian borders, but across from Lebanon as well'; and by late May 'The IDF's hands were tied; al-Fatah could attack at will' (*SDW*:

pp. 24, 27, 31, 45, 48, 63; cf. pp. 25, 28, 29, 42, 46, 53). After these cumulatively overwhelming statistics, it comes as something of a shock when Oren quotes Moshe Dayan from an October 1966 Knesset speech to the effect that 'There is no major wave of infiltration today. Just because several dozen bandits from al-Fatah cross the border, Israel does not have to get caught up in a frenzy of escalation' (*SDW*: p. 81). In fact, a former head of Israeli military intelligence, Yehoshaphat Harkabi, concluded shortly after the war in a sober balance-sheet – not cited by Oren – that the 'operational achievements' of the Palestinian commando raids 'in the *thirty* months from [their] debut to the six-day war are not impressive by any standard' (italics in original). Emphasizing that the few successful sabotage operations and few Israeli casualties in that period (a total of fourteen civilians, police and soldiers) 'did not endanger Israel's national life', he recalled that 'to hide its mediocre results, Fatah inflated communiqués which bore no resemblance to what actually took place. Often, reported actions did not take place at all, and the Israeli authorities had difficulty identifying them' (p. 133 in this volume). Inflating the threat posed to Israel, Oren cites as if credible these communiqués bearing 'no resemblance' to reality. Elsewhere Oren mockingly reports that after the June war 'in a communiqué issued from Damascus, al-Fatah claimed credit for killing Prime Minister Levi Eshkol with a surface-to-surface missile' (*SDW*: p. 317). One wonders why Oren didn't credit this communiqué as well.

## 4

In the first weeks of May 1967 Israel's Cabinet reportedly decided to attack Syria and numerous Israeli officials openly called for massive retaliation. Although Oren acknowledges these very real threats and even quotes Ben-Gurion and Dayan as deploring such bellicose provocations, he nonetheless reckons them as 'efforts to forestall a major confrontation with Syria' (*SDW*: p. 53; cf. p. 51). The Soviets apparently got wind of the Israeli Cabinet decision and conveyed a warning – albeit overblown – to Nasser. Maintaining that 'the reasons for the Russians' warning would remain obscure', Oren offers multiple tortured speculations in the body of the text such as 'the tendency of Communist decision-makers to be influenced by their own propaganda on imperialist and Zionist perfidy', and tucks away in a footnote the most obvious explanation: that Israel was in fact planning an attack (*SDW*: pp. 54–5, p. 342 n. 52). Indeed, just a few pages after reporting the Israeli decision to strike, he dismissively refers to 'yet another Soviet claim of threats against Syria' (*SDW*: pp. 51, 59).

Ridiculed in the Arab world for standing idly by after the Samu raid and the downing of Syrian aircraft, Nasser reacted in mid-May to the new Israeli threats by moving Egyptian troops into the Sinai and ordering the removal of UNEF from Sinai, Gaza, and Sharm-el-Shaykh overlooking the Straits of Tiran. To dampen tensions on the Sinai front, UN Secretary-General U Thant proposed (with the support of Israel's closest allies, the US and Canada) the repositioning of UNEF on the Israeli side of the border. Oren defends Israel's peremptory rejection of U Thant's initiative on the grounds that 'incorporating contingents from countries hardly sympathetic to Israel, UNEF would be less likely to stop aggression than to limit Israel's response' (*SDW*: p. 72). Oren doesn't offer a jot of evidence to support this allegation of UNEF's partisanship (there isn't any), but acknowledges earlier on that 'the mere presence of UNEF had sufficed to deter warfare during periods of intense Arab–Israeli friction, to keep infiltrators from exiting Gaza and ensure free passage through the Straits of Tiran' (*SDW*: p. 67).[12] In addition, he repeatedly suggests that Nasser's decision to remove UNEF (as well as U Thant's acquiescence in it)[13] put the Egyptian leader in a position to 'threaten' peace (*SDW*: pp. 67ff). It's hard to understand, however, why stationing UNEF on the Egyptian side of the border preserved peace while stationing it on the Israeli side wouldn't have or, put otherwise, why UNEF would deter Egyptian aggression on the Egyptian side but not on the Israeli side.[14] Oren also rapidly disposes of U Thant's stopgap proposal enthusiastically supported by Nasser (although Oren never mentions this) but firmly rejected by Israel to reactivate the Egyptian–Israeli Mixed Armistice Commission (EIMAC) (*SDW*: p. 74).[15]

Following the removal of UNEF from Sharm-el-Shaykh, Nasser declared the Straits of Tiran closed to Israeli vessels (and foreign vessels carrying 'strategic' cargo) bound for the Israeli port city of Eilat. Although acknowledging that 'few Israeli-flag vessels in fact traversed the Straits', Oren designates them a 'lifeline of the Jewish state' and Eilat a 'thriving port' (*SDW*: pp. 81, 83). In fact, only 5 per cent of Israel's trade passed through Eilat, and oil, which was the only significant commodity possibly affected by the blockade, could have been re-routed (if circuitously) through Haifa. Oren reports extensively on the 'frightful' news that Egypt had mined the Straits and otherwise forcibly implemented the blockade, only to note later in passing that actually 'the waterway remained mine-free' (*SDW*: pp. 84, 90, 95; cf. p. 166). Indeed, he makes no mention that just a few days after Nasser announced the blockade, vessels using the Straits apparently weren't any longer even being searched (p. 139 in this volume).

Oren maintains that Israel had won 'international recognition of its right to act in self-defense if the Straits were ever blockaded' and, even more emphatically, that the US had 'pledged' to 'regard any Egyptian attempt to revive the Tiran blockade as an act of war to which Israel could respond in self-defense under Article 51 of the UN Charter' (*SDW*: pp. 81, 12). Yet the actual documentary record shows that Israel obtained from the US and other maritime states support only for its right of 'free and innocent' passage in the Straits; that the US called for 'any recurrence of hostilities or any violation by any party' to be referred back to the UN; and that even US officials and legal scholars, not to mention UN secretaries-general Dag Hammarskjöld and U Thant, stressed that this was a 'complicated' jurisdictional dispute warranting mediation (there's a passing reference by Oren on p. 141 to the 'murky legal waters of Tiran'). It would seem that Oren conflates Israel's declared policy – 'Interference, by armed force, with ships of Israel flag exercising free and innocent passage in the Gulf of Aqaba and through the Straits of Tiran will be regarded by Israel as an attack entitling it to exercise its inherent right of self-defence under Article 51 of the United Nations Charter and to take all such measures as are necessary ... ' – with that of the US and the international community.[16]

Reaching Cairo just after the blockade was announced, U Thant elicited a 'very significant' (his words) assent from Nasser to a new diplomatic initiative: the appointment of a special UN representative to mediate the crisis, and a two-week moratorium on all belligerent acts in the Straits. Israel peremptorily rejected both of U Thant's proposals.[17] Its dismissal of the moratorium proposal rates only a scant mention in Oren's account (he never bothers to mention Egypt's acceptance and Israel's rejection of a special mediator), while Nasser's repeatedly expressed willingness to submit the Straits dispute to the World Court (for Israel inconceivable) is dispatched in a single, negatively charged phrase (*SDW*: pp. 126, 144; p. 129 and sources cited in this volume).

Alongside U Thant, the US also tried its hand at mediation in late May and early June. In what Oren rightly describes as 'precisely the opening the White House sought', Nasser agreed to send his vice-president to Washington to explore a diplomatic settlement (*SDW*: p. 145). Just two days before the Egyptian's scheduled arrival, however, Israel attacked. Recalling that the US was 'shocked ... and angry as hell', Secretary of State Dean Rusk speculated that 'We might not have succeeded in getting Egypt to reopen the straits, but it was a real possibility' (p. 129 in this volume; *SDW*: p. 196). Even *Middle East Record*, a semi-official Israeli compilation, observed after the June war that 'a number of facts seem to indicate Abdel Nasser's belief in the possibility of terminating ... the conflict through diplomacy' – pointing in particular to his 'suggestion' that the World Court arbitrate the Straits dispute, his 'vagueness' on the blockade's enforcement, and his 'willingness' to revive EIMAC (pp. 129–

30 in this volume). One would never guess from reading Oren that such a 'real possibility' existed for 'terminating ... the conflict through diplomacy', if only because the crucial facts enumerated in this mainstream Israeli compilation enter just barely or not at all in his uniquely comprehensive and impartial history of the June war.

## 5

A major thrust of Oren's account suggests that Israel launched its preemptive strike in the face of an imminent and overwhelming Arab attack. Basing himself on a few self-serving postwar Egyptian memoirs, Oren gives over many pages to 'Operation Dawn', a pre-emptive strike allegedly planned for near the end of May by Nasser's powerful defense minister, 'Abd al-Hakim 'Amer, and said to be abruptly aborted by Nasser. Yet, even mainstream American and Israeli historians crediting Operation Dawn typically consign it to a footnote or a phrase, whereas Oren, citing the same Egyptian memoirs, turns this ephemeral and inconsequential alleged episode into a centerpiece of his history, thereby magnifying the threat Egypt posed.[18] Fabricating a mammoth speculative edifice on an already flimsy evidentiary foundation, Oren professes to divine Nasser's subtle calculations for supporting Operation Dawn (*SDW*: pp. 95, 120), even after acknowledging that it is unclear whether 'Nasser even knew about the plan' (*SDW*: 92).[19] Oren further observes that the 'Egyptian first strike' posed a 'potentially greater threat' to Jordan than an Israeli attack because an unsuccessful Egyptian offensive would be blamed on Jordan, undermining Hashemite rule, while a successful Egyptian offensive might 'continue onward to Amman'. 'The predicament, as defined by royal confidant Zayd al-Rifai', Oren continues, 'was mind-boggling: "Even if Jordan did not participate in a war ... it would be blamed for the loss of the war and our turn would be next"' (*SDW*: p. 128; the ellipsis is Oren's). Turning to the source Oren cites, we read that King Hussein feared an *Israeli* attack in the event of a regional war 'no matter what Jordan did'. To document Jordan's worry, the source quotes al-Rifai: 'Even if Jordan did not participate directly in a war *that was started by Israel* it would not only be destroyed by the Arab world and even blamed for the loss of the war but our turn would be next' (my italics).[20] It would seem that the 'predicament' posed by an 'Egyptian first strike' to Jordan wouldn't have been quite so 'mind-boggling' if Oren hadn't excised the phrase 'that was started by Israel'.

At one point in his chapter on the 'countdown' to the June war Oren implies that Nasser had resolved not to attack on the eve of Israel's pre-emptive strike (*SDW*: p. 158). This acknowledgment easily gets lost, however, amid a barrage of alleged contrary indications. For example, he solemnly quotes the 4 June Israeli Cabinet decision to 'launch a military strike aimed at … preventing the impending assault by the United Arab Command' and, citing the UNEF commander that Egyptian troops stood poised for an 'offensive' as well as the renewed hopes of 'Amer 'to launch an air and ground offensive in the Negev', he closes the chapter by invoking Eshkol's plea on 5 June that 'all Israel strove for was an end to the immediate threat' (*SDW*: pp. 158, 167, 160, 169; cf. p. 99). In fact, there almost certainly wasn't an impending Egyptian assault. 'The Egyptian buildup in Sinai lacked a clear offensive plan', Avraham Sela, a colleague of Oren's at the Shalem Center, reports, 'and Nasser's defensive instructions explicitly assumed an Israeli first strike.' Oren doesn't adduce any evidence refuting this standard view. Even Menachem Begin, a member of the Israeli cabinet in June 1967, publicly admitted: 'The Egyptian army concentrations in the Sinai approaches do not prove that Nasser was really about to attack us. We must be honest with ourselves. We decided to attack him.' Oren omits any mention of Begin's remarkable testimony.[21]

Citing mostly public statements and tendentious memoirs, Oren suggests that Israel's security was rapidly deteriorating and, on the eve of the pre-emptive strike, Arab armies posed an 'existential threat' (his phrase): 'It is now a question of our national survival, of to be or not to be' and 'The noose is closing around our necks' (Yitzhak Rabin, IDF chief of staff); 'Eshkol now understood that time was not on Israel's side'; 'The news in the interim was frightful. Egypt's fourth division had completed its deployment in Sinai'; '[T]he general staff determined that "every day is a gamble with Israel's survival"'; 'Should Egypt attack first, "Israel has had it"' (Avraham Harman, Israel's ambassador to Washington); '[Israel's] one chance for winning this war is in taking the initiative and fighting according to our own designs. … God help us though if they hit us first' (Dayan); '"This is Egypt's greatest hour", … the combined Arab armies could push Israel back to the UN partition lines, or further … ' (Aharon Yariv, chief of military intelligence), and so forth (*SDW*: pp. 153, 86, 87, 90, 97, 147, 149, 150–1; cf. pp. 100, 106, 156, 157, 164, 168, 210).

Yet, these avowals are flatly contradicted by what intelligence agencies and officials were privately reporting: Israel's security situation was in fact steadily improving and it would win a quick and easy victory regardless of which side initiated hostilities. Indeed, Oren cites portions of this confident internal record in the very same passages that he uncritically reports the panicky pretenses. US intelligence predicted that 'the IDF would win a war in two weeks even if attacked on three fronts simultaneously – one week if Israel shot first', and, according to Oren, US and Israeli intelligence estimates 'agreed entirely'. The US ambassador to Israel reported back to Washington that '[the Israelis] feel they can finish Nasser off'. Labor Minister Yigal Allon expressed to the Cabinet 'total faith in the IDF's ability to beat the Egyptians', Chief of the Central Front, Uzi Narkiss, dismissed the Arab forces as a 'soap bubble – one pin will burst them', and Divisional Commander Ariel Sharon declared that 'The army is ready as never before to repel an Egyptian attack ... to wipe out the Egyptian army.' Mossad chief Meir Amit assured Eshkol that 'If [Nasser] strikes first, he's finished' and he also told US Defense Secretary Robert McNamara that 'the war would be over in two days'. In this regard it also bears notice that Oren cites the premonition of Quartermaster General Mattityahu Peled that 'the Egyptian threat had to be eliminated at once if Israel were to survive' but not Peled's subsequent admission that this posture had been a 'bluff', and he quotes statements by IDF chief of operations Ezer Weizman that 'We must strike now and swiftly ... we must deal the enemy a serious blow, for if we won't other forces will soon join him', and 'All the signs indicate that the Egyptians are ready to strike. We have no option but to attack at once', but not Weizman's later acknowledgment that actually 'there was no threat of destruction' and the Egyptians would have 'suffered a complete defeat' even if they 'attacked first' (*SDW*: pp. 110, 139, 146, 147, 122, 133–4, 151, 87, 99; cf. pp. 104, 152, 159, 165, 172).[22] Far from panicking on the eve of the June war, the 'IDF under Rabin' was – in the words of Israeli military historian Martin van Creveld – 'at the peak of its preparedness', 'confident in its power' and 'spoiling for a fight and willing to go to considerable lengths to provoke it'.[23]

# 6

Because he portrays Israel as reacting to an 'existential threat' in June 1967, Oren devotes relatively little space to its *political* motives for attacking. He briefly recalls that, like France during the Algerian war, Israel was 'at war with Arab nationalism', and that Ben-Gurion's 'nightmare' from the early 1950s onward was that Nasser might emerge as 'another Ataturk' uniting the Arab world (*SDW*: p. 10). He also points up (but without probing its meaning) Israel's fear of losing its 'deterrence power' (*SDW*: pp. 79, 81, 87–9, 123). In effect, Israel conceived any independent, modernizing movement in the Arab world as potentially undercutting its regional dominance and accordingly threatening its existence. The emergence of Nasser – and Nasserism – incarnated this challenge of 'Arab nationalism' to Israel's 'deterrence power'. To meet this threat Israel sought to cut Nasser down in 1956, but failed owing to US opposition. In June 1967 a new opportunity arose: 'Our objective is to give Nasser a knockout punch', Rabin declared on the eve of the war. 'That, I believe, will change the entire order of the Middle East' (*SDW*: p. 151). With US officials finally blessing this goal at the end of May and early June, the last obstacle to administering the 'knockout punch' was removed (pp. 142–3 in this volume).

Oren maintains that Israel's sole objective in the June war was 'eliminating the Egyptian thrust and destroying Nasser's army'. The conquests of the Sinai Peninsula, Gaza, West Bank and Golan Heights weren't 'planned or even contemplated'. In formulations strikingly reminiscent of Benny Morris's account of the origins of the Palestinian refugee problem ('born of war, not by design'), Oren avows that the Israeli offensives had been 'determined less by design than by expediency' and by 'the vagaries and momentum of war, far more than by rational decision making'. In fact, just as Morris's formulation apologetically distorted the dynamics of the 1948 expulsions, so Oren's formulations apologetically distort the dynamics of the 1967 conquests (*SDW*: pp. 311–12, 259–60; cf. p. 291).[24]

Unsurprisingly, many external circumstances shaped the course of Israel's offensives: Arab resistance (or the lack thereof), international public opinion, UN diplomacy, Soviet threats and American responses, and so on. There also wasn't a tactical or strategic consensus among Israelis on exactly how to proceed with the offensives. For example, despite pressures, Dayan temporarily held off conquering the West Bank and Golan Heights apparently because, attaching top priority to the Egyptian Sinai, he dreaded a multi-front war (*SDW*: pp.187, 190–1, 195, 232, 253, 260–2, 276, 279). Finally, Israel required pretexts – however flimsy – to launch the offensives: on the Egyptian front it alleged that Nasser's belligerence justified a pre-emptive strike, while on the Jordanian and Syrian fronts it pointed to armed hostilities.[25] Oren dramatically reenacts the Jordanian actions – 'Two batteries of the American-made 155 mm "Long Tom" guns went into action, one zeroing in on the suburbs of Tel Aviv. ... The Jordanians gradually escalated the fighting, ... introducing 3 inch mortars and 106 mm recoilless rifles. ... Arab Legion howitzers launched the first of 6,000 shells on Jewish Jerusalem' (*SDW*: pp. 184–7) – whereas in van Creveld's rather more sober balance-sheet Hussein responded to Israel's preemptive strike against Egypt with 'two symbolic thrusts', and a 'few' artillery shells and air attacks (against Israeli airfields) because 'he had no choice but to do something, all the while hoping to avoid serious retaliation'. And, for all his purple prose depicting a 'massive artillery barrage' here and a 'Syrian thrust' there, Oren seems to concede that Syrian hostilities were largely symbolic (to ward off the accusation that 'Syria was willing to fight to the last Egyptian'), and that Israel desperately sought the 'right pretext' to attack Syria (*SDW*: pp. 229–31, 260, 262, 276, 278, 291).[26]

Although a plurality of circumstantial factors plainly came into play during Israel's offensives, it's plainly untrue that these offensives weren't 'planned or even contemplated'. Rather the contrary; with external constraints temporarily in abeyance, internal differences provisionally resolved and just barely credible pretexts in hand, Israel implemented – albeit hesitantly and in piecemeal fashion – long-incubating plans to conquer the Sinai, Gaza, West Bank and Golan Heights. Ironically, Oren himself copiously documents that Israeli elites had contemplated and meticulously prepared for these offensives over many years. He reports that on the southern front 'contingency plans' had been developed after conquering the Sinai in 1956 'for moving tanks over desert wastes that were widely believed insurmountable'; on the eastern front 'the dream of completing the War of Independence and freeing the Land of Israel' had 'guided' the 'military planning' of 'all' Israeli commanders, and 'a drawer full of plans' had been developed to 'knock out Jordanian artillery concentrations on the West Bank and lay siege to East Jerusalem'; and that on the northern front an 'array of contingency plans for dealing with Syria' had been developed 'from a limited assault on the Golan ridge ... to ... conquering the entire Heights', and 'to conquer[ing] the enemy's capital within eighty hours' (*SDW*: pp. 211, 155, 154, 302; cf. p. 284). Even as Oren claims that Israel never 'even contemplated' anything beyond neutralizing the Egyptian military threat, he reports that in the weeks leading up to the June war (or before hostilities actually broke out on the Jordanian and Syrian fronts), different IDF commanders expected to 'conquer Gaza'; 'strike Egypt, and then we'll fight Syria and Jordan as well'; 'advanc[e] into Sinai and ... to the Jordan headwaters in the north and the Latrun corridor leading to Jerusalem'; 'advance westward to al-'Arish and, time permitting, beyond in the direction of the Canal'; 'take care of the Syrians'; 'eliminate the Egyptian army and ... seize the initiative on other fronts as well'; 'get to the Canal and to Sharm al-Sheikh'; 'eliminat[e] the Jordanian air force even without provocation'; and 'take Jenin' in the West Bank. With his eye riveted on conquering 'all of the Sinai Peninsula', Dayan declared in early June, according to Oren, that 'Our success ... will be judged not on the number of Egyptian tanks we destroy ... but on the size of the territory we'll seize' (*SDW*: pp. 81, 87, 90, 91, 122, 133, 155, 187, 208, 153; cf. 88, 152).

Oren uncritically quotes Yigal Allon's avowal that 'Israel sought no territorial gain' (*SDW*: p. 122). Yet, he ignores Allon's seminal article written just before the June war analyzing Israel's prospects in the event of a preemptive strike: 'In case of a new war, we must avoid the historic mistake of the War of Independence and, later, the Sinai Campaign. We must not cease fighting until we achieve ... the territorial fulfillment of the Land of Israel.'[27] Oren reports that just after the June war Allon 'led' the Cabinet ministers urging retention of the occupied territories (*SDW*: p. 314). It seems he didn't exactly undergo – as Oren's account suggests – an overnight conversion. In fact, the planning for and anticipations of the June offensives reflected Israel's long-standing territorial desiderata. From just after the first Arab–Israel war, many Israeli leaders lamented not conquering the West Bank and Gaza, and accordingly envisaged as part of the 1956 'Sinai campaign' annexing them, as well as the Egyptian Sinai.[28] In many respects, 1967 was simply a replay of 1956 – but, crucially, with the US now on board.[29] Oren himself reports that Weizman reputedly claimed 'the right to Hebron and Nablus and all of Jerusalem'; that Chief of Central Command Uzi Narkiss 'regretted Israel's inability to seize the West Bank and Jerusalem in 1948' and saw the June war as an 'opportunity to rectify Israel's failure in 1948, a miraculous second chance', declaring at a postwar briefing that 'Central Command fulfilled its natural aspirations and established Israel's borders on the Jordan'; that 'shortly before the outbreak of hostilities' Rabin exhorted troops on the Jordanian front to 'complete what we were unable to finish' in 1948, and 'many' officers 'shared that sentiment'; and that already on the third day of the war Israel contemplated retaining the West Bank, Gaza and the Sinai (*SDW*: pp. 135, 155, 192, 257, 191, 253–5). Oren also quotes uncritically Eshkol's claim that 'Of course, we don't want a centimeter of Syrian territory.' Yet he himself repeatedly notes that Eshkol 'went a little crazy' coveting the Jordanian headwaters in the Golan (*SDW*: pp. 122, 228–9, 261; cf. p. 23, 280), while Moshe Dayan – in a postwar interview not quoted by Oren – stated with 'absolute certainty' that the main impetus behind Israel's seizure of the Golan was not Syrian shelling but 'good land for agriculture. ... lust for that ground'.[30]

According to Oren, Israel's territorial conquests during the June war 'came about largely through chance': they just happened (*SDW*: p. 312). To judge by the historical record, however, they were just *waiting to happen*.

## 7

Oren's account of events attendant on the June war frequently descends to vulgar propaganda. Deeming the Israeli combined air and naval assault on the USS *Liberty*, in which 34 US Navy men were killed and 171 wounded, an 'accident' and an 'incident [of] faulty identifications', Oren rehashes official Israeli tales and embellishes on them with his own whoppers. He avers that Israeli reconnaissance pilots flying just overhead on a cloudless morning missed noticing the *Liberty*'s five-by-eight-foot American flag fluttering in the wind because they 'were not looking for the

*Liberty*, but rather for Egyptian submarines'; that 'the IDF could have easily sunk the *Liberty*', although with the IDF's extended air attack using missiles, cannon and napalm, followed by a torpedo attack followed by sustained fire on the crippled vessel that left two-thirds of the crew dead or wounded, the miracle is that the *Liberty* managed, just barely, to stay afloat; and that Israeli ships, after torpedoing the *Liberty*, 'ceased firing the instant the mistake was realized and offered to assist the ship', although surviving members of the crew uniformly testify that the Israeli ships fired from close range after the torpedo explosion and after stopping near the fantail, where the *Liberty*'s name and hull number appeared in large letters (a new oversized American flag had also been unfurled), finally firing on the life rafts in the water, and then left the area for more than an hour before returning to offer assistance (*SDW*: pp. 264, 271).[31]

Oren claims that the IDF, unable to handle the throngs of Egyptian prisoners, dispatched them toward the Canal and was at pains not to harm them, and 'no evidence was found' that Israel executed Egyptian POWs (*SDW*: pp. 259, 270–1). He is apparently unaware of the national debate that erupted in Israel a few years ago after the publication of unimpeachable eyewitness testimonies of Israeli soldiers as well as the testimony of an Israeli military historian that the IDF executed scores of Egyptian POWs during the June war.[32] Oren also claims that only a 'few' of the Palestinians who fled during the June war sought repatriation after it ended (*SDW*: 306), whereas a conservative Israeli scholarly source reports that fully 120,000 of these Palestinian refugees (half the total number) applied to return but only 21,000 were allowed to do so.[33] Finally, in his survey of developments since the June war, Oren recalls that in the post-Oslo period 'Palestinian terrorists killed dozens of Israeli civilians' (*SDW*: p. 313), but neglects to mention that Israeli forces killed a far greater number of Palestinians and that the 'vast majority' of these killings were 'unlawful' (Amnesty International).[34]

Whenever Israel faces a public relations crisis in the US – i.e., a jot of the reality of its brutal policies manages to break free of ideological controls – a new propaganda initiative is launched to lift the spirits and close the ranks of the Zionist faithful. After Israel's bloody invasion of Lebanon in June 1982, the Zionist book of the month was Joan Peters's *From Time Immemorial*.[35] Soon after the Palestinians entered into revolt in September 2000 and Israel unleashed a new round of violent repression, *From Time Immemorial* – although definitively shown to be a hoax – was reissued and soared to the top of the Amazon list, soon followed by Oren's book (Amazon frequently featured them together). While certainly a much more sophisticated enterprise, *Six Days of War* serves the same political agenda as *From Time Immemorial*. In the introduction Oren states as his goal that the June war 'never be seen the same way again'. In fact he simply repeats the same old, tired apologetics. Like *From Time Imme-morial*, its real purpose is to reclaim the lost world of Zionist heroism and innocence. With so much water under the bridge, however, except among true believers (admittedly not a small number) it's unlikely to succeed.

*November 2002*

# Notes

## Introduction to the Second Edition

1. See pp. 7–12 in this volume. The envisioned Jewish state would tolerate an Arab minority of no more than 15 per cent (Simha Flapan, *The Birth of Israel* (New York: 1987), p. 104).

2. For the crucial political repercussions on the Zionist movement of its reliance on Great Britain, cf. this volume, pp. 16–20.

3. See Chap. 2 in this volume.

4. Zeev Sternhell, *The Founding Myths of Israel* (Princeton: 1998), pp. 43–4. Benny Morris, *Righteous Victims* (New York: 1999), p. 91 (Shertok). Simha Flapan, *Zionism and the Palestinians* (London: 1979), p. 143 (Ben-Gurion). For further discussion and documentation, cf. this volume, pp. 98–110.

5. Walter Laqueur, *A History of Zionism* (New York: 1976), p. 597 (for discussion, cf. this volume, p. 233, note 13). Outright annexation of conquered territory had also ceased to be a political option – which crucially accounts for Great Britain's decision to issue the Balfour Declaration (cf. Isaiah Friedman, *The Question of Palestine* (New Brunswick, NJ: 1992), esp. pp. 175, 188–9, 288).

6. Benny Morris, 'Revisiting the Palestinian exodus of 1948', in Eugene L. Rogan and Avi Shlaim (eds), *The War for Palestine* (Cambridge: 2001), pp. 39–40.

7. Yehoshua Porath, *The Emergence of the Palestinian-Arab National Movement, 1918–1929* (Frank Cass: 1974), p. 147 (Congress). Tom Segev, *One Palestine, Complete* (New York: 2001), pp. 404–5; cf. pp. 403, 406–7, 508. Morris, 'Revisiting the Palestinian Exodus', p. 42 (Ben-Gurion); for timing, cf. also Shabtai Teveth, *Ben-Gurion and the Palestinian Arabs* (Oxford: 1985), p. 35. For further discussion and documentation of Zionist expulsion plans, cf. this volume, pp. 16, 103–4, and esp. Morris, *Righteous Victims*, pp. 139–44, 168–9.

8. Morris, *Righteous Victims*, p. 37. Porath, *Emergence*, pp. 59, 62.

9. Neville J. Mandel, *The Arabs and Zionism* (Berkeley: 1976), p. 40. Yehoshua Porath, *The Palestinian National Movement: From Riots to Rebellion* (London: 1970),

pp. 91–2, 165–6, 297.

10. See Chap. 4 in this volume.

11. Yosef Gorny, *Zionism and the Arabs, 1882–1948* (Oxford: 1987), p. 176; for detailed analysis of Gorny's study, cf. this volume, Chap. 1. Teveth, *Ben-Gurion*, p. 155.

12. Uri Ben-Eliezer, *The Making of Israeli Militarism* (Bloomington: 1998), p. 89 ('fusion') (cf. p. 62). Martin Gilbert, *Israel: A History* (New York: 1998), p. 312 (Dayan). For discussion, cf. this volume, p. 106.

13. David Ben-Gurion, *My Talks with Arab Leaders* (New York: 1973), p. 3. (For Ben-Gurion's private recognition of the real motives behind Arab attacks, cf. this volume, pp. 108, 110.) Norman G. Finkelstein, *The Holocaust Industry* (New York: 2000), pp. 49–53, 62–3.

14. Segev, *One Palestine*, p. 182.

15. Saul Friedlander, *Nazi Germany and the Jews*, vol. I (New York: 1997), p. 219. On related resettlement schemes, cf. Michael J. Cohen, *Churchill and the Jews* (London: 1985), pp. 236, 249–51, and Philippe Burrin, *Hitler and the Jews* (New York: 1989), pp. 59–61.

16. For population transfers from interwar through postwar period, cf. Joseph B. Schechtman, *European Population Transfers, 1939–1945* (New York: 1946), and *Postwar Population Transfers in Europe, 1945–1955* (Philadelphia: 1962), Alfred M. de Zayas, *Nemesis at Potsdam* (London: 1977), Andrew Bell-Fialkoff, *Ethnic Cleansing* (New York: 1996), Norman M. Naimark, *Fires of Hatred* (Cambridge: 2001). Segev, *One Palestine*, pp. 406–7 (Jabotinsky) (cf. also Gorny, *Zionism*, pp. 270–1). See this volume, p. 103 for 'positive experience'. Nur Masalha, *Expulsion of the Palestinians* (Washington: 1992), pp. 157–61 (Labor Party). Bertrand Russell, 'The Role of the Jewish State in Helping to Create a Better World' (1943), reprinted in *Zionism* (1981). Calling just before his death in 1970 for 'an Israeli withdrawal from all the territories occupied in June 1967', Russell, in a change of heart, particularly deplored the fate of the Palestinians: 'No people anywhere in the world would accept being expelled en masse from their country; how can anyone require the people of Palestine to accept a punishment nobody else would tolerate?' (*Spokesman*, no. 2 (Nottingham: April 1970), excerpted in Ronald Clark, *The Life of Bertrand Russell* (New York: 1975), p. 638).

17. Sasson Sofer, *Zionism and the Foundations of Israeli Diplomacy* (Cambridge: 1998), p. 367 ('social order'). Richard Crossman, *Palestine Mission* (London: 1947), pp. 33, 152, 167. Kenneth Ray Bain, *The March to Zion* (London: 1979), p. 35 (Wallace) (cf. pp. 34–6 for Americans' identification of Zionist settlement with American West). For a detailed comparison between Zionist and American conquests, cf. this volume, pp. 89–98, and esp. Norman Finkelstein, *The Rise and Fall of Palestine* (Minn.: 1996), pp. 104–21 (hereafter *R&F*).

18. See Chap. 3 in this volume; for further evidence supporting the argument in this chapter, cf. Laila Parsons, 'The Druze and the birth of Israel', in Rogan and Shlaim, *War*, chap. 3, and Ben-Eliezer, *Making*, pp. 170–81. For comparisons recently evoked by mainstream Israelis with the Serb expulsion, cf. Finkelstein, *Holocaust*, pp. 70–1.

19. Sternhell, *Founding Myths*, p. 173 (Katznelson; for Katznelson's effective support of forced transfer, cf. p. 176). Theodore Roosevelt, *The Winning of the West*

(New York: 1889), vol. 4, p. 54.

20. Wm. Roger Louis, *The British Empire in the Middle East, 1945–1951* (Oxford: 1984), pp. 117, 448, 614. Michael J. Cohen, *Palestine and the Great Powers, 1945–1948* (Princeton: 1982), pp. 197–8, 201.

21. See pp. 10–11, 15, 102–3 in this volume. Teveth, *Ben-Gurion*, p. 101 (cf. pp. 129, 187–90). For copious evidence that, even in the absence of Arab aggression, the Zionist leadership never intended to respect the 1947 Partition Resolution borders, cf. Ben-Eliezer, *Making*, pp. 144, 150–1.

22. For the June war, cf. this volume, Chap. 5.

23. For Zionist territorial imperatives after 1948, cf. this volume, p. 143. Martin Gilbert, *Israel: A History* (New York: 1998), p. 393. Michael Oren, *Six Days of War* (Oxford: 2002), p. 312. Sternhell, *Founding*, p. 330. For a critical review of Oren's study, cf. Appendix to this volume, 'Abba Eban With Footnotes', pp. 184–98.

24. An influential Zionist official during the 1948 expulsion, Yosef Weitz, typically warned after the conquests of the June war of the need to preserve Israel's Jewish character by keeping the 'non-Jewish minority limited to 15%' (Nur Masalha, *A Land Without A People* (London: 1997), p. 79).

25. M. Cherif Bassiouni, *Crimes Against Humanity in International Criminal Law* (Boston: 1999), pp. 312 ('unequivocally'), 322 (cf. pp. 312–27 for the historical development of international law regarding deportation).

26. See pp. 144–7 in this volume.

27. See p. 257, note 63 in this volume.

28. See Chap. 6 in this volume.

29. Geoffrey Aronson, *Creating Facts* (Washington: 1987), pp. 14ff. (Allon Plan). Sofer, *Zionism*, p. 385. Finkelstein, *Holocaust*, pp. 47–8.

30. See pp. 147–8 in this volume.

31. For the Jarring mission, cf. this volume, pp. 151ff.

32. *Foreign Relations of the United States, 1964–1968*, Volume XX (Washington, DC: 2001), pp. 619, 634–5 ('meant'/'never meant'), 639, 639 ('large chunks'/'non-starter'), 641, 654 ('unacceptable'), 655, 699.

33. Noam Chomsky, *The Fateful Triangle* (Boston: 1983), pp. 65–6. For the strategic motives behind this US policy shift and its repercussions for American Jewry, cf. Finkelstein, *Holocaust*, chap. 1.

34. For a comprehensive record through 1990 of lone US vetoes in the Security Council and lone US–Israel negative votes in the General Assembly on the Middle East conflict, cf. Finkelstein, *R&F*, pp. 53–7. For the 2002 General Assembly resolution 'Peaceful settlement...' (A/57/L. 37), cf. www.un.org/News/Press.docs/2002/ga10111.doc.htm; for Syrian and Israeli ambassadors, cf. www.un.org/News/Press/docs/2002/gaspd255.doc.htm. Marc Weller and Dr. Barbara Metzger, 'Double Standards' (Negotiations Affairs Department, Palestine Liberation Organization: 24 September 2002). Uri Savir, *The Process* (New York: 1998), p. 6 ('must drop').

35. Avner Yaniv, *Dilemmas of Security* (Oxford: 1987), p. 20 ('compromising'), p. 70 ('peace offensive'). For further discussion and documentation, cf. *R&F*, pp. 44–5.

36. For extensive documentation of Israel's repression, cf. *R&F*, chap. 3.

37. Savir, *Process*, pp. 5, 25. For the precedent of British rule in Palestine, cf. Baruch Kimmerling and Joel S. Migdal, *Palestinians: The Making of a People* (Cam-

bridge: 1994), pp. 86, 90–1, and Porath, *Emergence*, p. 202. The British first implemented indirect rule in its empire after brutally crushing the 1857 Indian Mutiny. Victor Kiernan's commentary on this British strategy could easily serve as an epigraph for the Oslo process: 'Rulers of the kind lately vilified as Oriental tyrants were now eulogized as natural leaders of their people. Leaving a third of the country under princely rule could be speciously represented as a concession to Indian feeling; and if, as was increasingly the case, conditions were worse there than in British India, nationalists could be invited to contemplate the consequences of self-government' (*The Lords of Human Kind* (Boston: 1969), p. 52).

38. Meron Benvenisti, *Intimate Enemies* (New York: 1995), pp. 218, 232. Savir, *Process*, p. 147. For detailed analysis of the Oslo Accord, cf. Chap. 7 in this volume, pp. 172–183. For a comprehensive overview of post-Oslo developments, cf. Nicholas Guyatt, *The Absence of Peace* (London: 1998).

39. May 2002.

40. Daniel Williams, 'Settlements expanding under Sharon', in *Washington Post* (31 May 2002). 'UN expert says settlements, house demolitions are war crimes', in *Haaretz* (15 June 2002). Jackson Diehl, 'Making a Palestinian state impossible', in *Washington Post* (23 July 2002).

41. Amira Hass, 'Donors are funding cantonization', in *Haaretz* (22 May 2002). Brian Whitaker, 'UN to feed 500,000 needy Palestinians', in *Guardian* (22 May 2002). *Report on UNCTAD's Assistance to the Palestinian People* (UNCTAD secretariat: 26 July 2002) (unemployment, poverty line). Justin Huggler, 'Palestinians face disaster, warns US government group', in *Independent* (6 August 2002) (malnutrition). Judy Dempsey, 'Israel blocking aid, says Brussels', in *Financial Times* (30 October 2002). 'Palestinian children "malnourished"', in BBC (18 November 2002), at http://news.bbc.co.uk/2/hi/middle_east/2489985.stm. Thomas O'Dwyer, 'Nothing Personal: Parts and Apartheid', in *Haaretz* (24 May 2002) ('appalling'). The *UNCTAD* report gives the Palestinian Authority generally high marks for its handling of the economy, and stresses that the dysfunctions 'arise from the legacy of 35 years of occupation and distorted economic relations with Israel and isolation from regional and global markets, much more than from the experience of its limited, and by design, provisional, interim period of self-government arrangements' (pp. 8, 9).

42. See Norman G. Finkelstein, 'Securing Occupation: The Meaning of the Wye River Memorandum', in *New Left Review* (November/December 1998), and esp. Mouin Rabbani, 'A Smorgasbord of Failure', in Roane Carey (ed.), *The New Intifada* (Verso: 2001), chap. 3.

43. Hussein Agha and Robert Malley, 'Camp David: The Tragedy of Errors', 'Camp David and After: An Exchange – A Reply to Ehud Barak', 'Camp David and After – Continued: Robert Malley and Hussein Agha reply', in *New York Review of Books* (9 August 2001, 13 June 2002, 27 June 2002). (Malley quotes from second article) David Clark, 'The brilliant offer Israel never made', in *Guardian* (10 April 2002) (British diplomat).

44. For text of the Saudi plan, cf. *Guardian* (28 March 2002); for its revision on the 'right of return', cf. Suzanne Goldenberg, 'Arab leaders reach agreement by fudging refugee question', in *Guardian* (29 March 2002). Aviv Lavie, 'So what if the Arabs want to make peace?', in *Haaretz* (5 April 2002). Uzi Benziman, 'Distorting

the map', in *Haaretz* (27 October 2002) ('road map'). For insightful commentary, cf. Uri Avnery, 'How to torpedo the Saudis' (4 March 2002) at www.counterpunch. org/avnerysaudis.html.

45. Amira Hass, 'The mirror does not lie', in *Haaretz* (1 November 2000). *Jane's Foreign Report* (12 July 2001). Robert Fisk, 'One year on: a view from the Middle East' in *Independent* (11 September 2002). Fisk rightly points to the imperial order imposed on the Arab world by the British and French after World War I as the relevant precedent.

46. Shulamit Aloni, 'You can continue with the liquidations', in *Yediot Aharonot* (18 January 2002); cf. Tanya Reinhart, 'Evil unleashed' (19 December 2001) at www.zmag.org.

47. For background to Lebanon war, cf. *R&F*, pp. 44–5 and sources cited. Official Israeli figure at www.ou.org/yerushalayim/yomhazikaron/default.htm.

48. Israel claimed that Palestinian ambulances had been misused to ferry around terrorists and suicide belts. In fact, there was only one alleged case of such misuse and, according to Amnesty International, 'several suspicious circumstances' suggest that even it was staged by the IDF (Amnesty International, 'Shielded from scrutiny: IDF violations in Jenin and Nablus' (November 2002); cf. Larry Derfner, 'Bad war, bad medicine', in *Jerusalem Post* (8 November 2002)).

49. Amir Oren, 'At the gates of Yassergrad', in *Haaretz* (25 January 2002), and Uzi Benziman, 'Immoral imperative', in *Haaretz* (1 February 2002) (Israeli officer). Chris Hedges, *War is a Force that Gives Us Meaning* (New York: 2002), p. 94; cf. his article, 'A Gaza Diary', in *Harper's* (October 2001). Jessica Montell, 'Operation Defensive Shield: the propaganda and the reality', at www.btselem.org (90 per cent). *Guardian* (2 August 2002) (wounded). Amnesty International, 'Shielded from Scrutiny' (November 2002) (statistics). *Report on UNCTAD's Assistance* (property damage). Hedges's experience merits extended quotation: 'I had seen children shot in other conflicts I have covered – death squads gunned them down in El Salvador and Guatemala, mothers with infants were lined up and massacred in Algeria, and Serb snipers put children in their sights and watched them crumple onto the pavement in Sarajevo – but I had never watched soldiers entice children like mice into a trap and murder them for sport.'

50. Recalling reports while Jenin was under siege that Israel had committed a 'massacre', Amnesty writes: 'During the fighting Palestinian residents and Palestinian and foreign journalists and others outside the camp saw hundreds of missiles being fired into the houses of the camp from Apache helicopters flying sortie after sortie. The sight of the firepower being thrown at Jenin refugee camp led those who witnessed the air raids, including military experts and the media, to believe that scores, at least, of Palestinians had been killed. The tight cordon round the refugee camp and the main hospital ... meant that the outside world had no means of knowing what was going on inside the refugee camp. ... It was in these circumstances that stories of a "massacre" spread. Even the IDF leadership appeared unclear as to how many Palestinians had died; General Ron Kitrey said that hundreds had died in Jenin before correcting himself a few hours later saying that hundreds had died or been wounded' (Amnesty International, 'Shielded from Scrutiny').

51. Human Rights Watch, 'Jenin: IDF Military Operations' (May 2002). Amnesty International, 'Shielded from Scrutiny'. For Nablus and elsewhere, cf. Suzanne

Goldenberg, 'Across West Bank, daily tragedies go unseen', in *Guardian* (27 April 2002), and Edward Cody, 'Unnoticed Nablus may have taken West Bank's worst hit', in *Washington Post* (21 May 2002). Reuven Pedatzur, 'The wrong way to fight terrorism', in *Haaretz* (11 December 2002) ('deterrent', 'fighter'). For Nazi justification, cf. this volume, p. 107.

52. 'Camp David and After: An Exchange – An Interview with Ehud Barak', in *New York Review of Books* (13 June 2002) (Barak). For Wiesel, cf. Megan Goldin, *Reuters* (11 April 2002), Greer Fay Cushman, 'Wiesel: World doesn't understand threat of suicide bombers', in *Jerusalem Post* (12 April 2002), *CNN* (14 April 2002), Caroline B. Glick, 'We must not let the hater define us', in *Jerusalem Post* (19 April 2002), Elie Wiesel interview with Gabe Pressman on 'News Forum' (21 April 2002). Wiesel subsequently served as a major cheerleader for a US attack on Iraq: 'I am for intervention. ... I think the choice is simple' – especially if the bombs aren't dropping on your head ('The Oprah Winfrey Show' (9 October 2002)); cf. Elie Wiesel, 'War is not the only option', in *Observer* (22 December 2002).

53. Tsadok Yeheskeli, 'I made them a stadium in the middle of the camp', in *Yediot Aharonot* (31 May 2002). Montell, 'Operation Defensive Shield' (B'Tselem). Amira Hass, 'Someone even managed to defecate into the photocopier', in *Haaretz* (6 May 2002). Chomsky, *Fateful Triangle*, pp. 298–9 (Beirut).

54. Justin Huggler, 'Ten killed in Israeli air strike on home of Hamas chief', in *Independent* (23 July 2002). Uli Schmetzer, 'Israeli strike kills at least 12 in Gaza', in *Chicago Tribune* (23 July 2002). Bradley Burston, 'Background/Shehada 'hit' sends shockwaves back to Israel', in *Haaretz* (24 July 2002) (Meretz leader). Akiva Eldar, 'How to cease from a cease-fire', in *Haaretz* (25 July 2002). Gideon Samet, 'It's a horror story, period', in *Haaretz* (26 July 2002). Graham Usher, 'Sharon accused of shattering ceasefire', in *Guardian* (27 July 2002). Akiva Eldar, 'If there's smoke, there's no cease-fire', in *Haaretz* (30 July 2002). 'Letter for an American editor', in *Haaretz* (30 July 2002) (text of planned public statement). Cameron Barr, 'Israel stokes a cooling conflict', in *Christian Science Monitor* (8 October 2002). Amos Harel and Aluf Benn, 'Full Gaza invasion is "just a matter of time", Israel says', in *Haaretz* (8 October 2002). For crucial background and subsequent developments in the July attack, cf. Mouin Rabbani's typically brilliant analysis, 'The Costs of Chaos in Palestine', at www.merip.org.

55. Amira Hass, 'Making life difficult for the Palestinian peace camp', in *Haaretz* (14 August 2002).

56. Chap. 7 in this volume, pp. 172–183.

57. 'Israel must end the hatred now', in *Observer* (15 October 2000). Haroon Siddiqui, 'Tutu likens Israeli actions to apartheid', in *Toronto Star* (16 May 2002) (Brzezinski). Desmond Tutu, 'Apartheid in the Holy Land', in *Guardian* (29 April 2002).

58. Jonathan Steele, 'The Bush doctrine makes nonsense of the charter', in *Guardian* (6 June 2002) ('mortal blow'). George Monbiot, 'The logic of empire', in *Guardian* (5 August 2002); for the US 'developing a new generation of weapons that undermine and possibly violate international treaties on biological and chemical warfare', cf. also Julian Borger, 'US weapons secrets exposed', in *Guardian* (29 October 2002). The US has displayed equal ruthlessness on the economic front,

*New York Times* economic affairs columnist, Paul Krugman, observing, e.g., that the steel tariffs imposed by the Bush administration 'demonstrate an unprecedented contempt for international rules' ('America the Scofflaw' (24 May 2002)).

59. 'Many Israelis content to see Palestinians go', in *Chicago Sun–Times* (14 March 2002). Ari Shavit, 'Waiting for the sign', in *Haaretz* (22 March 2002). Tom Segev, 'A black flag hangs over the idea of transfer', in *Haaretz* (5 April 2002). Gil Hoffman, 'Fight on the right', in *Jerusalem Post* (10 May 2002). Lily Galili, 'A Jewish demographic state', in *Haaretz* (28 June 2002). Boaz Evron, 'Demography as the enemy of democracy', in *Haaretz* (11 September 2002). Henry Siegman, 'Sharon's real purpose is to create foreigners', in *International Herald Tribune* (25 September 2002). 'Thin excuse', in *Haaretz* (27 September 2002). Nicole Gaouette, 'Palestinian statehood fades', in *Christian Science Monitor* (23 October 2002). Danny Rubinstein, 'The tangible fear of transfer', in *Haaretz* (28 October 2002). Zeev Schiff, 'The army must stop the olive thieves', in *Haaretz* (30 October 2002). Amira Hass, 'Will you just stand on the sidelines?' in *Haaretz* (6 November 2002); for the settler attacks on Palestinian olive groves, cf. also Amira Hass, 'It's the pits', in *Haaretz* (26 October 2002). For 'transfer' in Israeli political discourse since the state's founding, cf. Masalha, *Land*.

60. For the 'new' historians', cf. this volume, Chap. 3.

61. 'Interview with Benny Morris', by Baudouin Loos at http://msanews. mynet.net/Scholars/Loos/morris2001 (25 February 2001) ('mistake', 'complete', 'hundred', 'bomb'). 'The Arabs Are The Same Arabs', interview with Meron Rappaport in *Yediot Aharonot* (11 November 2001), reprinted in *Between the Lines* (December 2001) ('shooting', 'existential', 'leave', 'strategic', 'removing', 'defective', 'erection', 'happy'). Morris, 'Peace? No chance', in *Guardian* (21 February 2002) ('claim', 'enterprise', 'restraint', 'kingdom', 'straight'). 'Benny Morris, le nouvel historien, a rejoint le consensus israelien', interview with Sylvain Cypel in *Le Monde* (30 May 2002) (justifies expulsion, 'isn't room', 'sick, psychotic'). Morris, Ehud Barak, 'Camp David and After – Continued', in *New York Review of Books* (27 June 2002) ('no army', 'several dozen', 'journalists', 'torrent'). Morris, 'A new exodus for the Middle East', in *Guardian* (2 October 2002). 'Population Transfer: Is Israel considering expelling Palestinians to Jordan under cover of Iraq war', interview with Amy Goodman on 'Democracy Now' at http://www.pacifica.org/programs/democracy_now (18 September 2002) ('immoral and unjust', 'peace camp', 'learned some lessons'); in the Goodman interview Morris denied justifying an expulsion in the event of war and avowing that there was room only for Israel between the Jordan and Mediterranean. Yoel Marcus, 'Everybody loves Arik', in *Haaretz* (12 November 2002) ('pulp'). For 'right of Warre', cf. *R&F*: p. 106.

62. Yael Zerubavel, *Recovered Roots* (Chicago: 1995), p. 183; cf. p. 14. Teveth, *Ben-Gurion*, p. 36 (Balfour 'miracle'). Louis, *British Empire*, p. 487 (Partition 'miracle'); cf. pp. 395, 445, 460. James McDonald, *My Mission to Israel* (New York: 1952), p. 176 (1948 'miraculous simplification').

63. 'Hardball with Chris Matthews', *Transcript* (1 May 2002) at www.adc.org/action/2002/02May2002.htm (DeLay and Armey). 'Peace in the Middle East', Senate Floor Statement by US Sen. James M. Inhofe (R-Okla), at http://inhofe.senate.gov/fl030402.html (4 March 2002). Ali Abunimah, 'The growing clamor for ethnic cleansing', in *Electronic Intifada* (28 August 2002) (Clinton). Ami Eden, 'Top Lawyer

Urges Death For Families of Bombers', in *Forward* (7 June 2002). Alan Dershowitz, 'New response to Palestinian terrorism', in *Jerusalem Post* (11 March 2002). Alan Dershowitz, *Shouting Fire* (New York: 2002), pp. 476–7. Benny Morris, *Israel's Border Wars, 1949–1956* (Oxford: 1993), chap. 8 (Qibya massacre). Ritchie Ovendale, *Britain, the United States and the Transfer of Power in the Middle East, 1945–1962* (New York: 1996), p. 97 (American newspapers). James D. Besser, 'Jewish Law Comes to D.C.', in *Jewish Week* (6 December 2002). Boris Shusteff, 'The Logistics of Transfer' (3 July 2002) at www.gamla.org.il/english/article/2002/july/b1.htm (cf. section 'E. Israel's Actions in Yesha and the relocation itself'). For the mainstream Zionist resort to terrorist retaliatory strikes during the late Mandate years, cf. this volume, pp. 112–14, and Ben-Eliezer, *Making*, chaps. 1–2.

64. See Chap. 2 in this volume.

65. Quoted phrases and information about film project come from 'The Rehabilitation of Joan Peters: Discredited Author Finds a New Audience', in *The Rittenhouse Review* (19 June 2002) at http://rittenhouse.blogspot.com/2002_06_16_ritenhouse_archive.html. For Peters's web page, cf. www.israelunitycoalition.com/Speakers_Bureau/j_peters.htm. For propagation of the Peters myth by Canadian Jewish organizations, cf. Myron Love, 'Arab journalist puts lie to Palestinian claims', in *Canadian Jewish News* (21 February 2002). For the Christian Coalition and Pat Robertson, cf. 'Christians Hail Rightist's Call To Oust Arabs', in *Forward* (18 October 2002).

66. 'Sharon's plan is to drive Palestinians across the Jordan', in *Sunday Telegraph*, 28 April 2002 (Creveld). Menachem Shalev, 'Netanyahu recommends large-scale expulsions', in *Jerusalem Post* (19 November 1989). Meron Benvenisti, 'Preemptive warnings of fantastic scenarios', in *Haaretz* (15 August 2002). Rubinstein, 'The tangible fear of transfer.' 'Sharon embarks on ethnic cleansing', in *Jane's Foreign Report* (24 October 2002).

67. Boas Evron, *Jewish State Or Israeli Nation?* (Bloomington, IN: 1995), pp. 169, 237. Sternhell, *Founding Myths*, p. 331. Martin van Creveld, *The Sword and the Olive* (New York: 1998), pp. 123–5, 154.

68. Zeev Sternhell, 'Balata has fallen', in *Haaretz* (8 March 2002).

69. Cohen, *Palestine*, pp. 247, 249. Lewis, *British Empire*, pp. 467, 476. Prof. Ephraim Yaar and Dr. Tamar Hermann, 'The Peace Index', in *Haaretz* (8 October 2002). For contrary indications, suggesting that Israelis would make significant additional concessions if 'the solution will end terror', cf. Akiva Eldar, 'Winner takes out the garbage', in *Haaretz* (8 October 2002).

70. Cohen, *Palestine*, pp. 69, 79, 90–1, 230, 238–9. For further discussion, including American Jewish support for the Zionist terror campaign, cf. David Hirst, *The Gun and the Olive Branch* (London: 1977), pp. 108–23.

71. Crossman, *Palestine*, pp. 129, 169–70, 178–81.

72. Cohen, *Palestine*, p. 239, 245 (*Times* editorial).

73. van Creveld, *Sword*, pp. 57–61.

74. van Creveld, *Sword*, pp. 361–2.

75. Edward Said, 'A New Current in Palestine', in *Nation* (4 February 2002).

76. For more on the refusenik movement and dissident Israelis, cf. Roane Carey and Jonathan Shainin (eds), *The Other Israel* (New York: 2002); for insightful commentary on the Israeli public's roughly equal support (60–70 percent) for 'Sharon

and an "iron-fist" policy' as well as 'for immediate unilateral evacuation of most the territories and most of the settlements', cf. Tanya Reinhart, 'The Israeli Elections' (2 December 2002), at www.zmag.org/sustainers/content/2002–12/02reinhart.cfm.; cf. Yoel Marcus, 'Good morning to the victor', in *Haaretz* (29 November 2002).

77. Janine Zacharia, 'Poll shows Americans' support for Israel in decline', in *Jerusalem Post* (13 June 2002). Nathan Guttman, 'Israel's struggle for hearts and minds', in *Haaretz* (2 December 2002).

78. Alisa Solomon, 'Stop American Billions for Jewish Bombs', in *Village Voice* (26 December 2001). Liza Featherstone, 'The Mideast War Breaks Out On Campus', in *Nation* (17 June 2002). Karen W. Arenson, 'Harvard President Sees Rise in Anti-Semitism on Campus', in *New York Times* (21 September 2002). Tracy Wilkinson, 'Israeli Hawk Considers Run at a Wounded Dove', in *Los Angeles Times* (Ayalon). Desmond Tutu, 'Build moral pressure to end the occupation', in *International Herald Tribune* (14 June 2002), and Desmond Tutu and Ian Urbina, 'Against Israeli Apartheid', in *Nation* (15 July 2002).

79. Evron, *Jewish State*, p. 96 (Tal). Nicholas Watt, 'MP accuses Sharon of "barbarism"', in *Guardian* (17 April 2002).

80. Robert Fisk, 'There is a firestorm coming, and it is being provoked by Mr Bush', in *Independent* (25 May 2002).

# Introduction

1. Michael Walzer, 'Nationalism, Internationalism and the Jews', in Irving Howe and Carl Gersham (eds), *Israel, the Arabs and the Middle East*, New York 1972, p. 189; Noam Chomsky, *Towards a New Cold War*, New York 1982, pp. 241–2.

2. Norman G. Finkelstein, *From the Jewish Question to the Jewish State*, Politics Department, Princeton University, 1987.

3. Joan Peters, *From Time Immemorial*, New York 1984.

4. Benny Morris, *The Birth of the Palestinian Refugee Problem, 1947–1949*, Cambridge 1988; Anita Shapira, *Land and Power*, Oxford 1992.

5. For references, cf. Chap. 3 at pp. 51–2 below.

6. Benny Morris, *Israel's Border Wars, 1949–1956*, Oxford 1993.

7. Yehoshafat Harkabi, *Israel's Fateful Hour*, New York 1988, p. 101.

8. Leon Trotsky, *The Revolution Betrayed*, New York 1972.

9. The argument I make below is based mainly on my unpublished essay, 'Tribal Rumblings', June 1990. For two masterly critiques of Walzer's Zionist apologetics, cf. Noam Chomsky, 'An Exception to the Rules', *Inquiry*, 17 April 1978, and especially Edward Said, 'Michael Walzer's *Exodus and Revolution*', in Edward Said and Christopher Hitchens (eds), *Blaming the Victims*, London 1988.

10. Michael Walzer, *Just and Unjust Wars*, New York 1977.

11. Michael Walzer, *Spheres of Justice*, New York 1983.

12. Michael Walzer, *Exodus and Revolution*, New York 1985.

13. Michael Walzer, *The Company of Critics*, New York 1988. An acknowledgment reads that 'from my friends in Jerusalem I have learned the meaning of faithfulness in criticism, and that is why this book is dedicated to them.' One recalls Trotsky's stricture that

an officially registered 'friendship' for the Soviet Union is a kind of certificate of higher spiritual interests. ... [I]t makes it possible to live two lives at once: an everyday life in a circle of commonplace interests, and a holiday life elevating to the soul. From time to time the 'friends' visit Moscow ...

14. Benda observes that fascism marked a regression even from Machiavelli's politics. For the latter, 'evil, even if it aids politics, still remains evil.' Emblematic of fascist ideologues, by contrast, is the 'divinizing of politics': 'It is a great turning point in the history of man when those who speak in the name of pondered thought [maintain] that political egotisms are divine, and that everything which labors to relax them is degrading' – Walzer exactly (*The Treason of the Intellectuals*, New York 1969, pp. 107–9). On this point, cf. Adolf Hitler's *Mein Kampf*, New York 1971, where Germans who subordinate the 'rights of their own nationality' to 'objective' principles like 'internationalism' are chastised for 'a lack of devotion to our nation' (p. 113; cf. also pp. 177–8, 609–10).

15. Jules Roy, *The War in Algeria*, New York 1961, p. 127.

16. Albert Speer, *Inside the Third Reich*, New York 1970, p. 113.

17. Lamenting the lack of Israeli medical personnel abjuring complicity in the torture and ill-treatment of Palestinian prisoners, Human Rights Watch/Middle East observes that 'the small number ... is disappointing, particularly since, in contrast to the situation in many repressive countries, Israeli physicians do not risk imprisonment or worse for whistle-blowing' (*Torture and Ill-Treatment: Israel's Interrogation of Palestinians from the Occupied Territories*, New York 1994, p. 210). For the dire repercussions deterring resistance to the Nazi holocaust, cf. Sarah Gordon, *Hitler, Germans and the 'Jewish Question'*, Princeton 1984, esp. pp. 185, 296, 301–2. Interestingly, Gordon concludes that 'most surprising ... in some ways is the number of ordinary Germans who actually did something for Jews in the face of Hitler's police state'.

## Chapter 1

1. Yosef Gorny, *Zionism and the Arabs, 1882–1948: A Study of Ideology*, Oxford 1987.

2. The arguments presented in this chapter are more fully developed and documented in my doctoral dissertation, *From the Jewish Question to the Jewish State*, Princeton University, June 1987.

3. Cf. Arthur Hertzberg, *The Zionist Idea*, New York 1977, p. 33, 'Any version of Zionist theory must necessarily imply some sense of a loss of hope in the future total acceptance of the Jew as an individual by the majority society.'

4. Hans Kohn, 'Zion and the Jewish National Idea', in Walid Khalidi (ed.), *From Haven to Conquest*, Beirut 1971, p. 817. George L. Mosse's *The Crisis of German Ideology*, New York 1964, remains the best study of political Romanticism, providing also the crucial ideological context of Zionist thought.

5. Gorny quotes Herzl's closest collaborator, Max Nordau, to the effect that 'as long as the Jews constituted the minority [in Palestine], their moral and historical *proprietorship* was in question' (p. 157; emphasis in original).

6. It followed that, ideally, workers' organizations should be segregated along national lines. Much nonsense has been written on this topic. For instance, Amnon Rubinstein, *The Zionist Dream Revisited*, New York 1984, asserts that labor Zionism relentlessly sought solidarity with the Arab working class. 'Thus class interests would cut across national barriers put up by the scheming effendis'; but these noble labor Zionist efforts invariably 'crashed against the wall of Arab rejection' (pp. 60, 62). Yet, on those exceptional occasions when labor Zionism did preach bi-national cooperation between the Arab and Jewish laborers in Palestine, it was almost always with the explicit understanding that the proposed workers' syndicates would have to be organized separately on a national basis. In any case, opposition within the ranks of Jewish labor to these rare proposals was so strong that nothing ever came of them. The leftist Hashomer Hatzair mildly dissented from labor Zionism's exclusivist policies in the mid-1930s. Only Left Poalei Zion generally favored admitting Arabs to the Histadrut labor federation and organizing them in a single workers' organization with Jewish workers; Poalei Zion's political importance, however, was, to use Gorny's word, 'marginal'. Indeed, not only did labor Zionism not in principle want to 'cut across national barriers', but it was the aspiration of Arab workers (as well as extreme left Zionist elements) in the Histadrut to do so that 'crashed against the wall of Jewish rejection'. On these points, see pp. 134, 138, 143, 228–31, and Shabtei Teveth, *Ben-Gurion and the Palestinian Arabs*, New York 1985, pp. 64f. Cf. also Chap. 4 at p. 108 above.

7. The only politically significant discordant voices within the ranks of labor Zionism were the socialist 'pioneers' organized in Hashomer Hatzair. To be sure, they, too, insisted on the Jews' right to form a majority in Palestine, but only as the prelude to the territorial concentration of the Jews. They rejected the notion of an exclusivist Jewish state, championing bi-nationalism instead. (In the aftermath of World War II, Hashomer Hatzair reversed itself and eventually embraced the formula of a Jewish state.) See pp. 230–1, 292–3, 296–8. Berl Katznelson, the 'spiritual leader' of labor Zionism, stood fairly close, ideologically, to the left-wing socialist Zionists. In the early 1930s, he articulated a principled defense of bi-nationalism, characterizing (in Gorny's words) 'the multinational state as a positive phenomenon ... [and] believ[ing] that national blocs would disappear, to be replaced by class combinations, and that class solidarity would counterbalance national separation' (p. 220). When, in 1940, he acquiesced to the demand for a Jewish state, it was apparently for instrumental, not ideological, reasons – that is, to facilitate and secure the territorial concentration of the Jews:

> [T]he state is not the point at issue for me. If it were possible to establish a regime which guaranteed free mass immigration and freedom to construct the Jewish society, I would not be so strongly drawn to this slogan. But what we have undergone in the past few years has shown us that no regime other than a Jewish state can guarantee this. (p. 301)

8. Others within the Zionist movement went one step further, arguing that unless the Jews formed a majority in Palestine, they would eventually be assimilated. Jabotinsky, for example, contended that the assimilatory power of the majority could not, as a rule, be resisted, even if its cultural level was lower than that of the minority (p. 171; for Ben-Gurion, who made much the same argument, see p. 217).

9. At least at times, Ahad Ha'am seemed to favor a bi-national state in Palestine, if only for pragmatic reasons (pp. 102–3).

10. It is unclear from Gorny's account whether Weizmann advocated that an administrative system based on parity should be maintained even after the Jews formed the majority or whether it was merely a scheme to facilitate the demographic (and political) transformation of Palestine while the Jews still formed a minority. In any case, by the mid-1930s, when the prospects for the Zionist enterprise brightened, Weizmann (like Ben-Gurion) abandoned the parity principle in favor of a Jewish state *tout court*. Henceforth, the 'sole significance' of the parity principle for Weizmann, according to Gorny, 'was as a convenient political means of rejecting British proposals for the establishment of a [democratic] legislative council' (p. 207; for Ben-Gurion, see pp. 227, 255).

11. Ben-Gurion made this point even more emphatically in his gloss of the 1950 'Law of Return' which, together with the 1952 'Nationality Law', granted every Jew who emigrated to Israel the automatic right of citizenship: 'This law lays down not that the State accords the right of settlement to Jews abroad but that this right is *inherent in every Jew by virtue of his being a Jew*' (my emphasis; cited in *Encyclopedia Judaica*, Jerusalem 1971, vol. 10, p. 1486). Cf. Ben-Gurion's address to the 1951 Zionist Congress in Jerusalem: 'This State is the only one in the world which is not an end in itself but serves as a means – a central and principal means – for the fulfillment of Zionism: the Ingathering of the Exiles and their coalescence into a free nation in an independent State' (cited in Mitchell Cohen, *Zion and State*, New York 1987, p. 216). Jabotinsky fully shared Ben-Gurion's ideological perspectives on the Jewish state in general and its relationship to the Diaspora in particular; see pp. 268–9. Recalling the 1989 Israel High Court decision that any political party advocating full equality between Arab and Jew can be barred from fielding candidates in an election, David Kretzmer of the Hebrew University infers that the Israeli state 'is the state of the Jews, both those presently resident in the country as well as those resident abroad. Even if the Arabs have equal rights on all other levels the implication is clear: Israel is not *their* state' (*The Legal Status of the Arabs in Israel*, Boulder 1990, pp. 30–1; emphasis in original).

12. Curiously, the one place where illusions were rampant was in the 'scientific', 'dialectical' and 'class' analyses of the Zionist left. The proletarian Zionists invariably saw behind Palestinian resistance the hands of Arab feudalists and effendis, insisting that the Arab workers would at some point make common cause with the Zionist movement; see, e.g., p. 300. The mainstream labor Zionist leader Moshe Shertok denounced the fancifulness of these formulations: 'For the sake of self-delusion we have made it all sound easy and simple – a handful of effendis against the masses of workers' (pp. 134–5).

13. Inexplicably, Gorny himself seems unable to grasp this point. Referring to Chaim Arlosorov's tentative proposal to establish a provisional Zionist dictatorship in Palestine to expedite the territorial concentration of the Jews and the establishment of a Jewish majority, he remarks: 'Arlosorov was broaching an idea totally at odds with the tradition of Zionist thought, namely that the Jewish minority had the right to dominate the Arab majority' (p. 224). I return to these themes in Chap. 4 below.

14. Cf. Shlomo Avineri's conclusion in *The Making of Modern Zionism*, New York

1981, p. 226, that – except in a Jewish state – Jews constitute a foreign element and accordingly cannot contribute to a collective life:

> the Zionist revolution is very basically a permanent revolution against those powerful forces in Jewish history ... which have turned the Jews ... into a community living at the margin of and sometimes off *alien* communities. Zionism is a revolution against the drift of Jewish history, which pushes so many Jewish people ... to look for relatively neat and easy occupations rather than confront the challenge of building a national society, whose meaning is an overall responsibility and not just caring for oneself and one's own. ... Zionism is an attempt to bring back into Jewish life the supremacy of the public, communitarian and social aspects at the expense of personal ease, bourgeois comfort, and the good life of the individual. (my emphasis)

Note that, to clinch his argument, Avineri must resort to the most ugly and tawdry demagogy: the Jew as a self-centered and self-indulgent parasite battening off alien communities. Isn't Avineri actually depicting the 'drift of Jewish history' as distilled through the anti-Semite's perverted imagination? Compare, e.g., Adolf Hitler's *Mein Kampf*, New York 1971, where Jews are repeatedly excoriated as a '*parasite* in the body of other peoples', driven by the 'crassest egoism' and suffering from an 'absolute absence of all sense of self-sacrifice' (pp. 301–10 passim, emphasis in original; cf. also p. 150).

15. Gorny himself tacitly subscribes to the premises of this argument. Referring to Palestine at the dawn of the Zionist movement, he observes: 'It should be recalled that with the exception of several tens of thousands, the Jewish people were not residing in *their* country' (p. 1; emphasis added).

16. The same argument is still invoked even in the most secular and sober of fora. Thus, in a joint work with a Palestinian interlocutor, Mark Heller of the Jaffee Center for Strategic Studies at Tel Aviv University writes that 'I am convinced that Israel's claim to this land, including the West Bank and Gaza, is essentially just and right' inasmuch as 'any collective Palestinian claim is based on possession stemming from conquest of what was stolen property' (Mark Heller and Sari Nusseibeh, *No Trumpets, No Drums*, New York 1991, p. 5).

17. After World War II, Ihud, the organizational successor to Brit-Shalom, moved closer to the mainstream view, if still not fully endorsing it. It held 'the historical rights of the Jews and the natural rights of the Arabs as equal under all conditions' (p. 288). I also return to these themes in Chap. 4 below.

18. Linguistically, the qualitative distinction made in the Zionist discourse on Palestine between 'residential' rights (enjoyed by all inhabitants) and 'historical' rights (to which Jews have exclusive title) is 'doubled' in the Zionist discourse on the Jewish state in the distinction made between 'civil' rights (enjoyed by all citizens) and 'political' rights (to which Jews have exclusive title). Zionist ideology borrows extensively from the language of liberalism, but in a manner that totally abuses the original meaning. The liberal concept of the state, for instance, precludes a hierarchy of rights among citizens. Similarly, there is a conceptual disjuncture between the liberal principle of 'majority rule', in which to be in the minority bears not at all on one's standing in the body politic, and the Zionist principle of 'majority rule', in which the majority (or, more exactly, the majority nation) enjoys exclusive title to the state.

19. The author is apparently unaware, however, of how deep the roots of this idea run in Zionism. For example, he makes much of the roseate vision of Arab–Jewish amity that Herzl limned in his utopian novel, *Old-New Land*, but fails to note the future that this same Herzl charted for Palestine's indigenous population in his diaries: 'We shall try to spirit the penniless population across the border by procuring employment for them in the transit countries while denying any employment in our country' (Raphael Patai, [ed.], *The Complete Diaries of Theodor Herzl*, New York 1961, I, p. 88).

20. Much nonsense has been written on this topic as well. In *Ben-Gurion and the Palestinian Arabs* (cf. note 6 above), Teveth argues that Ben-Gurion endorsed the tentative British proposal in 1937 to deport the Palestinian Arabs with great reluctance, 'carefully measur[ing] ... expediency ... against the claims of justice'. To document Ben-Gurion's profound sensitivity to Arab claims, he cites the following extract from Ben-Gurion's diary: 'The more I study the recommendations [for a compulsory population transfer] ... I see above all the terrible difficulty in uprooting, by foreign force, some 100,000 Arabs from villages which they have inhabited for hundreds of years' (p. 181). Terribly difficult is not the same as wrong. In fact, Ben-Gurion explicitly denied that a coercive exodus was intrinsically immoral and heartily seconded the British proposal: 'If [a] forced transfer were to be implemented, in so far as I know our history in this country, it would be an unparalleled achievement from the point of view of settlement, giving us a vast territory' (p. 261). Pointing at a Zionist Congress in 1937 to 'the growing Jewish strength in Palestine [that] will increase our possibilities for conducting a large scale transfer', Ben-Gurion, like Zisling, avowed that 'this method also contains an important Zionist and humanist idea – to transfer parts of the people to their own land' (cited in *Haaretz*, 4 February 1994). Unfortunately, Gorny lapses into non-sequiturs in his treatment of this highly sensitive issue. For instance, after describing the Zionist movement's enthusiasm (despite some tactical reservations) for a clause in the 1944 British Labor party platform supporting a massive compulsory population transfer of Palestinian Arabs, he writes:

> Although these were mere theoretical proposals, they help to illustrate the attitude of Zionist leaders towards the Arab population. In effect, the Zionist movement was resigned to living with a large Arab minority in the Jewish state, whether in all or part of Palestine. (p. 306)

For further discussion, cf. also Chap. 4 at pp. 103–4 above.

21. I will not discuss here the tactical differences within the Zionist movement, of which there were several – the proper balance between military preparations and constructivist efforts, the utility of public deception (i.e. 'watering down' Zionist objectives in official representations) and so on. On these points, see pp. 165–6, 176–7. These tactical disputes ultimately proved to be much less significant than the common strategic orientation in which they were inscribed.

22. On this point, cf. the excellent (but largely ignored) companion studies by Isaiah Friedman, *Germany, Turkey and Zionism, 1897–1918*, Oxford 1977, and *The Question of Palestine, 1914–1918*, London 1973.

23. In the event, even the British-backed satraps that ruled the Arab world during the interwar period were unwilling to enter into a federation with the Zionists, except on terms that the latter considered less than minimally acceptable. Abdallah,

Amir (later King) of Jordan, who, of all the Arab rulers, evinced the greatest inclination for compromise with the Zionists, had the least claim to popular legitimacy and was most in thrall to Britain. For a painstaking historical treatment of this topic, cf. Yehoshua Porath, *In Search of Arab Unity*, London 1986, esp. ch. 2.

24.  Note the irony that, whereas the Zionist left theorized that the class interests of the reactionary effendis placed them in opposition to Zionism while the popular Arab masses were its 'natural' allies (see above, note 12), regionally the exact opposite turned out to be the case.

25.  This, incidentally, is exactly how Zionism was perceived at the time in the Arab world – i.e. as a 'tool of [British] imperialism against the Arab peoples' and as a British 'weapon against emergent nationalist trends among the Arabs' (p. 226). The left-wing Arab critique of Zionism is not nearly so new (hence, opportunist) as is suggested, for example, by Bernard Lewis in *Semites and Anti-Semites*, New York 1986, passim.

26.  Somewhat inconsistently, Gorny elsewhere observes that, within the Zionist movement, 'there was a consensus, *which even Brit-Shalom did not dare to violate*, on the vital importance of ties between Zionism and Great Britain' (p. 176; my emphasis).

27.  Cf. Jacob Neusner's authoritative remarks in 'America is the Best Promised Land', *Manchester Guardian Weekly* (22 March 1987), where he observes:

> Zionism promised that the Jewish state would be a spiritual center for the Jewish people. But today, in all the Jewish world, who – as a matter of Jewish sentiment or expression – reads an Israeli book, or looks at an Israeli painting, or goes to an Israeli play, or listens to Israeli music? ... [Jews] do not look to Tel Aviv for stimulation or for imagination. ... The not-very-well-kept-secret is that ... Israeli scholarship is pretty dull. After Martin Buber, not a single major Israeli thinker has made a mark outside the intellectual village of Jerusalem. After Gershom Scholem, not a single Israeli scholar in the study of Judaism has won any audience at all outside of the State of Israel. Everyone can boast about locals. But who, today, is listening? No historians, no philosophers in Judaic studies have a hearing overseas. Israeli scholarship boasts no social scientists working on Jewish materials in a way that interests anyone but Jews. Israeli scholarship in Judaic studies is provincial, erudite, unimaginative, remarkably unproductive – just a lot of dull-witted fact-mongering by third-rate academic politicians. The level of academic discourse is easily grasped when you realize that character-assassination has replaced criticism of ideas.'

Israel's cultural horizon is instructively surveyed by statesman Ezer Weizman in his paean to 'our army' as 'the Jewish people's most original creation since returning to its homeland' (Ezer Weizman, *The Battle for Peace*, New York 1981, p. 155). If the army is the archetypical institutional embodiment of Israeli culture, then Ariel Sharon is its archetypical individual embodiment. Moshe Dayan reports in his memoir that 'Ben-Gurion had a specially soft spot for ... Arik'. He 'did not just like' Sharon, he 'positively adored' him. The 'principal reason' for Ben-Gurion's 'special regard' was that Sharon 'embodied the character of the Israeli Jew of his dream – a man of integrity...' (*Story of My Life*, New York 1976, p. 524)

28.  Even so arch an apologist for the Israeli state as Avineri concedes this point in *The Making of Modern Zionism* (p. 224):

Today, mainly due to the influx of Arab labor from the West Bank and Gaza, sizable sectors of the Israeli economy have seen the disappearance of Jewish workers from manual jobs and their substitution by Arab laborers. In whole areas of agriculture, the building industry, and certain menial service occupations, most of the manual work is done by Arabs. This is occurring at a time when the relatively advanced standard of living of Israeli society is being maintained through sizeable overseas grants, and the Jewish population of Israel is becoming more and more concentrated in white-collar occupations.

## Chapter 2

1. New York 1984. This chapter was completed and widely circulated in December 1984. The only substantive criticism of its content of which I am aware appeared in the June and October 1986 numbers of *Commentary* magazine. I have used this opportunity to reply to it. Otherwise, the text is basically unchanged, aside from the postscript.

2. The findings of a number of these authorities are cited by Peters on pp. 223–5 and 513, footnote 19. For a recent restatement of the conventional view, see Dov Friedlander and Calvin Goldscheider, *The Population of Israel*, New York 1979, where the authors write that Arab population growth during the British mandate period 'was almost entirely the result of high natural increase – high fertility and low, declining mortality' (p. 17). Friedlander is associate professor in the departments of demography and statistics and director of the Levi Eshkol Institute for Economic, Social and Political Research at the Hebrew University. Goldscheider is chair of the department of demography at the Hebrew University. On this point, cf. also Chap. 4 at note 26 below.

3. Peters attributes this view to John Hope Simpson, but there is nothing in the report he authored that even remotely suggests such a conclusion. On p. 170, Peters claims there is a 'profusion of evidence' that Palestine was 'uninhabited' on the eve of modern Zionist colonization.

4. Peters speculates (pp. 252–4) that, even as early as 1878–93, literally thousands of Arab immigrants and in-migrants may have been flocking to the Jewish settlements in Palestine because of their 'economic attractions'. Further, to judge by the base figures in her demographic study (p. 255, Table G), the Zionist colonies attracted, not thousands, but nearly a *half million* Arab immigrants during these years. Yet, according to Walter Laqueur, the impoverished first *aliya* settlements established in 1881 and thereabouts did not even become 'going concerns' until the first decade of the twentieth century (*A History of Zionism*, New York 1976, p. 79). Neville Mandel, in his authoritative study of the period, writes that 'only a limited number of Arab villagers and a few passing Bedouin could have directly felt the presence of the Jewish settlers during the years before 1908' (*The Arabs and Zionism Before World War I*, Berkeley 1976, p. 34).

5. Peters's handling of numbers throughout does not inspire great confidence. I will have more to say about this topic further on, but allow me one example here. Peters quotes five different 'authoritative' figures (pp. 223, 242, 244, 245 and 523, footnote 38), ranging from under 150,000 to 600,000, for the Palestinian Arab population on the eve of modern Zionist settlement, yet she hardly seems aware

of the wide discrepancy among them. For instance, the one significant calculation that Peters – or, rather, Ernst Frankenstein (see p. 44 above) – makes for this early period (ch. 12, pp. 244–5) is based on one of the untenably low estimates. Had Peters used any of the higher figures cited, she could not have sustained her argument in ch. 12 (which, in any case, is contradicted by the findings of every historian of the period).

6. Peters assumes that the rate of natural increase for the Arab population in the region of Jewish settlement was no higher than the one she calculated for the predominantly Arab areas in Palestine.

7. But not terribly original. Had Peters's reviewers spent less time enthusing about the magnitude of her research and devoted a little time to investigating her sources, they would have discovered that Peters relies heavily on – and plagiarizes extensively from – Ernst Frankenstein, who tried to prove the exact point more than forty years ago. In a 1975 Jerusalem symposium, the Israeli orientalist Yehoshua Porath ridiculed this stale theme of massive Arab immigration as a 'pointless legend' (cited in Noam Chomsky, *Towards a New Cold War*, New York 1982, p. 440, note 74).

8. The few scraps of 'original' archival material that Peters does cite to substantiate her thesis are worthless. Consider the following examples:

(1) To document the 'prevalence of illicit Arab immigration into Palestine', Peters reproduces (p. 270) a batch of the Mandatory's inter-office memoranda. For instance, she quotes the following 'urgent' order sent in 1925 to the 'Northern District Commissioner' from the 'Controller of Permits':

> Subject: Refugees from Syria
> … to the officer in charge at Ras-El-Nakurah. … Will you be so good as to … furnish him as speedily as possible with a mimeographed supply of the blank passes. (all ellipses in Peters's text)

This 'evidence' is presented by Peters without any context or comment.

(2) In her chapter, 'A Hidden Movement: Illegal Arab Immigration', Peters devotes eighteen pages (278–95) to the correspondence between various British officials on how to curb the influx of Arab 'provocateurs' during the 1936–39 Arab Revolt. Readers who wade through these tedious pages will finally discover that the exchanges have nothing whatever to do with the thesis that Peters is supposedly trying to prove: there isn't a jot of evidence in the memoranda pointing to the conclusion that these 'outside agitators' either intended to or actually did *settle* in Palestine.

9. Peters acknowledges this crucial point, but in her own fashion: 'According to all reports of the period, Arab 'recorded' immigration to Palestine was minimal, casual and unquantifiable' (p. 226). She has evidently 'erred' in two respects: (1) the British assessments were *explicitly not limited* to 'recorded' immigration; and (2) no report ever stated that 'recorded' immigration was 'unquantifiable'. Peters should have taken full credit for the latter, remarkable contribution to demographic science.

10. The Mandatory government pegged the Jewish immigration quota (a.k.a. the 'Labor Schedule') to Palestine's capacity for absorbing new permanent workers. The 'present practice' refers to the British policy of deducting a certain number of immigration certificates from the Labor Schedule in anticipation of illegal immigration.

11. Number of 'Travellers' Reclassified as Legal Immigrants in Selected Years

|        | Jews | Muslims | Christians[a] |
|--------|------|---------|---------------|
| 1926   | 611  | 149     | 300           |
| 1927   | 705  | 85      | 430           |
| 1928[b] | 1287 | 143     | 436           |
| 1932[c] | 3730 | 109     | 719           |
| 1933[c] | 2465 | 63      | 344           |

|        | Jews | Non-Jews (Muslims, Christians, etc.) |
|--------|------|--------------------------------------|
| 1934   | 4114 | 752                                  |
| 1935   | 3804 | 625                                  |
| 1936   | 1817 | 467                                  |
| 1937   | 681  | 431                                  |
| 1938   | 1427 | 421                                  |

[a]  In Peters's special universe, 'Christian'-Arab is a contradiction in terms, an 'Arab propaganda claim' (p. 250). In any case, the provenance of roughly two-thirds of the Christian immigrants to Palestine in any given year was the non-Arab world.

[b]  Totals include 'travellers and others who received permission to stay'.

[c]  Totals include 'persons who had entered Palestine as travellers or without permission'.

*Source*: annual British reports to the League of Nations cited in Peters's bibliography.

12. According to Peters (p. 425), the British put the number of legally registered Arab immigrants at 27,300.

13. See p. 431 of Peters's text for a reproduction of the relevant British document. Note line 3: 'Including persons who entered as travellers and subsequently registered as immigrants.'

14. On these (and other) pages in her text, Peters employs the more vague expression 'Jewish-settled areas' to designate the region of Palestine that became Israel after the 1949 Armistice Agreements. She explicitly clarifies this peculiar usage elsewhere in her text (cf. p. 264 – 'what is now Israel, i.e., Jewish-settled areas').

15. Peters's apologists seem not to understand that, if in fact she were referring only to Area I, her 'revelation' is a meaningless tautology. The only germane demographic comparisons are between the Arab and Jewish populations in all of Palestine and, arguably, between the Arab and Jewish populations in the region of Palestine that later became Israel. Even if Peters's numbers were accurate (which they are not) and even if she were referring only to Area I (which she is not), all she would have 'proven' is that Jews were a majority where they were a majority.

16. Before 1930, these tabulations are collected under the chapter heading 'Immigration and Labour' or 'Immigration and Travel' in the annual British reports.

17. It is not without interest to compare Peters's treatment of this material with

the manner in which it is handled by another, equally partisan, author. In his openly apologetic tract, *Justice for My People* (1944), Ernst Frankenstein observed only that 'The Mandates Commission *discussed* in 1935 a declaration of the governor of the (Syrian) Hauran district that in 1934, in a few months, 30,000 Hauranese had entered Palestine and settled there' (pp. 128–9; my emphasis). Even in a book devoid of any scholarly pretensions, the documentary record is not mangled in so scandalous a fashion as in Peters's work. Virtually all the reviewers who acclaimed Peters's 'prodigious research' and 'brilliant detective work' highlighted her citation from the Mandates Commission hearing on the massive influx of Hauranis. It appears that Peters's find was neither especially original nor quite so difficult to track down. On Peters's intimate knowledge of Frankenstein's work, see pp. 24f. above.

18. See also the 1937 *Peel Commission Report* which states that 'The deputy Inspector-General of the Criminal Investigation Department has recently estimated that the number of Hauranis in the country at the present time is roughly 2,500.'

19. She asserts that a 'smaller number' of the Hauranis exited Palestine than had earlier entered but offers not a scratch of evidence to substantiate this claim. Cf. the *Survey of Palestine* observations already cited.

20. On pp. 253–4, Peters argues that the 1893 figure for Area I may itself include as many as 11,000 Arab immigrants and migrants (from other parts of Palestine) who settled in this region between 1870 and 1893, in which case 'anywhere from 45,000 to 350,000' of the Arabs counted as indigenous to Area I in 1947 may also have been relatively recent immigrants and migrants and their offspring. Yet, 2.7 times 11,000 equals 29,700. Peters offers no explanation for her bizarre projection of 45,000 to 350,000. On Arab immigration and migration to Area I before the turn of the century, see note 4 above.

21. In an appendix (pp. 427–8), Philip Hauser, the 'population expert' thanked by Peters for 'correcting, checking, and re-checking' (p. ix) the demographic study, certifies all her data for Area I. (Hauser is former director of the United States Census and director emeritus of the Population Research Center at the University of Chicago.) In the *Commentary* article cited in note 1, Erich and Rael Jean Isaac claim that I have used the wrong factor of natural increase. They allege that the correct multiple is 2.795. Yet, in Peters's text, 2.795 refers not to the factor of *natural* increase between 1893 and 1947, but to the factor by which the *total* Palestinian Arab population increased between 1893 and 1948, including, for example, the Arabs who immigrated into Palestine during those years:

$$\frac{1,303,800 \ \text{(total Arab pop. 1947)}}{466,400 \ \text{(total Arab pop. 1893)}} = 2.795$$

22. Peters reserves the term 'in-migration' for the movement of indigenous Palestinian Arabs from any other part of Palestine into the Jewish-settled area. Her handling of this – not terribly complex – concept is remarkably inept. See, *inter alia*, p. 245 (the same page on which her definition appears!), where Peters attributes the (alleged) aberrant growth in Palestine's *overall* Arab population between 1882 and 1895 to Arab immigration and *in-migration*; p. 376, where she condemns Britain's supposedly 'cynical policy' in Palestine, by which 'illegal Arab immigrants entered unheeded *along with Arab in-migrants*, and all were counted as "natives" unless they were "flagrant"'; and p. 157, where she surmises that, given the 'acute decline' that Palestine's population suffered before modern Jewish settlement, '[a]n

enormous swell of Arab population could only have resulted from immigration and *in-migration*' (my emphases).

23. In a footnote some 250 pages earlier (p. 16), we learn that the 430,000 figure Peters repeatedly uses as her low estimate includes only 'genuine refugees', i.e. those who were in need of relief after 1948. The source from which she took this figure put the total number of refugees in 1948 at 539,000.

24. In the *Commentary* article cited in note 1, the Isaacs offer an ingenious rationale for this omission: Peters need not have taken Area IV into account since historical evidence points to the conclusion that 'it is most unlikely' that Arabs out-migrated from that region. But, alas, if we are to believe Peters's demographic study, that is exactly what they did do. Either (1) the Isaacs' historical deductions are correct, in which case Peters's study is fraudulent or else (2) Peters's projection for Area IV is correct, in which case her conclusion is fraudulent. There is no third possibility.

25. In the *Commentary* article cited in note 1, the Isaacs claim I have miscalculated and that Peters's figure is correct. Yet, Peters's methodology (p. 256) yields the following results for Area IV:

| | |
|---|---|
| 87,400.0 | (1893 pop.) |
| × 2.7 | (factor of natural increase) |
| 235,980.0 | (projected 1947 pop.) |
| 125,100.0 | (actual 1947 pop. minus immigrants and nomads) |
| −110,880.0 | (net out-migration from Area IV) |

There can be no question about the manner of calculation since, for Area I, it yields the exact figure certified by Philip Hauser in Appendix VI, p. 428:

| | |
|---|---|
| 92,300.0 | (1893 pop.) |
| × 2.7 | (factor of natural increase) |
| 249,210.0 | (projected 1947 pop.) |
| 417,300.0 | (actual 1947 pop. minus immigrants and nomads) |
| +168,090.0 | (net in-migration to Area I) |

26. Peters received a copy of my findings on her demographic study in June 1984. In September 1984, Harper & Row issued the seventh printing of *From Time Immemorial*, which contained several 'minor corrections' in the demographic study (in the words of Aaron Asher, Peters's editor at Harper & Row). Specifically, Peters has emended the legend to the map on p. 246. Whereas she originally claimed that there was 'no Jewish settlement' in Areas III and IV, she has since discovered that there was 'some Jewish settlement' in those two areas. The legend for the map on p. 246 now technically corresponds to the bracketing in the legend on p. 424 *but*:

(a) This 'correction' still does not explain why Areas I, II and III are bracketed off from Areas IV and V.

(b) The legend to the map on p. 246 *contradicts* the data collected in the tables on p. 425. Area V, which is listed on p. 246 as having 'no Jewish settlement' still contained 6,500 Jews in 1947 according to the tables; Areas II and III, which are listed as having 'some Jewish settlement' on p. 246, contained no Jews in any years for which there is a breakdown in the tables. To conceal the data in Area IV, Peters evidently sacrificed internal consistency. Areas II–V of Peters's demographic study undergo a remarkable series of metamorphoses in the pages of *From Time Immemorial*. See Table A1 on p. 41 above.

27. By excluding from her calculations the 'out'-migrants from Area IV, Peters comes up with a figure for the 1948 indigenous Arab population within what became Israel that is some 110,000 short of the real number. From this figure, a second incorrect sum is derived (see column headed 'Arab settled population' in Table H, p. 257). These falsified numbers are then repeated elsewhere in the text (see, e.g., p. 262). For the correct figure, see my Table 2.4, column B: (Area I) 249,210 + (Area II) 105,030 + (Area IV) 235,980 = 590,220. Peters's falsified base figure is 483,000 (from which a second falsified figure is derived).

28. A full discussion of *From Time Immemorial*'s 'scholarly apparatus' would take us well beyond the scope of this chapter. I will therefore limit myself to a few brief remarks.

(a) *From Time Immemorial* has all the earmarks of a 'cut-and-paste' job, but with the additional shortcoming that quotes are repeatedly 'cut' from irrelevant sources. The result is a succession of arguments that are massively 'documented' yet completely unsubstantiated.

(b) For all her alleged research, Peters is apparently ignorant of even watershed developments in the political history of Israel, e.g. the 'Lavon Affair' (see pp. 49 and 458, footnote 125).

(c) Peters makes sixty explicit references to Jacob de Haas's 1934 popular 'history' of Palestine, eight to an entry in the 1911 edition of the *Encyclopedia Britannica*, nine to Ernst Frankenstein's 1942 tract, *Justice for My People*, eight to the 'works' of the former chair of the American Christian Palestine Committee (Carl Hermann Voss), twenty-one to Samuel Katz's *Battleground: Fact and Fantasy in Palestine*, etc., etc. These 'sources' have the combined scholarly weight of a classic comic book.

(d) Yehoshua Porath's standard two-volume work on the origins of Palestinian nationalism receives no mention in a book that devotes more than a few pages to this theme. Peters makes no reference to Erskine Childers's classic research on the 1948 Palestinian Arab exodus from Israel in her treatment of this topic. The findings of both authors completely contradict Peters's conclusions, conclusions that, in actuality, are nothing more than a rehash of the oldest and most tired Zionist apologetics without a shred of new evidence to support them.

(e) In a blurb for *From Time Immemorial*, Arthur Goldberg makes his little contribution to the myth of Peters's 'monumental' research: '*From Time Immemorial* is, to my knowledge, the first book in the English language which tells the story of the expulsion of Jews from Arab countries.' Had Goldberg bothered to consult Peters's footnote, he would have discovered that her entire discussion of this topic is based on a book by Joseph Schechtman and two pamphlets, and that all three of these references are in English.

29. For a more comical example of Peters's going awry because of hewing too closely to Frankenstein's line, see Alexander Cockburn's column in the 13 October 1984 *Nation*, where he observes that:

Peters does acknowledge Frankenstein elsewhere, but not always in a manner that enhances either her credibility or that of her guide. On page 169 she writes: 'Kurds, Turcomans, Naim [sic] and other colonists arrived in Palestine around the same time as the Jewish immigration waves began. Eighteen thousand "tents" of Tartars, (207) the "armies of Turks and Kurds", whole villages settled in the nineteenth century of Bosnians and Moors and "Circassians" and "Algerians" and Egyptians, etc. – all were continually brought in to people the land called Palestine.' Footnote 207 reads: 'Makrizi, *Histoire des Sultans Mamlouks*, II, pp. 29–30, cited in Frankenstein, *Justice*, p. 122.' If we turn to R.A. Nicholson's *A Literary History of the Arabs*, we discover that Makrizi was born in 1364 and died in 1442. He is thus a dubious authority on matters of nineteenth-century population movement, though his work on the migration of Tartar hordes in the Middle Ages is no doubt beyond reproach. In view of Peters's assertion about material she has cited, we must assume that both she and Frankenstein made entirely coincidental blunders about the date and utility of Makrizi's work.

30. Though one that contradicts every serious historical and demographic study of the period. Cf. notes 4 and 5 above.

31. Peters is simply repeating Frankenstein when she observes that, even if an unusually high rate of natural increase is assumed, the point still stands. Yet, in her one oblique reference to Frankenstein (pp. 245 and 523, footnote 42), Peters has the audacity to write that (1) it is *Frankenstein* who assumes an unusually high rate of natural increase for the period, and (2) even if his 'unlikely' assumption is credited, the argument *she* has worked out on Arab immigration between 1882 and 1895 is still valid!

32. United Nations Security Council, 'Provisional Verbatim Record of the 1724th Meeting', 13 June 1973 (S/PV.1724). Cf. Marie Syrkin, 'The Claim of the Palestinian Arabs', in Mordecai S. Chertoff (ed.), *The New Left and the Jews*, New York 1971:

> All reports agree that prior to the Jewish return Palestine was a dying land. Throughout the nineteenth century the favorite adjectives of travelers describing the Holy Land, beginning with the French[man] Volney who visited the country in 1785, are 'ruined' and 'desolate.' Each successive writer mourns the further decline of the country. A. Keith, writing in *The Land of Israel* some decades after Volney, comments: 'In his [Volney's] day the land had not fully reached its last degree of desolation and depopulation', and he estimates that the population had shrunk by half. (p. 260)

33. For further evidence of plagiarism, compare pp. 17–19 of Peters's text with Joseph Schechtman, *The Refugee in the World*, New York 1963, pp. 200–8, 248–9.

34. An authoritative international committee – including historians Albert Hourani, Roger Owen and Simha Flapan, and demographer Justin McCarthy – agreed to weigh the findings. The respected Israeli historian Isaiah Friedman at first expressed some interest but subsequently reconsidered, averring that 'the book may be inaccurate in part but it is not a "hoax". Some of the points which she makes are not new and I accept them.' Friedman went on to 'attribute her errors to deficient craftsmanship and a lack of training in academic work rather than a deliberate intent to falsify'.

35. Cf. Hannah Arendt on the reception of the *Protocols of the Elders of Zion*:

if a patent forgery ... is believed by so many people ..., the task of the historian
is no longer to discover a forgery. ... [T]he chief political and historical fact of
the matter [is] that the forgery is being believed. This fact is more important
than the (historically speaking, secondary) circumstance that it is forgery. (*The
Origins of Totalitarianism*, New York 1972, p. 7)

36. Edward Said and Christopher Hitchens (eds), *Blaming the Victims*, London
1988, chs. 1–2.
37. Benjamin Netanyahu, *A Place Among the Nations*, New York 1993, p. 36.


## Chapter 3

1. David Ben-Gurion, *Israel: A Personal History*, Tel Aviv 1971, p. 149 (quoting
Sharett). Benny Morris, 'The Eel and History', *Tikkun*, January–February 1990.
2. The other Israeli scholars include: Simha Flapan, *The Birth of Israel*, New
York 1987; Ilan Pappé, *Britain and the Arab–Israeli Conflict, 1948–51*, New York
1988; and Avi Shlaim, *Collusion Across the Jordan*, New York 1988. The works of
non-Israeli scholars also deserve mention here, especially inasmuch as they have
been ignored in the ensuing debates. I would note in particular Mary Wilson's
elegant study, *King Abdullah: Britain and the Making of Jordan*, Cambridge 1988, and
Michael Palumbo's *The Palestinian Catastrophe*, London 1987. Palumbo makes extensive use of hitherto untapped UN archival sources.
3. New York 1988; hereafter cited as *Birth*.
4. Cf. Johns Hopkins professor Fouad Ajami's typically effusive review in *The
Washington Post Book World* (18 September 1988), which acclaims *Birth* as a

book of extraordinary power and integrity. ... Benny Morris takes that great
tale of flight and conquest and tells it ... with precision and moral economy,
with awesome detail and honesty. ... Hitherto this subject has been the realm
of publicists and protagonists. ... In Benny Morris this episode has its first
historian and chronicler – no axe to grind, no apologies to make.

5. Oxford 1990; hereafter cited as *1948*. The notices for this volume read more
or less like those for *Birth*; cf. Israeli professor Moshe Ma'oz's accolade for Morris's
'remarkable impartiality and detachment' in the *Times Literary Supplement* (22 March
1991). A 'revised and expanded' paperback edition of *1948* was put out by Oxford
University Press in 1994 after the draft of this chapter was completed. References
to the new material are designated *1948, revised*.
6. Morris cites (*Birth*, pp. 284, 297–8) the following estimates for the total
number of Palestinian refugees by 1949:

| | |
|---|---|
| UN-sponsored Palestine Conciliation Commission (PCC) | 711,000 |
| United Nations Relief and Works Agency (UNRWA) | 726,000 |
| UN Economic Survey Mission | 726,000 |
| British Government | 810,000 |
| British Foreign Office | 711,000 |

Walter Eytan, then Director General of the Israeli Foreign Ministry, referred to the
UNRWA registration of 726,000 as 'meticulous' and believed that the 'real number

was close to 800,000'. Officially, however, the Israeli government maintained that the total number of Palestinian refugees came to only a little over 500,000. Inexplicably, even after citing Eytan's testimony and conceding the cynicism behind Israel's public estimates, Morris writes that 'Israel sincerely believed that the Arab (and United Nations) figures were "inflated"'. William Roger Louis reports that 'by 1952, a secret British estimate calculated the total number of refugees at 850,000 with the following breakdown: 460,000, Jordan; 200,000, Gaza; 104,000, Lebanon; 80,000, Syria; 4,000, Iraq; and 19,000, Israel'; see *The British Empire in the Middle East, 1945–1951*, Oxford 1984, p. 588. (The British estimate may be slightly misleading since it perhaps includes natural increase between the years 1949 and 1952.) For an exhaustive survey of estimates on the number of 1948 Palestinian refugees, all of which fall around the 700,000–800,000 range, cf. Elia Zureik, 'Palestinian Refugees and Peace', *Journal of Palestine Studies*, Autumn 1994, Table 3 at p. 11.

7. Indeed, not only Arab claims. Meir Pa'il, the widely respected Israeli historian of the 1948 war, estimates that, of the total Palestinian refugee population, 'one third fled out of fear, one third were forcibly evacuated by the Israelis ..., [and] one third were encouraged by the Israelis to flee' (Palumbo, p. xviii). Palumbo's study reaches roughly the same conclusion as Pa'il. To be sure, Pa'il still holds the Arabs fully responsible for the refugee problem since they engaged in a 'premeditated conspiracy' to start the war. Ironically, even the chief exponent of the official Zionist faith and the 'new' history's main detractor, Shabtai Teveth (senior research associate at Tel Aviv University and Ben-Gurion's current biographer), gives more ground than Morris on the matter of expulsion. He concedes that, once the Arab armies attacked on 15 May, 'one may properly speak ... of expulsion by Israel' of Palestine's Arabs, who were henceforth perceived as 'declared enemies' ('Charging Israel With Original Sin', *Commentary*, September 1989, p. 28). The majority of the Palestinian population that ended up in exile was still *in situ* on the eve of the Arab invasion. One may, finally, note that Morris's own most recent capsule formulation of the Palestinian refugee question comes quite close to these as he refers to 'some 700,000 driven into exile' (Benny Morris, *Israel's Border Wars, 1949–1956*, Oxford 1993, p. 410).

8. In 'The Eel and History' (*Tikkun*, January–February 1990; hereafter cited as *Tikkun*), Morris explicitly exempts the Zionist leadership from moral culpability for the unfolding of events in 1948, arguing that no leader would or could have acted otherwise than Ben-Gurion did:

> [W]ere I pressed ... to morally evaluate the Yishuv's policies and behavior in 1948, I would be loath to condemn. ... Would any leader, recognizing the prospective large Arab minority's potential for destabilization of the new Jewish state, *not* have striven to reduce that minority's weight and numbers, and been happy, nay, overjoyed, at the spectacle of the mass Arab evacuations? Would any sane, pragmatic leader *not* have striven, given the Arabs' initiation of hostilities, to exploit the war to enlarge Israel's territory and to create somewhat more rational, viable borders? (pp. 20–1; emphases in original)

Perhaps it is true that no 'sane, pragmatic leader' would have acted differently; but that simply points up that – at any rate, by current standards – a 'sane, pragmatic leader' is not a moral leader. Morris also argues here that the 'inevitability in the unfolding of the events' in 1948 'renders somewhat incongruous any attempt at moral judgment against Jew or Arab'. For a truly absurd apologia, cf. Kenneth W. Stein, 'One Hundred Years of Social Change: The Creation of the Palestinian Refugee Problem', in Laurence Silberstein (ed.), *New Perspectives on Israeli History*, New York 1991, which argues that, due to its 'fractious nature' and 'steady dissolution over the previous century', the 'Palestinian Arab community had been significantly prone to dispossession and dislocation before the mass exodus from Palestine began'. By the standard of the main evidence Stein adduces – a demographic shift in Palestine from rural to urban areas – every society undergoing modernization is in process of 'dissolution' and 'prone to dispossession'.

9. Morris's search for the 'happy median' occasionally results in bizarre formulations. Consider his usage of the locution 'dovetail'. He describes the Palestinian evacuation of a village threatened with a Haganah massacre as 'a dovetailing of British, Haganah and Arab views – all parties concerned, for different reasons, being keen on a speedy Arab evacuation' and the IDF-ordered expulsion of Palestinians remaining in Lydda after the mass slaughter as a 'dovetailing, as it were, of Jewish and Arab interests and wishes – an IDF bent on expelling the population and a population ready, perhaps, even eager, to move to Arab-held territory' (*Birth*, pp. 319, 209). Do the interests of a torturer and his victim 'dovetail' when the latter finally confesses or succumbs?

10. Morris explains his decision not to make more use of interviews by observing that 'I was brought up believing in the value of documents. While contemporary documents may misinform, omit or lie, they do so, in my experience, far more rarely than interviewees recalling highly controversial events some forty years ago' (*Birth*, p. 2).

11. 'How the Zionist Documents were Doctored', *Haaretz*, 4 February 1994.

12. Another reason that Ben-Gurion's testimony cannot be trusted is that he was so extreme a racist, indeed, comically so. Thus, he observed that Arabs were not entitled to the same respect accorded Jews because 'so far no Arab Einstein has arisen. ... We are dealing here with a collective murderer' (*Birth*, p. 331, note 54). Incidentally, Morris's study reveals that even the findings of Zionists renowned for their sympathy with the Palestinian Arabs must be handled with some caution. Thus a Mapam leader and secretary of the League for Arab–Jewish Rapprochement and Cooperation, Aharon Cohen, early on in the Arab exodus sought to minimize the responsibility of the Haganah by faulting the British for 'sow[ing] panic' among the Arabs – a claim for which there is apparently no supporting evidence (*Birth*, p. 317, note 73; cf. *Birth*, p. 319, note 93). Cohen's contention in this regard is consistent with the central thesis of his major study, *Israel and the Arab World*, New York 1970, namely that the British were the villains of the Palestinian tragedy – a claim for which the evidence is equally scanty. Cohen and the Mapam became convinced by mid-1948 that the *de facto* Zionist leadership was engaged in a systematic expulsion policy; see pp. 74–5 above.

13. A similar pitch (joined to the 'Joan Peters' thesis) was made by Prime Minister Begin's adviser during the Camp David negotiations. As Moshe Dayan contemptuously recalls:

The purpose of his contribution was to give the Israeli position an ideological wrapping. His main 'ideological' argument was that most of the Palestinian Arabs were really new immigrants who had come to Palestine only in the last hundred years. The silliest part was his 'proof' that the Arabs were strangers in the land of Israel. It was almost certain ... that was the reason why so many Arabs had fled so easily in the 1948 war. Farmers rooted in their soil did not behave that way. The only Arabs who really belonged to the country were those who stayed, despite the war. (*Breakthrough*, New York 1981, p. 21)

One may add that, as Russians fled before the conquering German army, Hitler anticipated Ben-Gurion's 'major political conclusion': 'The Russians have not that love of homeland which is characteristic of the German peasant. ... One must realise that they are nomadic. The wanderlust is inherent in them...' (Hugh Trevor-Roper [ed.], *Hitler's Secret Conversations*, New York 1953, pp. 486–7).

14. 'Revisionist Zionist' refers to the right-wing trend in Zionism associated with Vladimir Jabotinsky and Menachem Begin.

15. Cf. Menachem Begin, *The Revolt*, London 1951, pp. 163–4, where the author asserts that his men sought 'to avoid a single unnecessary casualty'. To be sure, the first Haganah accounts of the massacre were scarcely more accurate. Haganah radio reported on 12 April that 'a group of Arab rebels left Deir Yassin today without expressing remorse for the abominable crimes which they had committed against their own people' (Palumbo, p. 58).

16. Curiously, the one place where Morris does exercise circumspection is in his rendering of the Deir Yassin massacre (*Birth*, pp. 113–14). He describes Deir Yassin as a 'generally' nonbelligerent village. In fact, the village, as early as 1942, signed and scrupulously observed a nonaggression pact with its Jewish neighbors, refused the protection of the Arab Higher Committee when the fighting broke out at the end of the Mandate, and even agreed to cooperate with Haganah intelligence. Morris writes that the Arabs were slaughtered in the course of a 'prolonged firefight', during which the dissident troops 'lost their heads'. By contrast, Flapan concludes that it was a cold-blooded massacre (p. 94), a view supported by David Hirst in *The Gun and the Olive Branch*, London 1977, pp. 124–9 and ch. III of Palumbo's book. For a recent account of Deir Yassin by a participant in the massacre, cf. 'In any case the myth will obscure the facts', in *Haaretz*, 25 April 1993. Testifying that 'I saw terrible things taking place, I cannot tell everything', the former Stern Gang intelligence officer does acknowledge that one soldier 'took two Arabs, tied them back to back, and placed a dynamite "finger" between their heads, then shot at the dynamite and their heads exploded', and that 'we did not want to bury' the several dozen Arab corpses 'because it was too much work, and therefore we burned them. ... We threw all the bodies into a well, poured gasoline on them and burned them'. A Mossad intelligence officer on the scene recalls that later on 'we witnessed a most horrible and dreadful scene. ... IZL men were throwing Arab corpses into a house from the roof, while a huge fire was burning. It was really like a crematorium. Besides that horror I saw many wood fires along the path on which corpses were burning. The stench in the air was unbearable.' Yet other testimonials remembered 'homes in which entire families had been shot', and 'women shot in their genitals' because – it was explained – 'Arab fighters were disguised as women and the IZL members wanted to check'.

17. Most and perhaps all the Israeli casualties that Morris lists for the entire operation were suffered in a firefight with the Arab Legion *before* the supposed 'sniping' commenced. Morris notes that '[t]he ratio of Arab to Israeli casualties was

hardly consistent with the later Israeli (and Arab) description of what happened as an "uprising"' (*Birth*, pp. 205, 206).

18. For background, see Christopher Hitchens's contribution, 'Broadcasts', in Edward Said and Christopher Hitchens (eds), *Blaming the Victims*, London 1988.

19. 'Plan Dalet: Master Plan for the Conquest of Palestine', in *Journal of Palestine Studies*, Autumn 1988, p. 5.

20. This finding is indirectly confirmed in the Israel Defense Forces (IDF) Intelligence Branch Report, 'The Emigration of the Arabs of Palestine in the Period 1/12/1947–1/6/1948', which makes no mention of a general appeal by the Arab leadership ordering Palestinians to flee their homes and puts at '5 percent' the figure of Arabs who fled because of Arab commands. (Morris recalculates that the actual percentage is higher, but 'no more than 10 percent'; cf. *1948*, pp. 85–6.)

21. Cf. Walid Khalidi, 'Why Did the Palestinians Leave?', *Middle East Forum*, July 1959; Flapan, p. 87; Palumbo, pp. 43, 65–6.

22. On the complex and contradictory impulses animating the Arab states in 1948, cf. Avi Shlaim's study. Shlaim likewise concludes that Abdullah, who sought to avoid any armed conflict with the Zionists, 'was alarmed by ... the growing flood of Arab refugees arriving in Jordan, and by the desperate appeals for protection from the Arabs who were holding on in the face of intense Jewish military pressure' (pp. 618–19).

23. The general point was recently made with admirable concision in the pages of *Haaretz*: 'Israelis like to argue whether the Arabs escaped voluntarily or were expelled by us. As if this made any difference. We could always have let them return after the war' ('The 1948 Refugees are the Original Sin of Israeli Society', 5 December 1993). Indeed, by virtue of international law ratified in United Nations resolutions, Israel was legally bound to let the refugees return (cf. Mallisons' study cited in Chap. 5 at note 31 below).

24. Morris is not entirely consistent on the dates of the so-called main wave. Usually he puts it April–May, but occasionally April–June or April–July.

25. Cf. Benny Morris, 'The Origins of the Palestinian Refugee Problem', in Laurence J. Silberstein (ed.), *New Perspectives on Israeli History*, New York 1991:

> Plan D ... called for clear main lines of communications and border areas. Given Palestinian topography, the geographic intermingling of the two communities, and the nature of the partition plan and Palestine's frontiers, there were few Arab villages that did not, arguably, fall into either (or both) of these headings: most villages could be seen as either 'strategically vital' or as lying within 'border areas'.

Morris also concedes that the designation 'potentially hostile' was 'indeed open to a very liberal interpretation' (pp. 45–6). For background to, analysis of and excerpts from Plan D, cf. Khalidi, 'Plan Dalet: Master Plan for the Conquest of Palestine', pp. 4–37. For a careful consideration of Plan Dalet that concludes it 'was, in many ways ... a master plan for the expulsion of as many Palestinians as possible', and that 'Jewish policy as exemplified by Plan D is the principal explanation for the departure of most of the Arabs of Palestine', cf. Ilan Pappé, *The Making of the Arab–Israeli Conflict, 1947–51*, New York 1992, pp. 94, 93. Plan Dalet's 'General Section' called *inter alia* for:

Mounting operations against enemy population centers located inside or near our defensive system in order to prevent them from being used as bases by an active armed force. These operations can be divided into the following categories:

– Destruction of villages (setting fire to, blowing up, and planting mines in the debris), especially those population centers which are difficult to control continuously.

– Mounting combing and control operations according to the following guidelines: encirclement of the village and conducting a search inside it. In the event of resistance, the armed force must be wiped out and the population must be expelled outside the borders of the state.

26. Cf. *Birth*, p. 131, where Morris observes that, 'in general, operational orders in Haganah attacks on both urban and rural targets did not call for the expulsion or eviction of the Arab civilian populations'. I take Morris to mean here explicit, written orders. Given what he has already conceded, this is plainly a distinction without a difference.

27. Morris cites a British observer who noted that, during the morning of 22 April, the Haganah was

continually shooting down on all Arabs who moved in Wadi Nisnas and the Old City. This included completely indiscriminate and revolting machinegun fire and sniping on women and children ... attempting to get out of Haifa through the gates in the dock. ... There was considerable congestion outside the East Gate [of the port] of hysterical and terrified Arab women and children and old people' on whom the Jews opened up mercilessly with fire. (*Birth*, p. 85)

28. Cf. Morris's article cited in note 25 above where the 'atrocity factor' is similarly redefined at p. 46.

29. In addition to Morris and Palumbo, see Walid Khalidi's important article, 'The Fall of Haifa', *Middle East Forum*, December 1959.

30. According to Morris, the British claim that 'the Jews of Haifa for economic reasons wanted the Arabs to stay put' was partially 'based on prejudice' (*Birth*, pp. 87–8). Yet, it was precisely this concern that Golda Meir registered at a Jewish Agency Executive meeting in early May (Palumbo, pp. 74–7). Morris quotes extensively from Meir's remarks at this meeting (*Birth*, pp. 132–3) but omits the crucial passages cited by Palumbo.

31. Cf. Ben-Gurion's account during a Mapai meeting of the Arab flight from Haifa. Expressing his 'surprise' at what had happened, Ben-Gurion deemed it inexplicable ('there was no necessity for them to flee') and mused that it was as if a 'dybbuk' had got into the Arabs' souls (*1948*, p. 43). Cf. also Ben-Gurion's 1 May diary entry for Haifa, in which he expresses his bewilderment that 'tens of thousands' should 'leave in such a panic – without sufficient reason – their city, their homes, and their wealth' (*Commentary*, p. 30). I will return presently to Ben-Gurion's surprise and bewilderment at the Arab flight.

32. Cf. Milstein:

Already in the second week of the war, on 10 December 1947, the leader of the Jewish community, David Ben-Gurion, became aware that military operations by the Haganah in Arab population centers would cause a mass flight. The experts on Arab affairs, Ezra Danin and Yehoshua Palmon, reported to him that, after an operation by the Haganah in ... Haifa, the inhabitants fled to Nablus and Jenin. ... Danin suggested to inflict casualties on the Arabs. Palmon estimated that the Arabs would evacuate Haifa and Jaffa because of the food shortage. Thus it was decided to drive the inhabitants out by means of attacks and starvation. ('No Deportations, Evacuations')

Cf. also Flapan, pp. 90–2, for pertinent extracts from Ben-Gurion's diaries. Flapan convincingly argues that it 'can hardly be doubted' that Ben-Gurion's ultimate aim was to evacuate as much of the Arab population as possible from the Jewish state,

> if only from the variety of means he employed to achieve this purpose: an economic war aimed at destroying Arab transport, commerce and the supply of foods and raw materials to the urban population; psychological warfare, ranging from 'friendly warnings' to outright intimidation and exploitation of panic caused by dissident underground terrorism; and finally, and most decisively, the destruction of whole villages and the eviction of their inhabitants by the army.

Denial of citizenship to facilitate expulsion was, incidentally, the Nazi strategy early on to resolve the 'Jewish Question'; cf. Philippe Burrin, *Hitler and the Jews*, London 1994, p. 43. (Burrin demonstrates that, until the abortive invasion of the Soviet Union unleashed Hitler's genocidal fury in late 1941, the Nazis preferred resolution of the 'Jewish Question' was also 'transfer'.)

33. More difficult to credit is Ben-Gurion's diary entry for 18 May on arriving at Jaffa: 'I couldn't understand: Why did the inhabitants of Jaffa leave?' (*Birth*, p. 101). For the extraordinarily brutal IZL assault on Jaffa, the explicit purpose of which was to 'create a mass flight' among the civilian population, see *Birth*, pp. 96ff. The Haganah despoliation of Jaffa's rural hinterlands was a contributing factor in the Arab flight (*Birth*, p. 100).

34. Referring to the summer of 1948 (the 'main wave' of the Arab exodus), Morris writes: 'It was ... a boom-time for private, semi-official, and official initiatives by single-minded, dogged executives – such as Weitz' (*1948*, p. 111).

35. Morris rather describes Weitz as a 'man of integrity, vision, and action' (*1948*, p. 142). Referring to the bedouins slated for expulsion in May, this 'man of integrity' observed that 'we must be rid of the parasites'. Referring to the destruction of an Arab village in June, he observed that 'I was surprised [as] nothing moved in me at the sight' (*1948*, pp. 98, 109). Morris claims to find in Weitz's remark 'in war – [act] as befits war' evidence of 'pangs of conscience' (*1948*, p. 98). Similarly, Morris claims to find in Foreign Minister Moshe Sharett's anxiety that the expulsion of Arabs 'stirs up the public ... perturbs its conscience ... [and thus might] lead to public rebellion against the government', evidence of his 'soul-searching' (*1948*, pp. 202–3). For recent evidence unearthed by Morris of Weitz's 'systematic censorship' of a diary documenting the more unsavory episodes of the 1948 war, cf. 'The censored diary of Nahmani', in *Haaretz*, 26 November 1993. Ironically, in an exchange some years back on *Birth* and *1948*, Morris severely faulted me for questioning Weitz's 'forthrightness and candor' as a witness on the 1948 war (cf. *Journal of Palestine Studies*, Autumn 1991 and my rejoinder in Winter 1992).

36. Even as the Zionist expulsion policy went into high gear, Weitz was still expressing bewilderment at the Arab flight. On 1 June he referred to it as a 'miracle' and on 5 June as an 'unexpected phenomenon'. Yet on 2 June he was soberly

predicting that the flight 'may continue as the war continues and our army advances' (*Birth*, p. 160; *1948*, pp. 103–4). In this connection, Morris reports that, according to a ranking Jewish representative in Tiberias, Moshe Tzahar, the Arab evacuation of that city, which was preceded by Haganah atrocities in the nearby village of Khirbet Nasir ad Din and a murderous Haganah attack using mortars and dynamite on Tiberias itself, came as a 'shock'. In the corresponding note, we learn that Tzahar's expression of 'shock' is from an interview with him in January 1982 (*Birth*, pp. 71, 313, note 25). Recall Morris's strictures about the dubious value of 'interviewees recalling highly controversial events some fifty years ago' (*Birth*, p. 2). (For recent, authoritative evidence unearthed by Morris putting chief responsibility for the deterioration of communal relations in Tiberias on the Jewish side, with the Arabs desperately suing for peace but the Jews engaging in repeated violent provocations and ultimately refusing all truce appeals because the Haganah command had already 'decided … to launch a major offensive with the aim of conquering Arab Tiberias', cf. *1948, revised*, ch. 5.) Finally, Morris cites a memorandum submitted to the US State Department by Israeli Foreign Minister-designate Moshe Sharett to document the 'Yishuv's astonishment at the [Arab] exodus' (*1948*, p. 70). Responding to Washington's growing anxiety at the Arab flight from Palestine, Sharett referred to it.as an 'astounding phenomenon', and said 'something quite unprecedented and unforeseen is going on'. This sort of 'evidence' requires, I think, no comment.

37.  Bechor Shitrit, the Minister of Minority Affairs, for example, warned the Cabinet that 'the army must be given strict instructions to behave well and fairly toward the inhabitants' of predominantly Christian Nazareth 'because of the great political importance of the city in the eyes of the world' (*Birth*, p. 202). Occasionally, Arab villagers with a long record of 'collaborationism' (Morris's word) with the Zionist movement and/or needed for harvesting Jewish crops were allowed to stay (or trickle back after being expelled). For details, cf. ch. 7 of *1948*. In *1948, revised*, Morris repeats an earlier claim that 'the large number of Arab inhabitants … left in place' proves that Israel did not pursue a systematic expulsion policy (p. 38). This genre of argumentation is not without instructive precedent. Thus, one of the more crude Nazi holocaust deniers asserts that the '500,000 concentration camp survivors' proves that the Third Reich did not pursue a systematic extermination policy. (Austin J. Epp, 'The "Holocaust" Put in Perspective', *Journal of Historical Review*, vol. 1, no. 1, 1980, p. 57, citing his publication *The Six Million Swindle*). For a full discussion of Morris's claim, cf. my 'Rejoinder' cited in note 35 above at pp. 67–8.

38.  The well-placed Zionist official, Yosef Nahmani, similarly inferred that the 'massacres were part of a general policy or campaign of expulsion, a means of prodding the villagers' (*1948, revised*, p. 193; Morris's paraphrase). On Ad Dawayima, cf. Palumbo, pp. xii–xiv. The village mukhtar estimated 580 civilians killed, Israeli sources, 100–350, and testimonies preserved in US State Department records, 1000; see Noam Chomsky, *Turning the Tide*, Boston 1985, p. 76. Palumbo puts the number at 'probably about 300'.

39.  Earlier in August, Ya'ari lamented that

the youth we nurtured in the Palmah [elite strike force], including kibbutz members, have [occasionally] turned Arabs into slaves; they shoot defenceless

Arab men and women, not in battle. ... Is it permissible to kill prisoners of war? I hoped that there would be some who would rebel and disobey [orders] to kill and would stand trial – and not one appeared. ... They are not against transfer. What does it mean ... to empty all the villages? ... What did we labour for ... ? (*1948*, p. 59)

(Morris reports that a few soldiers did refuse to carry out 'barbaric orders'.)

40. One of Morris's attendant observations on atrocities in the 1948 war merits quotation: 'Two of the three major Arab massacres of Jews ... were revenge attacks triggered by Jewish atrocities against Arabs. On the other hand, Jewish atrocities against Arabs ... were generally unconnected to or lacked any previous, direct Arab provocation' (*1948, revised*, p. 42). The full scope of the IDF's carnage during the war is suggested – perhaps unwittingly – by Morris in the March–April 1989 *Tikkun* when he observes that the IDF has 'progressively become a "cleaner" army', its 'record, when it comes to *tohar haneshek* [i.e. purity of arms]' being 'far better' during the 1982–85 Lebanon War than in 1948. For Israel's less-than-glorious Lebanon 'adventure' (Morris's word in *Tikkun*, p. 19), cf. esp. the grisly records assembled in Robert Fisk, *Pity the Nation*, New York 1990, and Noam Chomsky, *The Fateful Triangle*, Boston 1983.

41. 'Most of the destruction in the 350 villages', writes Morris, 'was due to vandalism and looting, and to deliberate demolitions, with explosives, bulldozers and, occasionally, handtools, by Haganah and IDF units or neighboring Jewish settlements in the days, weeks and months after their conquest' (*Birth*, p. 156).

42. Cf. *1948*, pp. 83–4: 'In general, the situation on the ground made it impossible in many cases to draw a clear distinction between a Haganah/IDF or IZL "military operation" which ended in villagers fleeing their homes and "expulsion orders", which had the same effect.'

43. For the mass expulsion from Lydda and Ramle, cf. also Benny Morris, 'Operation Dani and the Palestinian Exodus from Lydda and Ramle in 1948', *The Middle East Journal*, vol. 40, no. 1, 1986.

44. There may be some overlap in the Arab villages and towns I report as erroneously tabulated since Morris's textual references range from single sites to broadly inclusive regions. I did not spot any clear-cut cases in which Morris's tables incorrectly tally sites abandoned because of Arab orders. Several such sites are not listed in the tables but this is true for expulsion sites as well.

45. Beirut 1978. Morris explicitly attests to the reliability of Nazzal's findings in *1948, revised*, at p. 43.

46. Morris is also not always consistent in sorting out security from political factors. For example, he first argues that '[m]ilitary considerations had little to do with' the decision in mid-1948 to bar Arabs from cultivating 'abandoned' fields, 'except in the wider, strategic sense'; yet, he later asserts that the reason for this decision was 'in large measure ... military' (*1948*, pp. 186, 190).

47. Cf. note 8 above for Morris's strictures on the 'inevitability in the unfolding of events' cancelling moral responsibility on both sides.

48. Cf. note 7 above.

49. Cf. the countermeasures section of Plan Gimmel (Plan C), the precursor of Plan D that was operative between December 1947 and April 1948, for the extremities that were sanctioned. Plan C is excerpted in the Khalidi article on Plan D

cited in note 19 above.

50. Cf. *1948*, p. 10:

> Indeed, in the first months of the hostilities, according to the Yishuv's intelligence sources, the bulk of Palestine's Arabs wanted peace and quiet, if only out of a healthy respect for the Jews' martial prowess. But gradually, in part because of Haganah over-reactions, the conflict spread, eventually engulfing the two communities throughout the land.

Entering an even stronger qualification in *1948, revised*, Morris suggests on the basis of the Tiberias experience (cf. note 36 above), that the 'traditional, "Old" Zionist historiography of a peace-minded Jewish community prodded into militancy and conquest only by Arab provocation and extremism' was 'seriously' open to 'question' (p. 209).

51. Oddly, Morris specifically faults Yosef Weitz's transcription of the Nahmani diary (cf. note 35 above) for 'omitting all mention of the IZL bomb attack that had provoked the refinery massacre' (*1948, revised*, p. 171).

52. In a recent article, Morris evidences that 'although Ben-Gurion, Chaim Weizmann and other Zionist leaders wished for transfer, they usually expressed their opinion on that matter only in closed Zionist forums' and – more important – deleted these references to transfer in published protocols. 'The result was not only a rewriting of Zionist history but also a rewriting of Zionist documentation.' Ben-Gurion, for example, preached behind the closed doors of the Zionist Congress in 1937 the virtues of transferring Palestine's Arabs (cf. p. 69 and Chap. 1 at note 20 above), but in the printed text of his speech solemnly expatiates on creating 'one law for the foreigner and the citizen in a just regime based on brotherly love and true equality ... that will be a shining example for the world in treating minorities' ('How the Zionist Documents were Doctored', cited in note 11 above).

53. Cf. Chap. 1 for a fuller discussion of the issues addressed in the next two paragraphs.

54. Cf. Khalidi's view that only the intervention of the regular Arab armies blocked the Zionists' predisposition to achieve 'complete military dominance of the whole of Palestine'. He cites Yigal Allon in *The Book of the Palmah* to the effect that 'had it not been for the Arab invasion there would have been no stop to the expansion of the forces of the Haganah who could have, with the same drive, reached the natural borders of western Israel' ('Plan Dalet', p. 19).

55. Alas, the same cannot be said for Morris's impact on popular debate in the United States. Consider the following examples:

(1) Current Prime Minister Yitzak Rabin, who presided over some of the most ruthless expulsions of the 1948 war and freely admitted as much in his memoirs (cf. Peretz Kidron, 'Truth Whereby Nations Live', in *Blaming the Victims*), nonetheless observes in an interview in a liberal Jewish monthly that

> Haj Amin Husseini ... called upon the Arabs to leave in view of the invasion of the Arab armed forces in 1948. This brought the first disaster on the Palestinians and created the Palestinian refugee problem. (*Moment*, May 1988)

These utterances, incidentally, evoked not the slightest demurral from his interlocutor.

(2) Menachem Milson, the highly regarded (at any rate in the United States) professor of Arabic Literature at the Hebrew University and former head of the

Civil Administration of the West Bank, writes in a liberal Zionist periodical that 'the established version of the origins of the refugee problem is on the whole historically correct'. This 'established version' goes as follows:

> Under orders of their leaders, the Arabs left their homes in the towns and villages in the area which was to become Israel. These areas evacuated were those which were or were becoming battle arenas between Arabs and Jews. The reasoning behind these orders, rooted in Arab plans and expectations at the time, was that the Jews would soon be vanquished, and thus the Arabs would not only be able to return to their homes in a matter of days, but would even inherit the property of their Jewish neighbors. (*Jewish Frontier*, March–April 1988)

(3) In a memoir excerpted in a prominent liberal journal, the acclaimed Israeli author Amos Kenan describes his stint as 'a platoon commander of the 82d Regiment of the Israeli Army brigade that conquered the Palestinian town of Lydda'. Recall that Lydda was the scene of one of the bloodiest atrocities of the war (between 250 and 400 Palestinians were 'slaughtered'; *Birth*, p. 206) and that the single biggest outright expulsion occurred there (fully 30,000 Palestinians were, on Ben-Gurion's orders, driven into exile; cf. note 43 above). Yet, in Kenan's fanciful account, 'we never really *conquered* Lydda. Lydda, to put it simply, fled', 'there was really no city to conquer. The whole place, except for George Habash and his sister and a few others, was empty', and so on (emphasis in original). Furthermore, except for 'those of us who couldn't restrain ourselves [and] would go into the prison compounds to fuck Arab women' (which, after all, was not so terrible since 'I want very much to assume, and perhaps even can, that those who couldn't restrain themselves did what they thought the Arabs would have done to them had they won the war'), the worst IDF sin committed at Lydda was that 'here they smashed a windowpane, there they killed a chicken' (*The Nation*, 6 February 1989; the journal refused to publish a brief letter that sought, citing mainstream Israeli sources, to set the factual record straight). Kenan's alibi that, given a chance, the Arabs 'would have done' the same or worse, is, incidentally, standard in the apologetic literature on conquest. Theodore Roosevelt, for instance, rationalized 'our ... grave wrong-doing' to the Creek Indians by observing that 'the Creeks themselves lacked only the power, but not the will, to treat us worse than we treated them, and the darkest pages of their history recite the wrongs that we ourselves suffered at their hands' (*The Winning of the West*, New York 1889, vol. i, p. 95).

(4) In a review article for a prominent literary magazine, rabbi and professor Arthur Hertzberg cites Morris's research as showing that 'more than half of the Palestinians left of their own accord, or in the hope of coming back with the invading Arab forces in victory' (*The New York Review of Books*, 25 October 1990).

## Chapter 4

1. New York 1986.

2. Oxford 1992. All parenthetical page references in the body of the text are to Shapira's book.

3. Marc Bloch, 'Towards a Comparative History of European Societies', in Frederic C. Lane and Jelle C. Riemersma (eds), *Enterprise and Secular Change*, Homewood 1953.

4. Francis Jennings; *The Invasion of America*, New York 1975, p. 15.

5. On 'territorial or locational right', cf. Michael Walzer, *Spheres of Justice*, New York 1983, p. 43.

6. David E. Stannard, *American Holocaust*, New York 1992, p. 235. As with many of England's conquest rationales in the North American context, the immediate precedent for this theme was the brutal subjugation of Ireland, regarded by the English as 'lieth waste or else inhabited with a wicked, barbarous and uncivil people' (Robert A. Williams, *The American Indian in Western Legal Thought*, New York 1990, pp. 140–3, 151–2).

7. Jennings, pp. 78–80; Williams, p. 218.

8. Stannard, pp. 235–6; Jennings, p. 82; John Locke, *Second Treatise of Government*, ch. 5, emphasis in original. Williams reports (pp. 246–9) that these notions of Locke were regarded as 'canonical' by the American colonists. Locke, incidentally, was far from a disinterested observer, acting as secretary to the proprietors of the Carolina colony (he helped to draw up the colony's first constitution), as well as to the Board of Trade. With the conquest of the Americas plainly in mind, Thomas More approvingly observes in *Utopia*:

> If the natives won't do what they're told, they're expelled from the area marked out for annexation. If they try to resist, the Utopians declare war – for they consider war perfectly justifiable, when one country denies another its natural right to derive nourishment from any soil which the original owners are not using themselves, but are merely holding on to as a worthless piece of property. (Book Two)

Cf. Kirkpatrick Sale, *The Conquest of Paradise*, New York 1992, p. 286, quoting an Englishman in 1636 that, 'We have done them no Injury by settling amongst them, we rather than they being the prime occupants, and they only Sojourners in the land.'

9. Albert Weinberg, *Manifest Destiny*, Baltimore 1935, pp. 77–8. The Vattel quote is cited here.

10. Williams, pp. 308–9, 296–8; emphasis in original. Jennings, p. 60; Wilcomb E. Washburn, 'The Moral and Legal Justification for Dispossessing the Indians', in James Morton Smith, *Seventeenth-Century America*, Chapel Hill 1959, p. 27. Weinberg, pp. 81f. Marshall ultimately found in favor of the Cherokee Indians, but the decision was without practical effect.

11. Andrew Jackson, 'Indian Removal and the General Good', in Louis Filler and Allen Guttmann (eds), *The Removal of the Cherokee Nation*, Lexington 1962, p. 50; Weinberg, p. 79; Washburn, p. 23.

12. On the demographic issue, see Stannard, appendix 1. Parkman and Turner are quoted in Jennings, p. 84. The Stannard quotes are on p. 12.

13. For the Native American precedent in Hitler's *Lebensraum* policy, cf. John Toland, *Adolf Hitler*, New York 1976, p. 702; Joachim Fest, *Hitler*, New York 1975, pp. 214, 650; H.R. Trevor-Roper (ed.), *Hitler's Secret Conversations, 1941–1944*, New York 1953, pp. 57, 257, 504, 574; cf. also Richard Rubinstein, 'Genocide and Civilization', in Isidor Wallimann and Michael N. Dobkowski (eds), *Genocide and*

*the Modern Age*, Westport 1987, p. 288. For Hitler's depiction of the East as virgin land, cf. Adolf Hitler, *Hitler's Secret Book*, New York 1961, p. 74; *Secret Conversations*, pp. 56, 91, 237, 265, 281, 344, 477, 501; Fest, p. 682; Max Weinreich, *Hitler's Professors*, New York 1946, p. 73. For the East as densely populated and Hitler's awareness, cf. Max Domarus (ed.), *Hitler: Speeches and Proclamations, 1932–1945*, London 1992, vol. 2, p. 966; Hermann Rauschning, *The Voice of Destruction*, New York 1940, pp. 33–7, 116–17; *Secret Conversations*, p. 477; Gerhard L. Weinberg, *Germany, Hitler and World War II*, Cambridge 1995, p. 42; Eberhard Jäckel, *Hitler's Weltanschauung*, Middletown 1972, p. 42. For Hitler's resolution of the 'demographic problem' in the East, cf. *Secret Conversations*, pp. 57, 237, 382, 477, 501–2; *Secret Book*, pp. 47–8; Fest, pp. 682–3; and the above-cited references in Jäckel, Rauschning and Weinberg. Dismissing Poland as a 'structure purporting to be a state ... incapable of existence ... artificially born ... lacking every national, historical, cultural and moral foundation', Hitler – in a familiar litany of conquest myths – further alleged on the morrow of the Nazi invasion that 'Poles laid claims to territory where they pretended to have a majority of 95 percent ... whereas ... the Poles actually had reached a figure of [only] 2 percent'; the Polish state in 1919 'took over ... provinces which had been developed through hundreds of years of hard toil, some of them being in a most flourishing condition', yet 'today, after the elapse of twenty years, they are at a point of gradually turning to steppes again. ... Towns as well as villages are in a state of neglect. The roads ... are badly out of repair and in a terrible condition' (Adolf Hitler, *My New Order*, edited with commentary by Raoul de Roussy de Sales, New York 1973, pp. 727–33 passim; cf. pp. 100f. above). Hitler, incidentally, could be much more instructive about the realities of conquest than many a professional historian. Compare, for instance, his recognition that 'there had never been spaces without a master ... the attacker always comes up against a possessor' with Walter Laqueur's insight that 'it was the tragedy of Zionism that it appeared on the international scene when there were no longer empty spaces on the world map' (*A History of Zionism*, New York 1976, p. 597).

14. Adolf Hitler, *Mein Kampf*, New York 1971, pp. 138–9; cf. pp. 649, 652, 675. Prefiguring his war of conquest in the East for *Lebensraum*, Hitler elsewhere observed: 'There is eighteen times less land per capita of the population in respect to the German being than, for instance, in respect to a Russian. It is understandable how hard the mere fight for one's daily bread must be and is [here]' (Domarus, vol. 2, p. 763).

15. *Secret Book*, pp. 15–16; cf. *Mein Kampf*, pp. 652–4. Theodore Roosevelt, *The Winning of the West*, New York 1889, vol. iv, p. 200. For the relevant passages in Nietzsche, cf. esp. *On the Genealogy of Morals*, essay I ('Good and Evil', 'Good and Bad'), section 11. One of Hitler's private wartime musings almost exactly echoed Roosevelt:

> If anyone asks us where we obtain the right to extend the Germanic space to the East, we reply that, for a nation, her awareness of what she represents carries this right with it. ... It's inconceivable that a higher people should painfully exist on a soil too narrow for it, whilst amorphous masses, which contribute nothing to civilisation, occupy infinite tracts of a soil that is one of the richest in the world. (*Secret Conversations*, p. 32; cf. p. 214)

On the American side, cf. Andrew Jackson's speech cited in note 11 above:

Humanity has often wept over the fate of the aborigines of this country, and Philanthropy has been long busily employed in devising means to avert it. ... But true philanthropy reconciles the mind to these vicissitudes as it does to the extinction of one generation to make room for another. ... Nor is there anything in this which, upon a comprehensive view of the general interests of the human race, is to be regretted.

16. Domarus, vol. 1, pp. 95–6; cf. *New Order*, p. 646. *Lebensraum* was accordingly conceptualized by Hitler not only as an absolute right of survival but also as a relative right of a commensurate Great Power:

> *It cannot be tolerated any longer that the British nation of 44,000,000 souls should remain in possession of fifteen and a half million square miles of the world's surface. They pretend to have obtained it from God and are not prepared to give it away. Likewise the French nation of 37,000,000 souls owns more than three and a half million square miles, while the German nation with 80,000,000 souls only possesses about 230,000 square miles.'* (*New Order*, pp. 774–5, emphasis in original; cf. pp. 740, 753, 874)

Mixing scorn and sarcasm, Hitler lambasted the Great Powers which had 'acquired a world by force and robbery', yet countered Germany's right to do so as well with 'moralizing theories', 'the cry that tyranny is the issue' or the smug declaration that 'there are nations which are "haves" and ... others on that account must always be "have nots"' (*New Order*, pp. 573, 785; cf. pp. 621, 875; Rauschning, pp. 122–3 and note 47 below).

17. Leonard Thompson, *The Political Mythology of Apartheid*, New Haven 1985, pp. 29, 60, 76–7, 83–4, 86–7, 93, 95–6, 199–201. On South Africa before the European invasion, cf. Leonard Thompson, *A History of South Africa*, New York 1990, ch. 1, which concludes that, 'By the beginning of the Christian era, human communities had lived in Southern Africa by hunting, fishing, and collecting edible plants for many thousands of years' and that 'By A.D. 1000 farmers were present in much of Natal, the Cape Province east of the Kei River, the Transvaal, Swaziland, eastern Botswana, and the northeastern Orange Free State.' Likewise in the course of the turn-of-the-century 'Scramble for Africa', Europeans, according to Thomas Pakenham, 'pictured most of the continent as "vacant": legally *res nullius*, a no-man's land'. Stanley, for example, described the Congo as 'a blank, a fruitless waste, a desolate and unproductive area. ... It has been our purpose to fill this blank with life, to redeem this waste, to plant and sow that the dark man may gather, to vivify the wide, wild lands so long forgotten by Europe.' Yet, Stanley himself had favorably compared the Congo's brisk commerce with Venice and put its population of 'champion traders' at some 40 million. The real figure probably stood nearer to 20–30 million. In any event, after two decades of European efforts 'to fill this blank with life, to redeem this waste', the 'most densely-populated regions of the Congo, with many large and flourishing towns' had, according to E.D. Morel, been 'reduced to a desert'. All told, 'a figure of ten million victims would be a very conservative estimate'. (Thomas Pakenham, *The Scramble for Africa*, New York 1991, pp. xxi, 159–60; cf. pp. 216, 372; E.D. Morel, *The Black Man's Burden*, New York 1969, ch. 9.)

18. For a representative sample of this literature, cf. Ernst Frankenstein's tract

cited in Chap. 2 at p. 42 above.

19. David Ben-Gurion, *Israel: A Personal History*, New York 1971, pp. xx, 25, 47.

20. Izhak Ben-Zvi, 'Under Ottoman Rule', *The Jews in their Land*, New York 1966, passim.

21. Abba Eban, *My Country*, New York 1972, pp. 26, 28.

22. Laqueur, *History of Zionism*, pp. 40–2, ch. 5; Jennings, p. 15.

23. New York 1984. One would want to stress that the novelty of Peters's book was not her thesis but the effort to prove it systematically. Thus, even the dovish Zionist historian Amos Elon reported in his much-acclaimed *The Israelis* (New York 1981), p. 89, that 'the population of Palestine probably more than tripled in the nineteenth century, mostly as a result of Arab immigration from neighboring countries'.

24. Norman Cohn, *Warrant for Genocide,* New York 1969, p. 71. Regarding the outlook reflected in the *Protocols*, Cohn relevantly notes (p. 174) that, as 'irrational, unscientific, and demonstrably nonsensical' as it was, it was 'nevertheless the specialty of the educated'. Cf. Bernard Lewis, *Semites and Anti-Semites*, New York 1987, p. 108: 'Any rational modern reader of the *Protocols* cannot but wonder at the crudity of this text, and the credulity of those who believed it.' Yet, for Lewis's own odd posture throughout the Peters hoax, see *Times Literary Supplement*, 'Letters', 21 June 1985, 26 July 1985, 16 August 1985, and Christopher Hitchens's running commentary in the 'American Notes' of the *TLS*; cf. also postscript to Chap. 2 above. The massive scholarly apparatus adorning *From Time Immemorial*, incidentally, cannot explain the initial gullibility of its sponsors. After all, Arthur Butz's unheralded *The Hoax of the Twentieth Century*, Torrance 1976, denying the Nazi holocaust, was similarly packaged with hundreds of footnotes plus multiple appendices, plates and diagrams. Historian Pierre Vidal-Naquet's description of *The Hoax* applies with equal force to *From Time Immemorial*: 'the *appearance* of a historical narrative, better still, of a critical investigation, with all the external features defining a work of history, except for what makes it of any value: truth'. Unlike Peters, however, Butz is 'admired by a minuscule sect and completely unknown to those ... who practice the historian's craft' (*Assassins of Memory*, New York 1992, pp. 98, 2; emphasis in original).

25. For Martin Peretz's accolade and the general reception accorded *From Time Immemorial* in the United States, cf. Chap. 2 above, and esp. Edward Said and Christopher Hitchens (eds), *Blaming the Victims*, London 1988, ch. 1.

26. Robert Friedman, *Zealots for Zion*, New York 1992, p. 194. For the population of Palestine on the eve of Zionist colonization and its growth thereafter, cf. esp. Justin McCarthy, *The Population of Palestine*, New York 1990. McCarthy's exhaustive analysis of the demographic data reaches the following conclusions: (1) Palestine's population in 1880 was roughly 450,000, of which less than 5 per cent (15,000) was Jewish – even after the 'great migrations' of the first and second aliyas, Jews still constituted in 1914 only 5 per cent (38,000) of the total population of about 710,000; (2) there is no evidence of any significant Arab immigration into Palestine during the Ottoman or Mandatory period; (3) there is no evidence of any significant Arab internal migration in Palestine due to Jewish enterprise; and (4) Palestine was 'underpopulated' only by 'modern standards ... where rapid population growth is endemic'. Peters's book is deemed 'demographically worthless' –

under the circumstances, a generous verdict. McCarthy's findings are generally supported by reputable Israeli scholars; cf. Chap. 2 at note 2 above. Cf. also Alexander Schölch, 'The Demographic Development of Palestine, 1850–1882', *International Journal of Middle East Studies*, November 1985. For Palestine's impressive economic balance-sheet in the Late Ottoman period, especially in the agricultural sector, cf. Alexander Schölch, 'European Penetration and the Economic Development of Palestine, 1856–1882', in Roger Owen (ed.), *Studies in the Economic and Social History of Palestine in the Nineteenth and Twentieth Centuries*, Carbondale 1982. Schölch's pioneering studies are collected in *Palestine in Transformation*, Washington, DC 1993.

27. E.g. to document the 'prevailing consciousness' of Palestine's Arabs on the morrow of the Young Turk revolution (p. 379, note 60).

28. Cf. pp. 317–18: 'While in Ha-Noar ha-Oved, the Masada cult of heroism was characterized by an extremely high level of pathos, it was integrated in Ha-Mahanot ha-Olim within a methodical program of education, aimed at inculcating patriotism, along the lines of *Bi-Vritekh*.'

29. Shapira's ambivalent relationship to Zionist mythology is signalled in small ways as well as big. Thus, she observes that the Yishuv leadership in 1936 used the locution 'disturbances' as against 'rebellion' to deny that the unfolding Arab revolt was an authentic national movement (p. 225). Yet, Shapira herself seems unable to decide what happened then, vacillating between 'disturbances' and 'rebellion' to describe these events (pp. 224, 227, 228, 264, 270). Cf. also Shapira's use of such hackneyed Zionist phraseology as 'Arab terrorist gangs' (pp. 247, 250).

30. In conformity with most recent scholarship, Shapira argues that strictly tactical considerations dictated the mainstream Zionist movement's public endorsement of a bi-national state and its public disavowal of a Jewish state until 1942 (pp. 167, 170, 189–93, 280). For a dissenting view, cf. Susan Lee Hattis, *The Bi-National Idea in Palestine During Mandatory Times*, Haifa 1970. On the 'Romantic-exclusivistic' roots of Zionism, cf. Chap. 1 above.

31. Walter LaFeber, *The American Age*, New York 1989, p. 45; Weinberg, p. 112; Arnold Toynbee, *A Study of History*, London 1954, vol. viii, p. 310.

32. In labor Zionism, Shapira notes, the Jews' historical writ established a 'primary right' to settle in Palestine, but that 'primary right' still had to be redeemed by actual labor on the land (p. 65). For the roots of Zionism's 'historical right' in German Romanticism, cf. esp. Mosse's study cited in Chap. 1 at note 4 above.

33. The one partial exception was, oddly, Hitler himself, who asserted in his *Secret Book*, p. 15, that 'there is no spot on this earth that has been determined as the abode of a people for all time, since the rule of nature has for tens of thousands of years forced mankind eternally to migrate'; cf. *Mein Kampf*, pp. 388, 390, 652–3. Cf. also Bernd Wegner, *The Waffen-SS*, Cambridge 1990, p. 25, in which a contrast is drawn between Himmler's 'romantic' ideology and Hitler's 'more rational instincts about strategic questions'. Yet, Hitler was not averse to also staking a claim based on Germany's 'historical right'. Thus Germany had a 'right' to Belgrade and Russia ('the German past, in its totality, constitutes our own patrimony ... [We] must be in a position to bring out from a drawer every historical date that justifies a German claim'), to Crimea ('basically, the population consisted firstly of the Germanic element, of Gothic origin; then of Tartars, Armenians, Jews; and Russians

absolutely last. We must dig our roots in this soil'), to Castile and Croatia ('they're the descendants of the Vandals. ... We need titles that will establish our rights back over two thousand years'), even to South America ('the Fuggers and Welsers had possessions there') (*Secret Conversations*, pp. 34, 91, 98, 504–5; Rauschning, p. 62).

34. Michael Burleigh, *Germany Turns Eastwards*, Cambridge 1988, pp. 25–31, 132, 151, 197–8, 105–6, 240, 242, 267 (the Brackmann quote is on p. 151); Michael Burleigh and Wolfgang Wipperman, *The Racial State*, Cambridge 1991, pp. 26–7; Theodor Herzl, *The Jewish State*, New York 1970, p. 52. Cf. Hitler's vindicatory speech on the morrow of the Nazi occupation of Czechoslovakia:

> The Czechs have never been an autonomous people. ... Bohemia was a German electorate in the Middle Ages. The first German university was founded in Prague two hundred years before the days of Queen Elizabeth. The modern German language itself was derived from the language of the diplomats who served in the governmental offices of that city, the site that the German Emperor had made his capital for a time. Only in the course of the Hussite wars were the Czechs independent for any period of time. ... The creation of this hetero-geneous Czechoslovakian Republic after the war was complete insanity. It does not have any characteristics of a nation, either from an ethnological or linguistic point of view, or from an economic or strategic one ... (Domarus, vol. 2, pp. 1168–9; cf. p. 1187).

Remarkably, England in the 'discovery' era asserted a 'historical right' to North America on the basis of an alleged twelfth-century colony founded by a Welsh prince in 'Terra Florida' (Williams, pp. 169–71).

35. For a fuller exposition of this argument, cf. Chap. 1 above.

36. Ze'ev Sternhell, 'Farewell to the Tombs of the Forefathers', *Haaretz*, 25 March 1994.

37. Cf. Walzer, ch. 2. Unfortunately, Walzer's discussion in this chapter, as throughout the book, is marred by what are plainly apologetics for Israel and Zionism, although neither is ever mentioned by name; cf. my unpublished ms., 'Tribal Rumblings', June 1990.

38. For extensive documentation of the arguments in these two paragraphs, cf. Gorny's study reviewed in Chap. 1 above, as well as Shabtai Teveth, *Ben-Gurion and the Palestinian Arabs*, Oxford 1985, pp. 187–9, and Simha Flapan, *Zionism and the Palestinians*, New York 1979, pp. 265–6. Equally disingenuous is Shapira's juxtaposition of the 'pragmatic' Zionist elder statesmen against the 'impassioned' Zionist youth, the latter supposedly unique in their opposition to 'sharing [Palestine] with another people' and in their certainty 'that all of Palestine was their country ... the land was theirs, theirs alone', etc. (pp. 271–5). For the mainstream Zionist movement's commitment to a Jewish state in all of Palestine in 1947 as well, despite the Jewish Agency's formal endorsement of the United Nations partition resolution, cf. Simha Flapan, *The Birth of Israel*, New York 1987, p. 33, and Avi Shlaim, *Collusion Across the Jordan*, New York 1988, p. 16.

39. The most extensive study to date of Zionist 'transfer' policy is Nur Masalha, *Expulsion of the Palestinians*, Washington 1992. Masalha's conclusion, amply documented, is that the 'transfer' concept 'occupied a central position in the strategic thinking' of the Zionist movement from its inception. For Zionist cognizance of

the brutality of the often cited Turkish–Greek precedent, cf. pp. 29, 70, 88–9 of Masalha. For Katznelson's views, cf. pp. 71, 114, 136 of Masalha, and Chap. 1 at p. 16 above. (Shapira similarly misrepresented Katznelson's views in her hagiographic biography *Berl*, Cambridge 1984, p. 292.) For Ben-Gurion's support of forcible 'transfer', cf. Chap. 1 at note 20 and Chap. 3 at p. 69 and at note 52 above. There is no evidence whatsoever that Ben-Gurion underwent a change of heart in the 1940s, although for reasons of political expedience he did mute his views in public fora; cf. pp. 128–9 of Masalha. For Ben-Gurion's emphatic implementation of 'transfer' in 1948, cf. Chap. 3 above.

40. Benny Morris, *The Birth of the Palestinian Refugee Problem, 1947–1949*, Cambridge 1987, p. 25. Cf. also Gorny's similar conclusion reported in Chap. 1 at p. 16 above. These assessments are fully supported by Masalha's study, which demonstrates that, by the late 1930s, the full spectrum of the Zionist movement (with the notable exception of Hashomer Hatzair) embraced the morality and necessity of compulsory 'transfer', debate focusing only on the modalities for implementing it; cf. chs 2–3. Yet, Abba Eban avows in his recent memoir, *Personal Witness*, New York 1992, p. 65, regarding the Zionist leaders that 'hardly any of them in their senses believed that it would be possible or morally justified to have the Arabs move out' of Palestine.

41. Arthur A. Goren (ed.), *Dissenter in Zion*, Cambridge 1982, p. 382.

42. Interestingly, right-wing Zionists (e.g. Jabotinsky) were least and extreme left-wing Zionists (e.g. Hashomer Hatzair) most given to the illusions of the 'defensive ethos' (pp. 185, 227).

43. For the enormous distance that Shapira has traveled in making these admissions, cf. Bernard Avishai's supposedly critical account, *The Tragedy of Zionism*, New York 1985, pp. 147f, where the 'anti-colonialist ethos' of labor Zionism is acclaimed, and the 'myth of Zionist colonialism' is contemptuously dismissed as a 'test of faith for the PLO's radical factions'. To be sure, Jabotinsky freely referred to Zionism as a colonizing enterprise. Mainstream, labor Zionism's preferred self-image was the morally more edifying and politically less incriminating one of the 'pioneer' (*halutz*).

44. Shabtai Teveth, *Ben-Gurion and the Palestinian Arabs*, Oxford 1985, pp. 198–9.

45. For Zionism establishing itself by virtue of 'foreign bayonets', see Teveth, p. 104. Shapira uses the euphemism 'buffer defense' to portray this crucial British function during the years of allegedly defensive Zionist settlement (p. 330). Ironically, Teveth entitles the chapter devoted to the period of Zionist settlement *after* 1930 'not by force alone', whereas for Shapira it was the period *before* 1930 that was 'not by force alone'. The fact is that force was deployed from the inception of Zionist colonization to its culmination in 1948. I return to this point below. Roosevelt, vol. ii, p. 160; vol. i, p. 160; vol. iii, p. 277 (emphasis added). *Secret Conversations*, p. 13.

46. Stannard, p. 120; Noam Chomsky, *For Reasons of State*, New York 1973, p. 114; Albert Camus, *Actuelles III: Chroniques Algériennes, 1939–1958*, Paris 1958, pp. 367, 370–1; Weinreich, p. 81; David S. Wyman, *The Abandonment of the Jews*, New York 1984, p. 53 (for Hitler's original 'prophecy', cf. *New Order*, p. 585, from a speech to the Reichstag in January 1939); J. Noakes and G. Pridham (eds), *Nazism: A History in Documents and Eyewitness Accounts, 1919–1945*, New York 1988, vol. 2, p. 1200. Cf. Richard M. Lerner, *Final Solutions*, University Park, Pennsylvania 1992, p. 44, quoting Otto Ohlendorf, director of the Reich Security Main Office:

It is very easy to explain if one starts from the fact that Hitler's order not only tried to achieve security, but *permanent* security, lest the children grow up and inevitably, being the children of parents who had been killed, they would constitute a danger no smaller than that of the parents. (emphasis in original)

47. Joseph Schumpeter, *Imperialism and Social Classes*, New York 1955, pp. 64– 98. Schumpeter, however, ascribes the need by modern ruling elites to depict all wars as defensive to the rationalizing effects of capitalism which turns wars into 'troublesome distractions' for the working classes. One may add that political rivals are adept at seeing through the hypocritical official pieties of each other, if not themselves. When Franklin Roosevelt in 1939 righteously exposed the aggressive designs behind Nazi Germany and Italy's 'defensive' maneuvers in Europe and Africa, Hitler riposted that Germany had 'played no part' in the 'twenty-six violent interventions and sanctions carried through by means of bloodshed and force' since the end of World War I whereas 'the United States alone carried out military interventions in six [of these] cases'; that 'it is not a question of one nation in Africa having lost its freedom [i.e. Ethiopia] – on the contrary practically all the previous inhabitants of this continent have been made subject to the sovereignty of other nations by bloody force, thereby losing their freedom. Moroccans, Berbers, Arabs, Negroes, etcetera, have all fallen victim to foreign might, the swords of which, however, were inscribed not "Made in Germany," but "Made by Democracies" '; that, despite Roosevelt's *'noble principle'* that 'unquestionable home defense' is the only valid grounds for waging war, 'there is hardly any possibility of doubt, for example, that America's entry into the Great War was not a case of unquestionable home defense … [but] ensued chiefly for exclusively capitalistic reasons'; that Roosevelt's 'belief that *every* problem can be solved at the conference table' rang hollow inasmuch as 'the statesmen of the United States, and especially her greatest, did not make the chief part of their history at the conference table but with the aid of the strength of their people', e.g. 'the innumerable struggles which finally led to the subjugation of the North American Continent as a whole'; that just as Roosevelt would reject German 'interference in the internal affairs of the American continent' in the name of the 'Monroe Doctrine' so 'Germans support a similar doctrine for Europe – and above all, for the territory and the interests of the Greater German Reich', etc. No less scathing as he exposed the hypocrisies of British officialdom, Hitler recalled that 'without so much as a thought for the opinion of the natives, they have led a drive for the bloody subjugation of entire continents. However, the minute that Germany mentions the return of its colonies, they declared that – out of concern for the indigenous population there – one could not possibly abandon the natives to so horrid a fate. At the same time, they did not distance themselves from dropping bombs out of planes onto their own colonies. And all this to use the force of reason to persuade the dear colored compatriots to submit to the foreign rule a bit longer. Of course, the bombs thus employed were bombs with civilizing warheads which one must absolutely not confuse with those brutal ones Italy used in Abyssinia'; that 'Britain said she was fighting for justice [in World War I]. Britain has been fighting for justice for 300 years. As a reward God gave her 40,000,000 square kilometers of the world and 480,000,000 people to dominate. That is how God rewards the people who fight for freedom; and, be it noted, those who also fight for self-determination. For

Britain fought this fight as well. ... For 300 years Britain has conquered people after people. Now she is satisfied; now there must be peace. ... If the British declare that they are fighting for freedom, then the British might have given a wonderful example by granting their own Empire full liberty'; that 'for 300 years ... they have always fought for God and religion. Never have they fought for the sake of material aims, but because they have only had ethical aims God has rewarded them with much riches. Britain has always pretended to be a fighter for truth and justice and the protagonist of all virtues. God has proved His gratitude for this. Within three centuries Britain conquered fifteen and a half million square miles of the globe, not for reasons of selfishness or lust for power. No! On the contrary, it was only in the execution of a mission entrusted to her by the Lord and for the sake of holy religion. ... The story of the conqueror of 15,500,000 square miles is a long chapter of oppression, tyranny, subjugation, and plunder. Things happened in the course of this great conquest which would have been impossible in any other State or in the case of any other nation. Britain waged war for any cause, be it to extend her trade or to make others smoke opium, or else because she wanted to obtain gold mines or diamond fields'; that 'for three hundred years, Britain had gradually formed her so-called Empire – not through the free choice of the peoples concerned, or through spontaneous demonstrations and aspirations on their part, but by force. Thus the Empire was built up. War after war was waged; people after people were robbed of their liberty; State after State was crushed. ... Democracy was merely used as a mask in this process. Behind this mask lurked the enslavement of people, the oppression and gagging of individuals. ... [T]oday 46 million Britons in the home country dominate approximately one-quarter of the earth, in area and in population. ... It is important, my fellow countrymen, that we should constantly reiterate this fact, because shameless democratic liars stand up and maintain that the so-called totalitarian States wish to conquer the world. In reality, it is our old enemies who have always been the conquerors and aggressors'; that 'they say we have no right to do this or that. I should like to raise the counter-question: What right, for example, has England to shoot down Arabs in Palestine just because they defend their homeland; who gives them this right?'; that 'the idea of concentration camps was born in British brains [during the Boer war] ... The British put women and children into the concentration camps and 20,000 Boer women perished', etc., etc. (*New Order*, pp. 622, 657–77 passim, 750, 762–4, 772–3, 777, 902–3, emphasis in original; Domarus, vol. 2, pp. 1152–3). (For the British precedent with concentration camps – Hitler's contention was basically correct – cf. Thomas Pakenham, *The Scramble for Africa*, New York 1991, pp. 577–81.)

48. Raul Hilberg, *Perpetrators, Victims, Bystanders*, New York 1992, p. 10. Cf. Raul Hilberg, *The Destruction of the European Jews*, New York 1985, vol. 3, pp. 1018–21: 'The theory of world Jewish rule and of the incessant Jewish plot against the German people penetrated into all offices [of the German bureaucracy]. In the minds of the perpetrators, therefore, this theory turned the destruction process into a kind of preventive war.'

49. Chomsky, *For Reasons of State*, pp. 54–5. Flapan, *Zionism and the Palestinians*, p. 141. For the failure of the 'revisionist' West German historians to disentangle 'motive from myth', cf. Richard Evans, *In Hitler's Shadow*, New York 1989. West

German historian Ernst Nolte, e.g., has credited Hitler's perception of the invasion of the Soviet Union and his 'internment' of the Jews as acts of 'preventive war' inasmuch as Stalin had committed 'mental acts of war' against Germany and Weizmann had aligned the world Zionist movement with Great Britain.

50. In addition to Chap. 1 at note 6 above, cf. Baruch Kimmerling, *Zionism and Economy*, Cambridge 1982, pp. 81–2; Teveth, pp. 12, 44–5, 57–65; Flapan, *Zionism and the Palestinians*, ch. 6. Gershon Shafir, *Land, Labor and the Origins of the Israeli– Palestinian Conflict, 1882–1914*, Cambridge 1989, p. 87, observes that, for labor Zionism, 'National conflict was not seen … as a danger, as it was viewed by the property owners, but as the lever to the workers' own interest', and quotes Ben-Gurion's declaration at a party meeting in 1910 that '[Arab] national hatred is the reason that will force, and bit by bit is already forcing, Jewish farmers to take on Jewish workers, whom they hate so much'.

51. Ideological fanaticism could even obscure so basic a fact as this one. Thus the socialist Zionist leader Tabenkin, eager to reconcile Zionist dependence on Great Britain with his anti-imperialist sensibility, 'systematically refused to acknowledge the British role in the development of the national home. He contended that the growth in Jewish power in Palestine had taken place *despite* British policies, not by dint of them' (p. 226, emphasis in original).

52. To her credit, Shapira acknowledges that the Nazi holocaust did not decisively influence Zionist policy in this regard. Discounting 'the tendency to explain phenomena by using the Holocaust', she observes that the basic factors that shaped Zionist decision-making already 'existed prior to that event' (p. 342).

53. In the Sternhell article cited at note 36 above, the point is succinctly made: 'Occupation by force was only openly discussed beginning in the 1940s' by the Zionist movement 'because until then it wasn't a realistic option'.

54. V. Jabotinsky, 'The Iron Wall (We and the Arabs)', Berlin 1923.

55. Neil Caplan, *Palestine Jewry and the Arab Question, 1917–1925*, London 1976, p. 42, emphasis in original. With his usual lucidity and candor, Jabotinsky accordingly observed that, so far as force was concerned, only tactical differences divided him from mainstream Zionism: 'There is no meaningful difference between our "militarists" and our "vegetarians." One proposes an iron wall of Jewish bayonets, the other proposes an iron wall of British bayonets, … but we all applaud, day and night, the iron wall.' ('The Iron Wall').

56. Jean-Paul Sartre, *Anti-Semite and Jew*, New York 1965, pp. 46–7.

57. *Hair*, 6 May 1992. Historian Benny Morris further notes that 'pillage and looting … accompanied almost each Jewish conquest of an Arab urban neighborhood and town' (*1948 and After*, Oxford 1994, p. 210).

58. For France's use of the '*mission civilisatrice*' rhetoric to justify torture in Algeria, cf. Rita Maran, *Torture: The Role of Ideology in the French–Algerian War*, New York 1989. The racist conceits of the Zionist movement animated its non-Jewish partisans as well. Thus, expounding on the Jewish right to Palestine, Winston Churchill compared the Arabs there to a dog in a manger:

> I do not agree that the dog in a manger has the final right to the manger, even though he may have lain there for a very long time. I do not admit that right. I do not admit, for instance, that a great wrong has been done to the Red Indians of America, or the black people of Australia. I do not admit that a

wrong has been done to these people by the fact that a stronger race, a higher grade race, or at any rate, a more worldly-wise race, to put it that way, has come in and taken their place. (Clive Ponting, *Churchill*, London 1994, p. 254)

59. The belief that the 'natives' only understand the 'language of force' is a mainstay of conquest ideologies. Thus, as 'the beaten nigger groaned' in Joseph Conrad's *Heart of Darkness*, a clerk in the colonial outpost mused: 'Serve him right. Transgression – punishment – bang! Pitiless, pitiless. That's the only way. This will prevent all conflagration for the future.' On this theme, cf. also Chap. 6 below.

60. Just as Shapira disingenuously suggests that the Zionist youth were peculiarly hostile to partition (cf. note 38 above), so she disingenuously suggests that the Zionist youth were peculiarly given to the use of force (p. 360). The sentiments she ascribes to the supposedly impetuous 'new generation' – 'The lesson that Palestinian youth had learned from the history of the 1930s was that it was possible to build socialism only by the use of force'; 'basically, there was general agreement that the use of force was normative and that "power leading to socialism is moral"' (p. 306) – were scarcely alien to the Zionist elder statesmen.

61. Cf. pp. 161 and 308, where Shapira notes, respectively, that 'whoever reads through the contents of the educational program of Betar ... finds it difficult readily to pinpoint the differences between it and the Labor youth movements', and 'As to Jabotinsky, [the Labor youth] argued that the difference between him and the Labor movement was not in the approach to the use of force but in the method of building the land.' Cf. also p. 305.

62. Cf. Flapan, *Zionism and the Palestinians*, p. 115: 'Self-restraint ... was motivated by the fear that an escalation of riots and bloodshed would bring about the immediate cessation of immigration.'

63. Incapable of revealing a truth about labor Zionism without directly mitigating it with the conventional mythology, Shapira writes on p. 252 that 'Wingate was a revered commanding officer, especially popular with persons from labor settlements. ... Participation in one of his raids was considered a special privilege', but on p. 253 that 'a substantial amount of persuasion was required in order to convince people in the settlements to agree to give Wingate a quota from the ranks of their own people. ... The aggressive mentality of a combat based on mobility and firepower was alien to individuals who had been educated by the Tel Hai myth'.

64. Avraham Shapira (ed.), *The Seventh Day*, recorded and edited by a group of young kibbutz members, New York 1970. In his above-cited memoir, *Personal Witness*, Abba Eban recalls *The Seventh Day* as throwing 'a strong light on the ambivalent mood of Israeli youth. Our soldiers revealed themselves as capable of moral self-analysis. They brooded on the ultimate mysteries of life and death, as well as on the issue of their Jewish identity. They were often tormented by the complexity of their own attitude toward their Arab enemies' (p. 443). Even otherwise highly skeptical Israeli observers like Amnon Kapeliouk praised *The Seventh Day* as a 'moving testimony' by soldiers who 'hated war but felt they had no choice except to fight' (*Israël: la fin des mythes*, Paris 1975, p. 107).

65. The basic distinction can be traced back to Machiavelli's *The Prince*:

We can say that cruelty is used well (if it is permissible to talk in this way of what is evil) when it is employed once for all, and one's safety depends on it, and then it is not persisted in but as far as possible turned to the good of one's subjects. Cruelty badly used is that which, although infrequent to start with, as time goes on, rather than disappearing, grows in intensity. (ch. 8)

66. *The New Republic*, 30 November 1992. Parenthetically, Alter notes with apparent dismay that 'incidents' of torture such as the one Ben-Gurion condemned 'still do' occur in the occupied territories. Yet all major human rights organizations have similarly concluded that Israeli torture of Palestinian detainees is 'virtually institutionalized' (Amnesty International, *The Military Justice System in the Occupied Territories*, New York 1991), 'systematic and routine' (B'Tselem–Israeli Center for Human Rights in the Occupied Territories, Jerusalem 1991), 'a systematic pattern' (Human Rights Watch/Middle East, *Torture and Ill-Treatment*, New York 1994), etc. (For a detailed discussion of this topic, see my forthcoming *The Rise and Fall of Palestine*, Chap. 3) Alter's concern is seemingly limited, again, to 'gratuitous' torture. For earlier apologetics on behalf of Israeli torture in *The New Republic*, cf. Noam Chomsky, *Towards a New Cold War*, New York 1982, p. 454, note 5.

67. Heinz Höhne, *The Order of the Death's Head*, New York 1969, pp. 365–6, 382–3, 386; Joachim Fest, *The Face of the Third Reich*, New York 1970, pp. 115, 118, 119; Raul Hilberg, *The Destruction of the European Jews*, vol. 3, pp. 904, 1009–10. Cf. Hilberg, *Destruction*, vol. 1, p. 326:

> The killing of the Jews was regarded as historical necessity. The soldier had to 'understand' this. If for any reason he was instructed to help the SS and Police in their task, he was expected to obey orders. However, if he killed a Jew spontaneously, voluntarily, or without instruction, merely because he *wanted* to kill, then he committed an abnormal act, worthy perhaps of an 'Eastern European' (such as a Romanian) but dangerous to the discipline and prestige of the German army. Herein lay the crucial difference between the man who 'overcame' himself to kill and one who wantonly committed atrocities. The former was regarded as a good soldier and a true Nazi; the latter was a person without self-control, who would be a danger to his community after his return home. (emphasis in original)

In the Algerian case, torture was supposed to be administered 'without sadism but efficaciously ... without joy, but also without shame, done only because of concern with duty, this crude need so contrary to our habits as soldiers and as civilised men' (Père Delarue, chaplain to the main torture unit in Algeria); Maran, p. 96.

68. Rudolf Hoess, *Commandant of Auschwitz*, London 1974. The 'ultra-Nazi' epithet is Arno Mayer's in *Why Did the Heavens Not Darken?*, New York 1988, p. 364. In *Face*, Fest makes the interesting point that the sadists in the ranks of the SS condemned by Hoess were perhaps more human than his ideal of the passionless, fundamentally disinterested killer for whom murder was simply an administrative procedure: 'At least behind the ... enjoyment of brutality there lay an overwhelming social, intellectual or otherwise motivated personal reaction which, significantly, "appears to us like a last residue of humanly intelligible behavior"' (pp. 279–80; the inner quote is Hannah Arendt's from *The Origins of Totalitarianism*).

69. Höhne, pp. 364–6, 387; Fest, *Face*, p. 121; Hilberg, *Destruction*, vol. 1, pp. 332–3. One would want to note the paradox that Nazi ideology directly denied but indirectly affirmed the humanity of the Jews. Thus, Himmler hurled with frenzied conviction the most inhuman epithets at the Jews – the 'primordial substance of all things negative', the 'bacillus of all dangers which threaten the Ger-

man people', etc. (cf. Wegner, pp. 48–9) – yet shrunk from the 'bloody business' of having to murder them. On a related point, Nazism's primitive appeal to instincts clashed with its quintessentially modern cult of rationality. Specifically, for all the visceral hatred that Nazism conjured up in its war against the Jews, the Final Solution was supposed to be implemented without personal rancor or animus. Hence, Hoess's censure of the 'hate indoctrination' of Nazi officials because it caused 'torture and ill-treatment to be inflicted upon the prisoners'.

70. Höhne, p. 364; Fest, *Face*, p. 115.

71. Besides anguish, Hoess pleaded ignorance in his defense: 'Whether this mass extermination of the Jews was necessary or not was something on which I could not allow myself to form an opinion, for I lacked the necessary breadth of view.' One is reminded of the lucubrations of another tormented soul, Elie Wiesel, the Nobel Laureate and now founder of the Universal Academy of Cultures for 'men and women professionally dedicated to the service of truth and beauty who are also committed to the pursuit of good'. Asked in the early 1980s to comment on Israel's repressive policies in the occupied territories, Wiesel replied, 'What to do and how to do it, I really don't know because I lack the elements of information and knowledge. ... You must be in a position of power to possess all the information. ... I don't have that information, so I don't know.' As Israel embarked on the wholesale brutalization of Palestinians in the first months of the *intifada*, Wiesel extended his sympathies, indeed, his love – to Israel: 'Whatever happens in Israel and to Israel, I love Israel.' Regarding his 'love's' methodical breaking of Palestinian bones, Wiesel courageously chose silence: 'I refuse to see myself in the role of judge over Israel. The role of the Jew is to bear witness; not to pass judgment.' At any rate, on Jews. Wiesel does not miss a beat when it comes to passing judgment on Arabs, Russians, Germans, Poles, ... Hoess, incidentally, ultimately came to 'see ... that the extermination of the Jews was fundamentally wrong' but, alas, only because it did not conduce to the desired end: 'It in no way served the cause of anti-Semitism, but on the contrary brought the Jews far closer to their ultimate objective.' For Wiesel's Universal Academy, cf. *New York Times*, 30 January 1993, quoting the charter; for Wiesel's views on the Israeli occupation, cf. Noam Chomsky, *The Fateful Triangle*, Boston 1983, p. 16, and *Midstream*, December 1988 ('Israel [!] Under Siege').

72. The evidence suggests that, in many and perhaps most cases, it was, as it were, genuine. Cf. Höhne, pp. 363, 366, 374; Hilberg, *Destruction*, vol. 1, pp. 328–9, 332, and vol. 3, pp. 1008, 1010; and esp. Christopher R. Browning, *Ordinary Men*, New York 1992, passim. Browning followed the murderous itinerary of a German reserve police battalion dispatched to the killing fields in Poland. His conclusion is that a small percentage took sadistic pleasure in the killings and an equally small percentage refused to participate (incidentally, without incurring any formal penalties, as abstention was an explicit option). The overwhelming majority, he suggests, succumbed to the conventional pressures of career, peers, etc. as well as to the 'deeply ingrained behavior tendency' to defer to authority (the quoted words are Stanley Milgram's). Notably, Browning concludes that, for all its racist virulence, Nazi ideology did not 'explicitly prepare' Germans for 'the task of killing Jews'. But cf. Hilberg, *Destruction*, vol. 1, p. 327, 'Clearly, the killing operations ... brought into the open an uncomfortably large number of soldiers who

delighted in death as spectators and perpetrators.' On the other hand, Hilberg also stresses (p. 331) that 'psychological justifications were an essential part of the killing operations. If a proposed action could not be justified, it did not take place'.

73. The pose is typical of every conquest regime as it embarks on mass murder. For the US case during the Vietnam War, cf. Noam Chomsky, *Year 501*, Boston 1993, pp. 119, 251f, noting with ample documentation that 'It is a staple of the media, and the culture generally, that we were the injured party in Vietnam.' One could only add to Chomsky's depressing inventory that this view extends even to dissident scholarship. Thus, in his otherwise highly sympathetic comparative study of French and American antiwar intellectuals during, respectively, the Algerian and Vietnamese conflicts, *War and the Ivory Tower*, New York 1991, historian David L. Schalk still refers, e.g., to 'the terrible (*for both sides*) Christmas bombing offensive of 1972' (p. 138, my emphasis). In the Algerian case, the central moral drama of the brutal French colonial war that left some one million Algerians dead, was apparently the tortured soul of Albert Camus, the Algerian-born writer who embraced – naturally, with anguish – the French repression. In his standard multivolume history, *La guerre d'Algérie*, Yves Courrière typically observes that, 'A Paris un autre homme parle aussi de l'Algérie, l'un des plus grands noms de la littérature française contemporaine: Albert Camus. Déjà, selon un mot qui deviendra célèbre, il a mal à l'Algérie' – 'Camus is pained by Algeria' (*Le temps des léopards*, Paris 1969, p. 239). Camus defended his opposition to Algeria's independence, *inter alia*, on the grounds that it was never actually a nation but rather a heterogeneous mosaic of nationalities:

> On doit cependant reconnaître qu'en ce qui concerne l'Algérie, l'indépendence nationale est une formule purement passionnelle. Il n'y a jamais eu de nation algérienne. Les Juifs, les Turcs, les Grecs, les Italiens, les Berbères, auraient autant de droit à réclamer la direction de cette nation virtuelle. (*Actuelles III*, pp. 366–7)

As seen above (p. 101), the same argument was made in the Zionist and Nazi apologetics on, respectively, Palestine and Eastern Europe. Camus's hypocritical platitudes are subjected to withering scrutiny in Conor Cruise O'Brien, *Camus*, London 1970. In *The Company of Critics*, New York 1988, social critic Michael Walzer attempts to rehabilitate Camus's record during the Algerian War, averring that the 'moral anxiety ... right on the surface' of Camus's writings demonstrates that he was not acting from 'bad faith'. One wonders if Walzer would also want to apply this insight to the 'moral anxiety ... right on the surface' of Himmler's speeches. In fact, 'moral anxiety ... right on the surface' is almost always the surest sign of bad faith. Recalling Camus's famous statement regarding Algeria just after he received the Nobel prize, 'I believe in justice, but I will defend my mother above justice', Walzer specially credits Camus for putting 'his' people (the *pieds noirs*) before 'abstract morality' – in Walzer's view, the hallmark of a 'connected' critic. Thus Camus, who 'would not have said ... that French and Arab lives were of equal importance in his eyes', is favorably contrasted with Sartre and de Beauvoir, in whose 'ideologically flattened world', the 'lives of Moslems were of no less importance ... than those of ... fellow countrymen'. These remarkable sentiments passed without comment in the uniformly adulatory reviews that Walzer's book received in the United States. A similar effort at rehabilitation is undertaken by Tony Judt in the *New York Review of Books* (6 October 1994), with 'Camus the Just' acclaimed for his unique 'lucidity and moral courage' during the Algerian war. Expatiating upon Camus's tortured search for a 'middle way' between 'assimilationist colonialism' and 'militant nationalism', Judt manages not to mention any of Camus's 'lucid' insights: that Algeria did not rate a nation; that the Algerian independence struggle – or, in Judt's preferred usage, 'civil war' – actually constituted an Arab–Soviet plot to undermine the 'West'; that granting Algeria independence would result in the 'historic death of France', the 'encirclement' and a fate akin to Hungary for Europe, and the 'isolation' of the United States, etc. Judt praises Camus's 're-jection of violence, of terror in all its forms' during the Algerian war, but forgets to mention that Camus evinced no such scruples – rather the contrary – when it came to the French resistance to the Nazi occupation, the Hungarian resistance to the Soviet occupation, and the Anglo–French–Israeli attack on Egypt, not to mention that, as O'Brien observes, Camus's 'position was necessarily one of support' for France's murderous repression in Algeria since he 'consistently opposed' negotia-tions with the actual leaders of the rebellion and independence. The upshot of Judt's essay is that Algerians would have been better off under French tutelage; they are incapable of independence. With 'nothing but blood and ashes to show' in the post-colonial world, Camus 'had been correct all along. ... Thirty years after gaining its independence, Algeria is again in trouble, divided and bloodied.' No doubt a Tory apologist similarly lamented several decades after the American War of Inde-pendence (or, as it would have been put, with far greater justification, 'civil war') that – between the wars of extermination against the indigenous population and the looming fratricidal conflict over slavery – there is 'nothing but blood and ashes to show. ... America is again in trouble, divided and bloodied'. On these points, cf. *Actuelles III*, pp. 370–1; Courrière, *Le Temps*, p. 251; O'Brien, pp. 73–4, Simone de Beauvoir, *Force of Circumstances*, New York 1964, pp. 380–1, 383–4, 458–9, 460–1; and Herbert R. Lottman, *Albert Camus*, New York 1979, pp. 577, 618, 624. On the propagandistic recasting of an independence struggle as a 'civil war', cf. George McT. Kahin, *Intervention*, New York 1987, p. 26. Even Alistair Horne frankly ac-knowledges in his pro-French apologia, *A Savage War of Peace*, London 1977, that Algeria was a 'grand style "colonial war"', in the strictest sense of the words' (p. 14).

74. Höhne, p. 388; Fest, *Face*, p. 283.

75. 'The Kitsch of Israel', *The New York Review of Books*, 24 November 1988. Fyodor Dostoyevsky, *Notes from Underground*, London 1972, pp. 31–2. Cf. Tom Segev, *The Seventh Million*, New York 1993, p. 390, where *The Seventh Day* is described as 'an authentic but not unproblematic document. There is no way of knowing when the soldiers revealed their real feelings and when they simply repeated clichés contrived to sustain their image as sensitive fighters – shooting and crying their way through a just war. They may not have known themselves'. Segev un-wittingly proves his thesis as he quotes the 'intimate' reflections of an Israeli soldier to his girlfriend on the eve of the June 1967 war to the effect that he, the soldier, wants to be 'strong, strong to the point of tears; sharp as a knife; quiet and terrible' (p. 450) – the very same phrases that appeared in *The Seventh Day* (see p. 114 above). Ironically, just as inner torment is seen in Zionist culture as morally redeeming, so is the overcoming of it. The added irony is that the same paradox tugged at Nazism. Shapira recalls that, from its inception, Zionism viewed the diasporan Jew as a 'pathological individual, plagued by physical and mental problems'. Chief among these afflictions is the virtue that has been made of meekness and the

attendant sickly inhibition about physical force and violence. The Zionist counter-ideal to the proverbial 'gentle Jew' is the Jewish 'fighter'. Hence, the Yishuv damned in the same breath the 'sick sadism of the Nazi torturer – but also the bent-down sick nature of the tormented victim'. The poet Moshe Tabenkin declared in 1944 that 'a powerless people in the physical sense has no biological right to exist'. In the Nazi holocaust's aftermath, Israel viewed with disdain and shame the survivors, since they were an unwelcome reminder that the Jews had gone 'like sheep to slaughter'. Only the Jews who 'fought back' were accepted in the Zionist fold (pp. 11–14, 71, 326, 331f). (For an insightful discussion of this facet of Zionist culture as it has come to corrupt American Jewry, cf. Paul Breines, *Tough Jews*, New York 1990. On the Zionist attitude to the survivors of the Nazi holocaust, cf. esp. Segev's *The Seventh Million*.) The Nazis made a virtue of the angst that wracked them but also of the 'toughness' they displayed, which was seen as the antithesis of the sickly Christian norms of charity, mercy and humility. In his study of the Waffen-SS, Wegner pertinently observes (p. 27) that it was the determination of the SS 'to overcome the orthodox codes of values, to suppress deeply held moral scruples, in a word to conquer one's very moral self' that explains how Himmler was able to 'praise murders by his death commandos as paradigms of moral conduct'. Fest similarly notes in *Face* that, in the case of Hoess, the constant effort toward toughness 'stimulated his misguided idealism, so that in the 'cold, indeed stony' attitude which in his own words he demanded of himself', the Auschwitz comman-dant saw 'the result of moral struggle'. Hoess, he adds, was 'haunted by the fear' of being accused of meekness. The desire, 'bred by the perverted image of the National Socialist ideal man, "to be described as harsh", as Hoess remarked, "in order not be considered soft"', nipped in the bud any moral doubt he may otherwise have entertained (pp. 279, 284). Ironically, Hoess sneered with monumental disdain at the special detachments of Jews working the crematoria who allegedly 'carried out their grisly task with dumb indifference' and 'even the cremation of their near relations failed to shake them'. Yet, wasn't that the Nazi – his own – ideal?

## Chapter 5

1. E.L.M. Burns, *Between Arab and Israeli*, London 1962, pp. 17–18, 71. Kennett Love, *Suez*, New York 1969, p. 9. Donald Neff, *Warriors at Suez*, New York 1981, p. 33. These findings are fully borne out with exhaustive detail in Benny Morris, *Israel's Border Wars, 1949–1956*, Oxford 1993.

2. For a detailed discussion of the Samu raid, cf. Samir A. Mutawi, *Jordan in the 1967 War*, Cambridge 1987, ch. 4. United Nations Security Council Official Records, 16 November 1966, 1320th meeting. In view of the extensive reference I will make in this essay to the deliberations of the United Nations on the Middle East conflict, it is useful to recall Eban's own assessment that 'the overwhelming bal-ance' of the UN's 'influence on Israel's destiny and status is dramatically positive'. 'No nation involved in a struggle for legitimacy', he continued, 'has received such potent support from the overall jurisprudence of an international organization' (*Jerusalem Post*, international edition, 3 December 1988).

3. Burns (p. 21) observed that 'reprisals are entirely inconsistent with the par-ties' obligations under the General Armistice Agreements' and had been repeatedly

condemned by the Security Council. Regarding the deterrent value of reprisals, Burns added that 'the retaliation does not end the matter; it goes on and on. ... The retaliatory actions undoubtedly give some satisfaction to the Israeli public, or at least the newspapers, but the policy was not effective in relation to its professed aim' (p. 38). E.H. Hutchison, who served with the United Nations forces on the Jordan–Israel border, similarly observed that 'one thing is certain' about Israel's 'reprisal' policy: it 'had little lasting effect on infiltration; in fact, it gave rise to a new type of border trouble – the raid of revenge. ... A hatred was being created that would take years to erase completely' (E.H. Hutchison, *Violent Truce*, New York 1956, p. 104). Dag Hammarskjold, Secretary-General of the United Nations at the time of the Suez invasion, lamented that the Israeli government could 'never transcend its one-sided view' that only 'threats to use military force, and excessive military reprisals' were effective, and could not admit that its 'retaliation policy is no better means for reestablishment [of] order than the U.N. operations which [it] so high-handedly reject[s]' (Neff, pp. 311–12).

4. Odd Bull, *War and Peace in the Middle East*, London 1976, p. 61. Hutchison, p. 106; cf. pp. 104–5. Patrick Seale, *Asad*, Berkeley 1988, p. 124. Mutawi, pp. 66–7. Bull – who, incidentally, was lavishly praised at his tenure's end by Israelis for his impartiality – also notes that the impulse behind Palestinian infiltration from the West Bank was not pathological malice but real injury incurred:

> The main reason ... was that the boundary was so drawn that the Arabs in that area were the victims of great economic hardship, since their villages were cut off from the land which for generations had been the source of their livelihood. ... It is not difficult to picture the state of desperation to which they were driven when they were obliged to contemplate Israeli farmers exploiting the land which they and their forefathers had cultivated for so many hundreds of years. ... It was these sorts of people who were responsible for infiltration over the demarcation line, their aim being to steal from what had not so long ago been their own land, to carry out acts of sabotage, and so on. (p. 61)

On this point, cf. also Burns, pp. 49–50, and Hutchison, p. 11.

5. Seale, pp. 126–7. Mutawi, p. 83.

6. Andrew and Leslie Cockburn, *Dangerous Liaison*, New York 1991, p. 137. John K. Cooley, *Green March, Black September*, London 1973, p. 160. Daniel Dishon (ed.), *Middle East Record* (hereafter *MER*), *1967*, Tel Aviv 1971–7, pp. 179, 186–7. *New York Times*, 12 May 1967. There is some dispute as to whether Rabin actually issued the quoted threat (cf. *MER*, *1967*, p. 186). Yet, given that 'there were enough verifiable statements by Israeli leaders during the period in question to create an impression that they were about to take serious military action' (Richard B. Parker, *The Politics of Miscalculation in the Middle East*, Bloomington 1993, p. 16), the point would seem to be academic.

7. United Nations Security Council, 19 May 1967, Report by the Secretary-General. U Thant, *View From the U.N.*, New York 1978, pp. 218–19. Maj.-Gen. Indar Jit Rikhye, *The Sinai Blunder*, London 1980, p. 166. Department of State telegram from Secretary of State to US Embassy, Cairo, 25 May 1967, in Parker, Document 2, at p. 224. UN memorandum of meeting between Secretary General U Thant and UAR Foreign Minister Mahmoud Riad, 24 May 1967, Cairo, in Parker, Document 5, at p. 228. Dishon, *MER*, *1967*, p. 188.

8. Abba Eban, *Personal Witness*, New York 1992, pp. 354, 356. Parker, pp. 16, 18–19. Michael Brecher, *Decisions in Crisis*, Berkeley 1980, p. 36. Much has been written about the Soviet intelligence report that Israel had mobilized ten to twelve brigades on the Syrian border. Although UN observers did not dispute Israel's denial of troop movements on its northern border (cf. Report of the Secretary General on the Withdrawal of the United Nations Emergency Force, 18 May 1967), Bull (p. 104) cautions that, 'it has to be remembered that Israel had acquired an almost legendary ability to mobilize its forces and concentrate them at the right time and in the right place'. (He also notes, p. 54, that UN inspection teams 'seldom unearthed anything of much significance because the authorities had time to remove anything they did not want to be seen'.) Ezer Weizmann, head of operations on the Israeli General Staff before and during the June war, acknowledged in 1972 that 'we did move tanks to the north after the downing of the [Syrian] aircraft' (David Hirst, *The Gun and the Olive Branch*, London 1977, p. 215; cf. Brecher, p. 45, where it is reported that Israel did not concentrate 'large forces' on the Syrian frontier, 'though some tank units were sent there as reinforcements after the 7 April flare-up'). Parker (pp. 8–11) convincingly demonstrates that Israel could not possibly have mobilized a force of the dimensions conveyed in the Soviet intelligence finding. The conclusion of Harold Saunders, a National Security Council Middle East expert, seems the most judicious: 'The Soviet advice to the Syrians that the Israelis were planning an attack was not far off, although they seemed to have exaggerated the magnitude. The Israelis were planning an attack – but not an invasion' (Donald Neff, *Warriors for Jerusalem*, New York 1984, p. 59).

9. Mutawi, pp. 85, 94.

10. For a careful sifting of the evidence, cf. Parker, pp. 63–76. Cf. also Rikhye, pp. 52–3, 160–3, 168, 181; Abdullah Schleifer, *The Fall of Jerusalem*, New York 1972, pp. 107–8, 130; Mohamed Hassanein Heikal, *The Cairo Documents*, New York 1973, p. 240; and William Quandt, *Peace Process*, Washington 1993, p. 509, note 9. U Thant's compelling defense of his actions can be found in the Report of the Secretary-General on the Withdrawal of the United Nations Emergency Force, 26 June 1967; cf. also Brian Urquhart, *A Life in Peace and War*, New York 1987, pp. 212f.

11. Eban, *Personal Witness*, p. 356. Neff, *Warriors for Jerusalem*, pp. 74–5. Bull, p. 104. Yitzak Rabin, *The Rabin Memoirs*, Boston 1979, p. 76. Cf. Parker, p. 60, Nasser 'could not do nothing. He had gotten away with that domestically, if not regionally, at the time of the Samu raid and the April 7 dogfight over Syria, but his prestige and Egypt's could not afford another such failure to react'. On this point, cf. also Jon Kimche, *There Could Have Been Peace*, New York 1973, p. 255, quoting a senior American official on 'the assessment of the general situation by the American and Israeli intelligence establishments':

> The move of the Egyptian troops into Sinai was interpreted by the Israelis as an Egyptian attempt to save their reputation in the Arab world. They really had no choice; they had to do something after Eshkol's warning to the Arabs otherwise they would have publicly displayed their total impotence.

12. United Nations Security Council, 19 May 1967, Report by the Secretary-General. Report of the Secretary-General on the Withdrawal of the United Nations Emergency Force, 18 May 1967. Thant, p. 250. UN memorandum of meeting

between Secretary General U Thant and UAR Foreign Minister, 24 May 1967, Cairo, in Parker, Document 5, at pp. 229–30. US Embassy Cairo telegram to Department of State, 2 June 1967, in Parker, Document 8, at pp. 234–5. Brecher, p. 147. Israel had also unilaterally withdrawn from the Israeli–Syrian Mixed Armistice Commission in an action criticized by the Security Council. It functioned only intermittently after 1956. (Cf. David Bowen and Laura Drake, 'The Syrian–Israeli Border Conflict, 1949–1967', *Middle East Policy*, vol. 1, no. 4, 1992, pp. 18–19.)

13. Rikhye, pp. 160, 180, 213–14, 232. Brecher, pp. 108, 112, 114. United Nations Security Council, 26 May 1967, Report by the Secretary-General. General Assembly, Fifth Emergency Special Session, 20 June 1967, 1527th Meeting. Report of the Secretary-General on the Withdrawal of the United Nations Emergency Force, 26 June 1967. Cf. paras 87–93 of this last document for a full discussion of the original intent of UNEF. It recalls 'Israel's persistent refusal to consent to the stationing and operation of UNEF on its side of the Line in spite of General Assembly Resolution 1125 (XI) of 2 February 1957 and the efforts of the Secretary-General'.

14. Thant, p. 223. Bull, p. 108.

15. Eban, *Personal Witness*, p. 363. General Assembly, Fifth Emergency Session, 19 June 1967, 1526th meeting. Abba Eban, *An Autobiography*, New York 1977, pp. 356–7. Fuad A. Jabber (ed.), *International Documents on Palestine, 1967*, Beirut 1970, p. 28.

16. United Nations Security Council, 26 May 1967, Report by the Secretary-General. U Thant, pp. 236–9. UN memorandum of meeting between Secretary General U Thant and UAR President Nasser, 24 May 1967, Cairo, in Parker, Document 6, at pp. 231–2. For U Thant's proposal, cf. also Heikal, *The Cairo Documents*, p. 243; Mohamed Hassanein Heikal, *The Sphinx and the Commissar*, London 1978, p. 176; and Rikhye, p. 73. Urquhart, p. 214. For Egypt's acceptance of the U Thant proposal, cf. also DAG – 1/5.2.2.1.2, Appendix 3, Box 3 (UN Archives), documenting that as late as the very end of May, Egypt still did 'not have any objection to a 2-week moratorium'. Eban's sanitized rendering of the episode reads that 'the Secretary-General had virtually brought nothing back with him from Cairo' (*Autobiography*, p. 360). Gideon Rafael, Israel's permanent UN representative in 1967, is roughly as credible a 'personal witness' as Eban. He reports that U Thant left Cairo 'empty-handed and down-hearted' as 'another diplomatic move had failed to dam the torrent of overflowing emotions released by a reckless dictator' (Gideon Rafael, *Destination Peace*, New York 1981, p. 142).

17. Neff, *Warriors for Jerusalem*, p. 179. Details of the Yost–Anderson meetings with Egyptian officials remain sketchy. According to David Nes, the *chargé d'affaires* of the US embassy in Cairo, Nasser agreed, *inter alia*, to completely lift the blockade pending a World Court decision. Cited in Schleifer, p. 149, and confirmed in a telephone interview, 7 July 1993. Anthony Nutting (*Nasser*, London 1972, pp. 411–13) reports that Nasser 'told Washington and other Western capitals' that he was 'perfectly prepared' to submit the Straits dispute to the World Court, and that the Egyptian foreign minister gave 'a broad hint' that Egypt 'might be prepared to allow the flow of oil to continue, provided that there was no appreciable increase in the tanker traffic to Elath'. After their respective meetings in Cairo, Anderson and Yost both reported in cables to the State Department that Egypt was adamant on its closure of the Straits to oil headed for Israel, but 'did not rule out completely possibility of a World Court review if it could be done speedily' (Anderson) and

'would see no objection to Israel presenting complaint on this issue to the International Court of Justice if it so desired' (Yost). US Embassy Cairo telegram to Department of State, 2 June 1967, in Parker, Document 8, at p. 234; US Embassy Lisbon telegram to Department of State, 2 June 1967, in Parker, Document 9, at p. 236; and US Embassy Cairo telegram to Department of State, 2 June 1967, in Parker, Document 10, at p. 238. Quandt (p. 45) notes the suspicion in Washington in early June that Nasser 'might propose referring the dispute over the strait to the International Court of Justice'. Charles Yost ('The Arab–Israeli War: How It Began', *Foreign Affairs*, January 1968, p. 316) states that 'unavailing efforts were made to persuade President Nasser to revoke, suspend or moderate the blockade but, the action once taken, he did not feel politically free to reverse it, even had he so desired'. The Yost–Anderson missions to Cairo were apparently not the first occasion that Nasser agreed to World Court adjudication. Rikhye (p. 74) reports that Nasser 'said he was ready to go to international arbitration, including the International Court at The Hague', during his meeting with U Thant on 23 May. Schleifer (p. 140, note 3) and Hisham Sharabi ('Prelude to War: The Crisis of May–June 1967', in Ibrahim Abu-Lughod [ed.], *The Arab–Israeli Confrontation of June 1967*, Evanston 1970, p. 52) both assert that Nasser had publicly expressed a willingness to turn the Straits dispute over to the World Court, while the Cockburns (p. 141) report that this intention of Nasser's was signalled to the CIA by the head of Egyptian intelligence. Parker (p. 90) confirms that 'Salah Nasr, Egypt's director of intelligence, told the CIA station chief in effect that referral to the court was the Egyptian ace in the hole, to be played at the right moment'. The author also notes (p. 90) that Egypt had already compiled a 'large briefing book' on the status of the Gulf of Aqaba and the Strait of Tiran in the event that the issue was referred to the World Court.

18. Dean Rusk, *As I Saw It*, New York 1990, pp. 386–7. In his last memo to US ambassadors in the Arab world before the June war, Rusk speculated that

> there may be some flexibility in what Cairo would be willing to do before major hostilities. … We shall not know details until further exploration of the problem with Cairo or intermediaries. … There might be some possibility of a breathing space if in fact passage were permitted for genuinely peaceful traffic, including crude oil. (Parker, Document 14, at p. 246)

Regarding Egyptian Vice-President Muhieddin's scheduled trip to Washington, Parker (pp. 58, 112–13) recalls that 'there was an audible sigh of relief from officers of the U.S. Embassy in Cairo, who saw this development as the first indication of a meaningful political initiative to resolve the crisis peacefully'. (Parker was a political counselor of the US embassy in Cairo at the time. Muhieddin told Parker in 1989 that he himself 'was not confident anything would come of it.') Yost (pp. 317–18) conjectures that 'it seems unlikely' that the Washington talks would have produced a breakthrough, but the reason he adduces – i.e. 'the support which the Soviet Union was providing its Arab friends' – is belied by recent scholarship. Rather the contrary, as Carl Brown ('Nasser and the June 1967 War: Plan or Improvisation?', in S. Seikaly et al. [eds], *Quest for Understanding*, Beirut 1991, p. 123) authoritatively concludes, 'the overwhelming weight of available evidence reveals the Soviet Union urging Egypt to dampen down the crisis'. Correcting for Yost's error in reasoning, his argument buttresses the view that a diplomatic settlement was within reach. Cf. also Rikhye, p. 169, 'the action by the United Nations, and its Secretary-General in particular, and the diplomatic interventions by the great powers indicated that Israel need not have gone to war at that time and should have allowed diplomacy to prevail'. On Eshkol's commitment to Johnson to delay military action, cf. Brecher, pp. 146–7.

19. Dishon, *MER, 1967*, p. 199. Questioned at a news conference on 28 May about what was meant by strategic materials, Nasser carefully skirted the issue; cf. Jabber, pp. 549f.

20. Eban, *Personal Witness*, pp. 365, 408. Cf. ibid., chs 18–19 passim for developments surrounding the multinational armada.

21. General Assembly, Fifth Emergency Session, 19 June 1967, 1526th meeting. Security Council Official Records, Twenty-Second Year, 13 November 1967, 1375th meeting. Eban, *Personal Witness*, p. 356. Brecher, pp. 95, 168; cf. p. 39. John Quigley, *Palestine and Israel*, Durham 1990, p. 163.

22. Eban, *Autobiography*, p. 342. Eban drew up the same bill of indictment in his initial presentation to the Security Council following the Israeli attack; cf. Security Council Official Records, Twenty-Second Year, 5 June 1967, 1347th meeting.

23. Eban, *Autobiography*, pp. 342, 313; Eban, *Personal Witness*, p. 347.

24. Bull, pp. 48, 50, 55. Bull notes (p. 67) that Israel indulged the same aggrandizing tactics in the other DMZs. Regarding the Jordan–Israel DMZ, he writes that 'one thing there can be no doubt about is that the status quo had changed in many respects over the years, and always in Israel's favor'. On Israeli violations of the armistice agreements in the Israeli–Syrian DMZ, cf. also Burns, p. 114:

> The Israelis in fact exercised almost complete control over the major portion of the demilitarized zone through their frontier police. This was directly contrary to Article V of the General Armistice Agreements and the 'authoritative interpretation' of it (by Dr Bunche) which formed part of the proceedings of the committee negotiating the armistice between the two countries, and had been agreed to by both sides.

For Israel's claim, contrary to the letter of the armistice agreements, to 'complete control and sovereignty' of the Israeli–Syrian DMZ, cf. Aryeh Shalev, *The Israeli–Syria Armistice Regime, 1949–1955*, Boulder 1993, pp. 40–1, 47, 68–9, 211, note 4.

25. Maj.-Gen. Carl Von Horn, *Soldiering for Peace*, London 1966, pp. 76, 86, 127–8.

26. Stephen Green, *Taking Sides*, New York 1984, p. 192.

27. Muhammad Muslih, 'The Golan: Israel, Syria, and Strategic Calculations', *Middle East Journal*, Autumn 1993, p. 619; Bowen and Drake, p. 27. Bull, p. 50.

28. Bowen and Drake, pp. 20–1. For the December 1955 Israeli attack, cf. also Muslih, p. 618. (Muslih observes that Israel 'had the edge' in the long-running confrontation with Syria 'in part because the kind of military power at the disposal of Syria was ill-suited to oppose or challenge the stronger and better-armed Israel'.) U Thant, p. 217. *Arab Report and Record* (hereafter *ARR*), 1967. Dishon, *MER, 1967*. One Israeli soldier was killed in the course of the aerial battle in early April discussed above.

29. Bowen and Drake, p. 26.

30. Rikhye, pp. 4–6. Cooley, p. 160.

31. U Thant, p. 214. Eban (*Personal Witness*, p. 178) argues that 'there is no such thing' in the December 1948 resolution as 'a right' of Arab refugees to return

irrespective of Israel's permission, since it uses the word 'permitted' which 'effectively put the determination in the hands of the ruling territorial power, which by then was Israel and no other'. Yet as Thomas Mallison and Sally Mallison (*The Palestine Problem in International Law and World Order*, London 1986, p. 179) point out, the resolution was 'written on the assumption that the principle of right of return was not in issue and that the central task was achieving practical implementation of repatriation'. Accordingly, the text '*instructs* the Conciliation Commission [of Palestine] to facilitate the repatriation' of the refugees (emphasis in original). The Mallisons further note that the conciliatory language reflected the assumption that Israel would act in good faith with the Commission and – in the words of the text – 'take all possible steps to assist in the implementation of the present resolution'. Eban (*Personal Witness*, p. 138) also argues that Israel bears no responsibility for the Palestinian flight in 1948 because 'it would not have taken place without the war and ... those who decide on war are responsible for the ensuing chain of consequence'. Remarkably, Eban seems unaware of the crucial distinction in international law, underlined at Nuremberg, between crimes against peace, on the one hand, and war crimes and crimes against humanity, on the other. On this matter, cf. Michael Walzer, *Just and Unjust Wars*, New York 1977, p. 21, where the medieval distinction between *jus ad bellum* (the justice of war) and *jus in bello* (justice in war) is recalled to make the elementary point that 'it is perfectly possible for a just war to be fought unjustly and for an unjust war to be fought in strict accordance with the rules'.

32. United Nations Security Council, 19 May 1967, Report by the Secretary-General. United Nations Press Release, SG/SM/708–9, 11 May 1967. Y. Harkabi, 'Fedayeen Action and Arab Strategy', *Adelphi Papers*, no. 53, London 1968. *Statistical Abstract of Israel, 1969*. Eban, *Autobiography*, p. 313; Eban, *Personal Witness*, pp. 346, 353. For the official Palestinian and Israeli figures on guerrilla attacks, cf. Fuad Jabber, 'The Palestinian Resistance and Inter-Arab Politics', in William B. Quandt et al., *The Politics of Palestinian Nationalism*, Berkeley 1973, pp. 169–72. Both sides evidently had a common stake – albeit for different reasons – in boosting these numbers. Regarding the Palestinian claims, Harkabi observes: 'To hide its mediocre results Fatah inflated communiqués which bore no resemblance to what actually took place. Often, reported actions did not take place at all, and the Israeli authorities even had difficulty in identifying them.' Israel reported one civilian casualty (on 14 January) and two military casualties (on 2 June) due to Palestinian guerrilla attacks for the six-month period leading up to the June war; cf. *ARR*, 1967, and Dishon, *MER, 1967*. Eban, *Personal Witness*, p. 346, claims multiple military fatalities in early 1967, but apart perhaps from Palestinian communiqués there is no known record of them. Total Israeli civilian and military casualties on all Arab fronts by regular and irregular Arab forces for the period 1956–1967 averaged one per month (David Korn, *Stalemate*, Boulder 1992, p. 215).

33. Cockburn and Cockburn, p. 152. Rabin, pp. 115, 264–5. Ezer Weizman, *On Eagles' Wings*, New York 1979, p. 257. Cooley, p. 162. Syria 'had kept successfully out of the war, for all practical purposes'. Dayan described the fighting on the northern front on the eve of the Israeli attack as 'terrorist harassment' which was 'a nuisance but not a cause of war' (Brecher, p. 277; *ARR*, no. 11, 8 June 1967).

34. Eban, *Autobiography*, pp. 395–6.

35. Security Council Official Records, Twenty-Second Year, 9 June 1967, 1352nd

meeting. Brecher, pp. 113, 118, 104. Quandt, p. 37. Eban, *Personal Witness*, p. 389, 395. Rikhye, p. 168. *New York Times*, 4 June 1967.

36. Cockburn and Cockburn, pp. 153–4. Dishon, *MER, 1967*, p. 202; cf. p. 199, 'Yet it is generally agreed [that] Nasser was sincere when he later said that he had no intention of launching an attack against Israel; on the contrary, as he said in his 23 July speech, he believed that "any attack on Israel would expose us [the UAR] to great dangers".' Regarding Rabin's admission, one may argue that the picture changed after 14 May as Nasser moved an additional five divisions into Sinai. Yet, Nutting (p. 410) observes that they were mostly 'held in reserve up to a hundred miles from the frontier'.

37. Eban, *Autobiography*, p. 360; Eban, *Personal Witness*, pp. 383, 395. Recently published Egyptian memoirs suggest that Marshall Amr, the powerful deputy commander-in-chief of the Egyptian armed forces, did authorize at one point in late May a limited strike, but the order was almost immediately countermanded by Nasser. Quandt, p. 512, note 38, and Parker, p. 252, note 25. Quandt adds speculatively that 'the Israelis must have gotten wind of this' because they complained to the United States through Eban of an imminent Egyptian attack. Yet Eban, *Personal Witness*, p. 382, never so much as even hints at such knowledge but, rather, dismisses as 'momentous irresponsibility' the 'eccentric' and 'hypochondriac cable' given him in late May that Egypt was poised for an offensive, averring that 'there had been no new development in the military alignment'; cf. Brecher, pp. 130–2.

38. Neff, *Warriors for Jerusalem*, pp. 140, 161. Eban, *Personal Witness*, pp. 385, 389. Robert S. McNamara, *In Retrospect*, New York 1995, p. 278. George W. Ball and Douglas B. Ball, *The Passionate Attachment*, New York 1992, p. 55. Eban, *Autobiography*, p. 371. Brecher, p. 160. Trevor N. Dupuy, *Elusive Victory*, New York 1978, p. 231. (Dupuy notes that Israeli officials 'recognized something that went unnoticed by most of the rest of the world, and was not given sufficient attention even by the Arabs: they had nearly as many first-line troops as the combined Arab forces'.) Cf. Brecher, pp. 100, 143, where Yigal Allon is quoted as having 'no shadow of a doubt' that Israel would 'not only check the enemy, but obliterate him', even if it had to fight on three fronts.

39. Eban, *Personal Witness*, p. 401; cf. Eban, *Autobiography*, pp. 380f. Eric Hammel, *Six Days in June*, New York 1992, pp. 38, 285–7.

40. Cooley, p. 161. Hirst, p. 210. Eban condemned the admission by Israeli generals that Israel faced no existential danger in June 1967, not because it was false, however, but because it was 'sabotage of the moral' – i.e. propaganda – 'basis of our political position' (*ARR*, 16–30 June 1972).

41. Security Council Official Records, Twenty-Second Year, 5 June 1967, 1347th meeting. Neff, *Warriors for Jerusalem*, p. 143. Quandt, p. 39. Eban, *Autobiography*, p. 383. Brecher, p. 153.

42. Eban, *Autobiography*, pp. 352, 371. Eban, *Personal Witness*, pp. 382, 385. Dupuy, p. 241.

43. General Assembly, Fifth Emergency Special Session, 19 June 1967, 1526th meeting. Eban, *Personal Witness*, p. 374.

44. Burns, p. 146.

45. Quandt, pp. 29, 509, note 13. United Nations General Assembly, Report by the Secretary-General, 24 January 1957. Report of the Secretary-General in Pur-

suance of Resolutions I and II Adopted by the General Assembly on 2 February 1957, 8 March 1957. Burns, pp. 251–3.

46. United Nations General Assembly, Report by the Secretary-General, 24 January 1957.

47. U Thant, pp. 250, 263–5. On learning of Nasser's decision to blockade the Straits – but before Nasser agreed to the 'breathing spell' – U Thant assumed that 'war was inevitable' (p. 234). Fisher's views were first published as a letter to the *New York Times* dated 9 June 1967.

48. Sharabi, 'Prelude to War'. Sharif Bassiouni, 'Some Legal Aspects of the Arab–Israeli Conflict', in Ibrahim Abu-Lughod (ed.), *The Arab–Israeli Confrontation of June 1967*, Evanston 1970. B. Selak, 'A Consideration of the Legal Status of the Gulf of Aqaba', *American Journal of International Law*, vol. 52, 1958, p. 646. Neff, *Warriors for Jerusalem*, pp. 187–8. *New York Times*, 29 May 1967. Parker, pp. 56, 111. Quandt, p. 45. A general defense of the Egyptian position can be found in Quigley, pp. 165–7, and esp. Bassiouni. Leo Gross ('The Geneva Conference on the Law of the Sea and the Right of Innocent Passage Through the Gulf of Aqaba', *American Journal of International Law*, vol. 53, 1959) effectively makes the case for Israel.

49. Jabber, *International Documents*, p. 9. Security Council Official Records, Twenty-Second Session, 31 May 1967, 1345th meeting. Eban, *Personal Witness*, pp. 374, 415. Security Council Official Records, Twenty-Second Session, 5 June 1967, 1347th meeting. Eban, *Autobiography*, p. 331. Recalling that Israel acquired Eilat in a land-grab that flagrantly violated the original Armistice Agreements with Egypt, Morocco's UN representative quipped that 'if Israel wishes to become stronger and to breathe, let it not breathe through another's lungs' (Security Council Official Records, Twenty-Second Session, 13 June 1967, 1358th meeting).

50. Rikhye, p. 78. An *Arab Report and Record* entry for 25 May states that two German vessels had been searched while an entry for 29 May states that arriving vessels 'had not seen any Egyptian controls'. Dishon, *MER, 1967*, p. 202, reports that Egypt claimed on 29 May that it had turned away a Liberian tanker but 'the incident was later denied by foreign sources'. Apart from this disputed case, there is no report after 25 May of a commercial vessel being stopped. Cf. Brecher, pp. 139, 152. Only 2.2 per cent of ship traffic (excluding oil tankers) and 2.1 per cent of freight unloaded (excluding oil in bulk) used Eilat in 1966 (*Statistical Abstract of Israel, 1967*, p. 437). In a cable to the State Department, Yost stated that he 'cannot believe' keeping the Straits open 'is vital to Israel's existence, especially recalling that Straits were closed prior to 1957'. He recommended that 'interim arrangements' be made 'to supply Israel with oil through other ports' until the complaint could be presented to the International Court of Justice. Parker, Document 10, at pp. 238–9.

51. General Assembly, Fifth Emergency Special Session, 22 June 1967, 1531st meeting, 21 June 1967, 1530th meeting, 20 June 1967, 1529th meeting, 23 June 1967, 1533rd meeting. Neff, *Warriors for Jerusalem*, p. 317. Walzer, p. 292.

52. Security Council Official Records, Twenty-Second Session, 5 June 1967, 1347th meeting. Security Council Official Records, Twenty-Second Session, 11 June 1967, 1356th meeting. Eban, *Autobiography*, p. 403. Eban (*Personal Witness*, p. 408) writes with coy circumspection: 'The air raid sirens let out their familiar howl. ... The action to which Nasser had been goading us for three weeks had now erupted. Israel was hitting back in the air.' Israel's London ambassador admitted already on 7 June that Israel had launched a preemptive strike.

53. Randolph S. Churchill and Winston S. Churchill, *The Six-Day War*, Boston 1967, p. 78. The 'friendly commentator' phrase is from Eban, *Autobiography*, p. 373.

54. For the green light thesis, cf. Cockburn and Cockburn, ch. 6; for the yellow light thesis, cf. Quandt, ch. 2. Eban, *Personal Witness*, pp. 368–9, 381. Nutting, p. 413. Parker, p. 255, note 42. Eban, *Autobiography*, p. 383.

55. Avi Shlaim, *Collusion Across the Jordan*, New York 1988, p. 343.

56. Neff, *Warriors at Suez*, pp. 439–40, 326–8. Morris, pp. 178–9, 278–81.

57. Neff, *Warriors for Jerusalem*, p. 230. Brown, p. 131. Brecher, p. 117, reaches basically the same conclusion as Heikal, although he casts it in terms more congenial to Israel:

> Nasser had challenged the basis of Israel's security policy, the concept of deterrence – that is, the capability of the IDF to prevent encroachments upon Israel's vital interests. The announcement of the decision to close the Straits was, for example, a major escalation; in fact, it was a point of no return on the path to war.

58. Eban, *Autobiography*, pp. 383, 369. Eban, *Personal Witness*, pp. 363–5. Egyptian Foreign Minister Riad similarly observed to U Thant respecting the Straits that 'the question is of prestige with Israel as it is with us' (UN memorandum of meeting between Secretary General U Thant and UAR Foreign Minister Mahmoud Riad, 24 May 1967, Cairo, in Parker, Document 5, at p. 228; cf. Document 8, at p. 234, where Yost quotes Riad as averring that 'Israel can be otherwise supplied and the problem is not economic but purely psychological').

59. Shlaim, pp. 16, 431. Neff, *Warriors at Suez*, p 37. Brecher, p. 100. For Israel's coveting of the West Bank from the early 1950s, cf. also Morris, pp. 11–12, 401, 410–11, where it is reported that

> A strong expansionist current ran through both Zionist ideology and Israeli society. There was a general feeling, shared by such prominent figures as Dayan and Ben-Gurion, that the territorial gains of the 1948 war had fallen short of the envisioned promised land. *Bechiya Le Dorot* – literally a cause for lamentation for future generations – was how Ben-Gurion described the failure to conquer Arab Jerusalem; leading groups in Israeli society regarded the Jordanian-controlled West Bank with the same feeling.

Pronouncing Jordan 'an artificial state' with 'no future' on the eve of the Suez war, Ben-Gurion proposed that it 'must therefore be dissolved, the East Bank must be annexed by Iraq ... and the West Bank must be organized as an autonomous Arab territory linked economically to Israel while Israel manages its defence and foreign policies'.

60. Burns, p. 290. Cooley, p. 161. Kimche, p. 244.

61. Security Council Official Records, Twenty-Second Year, 1382nd meeting, 22 November 1967.

62. Security Council Official Records, Twenty-Second Year, 13 November 1967, 1373rd meeting. Eban, *Personal Witness*, p. 457. Rafael, p. 188. Eban, incidentally, is not the first modern statesman to justify the revision of borders that are 'based on military considerations alone'. Adolf Hitler similarly called for the revision of Germany's pre-World War I borders on the grounds that 'they were not the result of a considered political action, but momentary frontiers in a political struggle that was by no means concluded' (*Mein Kampf*, New York 1971, p. 649; *Hitler's Secret*

*Book*, New York 1961, p. 88). Indeed, Israel's standard 'security' claim for retaining the occupied territories breaks no new ground either. Consider Hitler's argument for redrawing Germany's boundaries: 'Germany at the present time is encircled ... lies wedged between' hostile states, with 'militarily indefensible borders'; 'Berlin, the Reich's capital, is barely 175 kilometres from the Polish border. It lies scarcely 190 kilometres from the nearest Czech border. ... This means that Berlin can be reached by modern aircraft in less than one hour from these borders'; '[W]ith the present situation of the German borders, there is only a very small area embracing a few square kilometres which could not be visited by hostile aircraft within the first hour', etc., etc. (*Hitler's Secret Book*, pp. 125–7). One may add that Hitler's remonstrances concerning Germany's borders were not without merit; cf. Max Domarus (ed.), *Hitler: Speeches and Proclamations, 1932–1945*, London 1990, vol. 1, p. 323.

63. Eban, *Autobiography*, p. 451. Eban, *Personal Witness*, p. 458; cf. p. 500 for a slightly more cautious formulation, 'According to its sponsors and supporters, [the resolution] allowed for some degree of territorial revision' (Lord Caradon et al., *United Nations Security Council Resolution 242*, Washington 1981, p. 17). Although Eban equivocates on the extent of territorial revision allegedly sanctioned by 242, he does put certain definite limits on it. He states, for instance, that 'the resolution would certainly not be compatible with the idea that Israel could abandon Sinai and, in compensation, receive legitimacy for total control of the territories and populations in the West Bank and Gaza'; and, yet more emphatically, that Menachem Begin 'was absolutely right in his interpretation of 242' in a 1970 Knesset address that it required 'renunciation of the West Bank and Gaza' – 'not all of those territories, but undoubtedly most of them' (Eban, *Personal Witness*, pp. 458, 491). It is noteworthy that Eban's fellow Cabinet minister, Moshe Dayan, did not believe that 242 allowed for *any* territorial revision. In a June 1968 Cabinet meeting, Dayan urged that Israel not endorse 242 because 'it means withdrawal to the 4 June boundaries, and because we are in conflict with the Security Council on that resolution' (Dishon, *MER, 1968*, p. 247).

64. General Assembly, Fifth Emergency Session, 5 July 1967.

65. Introduction to the Annual Report of the Secretary-General on the Work of the Organization, 16 June 1966 – 15 June 1967. General Assembly, Official Records: Twenty-Second Session. Supplement No. 1A. United Nations, 15 September 1967. Para. 47; cf. para. 49, 'it is indispensable to an international community of States – if it is not to follow the law of the jungle – that the territorial integrity of every state be respected, and the occupation by military force of the territory of one State by another not be condoned.'

66. Eban, *Autobiography*, p. 440; cf. Eban, *Personal Witness*, p. 439.

67. Security Council Official Records, Twenty-Second Session, 20 November 1967, 1381st meeting. Brown's words were quoted from his speech at the Twenty-Second Session of the General Assembly, Plenary Meetings, 26 September 1967, 1567th meeting. At the Fifth Emergency Special Session, the British Foreign Secretary stated even more emphatically: 'I see no two ways about this; and I can state our position very clearly. In my view, it follows from the words of the Charter that war should not lead to territorial aggrandizement.'

68. Security Council Official Records, Twenty-Second Session, 22 November 1967, 1382nd meeting.

69. Caradon et al. Caradon specifically pointed to the 'annexation of East Jerusalem' and 'the creeping colonisation on the West Bank and in Gaza and the Golan' as 'in clear defiance' of (also: 'in direct contradiction' to) Resolution 242, and 'constituting an open rejection of the policy so widely supported in 1967'.

70. The most exhaustive study of the US approach to 242 is a still-classified State Department document entitled, 'The Withdrawal Clause in UN Security Council Resolution 242 of 1967', by Nina J. Noring and Walter B. Smith II. Unless otherwise indicated, I will be quoting from this study. The official US position in the immediate aftermath of the June war was for a full Israeli withdrawal to the pre-5 June borders; cf. DAG – 1/5.2.2.1.2, E9 (UN Archives).

71. Recall that Eban attributed the 'inadmissibility' principle to 'Latin American pressure'. Yet, even the Soviet–US draft resolution, which had no outside input, contained the identical wording. Eban's objections to the latter resolution are particularly unpersuasive. He pretends that issues other than its call for Israel's total withdrawal were at stake. For example, he feigns shock that 'even the fatal word, "Israel", did not appear in this draft, so that the Arab states would have no difficulty in making a general statement and then claiming its nonapplicability to Israel'. It is true that the Soviet–US resolution referred generally to the rights of 'all member states of the UN in the area' to peace and security. For Eban, Arab recognition of this last phrase would have constituted a 'meaningless historical gesture'. Yet, 242 also does not refer to Israel directly, speaking in even more general terms of the rights of 'every State in the area' and elsewhere of 'Member States'. Eban, however, heaped praise on 242 because it 'sanctified Israel's right, *as one of the states in the area*, to live in peace, secure from the threat or use of force'. Eban has also written that 242 'is quite explicit' in its recognition of Israel since 'the references to "member states" and "every state in the region" in a UN document leads inexorably to a booklet with a list of names of states'. What Eban evidently objected to in the Soviet–US draft – what made his 'concern leap to an astronomical height' – was not the generalized reference to Israel but its call on 'all parties to the conflict' to withdraw in accordance with that 'ominous' principle. (Eban, *Autobiography*, p. 443; Eban, *Personal Witness*, pp. 453–4, 457, my emphasis; Eban, *Jerusalem Post*, 3 December 1988.) The Arab states at first rejected the superpower draft; the Soviet Union accordingly dropped it, although still maintaining that it was 'sensible and should be pursued'. By late September, however, Egypt had come around, informing U Thant that it 'would now go along' with it (DAG – 1/5.2.2.1.2, Appendix 3, Box 3, E28, E37, E39) (UN Archives).

72. Donald Neff, 'The Differing Interpretations of Resolution 242', *Middle East International*, 13 September 1991. Rusk, p. 389; cf. p. 388, where Rusk deems Eban's embrace of territorial revision after Israel had committed itself on the first day of the war to no territorial ambitions a 'contentious and ever bitter point with the Americans'. (Rusk describes as 'equally authentic' the French version of 242, which includes the definite article.) Eban, *Autobiography*, p. 450; cf. Eban, *Personal Witness*, p. 458, where it is purported that 'only later under the Nixon administration' did the 'U.S. become accustomed to recommending the formula "minor changes"'. Henry Kissinger (*White House Years*, Boston 1979, p. 345), acknowledges that, to win King Hussein's support for 242, Goldberg promised that 'we would work for the return of the West Bank to Jordan with minor border rectifications and that we are prepared to use our influence to obtain a role for Jordan

in Jerusalem'. On US resistance to including the definite article, despite Soviet and British entreaties, cf. Rafael, pp. 188–9. Neff, *Warriors for Jerusalem*, pp. 334, 337–8, 405 confirms that all the US negotiators at the time (including Eugene Rostow) assumed that border changes would be at most 'minor' and 'reciprocal'. There is simply no evidence – indeed, all the evidence points to the contrary conclusion – that the United States dramatically altered its position on territorial revision between mid-summer and November 1967, as Korn (pp. 33–4) alleges. In fact, Korn himself makes the point that, just as the Johnson Administration was ending its term, the Israeli government was informed that the United States interpreted 242 to mean 'only very minor border changes, and any changes that did take place were not to reflect the weight of conquest' (pp. 73–4). Revealingly, Israel only discovered after the war that its pre-June 1967 borders constituted 'Auschwitz lines' (the phrase, incidentally, belongs *not* to Likud leader Benjamin Netanyahu but to the 'dovish' Eban; cf. Tom Segev, *The Seventh Million*, New York 1993, p. 393). Until the territorial conquests of the June war, Israel viewed its security requirements as fully compatible with 'minor frontier corrections by mutual agreement' (Ben-Gurion) – the exact language of the consensus interpretation of 242 rejected by Israel on security grounds (Burns, pp. 29, 124).

73. Eban, *Autobiography*, p. 21. Gershon Avner, who headed the Western Europe Department of the Israeli Foreign Ministry, was given to lament that Zionist diplomats 'always pushed to lie, to deceive, to resort to tricks ... , to lie ... even if it was unnecessary and brought no advantage'. Eban's memoirs recall to mind this propensity. For instance, the Nazis' crimes loom so large that any exaggeration is gratuitous. Yet, to invoke the horror of that era, Eban conjures up the apocrypha that a Jew's bones were 'crushed and melted down to make soap'. (Avner cited in Shlaim, p. 445; Eban, *Personal Witness*, p. 60; for the soap myth, cf. Raul Hilberg, *The Destruction of the European Jews*, New York 1985, vol. 3, p. 955.)

## Chapter 6

1. Daniel Dishon (ed.), *Middle East Record* (hereafter *MER*), *1969–70*, Tel Aviv 1971–7, pp. 169–70. Chaim Herzog, *The War of Atonement*, Boston 1975, p. 290.

2. The quoted phrases are, respectively, from Abba Eban, *An Autobiography*, New York 1977, p. 453; Shimon Shamir, 'Israeli Views of Egypt and the Peace Process', in William Quandt (ed.), *The Middle East*, Washington 1988, pp. 187–8; Abba Eban, *Personal Witness*, New York 1992, pp. 471, 589, 590, 492; Amnon Kapeliouk, *Israël: la fin des mythes*, Paris 1975, pp. 198–200; Ezer Weizman, *The Battle for Peace*, New York 1981, p. 81; Herzog, p. 290; Avraham Tamir, *A Soldier in Search of Peace*, New York 1988, pp. 203, 59; Moshe Dayan, *Breakthrough*, New York 1981, p. 284; Lawrence Whetten, *The Canal War*, Cambridge 1974, p. 330; Moshe Dayan, *Story of My Life*, New York 1976, p. 609; Gideon Rafael, *Destination Peace*, New York 1981 (title). Ze'ev Schiff, in *October Earthquake*, Tel Aviv 1974, p. 76, encapsulates Israel's strategic philosophy as 'Arabs only understand and respect the language of force'; for many examples culled from Israel's press and scholarship, cf. Kapeliouk's highly critical study of Israeli state policy prior to the 1973 war, pp. 198–200.

3. Neither a full withdrawal nor a peace treaty was explicitly spelled out in

Resolution 242, but both were clearly implied in the first preambular paragraph, which 'emphasiz[ed] the inadmissibility of the acquisition of territory by war and the need to work for a just and lasting peace in which every State in the area can live in security'. For the consensus interpretation favoring full Israeli withdrawal, cf. Chap. 5, pp. 144f. above. According to U Thant (*A View from the U.N.*, Garden City 1978, p. 336), the Soviet Union first accepted in mid-1970 the principle that the Arab states must sign a peace treaty in exchange for Israel's withdrawal; cf. Dishon, *MER, 1969–70*, p. 64. When Israel objected to Jarring's February 1971 proposal (see p. 157f. above) on the grounds that it set Israel's full withdrawal from Egypt as a 'precondition', Jarring pointedly observed that 'Israel had established its own precondition in talks with him, that peace should be established with Egypt by means of a binding contractual treaty. They had now had such an assurance and if they wished further progress they would have to pay for it by agreeing to withdrawal' ('Notes on a meeting with Sir Alec Douglas-Hume, Secretary of State for Foreign Affairs of the United Kingdom, 27 September 1971', in DAG – 1/5.2.2.1.2, Box 1, Envelope 3, Q18 [UN Archives]). In addition to a peace treaty, Israel had also demanded 'direct negotiations' with the Arab states. (Dishon, *MER, 1967*, pp. 274–5; cf. also Eban's gloss on the February 1971 Jarring initiative in Whetten, pp. 148, 174–5, that 'peace was never achieved by indirect proceedings' and only 'direct talks can rescue the Jarring mission'.) This 'precondition', however, was rejected by U Thant as both not called for by 242 and also 'unrealistic' (*Arab Report and Record* [hereafter *ARR*], 1–15 September 1969). Indeed, as Eban (*Personal Witness*, p. 592) forcefully observes, 'direct talks' figured barely at all in the negotiations that finally culminated in the Israeli–Egyptian treaty signed at Camp David; cf. William Quandt, *Camp David*, Washington 1986, p. 257. For Egypt's objection to 'direct talks' with Israel 'not because we simply chose to ignore its existence, but rather because … all such negotiations would necessarily be conditioned by the pressure and intimidation of actual military occupation', cf. Mahmoud Riad, *The Struggle for Peace in the Middle East*, New York 1981, p. 78. For Israel's insistence on direct negotiations as 'represent[ing] the defiant stand of a victor, not the pliable position of reconciliation its leadership often professed', cf. Whetten, p. 303.

4. For the 19 June cabinet proposal, cf. Yitzak Rabin, *The Rabin Memoirs*, New York 1979, p. 135, Eban, *Personal Witness*, p. 437, and Shimon Shamir, 'Nasser and Sadat, 1967–1973', in Itamar Rabinowich and Haim Shaked (eds), *From June to October*, New Jersey 1978, p. 216, note 8 (extensively quoting the proposal). Eban, *Personal Witness*, p. 451, describes the 19 June Cabinet proposal as 'non-annexationist', although its silence on an eventual withdrawal from the West Bank and Gaza was clearly not accidental, as Rabin (pp. 160–1) rightly observes, noting that 'never, in any of its decisions, has the Israeli government consented to withdraw from the West Bank'. (Gaza, incidentally, was referred to in the 19 June proposal as 'within the territory of the State of Israel'.) Dishon, *MER, 1967*, p. 275. 'Goldberg with U Thant, 22 June 1967', in DAG – 1/5.2.2.1.2, Box 3, E8 (UN Archives). Later that year in private talks with U Thant, Eban disingenuously represented Israel as possibly yet more flexible, suggesting that it was prepared to withdraw not only from Sinai and the Golan ('although in some places some frontier adjustment might be indicated'), but also perhaps – the formulation is highly ambiguous – from the West Bank as well, so long as all the evacuated areas were demilitarized ('Notes of meeting held in the Secretary-General's Office, 29 September 1967', in

DAG – 1/5.2.2.1.2, Box 3, E39 [UN Archives]). In yet another exchange of views at the United Nations, Eban was more firm that 'Israel will seek ... some territorial adjustments, particularly on the Syrian front and in Gaza' ('Notes of meeting held in the Secretary-General's Office on 30 October 1967', in DAG – 1/5.2.2.1.2, Box 3, E47 [UN Archives]).

5. Rabin, pp. 136, 159; cf. David Korn, *Stalemate*, Boulder 1992, p. 86, which also ascribes Israel's hardened stance to Khartoum (also Eban, *Personal Witness*, p. 446). Odd Bull, *War and Peace in the Middle East*, London 1973, p. 126; cf. Jon Kimche, *There Could Have Been Peace*, New York 1973, p. 262, confirming Israel's intransigence on the territorial issue 'even before the Prime Minister had been enabled to read the verbatim text of the discussions ... at Khartoum' (also Mohamed Heikal, *The Sphinx and the Commissar*, London 1978, p. 191).

6. Dishon, *MER, 1968*, pp. 122, 242–52 (cf. p. 250 for the background to the Allon Plan, first circulated in July 1967). *MER* notes parenthetically that 'Israeli leaders preferred to avoid the term "annexation" because of its historical connotations' (p. 252). Only the pre-1948 population of Gaza was to be granted citizenship once it was annexed, the 1948 refugees slated for removal to El Arish and the non-annexed areas of the West Bank (p. 252). *ARR*, 1–15 October 1968. 'Summary of Foreign Minister Eban's Remarks to Ambassador Jarring, October 15, 1968' (confidential), in DAG 1/5.2.2.1.2, Box 3, N8 (UN Archives). Korn, pp. 72, 130, 68. Eban, *Personal Witness*, p. 473. Eban effectively concedes that the real purpose of the 'moderate' nine-point peace plan was to 'encourage President Johnson to carry out promises that he had made ... concerning the supply of Phantom aircraft'. Yehuda Lukacs (ed.), *The Israeli–Palestinian Conflict: A Documentary Record*, Cambridge 1992, p. 178. U Thant, p. 282. For the background to Israel's acceptance of 242, cf. Rafael, ch. 21. Although Israel refused to officially specify the border changes it intended on the grounds that 'these cannot be presented until negotiations with the Arab countries concerned have come into effect', they were pretty much known by the main interlocutors; cf. Jarring's memorandum of 22 April 1968, 'P.M. on "Secure Boundaries"' (strictly confidential), in DAG – 1/5.2.2.1.2, Box 1, Envelope 3, N4 (UN Archives), but cf. also Jarring's memorandum of 1 August 1968, 'Provisions of the Resolution' (secret), in DAG – 1/5.2.2.1.2, Box 1, Envelope 3, N7 (UN Archives), which wrongly speculates that Israel was perhaps not firmly wedded to remaining in Sinai. For the frustration of U Thant and Jarring with Israel's refusal to explicitly state its position 'on the substance, that is, what does Israel mean by "secure boundaries"', cf. 'Notes on Meeting held in the Secretary-General's Office on 5 October 1968', in DAG -1/5.2.2.1.2, Box 3, F26 (UN Archives). For Jarring's analysis of the Israeli position as juxtaposed to the Egyptian one, cf. 'Report: Teheran, 22 April 1968' (strictly confidential), in DAG – 1/5.2.2.1.2, Box 1, Envelope 3, N2 (UN Archives), and the above-cited 'Provisions of the Resolution'. Jarring's nonpartisan conclusion was that 'with the firm attitudes taken by Israel and the UAR there seems to be no possibility for breaking the deadlock without their announcing substantial changes in their positions'. I return to the Egyptian position below.

7. *Security Council Official Records*, S/10070, Annex I. *ARR*, 1–15 June 1969. Michael Brecher, *Decisions in Israel's Foreign Policy*, New Haven 1975, pp. 460, 462. Dishon, *MER, 1969–70*, p. 114. Korn, p. 141. Michael Brecher, *Decisions in Crisis*, Berkeley 1980, p. 70. Kapeliouk, p. 17.

8. *New York Times*, 10 December 1969 (Rogers Plan; for an earlier, slightly different, version, cf. William Quandt, *Peace Process*, Berkeley 1993, pp. 437–40). Brecher, *Decisions in Israel's Foreign Policy*, pp. 481–6. Korn, p. 161. Rabin, p. 158. Rafael, pp. 210–11. Whetten, p. 88. For a detailed exposition of the Rogers Plan and the reaction to it, cf. *MER, 1969–70*, pp. 30–42, and Brecher, *Decisions in Israel's Foreign Policy*, ch. 8. Eban (*Autobiography*, p. 464) excoriates the Rogers Plan as 'one of the major errors of international diplomacy in the postwar era'. Eban, *Personal Witness*, p. 478, falsely claims that the plan called on Israel to make an 'important concession' (i.e. withdrawal) 'before Egypt had accepted the obligation to make peace with Israel'. As noted, the terms were mutually conditional. Rogers remained committed to the same basic formula throughout his tenure; cf. the 'Fundamental Principles' (top secret) presented by him to Jarring in September 1970, calling for a 'final and reciprocally binding accord' to be 'deposit[ed] with the UN' in which 'Israel would agree that the former international boundary between Egypt and the mandated territory of Palestine is not excluded as the secure and recognized boundary between Israel and the UAR', in DAG – 1/5.2.2.1.2, Box 1, Envelope 3, P10 (UN Archives). For Rogers's support of Jarring's comparable February 1971 initiative, see pp. 162f. above.

9. Brecher, *Decisions in Israel's Foreign Policy*, pp. 487–500. Dishon, *MER, 1969–70*, p. 77. *ARR*, 15–28 February 1970. The new Rogers proposal called for an 'Israeli withdrawal from territories occupied in the 1967 conflict', whereas the Cabinet's carefully crafted acceptance spoke of 'withdrawal of Israeli armed forces from territories occupied in the 1967 conflict *to secure, recognized and agreed boundaries to be determined in the peace agreements*' (my emphasis). The phrase 'secured and recognized boundaries' from 242 was often invoked by Israel to justify less than a full withdrawal. 'Agreed boundaries to be determined in the peace agreements', not in 242, was evidently included in Israel's reply with the same intent.

10. *ARR*, 16–31 August 1967, 1–15 September 1967, 1–15 November 1967. Lukacs, pp. 454–5 (Khartoum resolutions). Dishon, *MER, 1967*, pp. 256–67, 272. Jordan and Egypt subsequently maintained that Khartoum enjoined a 'peace treaty', not 'peace', with Israel; cf. DAG – 1/5.2.2.1.2, Box 3, E38 (UN Archives), and Dishon, *MER, 1967*, p. 269. DAG – 1/5.2.2.1.2, Box 3, E38 (UN Archives) (Egypt–Jordan agreement to Tito plan). For proposals similar to the Tito plan mooted by Jordan and Egypt in 1967, cf. Dishon, *MER, 1967*, pp. 266–7.

11. Dishon, *MER, 1968*, pp. 205, 209. 'Report: Teheran, 22 April 1968' (strictly confidential), in DAG – 1/5.2.2.1.2, Box 1, Envelope 3, N2 (UN Archives). 'From Ambassador Jarring, 1 August 1968, *Provisions of the Resolution*' (secret), in DAG – 1/5.2.2.1.2, Box 1 (?), N7 (UN Archives). Riad, p. 90. Regarding Egypt's views on other aspects of 242, Jarring reported that 'recognition that the Gaza Strip is not UAR territory ... no negative reaction to UN administration ... but no question of ceding [it] to Israel'. This was pretty much Israel's private view also as late as November 1968, Eban informing U Thant that his government considered Gaza to be in the Egyptian 'sector' but that Egypt 'should not return to Gaza, which should be left to the people of Gaza' ('Notes on Meeting in the Secretary-General's Office, 9 November 1968', in DAG – 1/5.2.2.1.2, Box 3, F31 [UN Archives]); cf. also 'Highlights of Ambassador Jarring's Report, 2 March 1968' (top secret), in DAG – 1/5.2.2.1.2, Box 3, F2 (UN Archives), where Jarring speculates that 'Gaza will not be returned to the UAR by Israel. There is a possibility that the

area will be placed under United Nations administration for some time'. Regarding the Egyptian position on the 1948 Palestinian refugees, Jarring reported that 'general indications that the most important aspect of the refugee question would not be repatriation, but compensation and rehabilitation'. A late December Soviet peace plan called only for a 'symbolic' return of a small number, the rest to receive financial compensation (*ARR*, 1–15 January 1969); cf. 'Highlights of Ambassador Jarring's Report, 2 March 1968' (top secret), in DAG – 1/5.2.2.1.2, Box 3, F2 (UN Archives), where Jarring reports that 'Jordan will be prepared to absorb most of the refugees in its territory'. Jarring drew up in August 1968 a 'Summary Statement of a Broad Estimate of Economic Costs of a Solution of the Arab Refugee Problem' (strictly confidential), estimating that the 'total net investment needed ... US $1.5 to US $2 billions', and that 'the back of the refugee problem should be broken within five years' (DAG – 1/5.2.2.1.2, Box 1, Envelope 3) (UN Archives). Jordan responded more or less as Egypt to Jarring's inquiries, adding that it would 'accept boundary rectifications' (the principle of 'minor border adjustments ... in a reciprocal way' was publicly agreed to in January 1969 [*ARR*, 1–15 January 1969]). Egypt publicly embraced 242 in March 1968, and the 'package deal' in October (Dishon, *MER, 1968*, pp. 213–14, *ARR*, 1–15 October 1968).

12. S/10070, Annex I. Dishon, *MER, 1969–70*, p. 15, quotes the *New York Times* to the effect that 'Israeli sources said the Arab answers to the questionnaire had taken an extreme position in referring to the 1947 partition lines as a basis for a settlement'. As seen above, this is at best a half-truth. Indeed, any ambiguity in the Arab position was removed in April 1969 with Hussein's 'six-point' peace plan, referring only to the June 1967 borders; see below.

13. For Hussein plan, cf. *ARR*, 1–15 April 1969, and Dishon, *MER, 1969–70*, p. 15. Regarding Hussein's proposal, U Thant (pp. 320–1) reports that 'Israel *for the first time* was offered an explicit public pledge of free navigation through the Suez Canal' (emphasis in original). For a 'five-point' Nasser initiative – 'declaration of non-belligerence', 'respect for the territorial integrity of all countries in the Middle East, including Israel, in recognized and secure borders', etc. – immediately condemned by Eban as a 'plan to liquidate Israel', cf. *Newsweek*, 10 February 1969, and *ARR*, 1–14 February 1969.

14. Quandt, *Peace Process*, pp. 81–3. Riad, pp. 110–11, 114. U Thant, p. 329. Egypt *unofficially* denounced the Rogers Plan from the outset as an unprincipled separate deal (*ARR*, 1–15 November, 16–30 November, 1–15 December 1969, and Mohamed Heikal, *The Road to Ramadan*, New York 1975, p. 91). For Egypt's subsequent statements on the Rogers plan, cf. *ARR*, 1–14 February 1970, and Korn, pp. 163–4.

15. Eban, *Personal Witness*, p. 484. *Le Monde*, 19 February 1970. Korn, pp. 240–1.

16. 'Comparison of the Papers of Israel and the United Arab Republic', in DAG – 1/5.2.2.1.2, Box 1, Envelope 3, Q2 (UN Archives). *ARR*, 16–31 January 1971.

17. William Quandt, *Decade of Decisions*, Berkeley 1977, p. 134; Quandt, *Peace Process*, p. 121. For a detailed account of the Jarring mission, cf. 'Report by the Secretary-General on the Activities of the Special Representative to the Middle East, 4 January 1971' (S/10070), and the updated 'Report of the Secretary-General under Security Council resolution 331, 18 May 1973' (S/10929). For the early phases of the Jarring mission, cf. also Dishon, *MER*, 1968, pp. 119–32. For the Jarring *aide-mémoire* submitted to Egypt and Israel, and their respective replies, cf.

'Report of the Secretary-General on the activities of the Special Representative to the Middle East, 30 November 1971' (A/8541 – S/10403).

18. Rafael, pp. 231, 256. The American minister in Cairo, David Bergus, was reportedly 'elated', commenting that 'here are the magic words' (Riad, p. 188).

19. Kapeliouk, p. 282, note 77. *Policy Background: The Components of a Secure Peace*, 10 March 1971, Embassy of Israel, Washington, DC (mimeo.) (UN Archives). Asked to comment on the sincerity of Egyptian peace overtures, Meir told an Israeli newspaper in late January: 'There is no sign which allows us to believe that the Egyptians take the Jarring negotiations seriously.' In an early February interview, Meir suggested that the test of Egypt's sincerity would be its willingness to sign a peace treaty (*ARR*, 16–31 January 1971, 1–14 February 1971). For background to Israel's reply to Jarring on the question of withdrawal, cf. Rafael, pp. 256–7. Decrying that Jarring had 'proposed certain territorial arrangements', Israel's UN representative, Yosef Tekoah, informed U Thant at an early February meeting that 'Israel regretted the submission of the aide-mémoire' and that 'it was impossible to proceed with the Jarring negotiations in such a manner' ('Notes on Meeting between Secretary-General and Mr. Yosef Tekoah, Permanent Representative of Israel to United Nations, 11 February 1971', in Middle East, 1970 [sic], H12 [UN Archives]). Deeming the call for withdrawal 'arbitrarily determin[ed]', the official March statement harshly declared that

> the authority of the UN Secretary General is defined by the United Nations Charter. It does not include the right to determine Israel's future boundary. It is not the UN Secretary General who will have to live with Egypt once these boundaries, whatever they are, are delineated.

The document also desperately sought to downplay the significance of Egypt's gesture, alleging that its 'acceptance of an invitation to "enter into a peace agreement with Israel"' was a 'tactical ploy' to 'drive a wedge between Israel and the United States', as well as a 'semantic' one that presented 'the term "peace agreement" as though it were an unprecedented concession', and that 'but for the expression of willingness to enter into a peace agreement, ... Egypt's position has not changed one iota from its traditional posture'. For Israel's opposition to the Jarring initiative on account of its call for full withdrawal, cf. also 'Notes on a Meeting with the Minister for Foreign Affairs of Israel, held in the Secretary-General's Office on Friday, 1 October 1971', in DAG – 1/5.2.2.1.2, Box 1, Envelope 3, Q18 and Q19 (UN Archives).

20. 'Further Report by the Secretary-General on the Activities of the Special Representative to the Middle East, 5 March 1971', para. 15 (S/10070/Add. 2). 'Introduction to the Report of the Secretary-General on the Work of the Organization, September 1971', in General Assembly Records: Twenty-Sixth Session, Supplement No. 1A (A/8401/Add. 1), paras 219, 221; cf. para. 223: 'Ambassador Jarring has clearly defined the minimum conditions that are required to move the peace talks ahead and, until those conditions are met, it is hard to see what else he can do to further his efforts.' In his memoir, U Thant similarly recalled:

> It was clear from the two replies that the U.A.R., for the first time in twenty-three years, officially committed itself to enter into a peace agreement with Israel, while Israel explicitly stated that it would not withdraw to the pre-June 1967 lines. Thus, Mr. Jarring was faced with a difficult dilemma. He had asked

the two governments to make parallel and simultaneous commitments. The U.A.R. said that it would, Israel said that it would not. (Thant, p. 347)

21. 'Implementation of Security Council Resolution 242 (1967) of 22 November 1967 For the Establishment of a Just and Lasting Peace in the Middle East, 11 February 1971', in DAG – 1/5.2.2.1.2, Box 1, Envelope 3, Q4 (UN Archives). *ARR*, 15–28 February 1971. For Jordan's consent to a peace treaty with Israel, cf. also the United Kingdom's intervention at the Security Council, 11 June 1973, where it is noted regarding Egypt's reply to Jarring's *aide-mémoire* that 'Jordan too has given an analogous undertaking' (S/PV.1721). Jordan repeatedly expressed its acceptance of 'minor and reciprocal border rectifications with Israel'; cf. *ARR*, 16–30 April 1971, and note 11 above. Jarring reported in March 1971 that Syria too had accepted the principle of 'minor rectifications' (and apparently the stationing of a UN force in the Golan) (DAG – 1/5.2.2.1.2, Box 1, Envelope 3, Q9 [UN Archives]). Yet, former president Carter writes in his memoir that Sadat's agreement at Camp David to 'some minimal deviation from the 1967 borders' was 'an important concession and, so far as I knew, unprecedented for an Arab leader' (Jimmy Carter, *Keeping Faith*, New York 1982, p. 283). Throughout 1972 and early 1973, Hussein made yet further concessions to reach an accord with Israel. Retreating from the demand for 'total recognition' of Jordan's rights to Jerusalem, Hussein proposed in March 1972 that Jerusalem become the 'capital of Israel and the capital of the Palestinian portion of Jordan. There is no reason why they cannot exist together' (*ARR*, 16–31 March 1972). Kissinger reports in his memoir that Jordan had directly offered Israel a peace treaty, border changes, as well as Israeli military outposts, even settlements, along the Jordan River (Henry Kissinger, *Years of Upheaval*, Boston 1982, pp. 219–20; cf. *ARR*, 16–31 March 1972, for indirect confirmation). Kapeliouk observes that Jordan's 'moderate policy' on the eve of the October war had 'no impact': 'Hussein proclaimed a desire for a separate peace with Israel, even at the cost of certain border modifications, but these proposals were completely rejected by Israel.' The government's duplicity was condemned in media commentary, the Labor Party weekly, *Ot*, editorializing that 'we demand of Hussein an unconditional surrender', and *Haaretz* that 'Israeli pretensions with regard to Hussein are hypocritical' (Kapeliouk, p. 64). Indeed, by March 1972, even Syria had announced its acceptance – albeit less compellingly – of 242 'when it is interpreted as providing for the withdrawal of the enemy from Arab territory occupied in 1967, and as a confirmation, assertion and realisation of the rights of the Palestinians' (*ARR*, 1–15 March, 1972; for details, cf. Khouri, 'United Nations Peace Efforts', in Malcolm Kerr [ed.], *The Elusive Peace*, Albany 1975, p. 79; Rabinowich, 'Continuity and Change in the Ba'th Regime in Syria', in Rabinowich and Shaked, p. 44). More generally, cf. Ambassador Yost's article in *Life* magazine, 9 April 1971, under the prophetic title 'Last Chance for Peace in the Mideast', reporting that Egypt and Jordan 'have in fact been ready for a year and a half' to enter into a 'binding peace containing firm reciprocal commitments'.

22. Quandt, *Peace Process*, p. 122. Indeed, for all that has been written on the 'peace process', apparently no previous researcher has ever even consulted the extensive file on the Jarring mission in the UN Archives.

23. Golda Meir, *My Life*, New York 1975, p. 398. *The Times* (London), 13 March 1971. Dayan, *Story of My Life*, pp. 453–4. *ARR*, 15–28 February 1971. Kimche, p. 305. Saadia Touval, *The Peace Brokers*, Princeton 1982, p. 137; cf. pp. 160, 163,

where the failure of the Jarring initiative is attributed, not to Israel, but to 'the incompatibility of the parties' positions and the firmness with which they held them', and also 'the structure of the conflict, which had come to overlap in part with the East–West struggle'. Eban, *Personal Witness*, p. 557. Herzog, p. 19. Whetten, p. 175; cf. p. 310, where the Arabs are taken to task for failing before the October war to 'demonstrate[ ] ... the will to make peace'. Shamir, 'Nasser and Sadat, 1967–1973', in Rabinowich and Shaked, pp. 195–6. Seth P. Tillman, *The United States in the Middle East*, Bloomington 1982, pp. 22–3 (emphasis added). Mark Tessler, *A History of the Israeli–Palestinian Conflict*, Bloomington 1994, p. 817, n. 30. More generally, cf. Carter, p. 276, which reports that before Camp David 'none of the Arab states was willing officially to acknowledge Israel's status as a nation or even its right to exist'.

24. United Nations General Assembly, Twenty-Sixth Session, Official Records, 1971 Plenary Meetings, 2000th Meeting, 6 December 1971, para. 89; cf. para. 99: 'how monstrous it is for the international atmosphere to be filled with the myth that Egypt had replied more affirmatively to Dr. Jarring's aide-memoire than had Israel'. Eban, *Personal Witness*, p. 499. Eban's 1992 assessment of the Jarring initiative appears under the chapter heading 'Could There Have Been Peace?' The only significant addition (apart from updating) to his 1977 memoir, the chapter is plainly a response to Kimche's study, *There Could Have Been Peace*, which had concluded that the February proposal 'opened [the door] sufficiently for a switch from political warfare to serious probing questions and discussions between Egypt and Israel with Dr. Jarring acting as go-between. But that was not how the matter was seen in Jerusalem'. Underlining the Labor government's reply that it 'will not withdraw', Kimche further observed that 'the Israelis seemed to be scaling up their demands as the Egyptians were inclined to scale theirs down' (pp. 300–2). Scrupulously silent in the first memoir on Egypt's consent to sign a peace treaty with Israel, Eban ascribed responsibility for the February initiative's failure to the Arabs ('While they were clear about what Israel should do about withdrawal, the Arab governments were not specific about what they would do in the direction of peace. ... The Jarring Mission thus came to a permanent end') and Jarring himself ('Dr. Jarring's mission had been paralyzed since his February 1971 memorandum, in which he had endorsed Egypt's territorial claims – and thereby lost Israel's confidence') (*Autobiography*, pp. 471, 486). In his more recent memoir, Eban puts the blame on the 'U.N.'s unique fantasy world' as well as Israel's principal interlocutors – 'If there was an embryo of peace in the 1971 exchanges, Jarring and the United States are mainly responsible for the miscarriage' (*Personal Witness*, pp. 501, 502).

25. 'Comparison Between the Commitments Requested in Ambassador Jarring's Aide-Mémoire of 8 February 1971 and the United Arab Republic Aide-Mémoire of 15 February 1971', in DAG – 1/5.2.2.1.2, Box 1, Envelope 3, Q6 (United Nations Archive). *ARR*, 15–28 February 1971. Riad, p. 214; cf. p. 189 for a more evasive formulation regarding the separate peace. The opening paragraph of the 'Framework for Peace in the Middle East Agreed at Camp David' states that the signatories invite 'other parties to the Arab–Israeli conflict to adhere to it', and the first main section ('Framework') begins that 'this framework as appropriate is intended ... to constitute a basis for peace not only between Egypt and Israel, but also between Israel and each of its neighbors which is prepared to negotiate peace

with Israel on this basis'. The preamble to the Egyptian–Israeli peace treaty reads that the 'framework as appropriate is intended to constitute a basis for peace not only between Egypt and Israel but also between Israel and each of its other Arab neighbors which is prepared to negotiate peace with it on this basis', and that the 'Treaty of Peace between Egypt and Israel is an important step in the search for comprehensive peace in the area and for the attainment of the settlement of the Arab–Israeli conflict in all its aspects'. Eban, *Personal Witness*, pp. 502–3; cf. Eban's intervention in the United Nations General Assembly, 26th Session, Official Records, 1971 Plenum Meetings, 2000th Meeting, 6 December 1971, para. 98. Rabin 'concede[s]' that Egypt's willingness to 'enter into a peace agreement with Israel' was a 'milestone', but then qualifies that the 'entire document bore Sadat's evasive imprint' as it also called for an Israeli withdrawal 'on all the other fronts as well'. Less categorical than Eban, Rabin leaves open whether 'there was a conditional link between the two sections of the answer or not' – as if Israel could not have put Sadat to the test if there were any genuine doubts on this score. Rabin further maintains that the real breakthrough ('political coup') of Sadat's 1977 Knesset speech was that he was 'prepared to make peace with [Israel] without waiting for the other Arab states to agree. ... [I]t was clear, without his spelling it out, that if the other Arabs rejected his terms for peace, Sadat would go it alone' (pp. 192–3, 323). Note that in the Knesset speech, Sadat repeatedly 'insisted' that he did not 'come here for a separate agreement between Egypt and Israel', that Israel must effect a 'complete withdrawal from the Arab territories occupied in 1967 ... including Arab Jerusalem', etc. Yet *then* it was 'clear' that Sadat 'would go it alone', but in 1971 it was not... Cf. also Dayan, *Story of My Life*, pp. 453–4, which reports Egypt's reply to Jarring as Israel must 'withdraw not only from Egyptian territory but also from the Gaza Strip and the rest of the Arab lands, retiring to the pre-war borders', and the authoritative Israeli government statement, *Policy Background: The Components of a Secure Peace*, 1971, Embassy of Israel, Washington, DC (mimeo.) (UN Archives), which reports it as 'Israel is required to carry out a total withdrawal from Sinai and the Gaza Strip, indeed from all the territories on every front'. Touval's 'standard work on mediation in the Middle East' (Eban) somewhat overstates that Egypt's 'readiness to conclude a peace agreement was conditional upon Israel committing itself to withdraw not only from Sinai but also from the Gaza strip (which Jarring had not requested)' – compare Jarring's more tentative formulation of Egypt's view regarding Gaza cited above – but does not pretend that Egypt was demanding a full withdrawal on all fronts (Touval, pp. 157–8). Not technically Egyptian territory, Gaza was excluded from Jarring's aide-mémoire. (Gaza had been placed under Egyptian administration in the 1949 armistice agreement pending the conclusion of a peace settlement.) The omission, however, was apparently without prejudice to Gaza as an Arab territory occupied by Israel that should eventually be de-occupied (cf. Egypt's intervention in S/PV.1721, 11 June 1973, and the Secretary-General's reply in S/PV.1725, 14 June 1973). Eban demurs that Jarring's view that 'Gaza should be restored to Arab rule and not left in Israeli hands' gave 'full endorsement' to the 'Arab territorial claims' (Eban, *Personal Witness*, p. 500). Yet Eban himself had earlier upheld the identical position; cf. note 11 above. One may further note that Eban interprets the Camp David Accords as meaning that Gaza was an 'area of indeterminate status unconnected to the sovereign territory of Israel', and that Israel had 'virtually signed' Gaza 'away' (Eban, *Personal Witness*, p.

600). The 1979 Egyptian–Israel treaty states simply that the Israeli withdrawal from Sinai would be 'without prejudice to the issue of the status of the Gaza Strip'.

26. I leave to one side Eban's more vacuous 'arguments' – e.g. 'The fact that Israel would seek some territorial revision was well known', and 'Sadat could have hoped that in vigorous negotiation he could get Israel' to offer 'all of Sinai for peace' (*Personal Witness*, p. 501). There was not only no basis in 1971 for the latter claim but it also flatly contradicts the former one. Meir similarly purports that throughout her tenure Israel held only that 'all of Sinai' would not be returned 'at once' to the Egyptians (p. 371). Cf. also Whetten, p. 330, claiming that Israel sought to 'negotiate away for six years' and 'intended to return' the Sinai.

27. United Nations General Assembly, Twenty-Sixth Session, Official Records, 1971 Plenum Meetings, 2000th Meeting, 6 December 1971, para. 90; cf. Eban, *Personal Witness*, p. 503. Dayan, *Breakthrough*, pp. 453–4, 610–11. Cf. also *Policy Background: The Components of a Secure Peace*, 10 March 1971, Embassy of Israel, Washington, DC (mimeo.) (UN Archives), which similarly purports that the Egyptian reply called on Israel to 'renounce its sovereign rights on the refugee issue and give entry to a mass Arab influx'. *Newsweek*, 22 February 1971. *ARR*, 15–28 February 1971. For the consensus view on the refugee question, cf. note 11 above. Rafael, p. 257. Shamir, 'Nasser and Sadat, 1967–1973', in Rabinowich and Shaked, p. 195.

28. United Nations General Assembly, Twenty-Sixth Session, Official Records, 1971 Plenum Meetings, 2000th Meeting, 6 December 1971, para. 91; cf. Eban, *Personal Witness*, p. 502, and Eban's intervention in the United Nations General Assembly, Twenty-Sixth Session, Official Records, 1971 Plenary Meetings, 2015th Meeting, 13 December 1971, para. 56 (also Meir's interview in *Newsweek*, 1 March 1971). Whetten, p. 144, reports that in January 1970 Egypt agreed to 'sign a declaration limiting its application of Article 10 of the Constantinople Convention, which had granted it authority to restrict passage of the Canal if there was a danger of war'. Eban similarly alleged that, regarding the Straits of Tiran, Egypt 'replied with an offer of "freedom of navigation … in accordance with the principles of international law." The last eight words are identical with those invariably invoked by Egypt to deny the international rights of navigation in the waterway'. Yet Sadat was prepared to ensure Israel's free passage even by permitting an international force to be stationed at Sharm-el-Shaykh – 'It could be any international force. It doesn't matter to me' – directly subject to, and removable only by a unanimous vote of, the Security Council. Indeed, such a provision was ultimately incorporated in the 1979 Egyptian–Israeli treaty (Article IV and Annex I). United Nations General Assembly, Twenty-Sixth Session, Official Records, 1971 Plenum Meetings, 2000th Meeting, 6 December 1971, para. 92; cf. Eban, *Personal Witness*, p. 502, and Eban's intervention in the United Nations General Assembly, Twenty-Sixth Session, Official Records, 1971 Plenary Meetings, 2015th Meeting, 13 December 1971, para. 56. *Newsweek*, 22 February 1971. In the *Newsweek* interview, Sadat reiterated several times over that he would 'guarantee' Israel 'freedom of navigation in the canal and the strait'. Cf. also Sadat's interview in *Newsweek*, 9 April 1973:

> We will agree to anything for Sharm and guarantee freedom of [Israeli] navigation [but not] Israeli occupation. We will turn it over to the international community under any formula they think desirable – the Big Four of the

Security Council, including China, with their troops, or neutral forces under their guarantee.

29. United Nations General Assembly, Twenty-Sixth Session, Official Records, 1971 Plenum Meetings, 2000th Meeting, 6 December 1971, para. 95. Eban, *Personal Witness*, pp. 502–3. 'Notes on a Meeting with Sir Alec Douglas-Hume, Secretary of State for Foreign Affairs of the U.K., 27 September 1971', in DAG – 1/5.2.2.1.2, Box 1, Envelope 3, Q18 (UN Archives). Eban also objected to Egypt's call for a UN peace-keeping force to be stationed adjacent to the international border, since 'no proposal of the kind suggested by Egypt is contained in Ambassador Jarring's aide-mémoire' (para. 96). Yet, precisely these provisions were incorporated into the 1979 Egyptian–Israeli treaty (Article IV and Annex I).

30. 'Notes on a Meeting between Secretary-General and Mr. Abba Eban, 18 March 1971', in Middle East, 1971, J70 (UN Archives). In a mid-March confidential letter to the foreign minister of the Netherlands, Eban pointed singularly to the issue of 'an agreed and secure boundary' as separating Egypt and Israel ('Letter from [sic] the Foreign Minister of the Netherlands, 14 March 1971' [top secret], in DAG – 1/5.2.2.1.2, Box 3, J68 [United Nations Archive]). Rafael reports that, in its consideration of the Jarring initiative, Israel was 'hard-pressed' by the 'objectionable territorial conditions'. He nonetheless credits Israel's negotiating posture at the time as 'contain[ing] all the elements of the future peace settlement between Israel and Egypt' (Rafael, pp. 256, 253).

31. Rabin, p. 194. *ARR*, 16–31 March 1971. *New York Times*, 17 March 1971. 'Notes on the Big Four Meeting on the Middle East on 24 June 1971', in Middle East, 1971, J100 (UN Archives). Thant, pp. 348, 349. DAG – 1/5.2.2.1.2, Box 1, Envelope 3, Q11 (UN Archives). DAG – 1/5.2.2.1.2, Box 1, Envelope 3, Q17 (UN Archives). On the Big Four and the Jarring initiative, cf. also Egypt's intervention at the 11 June 1973 meeting of the Security Council (S/PV.1721), and the Secretary-General's reply at the 14 June 1973 meeting (S/PV.1725). For Rogers's reportedly chilly reception in Israel when he confirmed that 'America was not prepared to modify its proposal for a near-total withdrawal', cf. *ARR*, 16–31 May 1971.

32. *United Nations Yearbook*, 1971, 1972, 1973. U Thant, pp. 352–3. *United Nations Security Council*, S/PV.1734. *ARR*, 16–31 July 1971. Quandt, *Decade of Decisions*, p. 128; Quandt, *Peace Process*, p. 116. For the best account of the UN record throughout the 1967–73 period, and background to the July 1973 Security Council resolution, cf. Khouri, 'United Nations Peace Efforts', in Kerr. Whetten, pp. 201–2, dismisses the UN condemnations as 'clearly … extraneous and distracting' – unlike, say, during the Gulf crisis. Quandt (*Peace Process*, p. 143) reckons Egypt's efforts to galvanize the UN machinery to achieve a settlement in accordance with the international consensus short of war as an attempt to 'forc[e] the United States into an anti-Arab posture'.

33. *Times* (London), 13 March 1971 (for the flap caused by Meir's *Times* interview within Israel, cf. *ARR*, 16–31 March 1971). *New York Times*, 17 March 1971. (Sympathetic to Israel's position, the *Times* nonetheless editorialized again on 8 October 1971 that its refusal to withdraw from Sharm-el-Shaykh was 'the real sticking point' in the diplomatic impasse.) Kimche, p. 304. Whetten, pp. 150–2. *ARR*, 1–15 January 1972, 16–31 January 1972, 1–15 February 1972, 1–15 March 1972, 1–15 April 1972, 1–15 June 1972, 1–15 April 1973, 1–15 March 1973.

Kapeliouk, p. 44. Lukacs, pp. 184–7 (Galili Plan). Geoffrey Aronson, *Creating Facts*, Washington 1977, pp. 33–4. Sadat apparently took special umbrage at the Yamit project. Heikal quotes him to the effect that 'Every word spoken about Yamit is a knife pointing at me personally and at my self-respect' (p. 205; cf. pp. 22, 24; cf. also Kapeliouk, p. 63, citing Sadat, 'Yamit, that signified war, at least for Egypt').

34. Eban, *Personal Witness*, p. 492; cf. p. 491 – 'Most of us had reached the conclusion [by August 1970] that Sinai, under Israeli occupation, was not a security asset, but a strangling millstone around our neck.' In a subsequent passage, Eban more accurately reports that 'on June 19, 1967, and in the ensuing *weeks* the Arab governments had before them Israeli offers to restore Sinai, the Golan Heights, and most of the West Bank territory to Arab rule' (p. 493, my emphasis).

35. Whetten, p. 326, concludes that 'a resumption of hostilities after six years of fruitless attempts to start negotiations ... was the harsh price the Israelis had to pay' for 'their demand for essentially an unconditional surrender'. Cf. Eban, *Personal Witness*, p. 528 – 'The idea of driving Egypt to a polarized option between accepting the status quo or negotiating on Israel's terms had proved baseless. There had been a third option – that of military assault'. Cf. also Korn, p. 274 – 'Only after [negotiations with Israel] had unmistakably failed did Sadat abandon diplomacy and turn toward war'. In June 1973, Nahum Goldmann, the maverick president of the World Jewish Congress, warned that the status quo would not endure forever:

> I do not agree with the Israeli leaders who believe that eventually everyone will just accept things as they are. This is not realistic. Sadat has taken a rather daring initiative. Despite opposition, he has declared himself ready to recognize Israel. If he gets no results, the army will have to launch a war. (Kapeliouk, p. 49)

36. Given the limited aim of liberating occupied territories and the exhaustion of all diplomatic options, not one government in the world – the United States included – charged Egypt and Syria with aggression in the October war (Eban, *Personal Witness*, p. 541; Quandt, *Peace Process*, p. 152; and 'Kissinger Meets Haikal' [interview], *Journal of Palestine Studies*, Winter 1994, p. 213, where Kissinger is quoted to the effect that 'You may have noticed that we have not given much attention to the question: Who fired the first shot?').

37. On the circumscribed nature of the October attack, cf. Hassan el-Badri et al., *The Ramadan War*, New York 1978, pp. 16–19; Trevor Dupuy, *Elusive Victory*, New York 1978, p. 387; Eban, *Personal Witness*, p. 589; Shamir, 'Nasser and Sadat', in Rabinowich and Shaked, p. 199; Saad el-Shazly, *The Crossing of the Suez*, San Francisco 1980, pp. 25f.; Tamir, pp. 195–6; Whetten, pp. 233–4, 283, 329–30. On the conflict between Egyptian and Syrian war aims, cf. Patrick Seale, *Asad*, Berkeley 1988, pp. 194–7. On Israel's failure to heed Sadat's threats, cf. Brecher, *Decisions in Crisis*, p. 53. Incidentally, Eban (*Personal Witness*, p. 529) reports that Arab leaders were unaware that the attack day fell on Yom Kippur, and that for Israel the choice was actually fortunate since reserves could be more easily mobilized when everyone was either at home or in synagogue (cf. Schiff, p. 12).

38. Eban, *Personal Witness*, p. 588. As against Eban's singling out of Dayan, Evron reports that 'the whole Israeli political position from 1970 on was based on the assumption that the status quo created after 1967 was stable' ('Two Periods in the Arab–Israeli Strategic Relations', in Rabinowich and Shaked, p. 111). Kapeliouk (p. 45) observes that 'one had to live in Israel in the last year before the Yom

Kippur war to know the atmosphere of euphoria, assurance and success that Israel's leaders created among the people. Just to suggest a true peace initiative meant to be immediately branded a utopian, a dreamer'.

39. Rabin, p. 327; cf. Dayan, *Breakthrough*, p. 180. Eban, *Personal Witness*, pp. 588, 601–2. Shamir, 'Israeli Views of Egypt and the Peace Process', in Quandt, *The Middle East*, p. 202 (for details on the 'cold peace' between Israel and Egypt, cf. pp. 200f.). Quandt, *Camp David*, pp. 254–5.

40. Rabin, pp. 198, 324. Cf. Eban, *Personal Witness*, p. 502, where it is purported that 'the absence of any celebratory or dramatic accompaniment to the Sadat proposal' in 1971 accounted for its failure.

41. Tamir, pp. 17, 22, 27; but cf. p. 61, where even Tamir cannot resist repeating the fairy-tale that 'until he came to Jerusalem to launch his peace initiative, Sadat had appeared to us as an uncompromising enemy with whom we had no chance of reaching peace during our generation'. Tamir also relevantly notes that the electoral platform on which Likud came to power in May 1977 already called for the 'return of the whole of Sinai to Egypt, on certain conditions' (pp. 16–17). For Tamir's key role in Israel's strategic planning after the October war, cf. pp. 222f.; for confirmation, cf. Weizman, pp. 149–50, describing Tamir as 'one of the architects of the Israeli–Egyptian peace treaty'. For the crucial Israeli concessions before Sadat's trip, cf. also Martin Indyk, *To the Ends of the Earth*, Cambridge 1984, pp. 35, 37; Quandt, *Peace Process*, p. 268; and Seale, p. 303. No doubt because it meshes so poorly with the supposed miracle worked by Sadat's trip, the Sinai concession made at the secret preliminary talks with Egypt is absent from Dayan's otherwise detailed account of the proceedings. Rather, the pretense is maintained that Sadat went 'to Jerusalem unaccompanied by any preconditions' (*Breakthrough*, p. 77). Lukacs, pp. 136–46 (Sadat's Knesset speech).

42. On Israel's effort to keep the settlements, airfields and oil refineries, and the motives behind this effort, cf. Carter, pp. 333–4, 382; Dayan, *Breakthrough*, pp. 93-4, 180, 214, 232, 277–80; Quandt, *Peace Process*, p. 279; Adel Safty, *From Camp David to the Gulf War*, Montreal 1992, pp. 68–70 (arguing that Begin used the Sinai settlements mainly as a bargaining chip to extract concessions from Sadat on the Palestinians and Syria); Weizman, pp. 90, 98, 139, 144 (Weizman purports to have believed all along that Sharm-el-Shaykh was a 'beauty spot' of 'no more than political importance'). Schiff, p. 166; cf. Weizman, p. 615.

43. Kapeliouk, ch. 6. Avi Shlaim, 'Failure in National Intelligence Estimates', *World Politics*, April 1976, p. 362. Eban, *Personal Witness*, pp. 517–19. Schiff, p. 58. Dupuy, p. 410.

44. Matti Golan, *The Secret Conversations of Henry Kissinger*, New York 1976, pp. 144–5.

45. Tamir, p. 190. Schiff, pp. 92, 172, 299. Eban, *Personal Witness*, p. 531. Dupuy, pp. 433, 566. Dupuy calculates Israel's losses as, with respect to population, more than thirty times as great as the United States' in World War II. His judicious comprehensive assessment is that

> if war is the employment of military force in support of political objectives, there can be no doubt that in strategic and political terms the Arab states – and particularly Egypt – won the war, even though the military outcome was a stalemate permitting both sides to claim military victory. (p. 603)

46. Shlaim, p. 349. Schiff, p. 311; cf. p. 299:

Questions that had been perpetually pushed off at a tangent, resurfaced. Will we always live by our swords? Can we withstand more wars, when the quantity gap is ever widening to the Arab benefit? Israel returned overnight to stage one – the State's existence was again threatened.

47. Weizman, p. 197. Schiff, pp. 314, 318. Cf. Tamir, p. 58. Not every Israeli was sobered up by the October war, however. Acclaiming Israel's 'incredible military victory', military historian and former Israeli president Chaim Herzog contemplated that the only 'danger' was that the Arabs 'will not draw the correct lessons and conclusions from the war, carried away as they are in a euphoria of victory which is imaginary'. This insight may be usefully coupled with the one that Arabs 'never excelled in attack, because this type of warfare calls for an ability to think quickly' (pp. 285, 190, 273).

48. Quandt, *Peace Process*, pp. 147, 177–9. 'Kissinger Meets Haikal' (interview), *Journal of Palestine Studies*, Winter 1994, p. 214. Cf. Kissinger's explanation, as reported by Heikal, for why the United States moved only in the war's aftermath to implement 242: 'Kissinger said that, quite frankly, the reason was the complete military superiority of Israel. The weak, he said, don't negotiate. The Arabs had been weak; now they were strong. The Arabs had achieved more than anyone, including themselves, had believed possible' (p. 233).

49. Dupuy, p. 602. Schiff, pp. 233, 310–11. Louis Williams (ed.), *Military Aspects of the Israeli–Arab Conflict*, Jerusalem 1975, pp. 199, 212, 216, 217.

50. Williams, p. 221. Quandt, *Peace Process*, pp. 268, 315. Carter, p. 275. Cf. Seale, p. 256. Cf. also Quandt, *Camp David*, p. 330: 'For most Israelis ..., the idea of separating Egypt from the other Arabs was a long-held objective. Without Egypt as a belligerent, Israel could manage to cope with threats from other Arab states.'

51. Quandt, *The Middle East*, p. 8. Eban, *Personal Witness*, p. 591. İndyk (p. 38) purports that Israel opted for a separate peace with Egypt to free negotiations from the 'demands of the more intractable states' – for example, Jordan which, unlike Egypt, had agreed to significant territorial concessions (cf. note 21 above).

52. For Camp David freeing up Israel's hand to consolidate control of the West Bank and Gaza, cf. Eban, *Personal Witness*, pp. 587, 595, 597; Quandt, *Camp David*, pp. 256, 323, note 3; Shamir, 'Israeli Views of Egypt and the Peace Process', in Quandt, *The Middle East*, p. 193; Weizman, pp. 190–1. For the direct causal link between the neutralization of Egypt at Camp David and the Lebanon invasion, cf. Eban, *Personal Witness*, pp. 597, 602; Quandt, *Camp David*, p. 321 (for a more equivocal view, Quandt, *The Middle East*, p. 10); Shamir, 'Israeli Views of Egypt and the Peace Process', in Quandt, *The Middle East*, p. 190; Tamir, pp. 56, 126. For the crushing of Palestinian resistance to the Israeli occupation as the aim of the Lebanon war, cf. Tamir, pp. 93, 116, 117, 122; Shamir, 'Israeli Views of Egypt and the Peace Process', in Quandt, *The Middle East*, p. 207.

## Chapter 7

1. Edward Said, *Peace and its Discontents* (New York: 1996); Meron Benvenisti, *Intimate Enemies* (New York: 1995). This chapter is a slightly edited version of an article that appeared under the title 'Whither the "Peace Process"?' in the July–

August 1996 issue of *New Left Review*.

2. Said, *Peace and its Discontents*, pp. 147, 12.

3. Benvenisti, *Intimate Enemies*, p. 218.

4. *Israeli–Palestinian Interim Agreement on the West Bank and Gaza Strip* (Washington, DC: 28 September 1995).

5. Article XXXI.

6. Said, *Peace and its Discontents*, p. 11.

7. Ibid., p. 63.

8. Ibid., pp. 27–8.

9. Article XXXI.

10. Said, *Peace and its Discontents*, p. xxix.

11. Article XI.

12. Conceived soon after the June 1967 war, the Allon Plan projected Israel's incorporation of roughly half the West Bank, the remaining areas of 'dense Arab settlement' bisected and consigned to some kind of self-rule.

13. Annex III, Appendix I, Article 40; Schedule 8, 'Joint Water Committee'.

14. Per capita water allotment for an Israeli is thus four times that of a Palestinian; cf. *Davar* (25 October 1993).

15. Annex III, Appendix I, Article 40.

16. Noam Chomsky, *World Orders Old and New* (New York: 1994), p. 210.

17. Said, *Peace and its Discontents*, p. 103; see also pp. xxviii–xxix, 9, 18, 66, 154.

18. Article XX.

19. Said, *Peace and its Discontents*, pp. xxxii, 103.

20. Article 10.

21. Article XVII.

22. Annex IV, Article I, paras. 2, 7a.

23. Article XVIII, paras. 4–6.

24. Annex III, Article 29.

25. Article XXXI.

26. Articles X, XII.

27. Annex I, Article V; cf. Annex I, Article XI, para. 3b for application of this provision even to 'territory under the security responsibility of the Council.'

28. Article XV, Annex I, Article II.

29. Annex I, Article XI, para. 4d; cf. Annex I, Article V, para. 3b2.

30. Annex I, Article IX; cf. Annex V, Article VII.

31. Said, *Peace and its Discontents*, p. 53.

32. Annex I, Article VIII, Annex I, Appendix V, Section F.

33. Annex III, Appendix I, Article 28.

34. Article XI.

35. Annex III, Appendix I, Articles 16, 22.

36. Said, *Peace and its Discontents*, p. xxv.

37. Ibid., p. xxiii.

38. Ibid., pp. 7–8, 73, 82–3, 120, 180–1.

39. No one knows better than Said that the impetus behind Israel's 1982 Lebanon invasion was not PLO 'folly' but rather its 'peace offensive' (Israeli strategic analyst, Avner Yaniv); for sources, cf. p. 272 n.52 in this volume, and Norman G. Finkelstein, *The Rise and Fall of Palestine* (Minneapolis, MI: 1996), p. 45 and sources cited. For the more complex issue of the Palestinians' stance during the Gulf crisis,

see *Rise and Fall*, chap. 4 and Epilogue.

40. Said, *Peace and its Discontents*, p. 127.

41. For details, cf. Chap. 6 in this volume.

42. Said, *Peace and its Discontents*, pp. 35–7.

43. Said, *Peace and its Discontents*, pp. 70, 147. Benvenisti, *Intimate Enemies*, p. 232. Indeed, the Bantustan precedent is plainly uppermost in the minds of all the signatories to as well as dissenters from the Oslo agreement; see Graham Usher, *Palestine in Crisis* (London: 1995), pp. 8, 10, 85n 6.

44. Said, *Peace and its Discontents*, p. 95; emphasis in the original.

45. Ibid., p. 155.

46. Verwoerd hoped that political separation would, in his words, provide a 'basis for the Western members ... to prevent action against South Africa in the UN' (Gerhard Mare and Georgina Hamilton, *An Appetite for Power* (Bloomington, IN: 1987), p. 29).

47. Roger Southall, *South Africa's Transkei* (New York: 1983), p. 149. Forming a lobby and aligning with the opposition political party, the white settlers resisted government plans. Ultimately, however, most returned to South Africa.

48. Jeffrey Butler, Robert I. Rotberg and John Adams, *The Black Homelands of South Africa* (Berkeley: 1971), p. 31.

49. Christopher R. Hill, *Bantustans* (Oxford: 1964), p. 59.

50. Ibid., p. 57.

51. Newell M. Stultz, *Transkei's Half-Loaf* (New Haven: 1979), pp. 93, 96.

52. Said, *Peace and its Discontents*, p. 153. See also Usher, *Palestine in Crisis*, pp. 38–40 and Chomsky, *World Orders*, p. 254.

53. As in Transkei, the real purpose of the January 1996 election in the West Bank and Gaza was for the subject population to 'democratically' ratify the annulment of its basic rights and to 'democratically' install a Quisling leadership. In neither case was the derisory settlement subject to a public referendum. Rather, the electoral victory of, respectively, Matanzima and Arafat was 'interpreted' as acclamation of it. Thus, a vote for Arafat purportedly signaled support for Oslo. The actual facts suggest otherwise. For an analysis of the Transkei election, the modalities of which exactly prefigured the 1996 Palestinian election, see Southall, *South Africa's Transkei*, pp. 120ff. For the Palestinian election, see Norman G. Finkelstein, 'Arafat Victory Doesn't Equal Real Reconciliation', *Christian Science Monitor* (31 January 1996).

54. Trumpeting the abolition of apartheid within Transkei, the Matanzima regime claimed to have done more for black freedom in South Africa than any of the more militant liberation movements: 'The Transkei has ... liberated 18,000 square miles ... from the grips of apartheid – the pass laws, job-reservation, apartheid at our post offices and segregation at the numerous beaches along our ... coast' (Southall, *South Africa's Transkei*, p. 254). Arafat's Palestinian Authority contrived a similar defense against its principled critics.

55. Said, *Peace and its Discontents*, p. 172; cf. p. 157.

56. Although perhaps sincere, such fulminations also served Matanzima as 'proof' that he was not a South African stooge. For that same reason, South Africa quietly abided them.

57. Mare and Hamilton, *Appetite for Power*, pp. 3, 35–9; cf. p. 82: 'We have

created a springboard from which we can go forth to conquer in ever widening circles. We have created for our Black South Africa a liberated zone from whence we can mount our strategies and attacks on apartheid which are vital to the country as a whole.' See also Butler et al., *Black Homelands*, p. 35, quoting Buthelezi on 'self-rule': 'It may be a contribution to the unraveling of the problem, insofar, as, if we attain full independence, our hand will be strengthened.' Echoing Buthelezi's rationale, Arafat told a crowd in Gaza upon his return: 'I know many of you think Oslo is a bad agreement. It is a bad agreement. But it's the best agreement we can get in the worst situation.' And his deputy maintained that Oslo 'will not automatically lead to national independence, but the political space it opens up enables us to set off an irreversible dynamic towards independence through the new national mechanisms we set in place' (Usher, *Palestine in Crisis*, pp. 1, 9–10; cf. Said, *Peace and its Discontents*, p. 8).

58. Even Bophuthatswana, the one Bantustan initially protective of individual rights, ended up as a police state.

59. Said, *Peace and its Discontents*, pp. 173–4.

60. Stultz, *Transkei's Half-Loaf*, pp. 133–4; emphasis in the original.

61. Benvenisti, *Intimate Enemies*, p. 222.

62. A case can plainly be made that the two-state settlement allotting the indigenous Palestinian population 20 per cent of Mandatory Palestine and the Jewish settlers who displaced them 80 per cent is also far from equitable. Arguably, however, this proposal is a pragmatic application of justice, that is, an application of Max Weber's formula, 'Given the existing conflict, how can one solve it with the least internal and external damage for all concerned?' (H.H. Gerth and C. Wright Mills, eds, *From Max Weber: Essays in Sociology* (New York: 1975), p. 9). Granting Palestinians independence in the derisory areas of 'self-rule' sketched in Oslo II cannot, I think, be plausibly justified by any standard of justice.

63. Hill, *Bantustans*, pp. 5, 41. It is an open question whether the *apartheid* regime ever actually envisaged a total separation. 'The dominant Republican Afrikaner attitude to race relations', T.R.H. Davenport observes, 'held in tension the conflicting notions of territorial separation (as an insurance against numerical swamping) and domination *(baasskap)* to ensure control over labour' (*South Africa, A Modern History* (Toronto: 1991), p. 518). At any rate, one cannot but be struck by the identity of socioeconomic visions between the masterminds of apartheid and the Oslo accord. Verwoerd projected 'one national economy [with] the opportunity of separate government, the opportunity of living separately', while Shimon Peres calls for a 'political divorce and an economic marriage' (Mare and Hamilton, *Appetite for Power*, p. 30; Usher, *Palestine in Crisis*, p. 35).

64. Nearly 10 per cent of the South African budget was earmarked for the Bantustans. 'Rather surprisingly', reported the authors of one standard study, 'the rapid growth of spending on the homelands ... has not been challenged by white public opinion or politicians' (Butler et al., *Black Homelands*, p. 143).

65. Benvenisti, *Intimate Enemies*, p. 221.

66. Said, *Peace and its Discontents*, pp. 3, 20, 119, 125. To be sure, Said reports (p. 174) that he too endorsed the two-state settlement with great reservations, although apparently not because of doubts about its viability.

67. Ibid., pp. 163–4.

## Appendix

1. Oxford: 2002 (hereafter: *SDW*).

2. Gary J. Bass, 'Days That Shook the World', in *New York Times* (16 June 2002), Richard Bernstein, 'Short Conflict, Far-Reaching Consequences', in *New York Times* (17 July 2002), Edward Rothstein, 'Six Days of Confusion That Rearranged World Politics', in *New York Times* (6 July 2002). Howard Fineman, 'Bush Studied '67 Preemptive Strike', in *Newsweek* (9 October 2002), at www.msnbc.com/news. The back cover of the hardbound edition is studded with advance acclaim from partisan figures such as former Israeli Prime Minister Ehud Barak and *New Republic* publisher Martin Peretz, but also from respected authorities such as historian Wm. Roger Louis and former US ambassador Richard B. Parker.

3. A fellow of the Shalem Center, a conservative research institute in Jerusalem, Oren has in recent months praised Prime Minister Sharon's 'restraint', urged the US to 'allow Israel to finish rooting out the terrorist infrastructure in the territories', and opined that the 'good part' of President Bush is 'when he is Manichean – when he's saying that there are good guys and bad guys and you're with us or against us' ('For Sharon, a Lesson from 1967', *Jerusalem Report* (3 June 2002), 'Don't Hold Israel Back', in *Wall Street Journal* (9 April 2002), Suzy Hansen, 'Six Days that Shook the World' (interview) at www.salon.com/books/int/2002/06/12/oren).

4. Oren mistakenly states in the *Salon* interview that the UN archive 'works under the 30-year rule' of declassification; in fact it operates under the 20-year rule and its documentation on the June war has already been consulted by prior researchers; cf. Chap. 5 in this volume.

5. An interesting ancillary question Oren never explores is the split between the White House and the State Department on the pre-emptive strike (apparently President Johnson approved, Secretary of State Dean Rusk didn't). The volume of the *Foreign Relations of the United States* series on this period is scheduled for publication in early 2004. The volumes covering the periods preceding and succeeding the months May-November 1967 have already been published. The sensitivity of the materials covered in these months has presumably held up publication.

6. Checking Oren's evidence also poses a challenge: an endnote incorporating tens of references frequently corresponds to many paragraphs of text incorporating tens of quotes, making it nearly impossible to match reference against quote.

7. For the Qibya massacre, see Benny Morris, *Israel's Border Wars* (Oxford: 1993), pp. 244ff. (Morris dismisses Sharon's account as 'pure invention': p. 246 n. 86); for the Israeli firebombing in Egypt, see David Hirst, *The Gun and the Olive Branch* (London: 1977), pp. 166–8. Oren plainly knows the actual content of this 'vandalizing' since three sentences later he refers to Egypt's refusal to 'pardon the arsonists'.

8. For background on the DZs and further documentation, see Muhammad Muslih, *The Golan* (Washington, DC: 1999), chaps. 1–2. Oren seeks at one point to discredit Bull on the grounds that he was 'ill-disposed toward Israel'. He quotes from Bull's memoir that, when Israel summoned him on 5 June to warn Jordan not to attack or else Israel would react in kind, Bull responded: 'This was a threat, pure and simple, and it is not the normal practice of the UN to pass on threats

from one government to another.' Bull does appear grossly derelict from Oren's snippet, but the very next sentence of his memoir – omitted by Oren – reads: 'But this message seemed so important that we quickly sent it ... and King Hussein received the message before 10:30 the same morning' (*SDW*: p. 184; Odd Bull, *War and Peace in the Middle East* (London: 1976), p. 113).

9. 'Interviews on the Golan Heights and on Jewish Settlements in Hebron, 22 November 1976 and 1 January 1977', reprinted in *Journal of Palestine Studies* (Autumn 1997), p. 145 (the interviews originally appeared in *Yediot Ahronot*).

10. Martin van Creveld, *The Sword and the Olive* (New York: 1998), p. 172.

11. For the record, the cited work actually states 'between 23 February 1966 and 15 May 1967', and the figures emanated not from Syria but 'Israeli sources' (Moshe Ma'oz, *Syria and Israel* (Oxford: 1995), p. 89; Yacov Bar Siman-Tov, *Linkage Politics in the Middle East* (Boulder: 1983), pp. 151–2).

12. In addition to its alleged pro-Egyptian bias, UNEF – according to Oren – inspired 'little faith' regarding its 'ability to prevent Egypt–Israeli hostilities', and was viewed 'with skepticism' by 'Western states disaffected by the UN's increasingly pro-Soviet stance' (*SDW*: p. 67). To support these disparaging claims, Oren directs the reader specifically to Brian Urquhart's memoir, *A Life in Peace and War* (New York: 1978). Yet, on the cited pages Urquhart says nothing of the sort. For example, recalling the establishment of UNEF after Israel withdrew from the Sinai in 1957, Urquhart writes: 'The Israelis withdrew with a bad grace, destroying roads and railway communications and leaving uncharted minefields in their wake, all of which caused considerable grief and trouble to UNEF. They started a vitriolic campaign about Hammarskjold's and UNEF's alleged partiality to Egypt. Israel also refused to allow UNEF to be stationed on the Israeli side of the line, a grave weakness for a peacekeeping force. The Israeli attitude to UNEF changed a few months later when they realized that the force, in its impartial way, had achieved peace on what had formerly been their most violent and bloody frontier' (p. 136).

13. Oren dubs U Thant 'one of the greatest obstacles to UNEF's survival' and quotes the Israeli Foreign Ministry to the effect that 'it is still unclear what diplomatic consideration or defect of character brought him to make this disastrous move' (*SDW*: pp. 71, 75). Yet U Thant's detailed factual accounting (seconded by his UN colleagues) makes plain that he had no alternative (see p. 249 n. 10 in this volume for references). Although judging by the documentary record a man of remarkable integrity and decency, U Thant comes off very badly in Oren's book – 'emotionless and moon-faced ... rather simple-minded' (citing an anonymous source), 'anti-American and, perforce, pro-Soviet' and exhibiting 'the psychology of the Asian ... a built-in reaction against the white man' (citing American officials), as well as in thrall to his horoscope – presumably because, like Odd Bull, he preserved on the Israel-Arab conflict an independent cast of mind (*SDW*: pp. 71–2, 75). Both U Thant and Odd Bull later speculated that if Israel had agreed to station UNEF on its side, the June war might have been averted.

14. Israel's apologists have always strained to reconcile its opposition to stationing UNEF on the Israeli side of the border with the claim that Israel did all it could to avert war. Israel's UN ambassador, Gideon Rafael, subsequently maintained that on the Egyptian side of the border UNEF served 'as a neutral factor or restraint and a kind of, I would say, shock absorber between the two countries' but

on the Israeli side would have served 'no purpose whatsoever' (Richard B. Parker, *The Six-Day War* (Gainesville, FL: 1996), pp. 105–6; for Abba Eban's equally contrived rationale, see p. 128 in this volume).

15. An integral part of the 1949 armistice agreement, EIMAC was disbanded by Israel after its 1956 Sinai invasion 'unilaterally' and 'in clear defiance of U.N. resolutions' (U Thant) (for details, see pp. 127–8 in this volume). Oren incorrectly refers to EIMAC as the 'Mutual Armistice Commission'.

16. It also bears notice that the US officially hedged its support of Israel's right of passage with the conditional phrase 'In the absence of some overriding decision to the contrary, as by the International Court of Justice', and that President Eisenhower explicitly stated after the Sinai invasion that Egypt's 'exercising [of] belligerent rights in relation to Israeli shipping' in the Straits 'constitute[d] no justification for the armed invasion of Egypt by Israel'. (For background and documentation, see pp. 137–9 in this volume, and John Norton Moore (ed.), *The Arab–Israeli Conflict, Vol. III: Documents* (Princeton: 1994), section IV, esp. pp. 639, 661 ('passage', 'absence of'), 663 ('recurrence'), 655 (Israeli policy), 649 (Eisenhower); see also Parker, *The Six-Day War*, pp. 295–6.)

17. Basing himself on the wholly unreliable memoir of Israel's UN representative, Gideon Rafael, and the anecdotal recollections twenty-five years later of U Thant's aide, Brian Urquhart, Oren suggests that Egypt suddenly reneged on the terms of the moratorium at the end of May, and accordingly the proposal was not submitted to Eshkol (*SDW*: p. 126). Yet U Thant's meticulous account running through early June of these negotiations reports Rafael's explicit rejection speaking for the Israeli government and makes no mention at all of an Egyptian volte-face on the moratorium's terms (on the contrary, he was still citing Nasser's support on 1 June), while Urquhart's own memoir closely follows U Thant (see p. 129 and sources cited on p. 250 n. 16 in this volume, for U Thant's account and Urquhart's memoir, as well as supplementary UN documentation and Rafael's unreliability; and Parker, *The Six-Day War*: pp. 94–5, for Urquhart's anecdotal recollection).

18. For historians who credit Operation Dawn (usually dated 25–27 May) but attach slight significance to it, see p. 254 n. 37 in this volume, and Avraham Sela, *The Decline of the Arab–Israeli Conflict* (Albany: 1998), p. 90; for an historian who altogether doubts its existence, see Benny Morris's review of Oren's book in *Jerusalem Report* (21 August 2002). Even assuming an Egyptian attack was planned and leaving aside that the alleged plan was aborted well before 5 June, it couldn't have influenced the Israeli decision to preemptively strike unless officials knew about it. Although circumstantial indications suggest that they might have known, it remains that both at the time and in his later memoirs Abba Eban emphatically dismissed all talk of a planned Egyptian attack as 'hypochondriac frivolities' and a 'cheap trick' designed to justify an Israeli attack, and neither British and US nor, for that matter, Israeli intelligence could detect in late May any evidence of an imminent Egyptian attack (for Eban's dismissal and the lack of any intelligence confirmation, see pp. 134, 254 n. 37 in this volume, and *SDW*: pp. 102–3, 107–8, 110, 114–15, 122).

19. Whereas historians crediting Operation Dawn argue on the basis of the Egyptian memoirs that it was 'Amer's secret brainchild and that Nasser almost immediately cancelled the plan upon learning of it, Oren manages to prove otherwise through tortured reasoning and by playing fast and loose with the already

problematic evidence: e.g., he reports an alleged statement by 'Amer complaining that the plan had been leaked abroad but omits Nasser's alleged reaction suggesting he knew nothing of it: 'Why is 'Amer upset? Does he think that we shall start the war?' (*SDW*: p. 120; Parker, *Six-Day War*, p. 45).

20. Samir A. Mutawi, *Jordan in the 1967 War* (Cambridge: 1987), pp. 100–1.

21. Sela, *Decline of the Arab–Israeli Conflict*: p. 91; for Begin and further supporting documentation, see pp. 134–5 in this volume. The UNEF commander quoted by Oren on Egypt's imminent attack, Indar Jit Rikhye, reports elsewhere in his memoir that Egyptian troops were in fact ambiguously positioned and he concludes that 'the Egyptian armed forces had eventually accepted the final decision of Nasser not to attack' (see p. 134 in this volume). In preparing this Appendix, I came across an error in Chap. 5 in this volume. I suggested that on the eve of Israel's pre-emptive attack Mossad chief Meir Amit denied Nasser's readiness for war (p. 134 in this volume). The statement I quote, however, was made before Nasser announced his intention to close the Straits of Tiran, and Amit might have subsequently changed his mind.

22. For Peled and Weizman, as well as further documentation on Israel's steadily improving and Egypt's steadily deteriorating military situation, and the certainty of an Israeli victory, see pp. 135–6 in this volume.

23. Van Creveld, *Sword and the Olive*, pp. 172, 176–7. To enhance the Arab threat, Oren gestures menacingly to Jordan's 'twenty-four Hawker Hunter' aircraft and 'eleven brigades – 56,000 men, 270 modern tanks, Centurions and Pattons' (*SDW*: p. 137). In fact military historians recall that the Jordanian army was a 'kind of showpiece' serving primarily as a 'palace guard' while the Jordanian air force was 'not a threat at all'; for details, see pp. 135–6 in this volume.

24. For Benny Morris and the Palestinian refugees, see Chap. 3 in this volume.

25. At first Israel feigned that Egypt also initiated armed hostilities – further evidence of how feeble its pretext for preemptive war was.

26. Van Creveld, *Sword and the Olive*, p. 188. Creveld similarly reports that Syria 'scarcely lifted a finger while their allies were being pulverized' and that 'any talk of a [Syrian] offensive was absurd, given that by the evening of June 6 most of their air force had been destroyed by the IAF' (p. 191).

27. Michael Brecher, *Decisions in Crisis* (Berkeley: 1980), p. 100 (see p. 143 in this volume).

28. For the West Bank and Sinai, see p. 143 in this volume, and sources cited (the page numbers for Donald Neff, *Warriors at Suez* (New York: 1981), should be 332 and 416, and for Morris, *Israel's Border Wars*, should include 179), and van Creveld, *Sword and the Olive*, pp. 105, 151.

29. For the remarkable congruencies between the build-ups to the respective wars, see p. 142 in this volume.

30. 'Interviews on the Golan Heights and on Jewish Settlements in Hebron, 22 November 1976 and 1 January 1977', reprinted in *Journal of Palestine Studies* (Autumn 1997), p. 145.

31. For background, see esp. James M. Ennes, Jr., *Assault on the Liberty* (New York: 1986), and John Borne, *The USS Liberty: Dissenting History vs. Official History* (New York University, PhD thesis: 1993), and for recently declassified supporting documentation, see James Bamford, *Body of Secrets* (New York: 2002), Chap. 7. Apart from Eugene Rostow, under secretary of state in the Johnson administration,

just about every official and intelligence agency on the American side eventually concluded that the Israeli assault was intentional. A well-known apologist for Israel, Rostow lectured to an academic conference on the June war that 'the prolonged Arab war against the Jewish political presence in the Middle East ... goes back to 1922, with the announcement of the Balfour Declaration'. As every beginner knows – but Rostow apparently doesn't – it was issued in 1917. (For Rostow's claim that the *Liberty* was a 'pure accident', and the Balfour Declaration, see Parker, *The Six-Day War.* pp. 176–7, 110; for US 'military and intelligence agencies ... unanimous in finding' that the Israeli attack on the *Liberty* was 'deliberate and unprovoked', see Raymond Garthoff, *A Journey through the Cold War* (Washington, DC: 2001) p. 214.)

32. See, e.g, Gabby Bron, 'Egyptian POWs Ordered to Dig Graves, Then Shot by Israeli Army' in *Yediot Ahronot* (17 August 1995), Michael Bar-Zohar, 'The Reactions of Journalists to the Army's Murders of POWs', in *Maariv* (17 August 1995), 'Israel Reportedly Killed POWs in '67 War', in *Washington Post* (17 August 1995), Barton Gelman, 'Debate Tainting Image of Purity Wrenches Israelis', in *Washington Post* (19 August 1995), Serge Schmemann, 'After a General Tells of Killing POWs in 1956, Israelis Argue Over Ethics of War', in *New York Times* (21 August 1995), Youssef M. Ibrahim, 'Egypt Says Israelis Killed POWs in '67 War', in *New York Times* (21 September 1995).

33. Shlomo Gazit, *The Stick and the Carrot* (Tel Aviv: 1985), p. 59. Gazit is former head of Military Intelligence.

34. According to B'Tselem (Israeli Information Center for Human Rights in the Occupied Territories), 356 Palestinians as against 251 Israelis were killed through 1998 (www.btselem.org/STAT/table.htm). Amnesty International, *Five Years After the Oslo Agreement* (September 1998). On a lesser note, Oren reports that Ben-Gurion 'cautioned against the demographic dangers of annexation' from right after the June war until his death in 1973 (*SDW*: p. 314). True enough, but this did not at all mean he favored returning the conquered territories. In a 19 June 1967 declaration, he called for Israel's retention of Gaza and an 'autonomous' status for the West Bank. Although in the very early 1970s he supported keeping only Jerusalem, the Golan Heights and possibly Gaza, by the end of 1972 he maintained more generally that because the Arabs were 'not ready to make peace, we are not committed to giving them back [all the territories]. We cannot take it upon ourselves to retain all we have conquered, but there are territories where this (i.e., keeping them) is possible' (Mordechai Gazit, *Israeli Diplomacy and the Quest for Peace* (London: 2002), pp. 150–1). In fact, Egypt and Jordan were already committed to a full peace treaty with Israel in exchange for full withdrawal by early 1971, but Israel refused (see Chap. 6 in this volume).

35. For details, see Chap. 2 in this volume.

# Index